EDITING AND DESIGN 2

Handling Newspaper Text

Harold Evans

Editor, *The Sunday Times*, London

A Five-volume Manual of English, Typography and Layout

Book Two
Handling Newspaper Text

Published under the auspices of the
National Council for the Training of Journalists

HEINEMANN : LONDON

William Heinemann Ltd
10 Upper Grosvenor Street, London W1X 9PA

LONDON MELBOURNE TORONTO
JOHANNESBURG AUCKLAND

Filmset by Keyspools Ltd, Golborne, Lancs.
Printed and bound in Great Britain by
Morrison & Gibb Ltd, London and Edinburgh

EDITING AND DESIGN

A Five-volume Manual of
English, Typography and Layout

To Ruth

Preface

Of all the craft elements in newspaper journalism none is more neglected by journalists than the typography of the text. Writers leave text
typography to deskmen, the sub-editorial serfs who transmute their
golden words to base metal. Deskmen, though they take care to give an
air of knowledge, leave much to the printer and, sometimes, worse, to
the artist. There is no debate about text typography. Newspaper giants
have clashed about the meaning of news; cosmic theories are advanced
about layout, and men will die for an intro, but to my certain knowledge
there has never, in our argumentative world, been a single cross word
about an x-height. This is good for our blood pressures, but bad for our
readers. It is also frequently bad for the writers whose words are made
harder to read by permutations of inappropriate type, setting measure,
spacing and inking, that no single philistine working alone could
possibly dream up.

These things just happen but they happen out of a combination of
ignorance and wild experiment. The ignorance need not be laboured;
I would guess that fewer than half of the deskmen setting type on any
newspaper know the name and characteristics of their own text type.
Not until Allen Hutt's masterly *Newspaper Design* did they really have
anywhere to go if they wanted to find out or make comparisons. Famous
books on sub-editing, like F J Mansfield's, had nothing to say on the
subject beyond indicating the various sizes of type. As for experiment,
there are two kinds. There is the artist's whose setting prescriptions
demand unparalleled feats from the human eyeball, but whose settings
are passed, unremarked, by deskmen journalists. And there are
engineers, running wild in the United States, who regard as infinitely
malleable letterforms that have survived and served two centuries.

Much of this book, therefore, deals with the typography of setting
newspaper text, and in that I include the racing results and classified
advertising. It is not a book of solely British practice; the observations
will travel as well, or as badly, as those in the other volumes on the use of
English, headlines, picture editing, and newspaper design. There is
one area, however, where I have drawn on British practice and that is
the analysis of the editing of a running story of some length and un-
predictability. It is a frequent challenge for newspapers all over the
world, but it is one task where I have never seen the Fleet Street sub
excelled.

My own initiation into the subbing of a running story was at the
Manchester Evening News and I have a debt which should be acknow-

ledged here to Norman Thornton, my chief sub-editor, who drilled us at all the disciplines. On typography, my deepest debt is not to a journalist but to a typographer, Walter Tracy of Linotype and Machinery Ltd, London, who has lightened my own areas of ignorance with courtesy and scholarship. He was also kind enough to read the manuscript of this book, as did Leslie Owens, of the London College of Printing, Herbert Spencer of the Royal College of Art, Walter Partridge of the Westminster Press, Robert Harling, and Matthew Carter, formerly with Mergenthaler Linotype Company (Brooklyn). All made most useful corrections and suggestions. I am additionally grateful to Mr Carter for letting me have material on his new design, Olympian.

An illustrated book like this would not be possible, of course, without the assistance of the type companies. Linotype and Machinery Ltd, Mergenthaler Linotype, Ludlow Industries (UK) Ltd, and Harris-Intertype Ltd, have all given the most generous assistance with illustrations and have gone to great pains to answer my requests.

Finally, I must thank the comps and printers I have worked with, notably in Manchester, Darlington and London, for always being ready to talk type. George Darker, the Head Printer at *The Sunday Times*, was especially helpful with this book.

I should add that not all of the people mentioned of course agree with me all of the time about all of the book, nor is any one of them responsible for my judgments.

Highgate, London   HAROLD EVANS

This has been an expensive book to produce. The author, the National Council for the Training of Journalists, and the publishers are deeply grateful to a number of national and regional newspaper managements who have made contributions so that some of the heavy costs involved can be absorbed.

Contents

1 The Typography of Text Setting

God has revealed to me the secret that I demand of Him . . . I have had a large quantity of lead brought to my house and that is the pen with which I shall write. —JOHANNES GUTENBERG

In *The Hound of the Baskervilles* Sherlock Holmes declares: 'There is as much difference to my eyes between the leaded bourgeois type of a *Times* article and the slovenly print of an evening halfpenny paper as there could be between your Negro and your Eskimo. . . .'

If Perry Mason or Maigret today wanted to impress those about him, he would allude to the 24pt Excelsior in the incriminating evidence and deduce that it could have been sent only by someone with access to filmsetting.[1] But if the terminology and technology have changed, Holmes is a good model. He had gone beyond feeling that *The Times* looked better, he had appreciated the importance of the type used for the text of the paper and the space between each line of type. Today it is necessary to be more precise than Holmes.

His 'bourgeois' type is the name of a size (and nothing to do with social classes). Today 'leaded bourgeois' would be specified as 9pt Times Roman on a 10pt body. The point system for measuring type has supplanted the romantic but undescriptive names for the various sizes of type, and even though the advent of photosetting requires modifications to the terminology, the typographic point remains the most convenient standard for indicating the size of both metal and filmset characters.

Changing one's mental arithmetic from inches to points may seem quite a task. It is surprising how easily it is done. Within a short time, a newspaperman interested in typography is thinking in points, just as the linguist learns to think in a foreign language. Some who have never quite grasped the type-measuring systems can, it is true, be seen covertly converting points into fractions of inches; inches should be forgotten for type. Conversion wastes time and introduces error; and printers will want instructing in points and their multiples. Newspapermen should acquire a type gauge as a twin to the ordinary inch ruler. The ruler is still required, of course, for the inch-measurements of pages and pictures.[2]

We will deal briefly first with the arithmetic of type measurement and the materials for setting it. The emphasis is on text setting but there is some common ground with display setting for headlines and this is included for convenience. We then examine in detail the requirements for readable newspaper text; anyone familiar with the mechanical side can go straight to that, beginning on p. 10.

Measuring Type

Text type and display type are measured with the same scale. The settings **opposite** give some feel for text sizings in the point system in general use in newspapers. The old names still survive in some places so these are given after the nearest point designations. A in brackets means this is the American expression, E the English.

> **4¾pt** (no name)
> **5pt: pearl**
> **5½pt: ruby (E), agate (A)**
> **6pt: nonpareil** (pronounced 'nomp' or 'nonprul' in composing rooms; abbreviated to 'Nmp' or 'Np' in written instructions)
> **6½pt: emerald**
> **7pt: minion** (abbreviated to min)
> **8pt: brevier** (pronounced 'breveer', shortened to 'brev')
> **9pt: bourgeois** (pronounced 'burjoyce', with the accent on the second syllable; abbreviated to 'Bjs' or 'BG')
> **10pt: long primer** (pronounced 'primmer', written as 'LP')
> **11pt: small pica** (pronounced with a long i as in pike—'piker')
> **12pt: pica** (an important name to remember, because this is the basic unit used in measuring type area—*see* below)

Here are the full areas occupied by different point sizes:

| 6pt | 7pt | 8pt | 9pt | 10pt | 12pt | 14pt | 18pt | 24pt |

The American point system, used throughout the English-speaking world, offers a very refined measurement. Every type size is an exact multiple or increment of every other type size. The *point*, the basic unit, is 0·013837 of an inch, so 72 points are almost an inch—0·996264 of an inch.[3] When you specify a 72pt type you are specifying a type whose metal occupies approximately an inch of vertical space.

5 point Ionic

On what does ease of reading depend? On the simplicity of the type design, on the length of the type lines, on their leading, on the spacing of words, and on a principle either misunderstood or sadly ignored: that of appropriate choice of type for the paper on which it is to be printed.

5½ point

On what does ease of reading depend? On the simplicity of the type design, on the length of the type lines, on their leading, on the spacing of words, and on a principle either misunderstood or sadly ignored: that of appropriate choice of type for the paper on which it is to be printed.

6 point

On what does ease of reading depend? On the simplicity of the type design, on the length of the type lines, on their leading, on the spacing of words, and on a principle either misunderstood or sadly ignored: that of appropriate choice of type for the paper on which it is to be printed.

7 point

On what does ease of reading depend? On the simplicity of the type design, on the length of the type lines, on their leading, on the spacing of words, and on a principle either misunderstood or sadly ignored: that of appropriate choice of type for the paper on which it is to be printed.

8 point

On what does ease of reading depend? On the simplicity of the type design, on the length of the type lines, on their leading, on the spacing of words, and on a principle either misunderstood or sadly ignored: that of appropriate choice of type for the paper on which it is to be printed.

9 point

On what does ease of reading depend? On the simplicity of the type design, on the length of the type lines, on their leading, on the spacing of words, and on a principle either misunderstood or sadly ignored: that of appropriate choice of type for the paper on which it is to be printed.

10 point

On what does ease of reading depend? On the simplicity of the type design, on the length of the type lines, on their leading, on the spacing of words, and on a principle either misunderstood or sadly ignored: that of appropriate choice of type for the paper on which it is to be printed.

12 point

On what does ease of reading depend? On the simplicity of the type design, on the length of the type lines, on their leading, on the spacing of words, and on a principle either misunderstood or sadly ignored: that of appropriate choice of type for the paper on which it is to be printed.

This is not the same as saying the printed image of the 72pt type will be one inch high. The image produced by metal type (the face) will almost always be somewhat less than its point size. Characters cast in relief on metal have to be supported on a rectangular metal body, and it is this body which is measured and not the character, though of course the bigger the body the bigger the character it can support. The reason for basing the system of measurement on the body size is simple. Letters have very different shapes. Some letters are short—like a, x, c. Some—like b, d, h, k, l—are tall with ascending strokes. Some have long descending strokes—g, p, q, y. The long letters f and j can have both ascenders and descenders. In any one design they all have to be accommodated on the same size of body and cast in the same mould. It is this body which is the constant factor, and hence the unit measured.

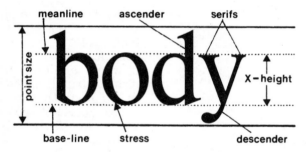

The point size in the word 'body' above is approximately the distance from the top of the letter 'b' to the bottom of the letter 'y'. Clearly a designer can make a great difference to the apparent size of a type by how much space he takes on the body with such ascenders and descenders. Types designed with short ascenders and descenders leave more room on the body for the short letters, and then we say these faces are big on the body, or that they have a large x-height. The x-height is the vertical measurement of the lower-case x and the other short letters without ascenders and descenders.

A type with a large x-height will appear bigger than a type of identical point size which has a small x-height. These characters are all of the same point size:

And the effects of these variations in x-height and appearing size can be seen when some of them are shown with their ascending or descending characters:

x y x y X h x h

This concept of x-height is of great importance in the newspaper's choice of a face for setting small text, since small type, other things being equal, is easier to read if it has a maximum face-to-body size.

So much for the significant dimensions of type. Character is something else; it is discussed in Book Three in this series, on headlines. Briefly, type is distinguished by the nature of the serifs, if any, the thick–thin relationship of the strokes, and the stress, which is the thickening in a curved stroke.

Text type, like headline type, is commonly classified in certain groups (**below**, l. to r.) *old style, transitional,* and *modern* and *egyptian* among the serif faces, which is all that need concern us here:

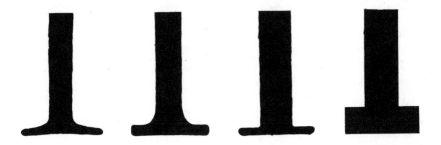

Old style is distinguished by oblique stress, modern by vertical stress. Old style serifs are attached to the stem by a curving bracket; modern serifs are unbracketed hairlines, and egyptian serifs are nearly equal in thickness to the main strokes. Modern has the sharpest thick–thin contrast.

The small scale of text type disguises the precise nature of the serif, the thick–thin contrast, the width and the stress; but though hardly discernible, these characteristics are just as relevant as in display type. They decide the legibility and colour (i.e. blackness) of the type in the page and hence the ease of reading it. For instance, the colour of a text is influenced not simply by the thickness of the strokes, but by the white remaining between them, notably in the counters. The 'captive' white dilutes the colour. The narrower the face, the smaller the counters must be, and hence the darker the type looks. The 8pt Ionic, for instance, has a bigger printing area than 8pt Corona, and therefore carries more ink, but Ionic does not *look* heavier. The reason is that its characters are wider than Corona and have more white in them. For instance, the height of the lower-case letter 'n' in 8pt Ionic is 0·0615 (61½ thousandths of an inch) against Corona's 0·5875 (58¾ thousandths), and the end of the Ionic serif is stronger, too. Those extra fractions add up to quite a bit more inking surface on a text page, but it is diluted by the white within the width of Ionic—the Ionic 'n' is 81 and the Corona 'n' only 71½ thousandths of an inch.

Measuring Print Area

Points describe the vertical dimensions of a piece of type. When we measure an area of type we use a unit called a *pica em*. This is as fundamental a unit as the point. It is 12 points square. When one hears a newspaper column being specified as 11 picas wide (US practice), it means 11 pica ems. In English newspapers the same measurement would normally be given as 11 ems, leaving the pica to be understood.

And the pica em is used to specify the depth of a type area. The following is the area of type produced by specifying a news intro to be 8 pica ems wide to a depth of 7 pica ems:

Strictly speaking, in typefounders' type, an em is the square of any given type size in points. Thus an 18pt em is 18 points high by 18 points wide, a 10pt em is 10 points by 10 points. But since the em varies with the point size, that would not, of course, give a constant standard. The standard is provided by the convention that type areas are measured in the em of the 12pt or pica type.

The size of type used in these measures is irrelevant. Whether it be 8, 9 or 24pt, the type set across 11 ems is set across 11 *pica* ems. Any type marked to be set to a depth of 4 ems is set 4 *pica* ems deep—though newspaper practice is to work in column-inches for depth or length.

To be precise one should always specify pica ems; in fact practices vary. In English print shops, including newspapers, the term 'em' is used by itself leaving the 12pt (a pica) to be understood; the American practice favours the term pica, leaving the 'em' to be understood.

The European system is similar, though the terms and specifications are slightly different.[4]

There is a half unit for the em. It is an *en*. It is one-half of the em in width, but the same as the em in depth, i.e. in 12pt instead of being 12 × 12 points it is 12 points × 6 points. This is how the 12pt em and en compare: ■ ▋

Can you forget about all ems other than 12pt ems? Not quite. There is one instance where the em and the en live up to their pure definitions as the square of the given body depth. This is when text type is being set with indentions of white space, as in tabular setting, to provide a straight gutter of white space down a newspaper column. The instruction then to indent one em or one en means to indent one em or en *of the type size being used*. Thus if the type is 8pt an instruction to indent one em on the left will be understood to mean an indent of one 8pt em, i.e. 8 points, not 12 points. An instruction to indent one en will produce an indention of one 8pt en, i.e. 4 points, not 6 points.

Em and en being awkward little words, easily confused, printers have cheerfully enlisted the terms *muttons* and *nuts* to refer to ems and ens.

When indicating indentions or body type spacing, the instruction is:

indent one mutton (one em)

indent one nut   (one en)

Here is a setting which sums up the terms used:

17 ems (i.e. 17 pica or 12pt ems wide)		
a b c d E f g h i J k l m		
8pt nut	All 8pt type	8pt mutton
indent		indent
(i.e. one		(i.e. one
8pt en)		8pt em)

Measuring printed body size

Sometimes a deskman needs to know the body size of a piece of print. This can be deduced by using the measuring units described above. Take a type gauge marked with a pica scale. Measure twelve lines of the printed text from baseline to baseline, ignoring the ascenders and descenders. Twelve lines of 9pt solid will measure nine picas; twelve lines of 7pt, 2pt leaded, or set on a 9pt body, will also produce a measurement of nine picas, of course. It is the body size, not the face size, which is revealed by the 12-line measurement.

Shaikh Mujib's success in the Bangladesh elections comes as no surprise except perhaps by its magnitude. Ever since his return to his liberated country he has been presented by his followers as the "father of the nation". The new experience of nationhood was arduous enough for the role to be welcomed, especially in a country so riven by hatreds and scarred by suffering. By his

9 picas

Although the existing Constitution states that Parliament consists of the Sovereign (the Governor General in this case as representative of the Queen), the House of Representatives and the Senate, it is believed that it is possible to amend the Constitution to do away with the Senate.

It would still be possible, if the Senate desires, for it to re-

American advertisement measure

There is one final complication in measuring area. United States practice, on the larger papers, is to measure advertising in terms of the number of agate lines in depth. Agate is the name for $5\frac{1}{2}$pt type (*see* p. 2), giving (roughly) 14 agate lines to a column-inch. The *New York Times* page is 305 agate lines deep.

Spacing

In letterpress printing everything that is to print stands in relief to a certain plane height (0·918 in., known as *type height*).

All white space in a letterpress newspaper is metal that is lower than type height. The newspaperman is mostly concerned with the space around display type (which is provided by metal spacing), and white between lines of type (either by separate metal spacing or space included in the cast body of type). The white between words (or letters) in a line of text type will concern the average newsman less from day to day, but anyone concerned with newspaper design should know something also of the way this white is provided by line-casting spacing on Linotype and Intertype machines, and the implications for efficient reading.

Space between lines

This can be obtained mechanically by setting the type on a bigger body or slug. Thus a 7pt type can be cast on an 8pt body to give an extra 1pt

of white space between the lines. When the type is set on its own body, it is said to be set *solid*. When it is set on a larger body, it is said to be '7 on 8' or '8 on 9', and so on, according to the permutation of type and body size, and the deskman's instruction to the printer is '7/8' or '8/9'— the body size coming second.

The manual way to introduce white between lines of type in hot-metal plants is by the use of a machine-cast spacing material called a *lead*— pronounced 'ledd'. The lead is a thin strip of metal, cut to the width of the column. It is inserted by hand between the lines of type. Leads may be of varying thickness, eg, 1pt, 1½pt, 2pt, 3pt.

In these presentations the leads have been raised to printing height so that you can judge character and dimensions:

1pt

2pt

3pt

4pt

Space around headlines
This is provided by thicker, foundry-cast leads, graduated in 6 points (again raised here to printing height):

6pt

12pt

18pt

24pt

Spacing between letters and words

Spacing between headline words or letters is provided on Ludlow and similar machines by a range of blank matrices from, say 1½pt to 18pt. The spacing for making special indentions in hand-set captions and other occasional matter is called a quadrat (*quad* for short). The widest quad is the em of the point size. The others are fractions of the em.

Now for line-casting spacing. When the Linotype or Intertype operator wants a white space between words he taps the space key on the machine and a tapered spaceband slides between the letter matrices. The spaceband can provide the smallest word-space consistent with good typography, say something like 0·007 in. But because it is tapered it can expand by infinite gradations to something like 0·098 in.

As the line-composing operator nears the end of the line he frequently discovers that he has space left for only one or two letters, and that the following word does not hyphenate. This spare white space at the end of the line is automatically redistributed along the line before it is cast.

The spacebands are pushed up between the words, forcing in extra white until all the spare space on the line is evenly filled up. Only occasionally does the expanding spaceband fail to provide sufficient space to fill out the line satisfactorily. The operator can then insert extra spacing by hand.

In tabular setting (i.e. matter set in columns not separated by rules), where an even distribution of white between words would not help, the operator can make use of three fixed spaces provided automatically (as matrices)—em, en, and thin (four-to-the-em in all but very small faces, when it is three-to-the-em).

The Mental Factors

So much for the moment for the raw material of text setting. We cannot begin to discuss the basic item of newspaper setting, the text types, until we have touched on the mental processes of reading itself. This is a complicated psychological and physiological process, and despite a lot of research there is an area of unresolved argument. Some of the results of research have to be treated with reserve because of the limited nature of the experiments. Those that are helpful will be indicated, and some general conclusions emerge, but the serious newspaper designer and text editor should read more widely on the subject[5] and attempt also to keep in touch with modern research.[6] Newspapers occasionally have to question or disregard a reading optimum, and in the next chapter we will examine the limitations of newspaper text setting, but it is as well to be aware of what is ideal. There are designers and text editors with sufficient genius to combine all the non-optimum factors in a way which really does drastically affect the legibility of the newspaper.

We do not read by identifying individual character after individual character and building a word at a time. We read by recognising the shapes of words and groups of words—this means by recognising the external outlines and the internal shapes as a totality. The eye does not move smoothly along a line, but in a succession of short jerks, looking at sections of the line in a series of 'eye-fulls'.

The eye-fulls are separated by pauses of about a quarter of a second, called fixations. It is in these fixations that the perception, the absorption of meaning, takes place. About 94 per cent of reading time is devoted to fixation pauses. At the end of each line the eye sweeps back swiftly to the beginning of the next line in a return sweep, and the process of perception by fixations begins again. The width of an eye-full and the duration of a fixation depends, within limits, on the skill of the reader and the simplicity of the material. A poor reader may proceed a word at a time with frequent regressive movements in which his eyes go back to what he has already seen. The practised reader may absorb the meaning of half-a-dozen words in a single fixation and makes fewer regressions; and it is an aim of good typography to reduce regressions and fixations.

One incidental practical sequel of the reading process is the difficulty of detecting printing errors. The literate adult reading familiar simple material often perceives some of the words only marginally. He infers meaning from sentence structure, past knowledge, context, and so on, and 'sometimes even reads what he expects to see instead of what is actually printed, overlooking misprints or the omission of whole words'. [7]

This is the real difficulty for the proof reader and the deskman checking a proof. For the process of checking you have mentally to recondition yourself to looking at individual letters and words; and that is a reason why a man who has written a story is not the best man to check the proof for small printing errors: he knows what he expects to read and without concentrating he may see it when it is not there.

For the newspaper there is no consolation in the tendency of the eye to skip individual letters. You cannot hope that all the readers all the time will overlook setting errors (*literals* or *typos*) and one literal produces a devastating squeak in the most resounding editorial.

Four practical conclusions emerge from the fact that we read by recognising the configuration of groups of words. One is the desirability of avoiding letterspacing, which weakens the unity of words. The other three conclusions are as follows:

1. Lower-case[8] type is essential for the mass of newspaper setting. All-capital words form a very similar shape but lower-case words have substantial variety of pattern, especially from having ascenders and descenders. All-caps setting takes about four times longer to read, occupies about 40 per cent more space, and the number of words perceived with each fixation is reduced.

2. In reading by recognising configurations, the upper part of the lower-case letter is more important than the lower part.[9] There are more distinctive patterns in the upper half—and not merely in the ascenders. This is demonstrated when you actually cut through a line, **below.** The upper half of the lower-case letter is hard to read, but it is possible to understand the words in the second line when they are represented by the upper halves of the letters. The actual words in each instance are

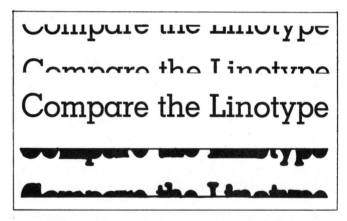

shown in the following two lines. The final two lines show again how much easier it is to comprehend even the outlines of the upper half of the words. The outlines of the lower half are much less distinguishable.

There is a lesson in this for the design of lower-case text type for newspapers. Because the point size must be small it is desirable to increase the x-height of the face by limiting the space taken by ascenders and descenders. But clearly it is the descenders which should bear the brunt of the squeeze. The ascenders can be abbreviated in newspaper text faces, to help improve x-height, but they must not lose their distinction. (In the first designs of Ionic for newspapers the x-height was increased too much to the detriment of the ascenders, with loss of readability.)

3. The third sequel to our habit of reading by total word shape (by silhouettes and internal patterns) is that the eye must not be distracted or the mind misled by letter shapes within the words. Capitals must be big enough only to be noticed; they must remain in harmony with the lower-case letters. In the lower-case letters, what Stanley Morison called 'the essential form' must predominate over any novel characteristics supplied for ornament. And the form of each of the letters must work together to aid the perception of whole words and phrases. The space between letters must be so distributed that it helps them to cohere into familiar word pictures we have grown used to over years of reading. However beautiful they are individually, or however scientifically designed, letters which are eccentric, or do not knit together, seriously compromise reading.

There is a simple rough test for readability of a face. If some unfamiliar element in the face catches your attention, then that is a mark against it. The fact that you have noticed the difference means that you have slowed down.

Helping the Reader

Reading research can give us valuable further guidance on the nature of a readable text face. Reading is hindered by letters with thin hair lines (as in Bodoni), or long or heavy serifs (as in some of the egyptian faces), or when there is marked contrast between thick and thin strokes.[10] Italic retards reading and is unpopular with readers.[11] These exclusions of strong egyptian faces and italic are, of course, for continuous text, and newspapers may well use italic sparingly for brief pieces of differentiated settings (such as distinguishing questions from answers, captions from text, and so on).

There is no case at all for anyone emulating the standard Continental custom of setting special full-length articles in italic, or indeed (need it be said) varying text faces from column to column. This bizarre habit takes away more in readability than it adds in typographic spice. The splendid *Le Monde*, for instance, is harder to read because of the random changes of text throughout the body of the paper, which vary between roman, bold, italic, egyptian and egyptian bold, so that the reader is invited continually to reorientate his visual memory. Page monotony has to be avoided by subtler methods than this.

Habit is the most powerful force in reading. It is one of the reasons why serifed letters are still rightly preferred to sans serif for continuous text, unadventurous though this may seem. Behind the serif there are centuries of reading experience; and most of our reading lives have been sustained by the serif. Such reading research as there is does not suggest there is any significant difference between speed of reading serif and sans serif[12], but Morison[13] and others[14] have argued more convincingly that the serif contributes to the uniting of separate letters into words and helps us to distinguish one shape from another. The serif undoubtedly helps to produce an identifiable distribution of white space in and around letters; and in small newspaper text types where a large x-height has been sought, the emphasis given by the serif to an ascender may play an important part in readability.

The serif terminates the straight line of the ascender in such a way as to give it maximum value as a black line on white paper: 'A straight line with no thickening or cross stroke at the end loses a fraction of its apparent length through halation from the paper'.[15] There are certainly obvious occasions when the serif helps the eye to make rapid distinctions between similar characters. Consider for instance:

Illinois!   Illegibility

The kind of momentary uncertainty produced by a sans serif in instances like this may, repeated over a long text, produce more regressions and require rather more concentrated effort than reading the more familiar and distinct serif letters, though the extra concentration required for sans will be hard to measure in reading research. The predominance of serif text faces may also be connected to Burt's claim that people read faster the typeface they prefer aesthetically,[16] for until relatively recently there have been few widely admired sans serif text faces. In addition to a few ambiguous letter forms, many have clearly lacked colour and cohesion.

This is not just a question of the aesthetic appeal of an individual letter form. Because sans letters are more even in colour they are, in a large unbroken area, more monotonous than serifed type.

Better sans faces for text are gradually being designed – for instance, Helvetica, in which the letters knit especially well into words. But Helvetica has such a large x-height that for long settings it needs 2 points of white between the lines for easy reading, and then it begins to lose its colour and economy:

This is how 8pt Helvetica looks when it is set solid. But there is a limit to the length that such setting should be allowed to run. With 2pt leading between the lines—as here—Helvetica is easier to read because of its large x-height, though of course there is a loss of colour and economy.

Further improvements in sans design will certainly come and with them perhaps acceptance of non-serif text faces. It may be a pointer that one piece of research[17] found a small legibility advantage for Gill Sans over Plantin, but only for adult readers.

Another piece of research[18] comparing the legibility of serif and sans serif found that Gill Medium had a 20 per cent advantage over the other newer faces (though it was not reliably better than the serif faces). Again this may be due to relative familiarity with Gill, compared with the other faces tested (Grot 215 and Univers); or possibly also that the general form of Gill is closer to the serifed typefaces we are used to reading. If the same experiment is repeated in ten years' time when Univers has been more widely seen it should, if the familiarity hypothesis is correct, improve its legibility rating.

If it is still comprehended less rapidly than Gill or serif faces, then it may be that the letters of this sans face do not have sufficient individual distinction to combine in perceptibly different shapes.

More fruitful innovations may well lie in the direction of Hermann Zapf's Optima, whose letter form has variations of stroke thickness with a flaring at the end of strokes which almost accomplishes the readability function of serifs. Optima can be described either as a calligraphic roman or a modified sans serif.

The newspaper designer will consider all the developing alternatives without prejudice – but with proper weight for tradition, for the ordered evolution which is the hallmark of viable change in typography.

Morison may have stuck his neck out too far when he said that 'it is safe to say no newspaper will ever be printed in sans serif',[19] but for the time being the choice is certainly from among the serif text faces; and we should certainly eschew the fashionable idea that sans, because it is newer, is therefore to be preferred as a symbol of dynamic modernity.

Preference for it is usually no more than the symbol of a designer's susceptibility to being trendy.

Special Newspaper Factors

These preliminary considerations of readability apply to all text setting. For newspapers there are two special factors: the imperatives of journalism and of production. Journalism requires economy of space. Production requires an especially robust type and, for many American papers, a type suited to remotely controlled automated setting.

The journalistic imperative of economy

Newspaper text type is inevitably in the smaller sizes from 10pt downwards: a great deal has to be communicated in a limited space. If a type small in point size is also small on its body, then it may be too small for comfortable reading, especially in the conditions in which newspapers are read. The newspaper text type must therefore have a large x-height. But this x-height must be achieved without damage to two other requirements. It must not, as we have seen, impair the clarity of the ascenders or it will lessen readability. And it must not be so wide that it consumes too much space. The famous Ionic, the first of the Legibility Group of types produced in 1926 especially for newspapers, was a brilliant success except in these two factors. The ascenders were too short and the admirably clear x-height lay in a square fat character that consumed excessive space.

Nor it is any answer to the newspaper problem of economy to gain space by squeezing the width of a letter to produce a really condensed face of low alphabet length. There are two reasons in hot-metal papers and one in filmset papers. First, in a condensed line-cast type there is less matrix metal around the relief letter: the sidewall, so called, is said to be thin. An ultra-thin sidewall wears out easily producing distortion of the printed image and the need for costly matrix replacement. Second, and this applies equally to filmset alphabets, there is a limit beyond which further condensation of set-width produces too much strain in reading for any length of setting. This, as we shall see, is one of the penalties of modern automatic setting methods in North America, but the general point on the difficulty of reading condensed letter forms can be illustrated here by Vogue Bold Condensed, an occasional newspaper face. Even for one-line caption settings it is a hard read:

Do you find your eye has to pause as you gaze across this line?

The alphabet length of a type is some guide to its legibility. The Vogue Condensed above has, in 10pt, an extraordinarily short lower-case alphabet length of 94 points, compared with 120 for Plantin and 138 for Corona Royal. Any 10pt below 110 points alphabet length, or 8pt below 90 points, is almost certainly too cramped for normal text.

This is only a rough guide—and certainly you should be cautious about judging set economy in newspapers too rigorously by competitive alphabet lengths. Here is a practical instance. The London *Daily Telegraph* used to set its news pages in Jubilee, an 8pt face with a lower-case alphabet length of 113 points. It reset a regular news page in a different 8pt type (Modern) with a larger face and an alphabet length of 118 points, a difference of five points which ought, in theory, to have produced an unwelcome amount of overmatter.

In fact the larger Modern resulted in only six extra lines in the whole page, and these were easily absorbed by small reductions of spacing here and there. Why was this? There are several reasons. The most important is that in this newspaper, made up in 11-pica columns, news items are written in fairly short paragraphs—rarely more than nine lines, more often six or seven. So there are plenty of short lines in a column, and it is these which take up the 'stretch'. Another reason is the English language itself. It is not *all* polysyllabic: there are many four-, five- or six-letter words which cannot be divided—which is why wide word-spacing in narrow measures is inevitable. In the specimen page much of the new setting (in the type with the longer alphabet length) ran line for line with the original.

The alphabet length of a text type is a more reliable guide to economy of setting when (*a*) paragraphs are longer and, or (*b*) the setting is across the wider 14- and 16-pica measures recently making a comeback in some American and British newspapers. The diminution in the number of breaklines then allows the narrower-set type to exploit its potential for economy. When judging types for economy, however, it is always a good idea to carry out comparative settings by the column.

2 Production imperatives:
(A) COLOUR AND CLARITY: The universal requirement is a type which survives into print with colour and clarity. A great deal has been achieved. There has been a remarkable improvement in colour and readability to meet changed production and reading conditions. The newspaper of today will be read in adverse conditions by many—in bad light or in motion travelling on bus, train and Tube. The vibration or bad light must be compensated for by size when possible but

also by maximum clarity of letters. Clear letters must form deftly and unambiguously into words.

And there must be reasonable colour to the printed image after printing with thin inks at high speed. Reading old newspapers puts a strain on the eyes because the text type is small, and also because it is so grey, swimming blearily in white. Modern text types have greatly improved here but even so this matter of *colour*[20] in the page is of increasing importance for newspapers all over the world. The weight or colour is a function of several conditions other than the thickness of the type—the tone of the newsprint, its quality, the relative blackness of the ink, the effects of stereotyping and printing, the amount of leading between lines, and the amount of white space in and around letters. The text type that was satisfactory on a short printing run with good newsprint is likely to fail when the run is long and the newsprint rougher. Increased circulations and increased paging have produced the need for longer runs; and increasing costs of newsprint and freight are forcing more newspapers to thinner newsprint.

The result, obvious in many newspapers, is text reproduction too thin for easy reading, especially in bad conditions. The naked eye is simply aware that the page is grey. Examination by microscope shows that fine serifs and thin letters on coarse newsprint are carrying insufficient ink; frequently serifs and thin strokes can be seen to have broken altogether under repeated mouldings and failed to print at all.

Here, for instance, is an enlarged comparison of several Times Roman

murder

murder

characters as they were designed—and as they appear after being set as text, cast, moulded, and run at high speed with thin inks on newsprint.

This shows the balance of judgments required from a newspaper typographer, for Times, particularly vulnerable to modern printing and paper, is the most economical newspaper face. The 8pt Times gives the journalist 5 to 7 per cent more space than, say, Royal.

But is it worth it if it is achieved, as it is nowadays in letterpress newspapers, at the expense of the colour and clarity of the text? The answer must be No. It is no good getting a lot in if it is irritating to read. Essentially the letterpress newspaper must have a text which will not suffer when cast into curved stereo plates from a papier-mâché matrix and printed at high speed for long runs on rough newsprint with ink which dries fuzzily by absorption into the newsprint fibres.

This means a type without fine lines and delicate serifs but with large counters, open bowls and an absence of the acute angles and narrow interstices that trap ink.

The designer works within strict limits. It is easy enough to thicken a letter, but if the type requires too much ink the newspaper may have problems drying it quickly. Then it may smear. Again, the colour required for news text must not be achieved at the cost of character differentiation, or *too much* space extravagance, or any assault on basic readability. Blackness achieved by reducing the white in the counters, for instance, affects the light cast within letters; and small counters are traps where thin inks collect and smear the text during printing. This is why the normal full boldface is not attractive for continuous newspaper text. The counter inside most boldfaces is smaller than that of roman characters and tends to fill up in letterpress printing on long runs. (Also, to be tolerable in large portions the ordinary body needs space-consuming interlinear white.)

Beginners in typography often worry about their inability to see small differences in letter style of the kind we have been discussing, like the biology student in James Thurber's story who could never see cells. Of course nobody should expect to notice subtle differences in letter formation when looking at type in a page. The effect can be seen when short sections of different faces are set side by side for comparison; but the detailed changes that produce the effect can only be seen in enlargements of key letters. It is worth examining two examples to emphasise both the limits of design and the cunning of the designer within his cage.

In the first the comparison is between a Bodoni letter and a Times letter. Bodoni is not a text face; it is used here merely because it provides an exaggerated contrast with Times, which hopefully will help anyone to grasp a general truth about the subtle possibilities of letter shapes.

e   e

The first 'e' is Times Roman and the second is Bodoni. Times Roman has a bigger x-height, of course, which is one important newspaper consideration, but the differing stress—*see* diagram, page 4— is another. The Bodoni is a modern face with vertical stress and the curves thickest at the vertical. The Times is an old face with the thickening of the curves on the diagonal. Increasing the colour in the modern face would mean thickening the strokes vertically, which means either widening the letter or diminishing the counters.

Both are disadvantages for a newspaper text. However, with Times the thicker parts of the curve can be made heavier at an angle without encroaching on the counter or increasing the width. Similarly, the Times old style stress produces a more distinct character when the letter 'b' is considered. Only in the lower left-hand part of this letter is the character distinct from the letter 'h'. In the Bodoni, below, the distinction depends on a thin vulnerable up-curling stroke. In the Times the 'b' is more distinct because of the thick old-style curve.

b   b

Compare now, from different faces, the letter 'd':

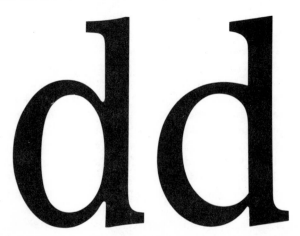

The Corona on the left looks more compressed than the Olympian on the right. But the broader appearance of the Olympian is an illusion.

The two letters are the same width, as is shown by this superimposition of outlines:

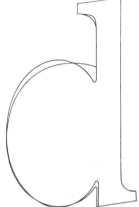

This illusion, which distinguishes the whole face, is useful, especially for the conditions for which Olympian was designed, of which more later. Again, like the Times–Bodoni comparison it is a distinction based on the stress of the letter and the resulting shape of the counter. I am indebted to Matthew Carter, who designed Olympian for Mergenthaler Linotype, for the following short sequence of drawings which make the point that it is the old-style nature of the 'd' of Olympian which gives it a more ample look than the modern-style 'd' of Corona. First the outlines of the letters:

Here, now, the counters are illuminated. Note the strong vertical stress of the Corona (left):

Here are the two counters side by side:

And here are the two counters superimposed:

The blacked-in parts are those by which the Olympian counter exceeds

other would not justify. The matrix of each character in the TTS fount is therefore assigned a width, one of eleven possible widths. Thus cap 'A' is 14 units and always 14 units whatever the design; lower-case 'a' must always be 11 units, whatever the design of the 'a'. These unit widths enable a typographer to produce fairly good letter proportions in unit matrices in 8pt faces to a lower-case alphabet length of 118·1 points for 11-pica columns. But since the standard was fixed in 1963 great numbers of American newspapers have abandoned 8pt in favour of 9pt. In 1969 there were 391 papers using 9pt, compared with 235 using 8pt. For an 11-pica column the justification answers in the wire tape will only produce lines of the correct length if composed to an alphabet length of 118·1 points (8-set). Therefore the 391 papers using 9pt have to use a 9pt type with the alphabet length of 118·1 points suitable for 8pt. They have to use what is called 8-set 9pt and 8-set 9pt must be an inferior typeface. This is how TTS 9pt (left) compares with regular 9pt:

The 8-set 9pt is forced to assume skyscraper proportions since the only room for enlargement is up and down.

On the Manhattan skyline that kind of enlargement is aesthetically satisfying but with type it can be disturbing, especially since the stereotyping processes condense type anyway. Most American newspapers have settled on good interlinear white; it is common practice to lead 1pt and that helps. But the worst damage to readability has arisen from the corruption—there is no other word—of Corona. It was not designed to be mangled by TTS, and the result of adopting 9pt Corona for 8-set is a heavy vertical emphasis which is not the easiest type to read for long, despite the gain from a large size. Corona is a modern type in that the axis of its curves is vertical. In the next example (**above, right**) the bowl of the 'd' is thickest along a section half-way up its height. A tangent to the curve at its thickest point would be vertical, parallel to the stem.

How do you compress this letter by 11 per cent to make it conform to the 9pt 8-set proportions? The answer was to move the thickest parts of the letter—and of all the letters in the line—closer together. As Matthew

Corona's in area. The apparent gain in width of Olympian is t
of turning the stress of the curves away from the vertical axis.

Teletype setting

Let us now turn to the second production imperative in the d
type, one which had a decisive influence in the creation of Ol
In teletypesetting (TTS), line-casting machines are operat
manually by a man sitting at the keyboard of the casting machi
automatically by the machine responding to a perforated tap
perforations in the tape have been produced at an earlier stage
operator at a keyboard. This gives two separate stages of prod
compared with the one of manual keyboarding and casting, but n
rates of setting are easily overtaken by TTS. This is because esp
fast line-casting machines can be operated without pause in respo
perforated tape.

TTS gives no real type-design problem when the tape is punch
the plant, but increasingly newspapers in North America have
feeding their machines with tape punched in Radio City, Manha
by the Associated Press and United Press International and then tr
mitted electrically to subscribing newspapers. More than 800 plan
North America reported to the American Newspaper Publis
Association Research Institute in 1969 (membership then 1,052 ne
papers in 858 plants) that they were using wire-service tape to ope
TTS. Most American newspapers depend on the agencies for tl
national and international news and TTS is obviously economical si
it combines the speed of line-casting from perforated tape with
economy of punching the tape centrally for hundreds of subscribe
The trouble is that TTS and a desire for larger body types have t
gether worked havoc with the readability of American newspaper text

This is how it has happened. If the wire-service tape is to be f
immediately on arrival into a tape-operated line-casting machine (
tape-operated photo-composing machine), it must be ready justifie
The wire-service centre therefore computes the justification while mor
than a thousand newspapers assemble the resulting line from matrice
and spacebands in their own line-casting machines. For the two settin
operations, national and local, to work independently like this but agree
in the result, the widths of matrices used for TTS composition have to
be brought to a single national standard.

Remote setting for everyone would not work if an 'e' punched on the
tape in New York produced a fat 'e' in the type used in a San Francisco
paper and a thin 'e' in the type used in a paper across the Bay. One or the

Carter has remarked[21]: 'The effect was to emphasise the verticality of the design and so produce a 'picket fence' of close-pitched serried thicks —a very mild form of the insistent rhythm of a Textura' (i.e. a Gothic blackletter with perpendicular stress). Whether the benefit of increased size is worth this distortion is questionable; a regular 8pt also has the advantage of consuming less space.

Mergenthaler Linotype fortunately decided in the early Sixties that TTS required a type designed as much as possible to overcome the skyscraper appearance produced by 8-set 9pt Olympian, designed by Matthew Carter, is the result. His clever use of the old face oblique stress —touched on earlier on pp. 21–23—has produced a type which looks less attenuated. Corona is the top line, with the stress shaded, and Olympian is the bottom line (of the same length):

bcdepq

bcdepq

That is a fine example of what good design can do in type, though, of course, Olympian remains a frankly condensed typeface. The ultimate answer in the US, when the majority of papers have moved to 9pt, will presumably be to change the TTS standard. In the meantime, and certainly while the majority are using 8-set 9pt Corona and suchlike, it has to be said that TTS is a pernicious design influence. It is easy to see why publishers have gone along. There are substantial gains in production time and in the United States in particular, where there is such a willingness to innovate, the result of production gains are measurable while the effect on design is a matter for judgment and argument.

What seems to be overlooked in North America is the medium-to-long-term effect on readers of newspapers as they find newspaper text frequently less inviting to read. The improvements in type-size and print and production standards are in danger of being lost by casual design standards: too much engineering and not enough art. The case of the *Waterbury Republican* and *Waterbury American* (Connecticut) is typical of both the virtues and vices of modern production. This efficient newspaper group converted to photo-composition and offset printing with significant production gains (composing time per page reduced by two hours, and a full six-day production reduced to a five-day week). But there has been a reduction in readability. The newspapers used to set 9pt Corona on 9½ body in 11-pica columns with 4pt column rule. They are now in 8½pt Aurora on 9¼ slug, Aurora being chosen because the extra weight is better for offset and there was no suitable 9pt. The photo-composed offset printing provides clearer images than the old hot metal, but the 8½pt is less satisfactory than 9pt, and the effect of the excessively cramped Aurora has been aggravated by the use of a SQU-7 width-compressing (squeeze) lens. Perforated tape comes out of a computer justified to an 11-pica column, but is run off on the photo-composing machines at a column width of 10·8 picas. The idea of that—to gain a 6pt column white—is laudable but the double squeeze on a normal character is not. There is only so much engineering one can do with the roman alphabet.

Making a choice

There is, as we can see, no simple answer to the production imperatives, still less to the production and journalistic imperatives combined. Eternal vigilance is the price of newspaper legibility. There has to be a nice judgment of priorities for a particular newspaper and particular technical conditions; there has to be enlightened pragmatism. This was the essential achievement of the Mergenthaler Linotype draughtsmen who, from Brooklyn in the Twenties and Thirties, under the direction of C H Griffith, inspired the revolution in text typography which gradually had its reviving influence on every part of newspaper design. In the Legibility Group of types that they produced they were responding not to some vision of Truth but to the weaknesses of newspaper text they saw before them; they improved colour and legibility and initiated the move towards larger sizes. Yet though the culminating type, Corona, today has wide appeal, it is very much in the tradition which bred it, which is to say that neither it, nor its Intertype equivalent Royal, is the answer for all papers because production conditions vary and so do the requirements of journalism.

To achieve the ideal balance of all the requirements of a newspaper text for any one paper indeed requires a designer who is a 'juggler extraordinaire'. A serious web offset paper with 14-em columns and a small print run will have to balance the advantages and disadvantages of a text type differently from a popular tabloid letterpress newspaper with 9-em columns and a long run. The popular newspaper, with short text, may be well served by a thick, chunky type of open character—to hold up well amid the big headlines and pictures. Hence the long retention of Ionic in London's *Daily Mirror* and *Sunday Mirror*. Such a text face will not be as good for sustained reading as another face, but if there is no sustained reading in the paper, the quality of readability is of reduced importance. Economy is another factor: a chunky type may be fine for a popular paper with lots of pages, but extravagant for a small sheet desperate for every word.

Designing a New Face

It will give some idea of the practical balance of factors if I indicate those that influenced Times Newspapers of London when it began to investigate the possibilities of designing a new face attractive enough for sustained reading to succeed both Times Roman at *The Times* and related papers at Printing House Square and Royal at *The Sunday Times*. The first rough brief went like this:

Proportions

1. The new face should not attempt the extreme word-economy of Times Roman (because of the thin matrix walls resulting and the unsatisfactory texture of the type after printing at high speed). The word-spacing of Royal/Corona at 8pt in 11 picas is considered satisfactory. Therefore make the new characters the same width as Corona/Royal—119 points for 8pt alphabet length against 109 points for Times Roman and 128 for Ionic.

2. The new face should have a better x-height than Times Roman and so appear larger, but it should not reach for the x-height of Corona/Royal with its penalties in reduced ascenders and character configuration. Therefore make the x-height of the new face between Times and Royal.
3. Caps occur frequently in news copy. Therefore make the caps less than the height of lower-case ascenders.

Colour

The overall colour should be much greater than Times Roman and fractionally greater than Corona/Royal, so as better to survive the long runs on thin newsprint.

Texture

Crisper than Ionic/Corona, but more even than Times. Therefore make the thick strokes a little thicker than Royal, thin strokes and serifs to be thinner. But make the serifs more robust than Times Roman.

General character

Old style
Transitional
Modern   } or a hybrid of these?
Egyptian
Clarendon

The Main Newspaper Text Faces

The principal newspaper text types number about twenty, though they are not all freely available internationally. Matrices made in Britain for line-casting machines (Linotype, Intertype) are struck to 'English' depth. Matrices made in the US and Germany are struck to American depth. This means the machines made in each country have different moulds and printers use one or the other. Canada, Australia, New Zealand, India, and Pakistan use American depth; so does most of Continental Europe. English depth is used in most of North Africa, Egypt, Lebanon, Iran and Malaysia.

1. Type designs made in Britain and the US

Linotype Ionic
    ,,   Excelsior
    ,,   Corona
    ,,   Times Roman

2. Designs made in the US only

Linotype Aurora   Intertype Regal
    ,,   Opticon   ,,   Rex
    ,,   Paragon
    ,,   Textype
    ,,   Olympian

3. Type designs made in Britain only

Linotype Jubilee   Intertype Ideal
    ,,   Telegraph Modern   ,,   Royal
    ,,   Times Europa   ,,   Imperial
    ,,   Plantin   ,,   Times Roman
                            ,,   Plantin

The American Newspaper Publishers Association Research Institute conducts a survey of production equipment each year among more than 1,000 newspapers (697 letterpress and 190 offset in 1970). These were the most popular faces for text:

Linotype Corona used in 349 newspapers
Intertype Imperial   79
Linotype Aurora   63
Intertype Regal   57
Intertype Royal   76

Similar figures are not available in Britain, but Intertype Royal (comparable to Linotype Corona) is also widely used.

Most newspaper text faces are available in a range of sizes up to 14pt and are duplexed in combinations of roman with italic and roman with bold; some are also duplexed with a sans serif. This means the operator can change from one style to the other as simply as a typist uses the shift key to produce capitals. The single matrix carries two versions of the same character. The manufacturers are always happy to supply catalogues of their current range—but the newspaperman must remember that at all times what matters is the characters as they reproduce.

Some general observations on reproduction strength will be made in the notes that follow, but newspapers contemplating a change of text type must always try the face in their own actual production conditions. After the machine trials of the matrices the specimen columns should be looked at and read first as a general reader would read them; and then photographic enlargements of sections of the printed type should be examined. Different sections of a page or column should be studied, not neglecting the corners.

Here first is a brief comparative showing of the text faces in 8pt (classified advertising faces are discussed later, pp. 73–77). A glance at this grouping gives an immediate sense of the differences in colour, stress and economy.

Ionic

Letterpress or relief printing is accomplished by inking a raised surface, then imposing a sheet of paper against this surface under pressure. There are four general types of presses for doing this. In the rotary presses used in most newspapers, the impression is taken from a curved printing plate which is fastened to a cylinder rotating against a continuous web of paper and pressure is *applied by a second impression cylinder.*

Ideal

Letterpress or relief printing is accomplished by inking a raised surface, then imposing a sheet of paper against this surface under pressure. There are four general types of presses for doing this. **In the rotary presses** used in most newspapers, the impression is taken from a curved printing plate which is fastened to a cylinder rotating against a continuous web of paper and pressure is applied by a second impression cylinder.

Excelsior

Letterpress or relief printing is accomplished by inking a raised surface, then imposing a sheet of paper against this surface under pressure. There are four general types of presses for doing this. In the rotary presses used in most newspapers, the impression is taken from a curved printing plate which is fastened to a cylinder rotating against a continuous web of paper and pressure is applied by *a second impression cylinder.*

Times New Roman

Letterpress or relief printing is accomplished by inking a raised surface, then imposing a sheet of paper against this surface under pressure. There are four general types of presses for doing this. In the rotary presses used in most newspapers, the impression is taken from a curved printing plate which is fastened to a cylinder rotating against a continuous web of paper and pressure is applied by a second *impression cylinder.*

Imperial

Letterpress or relief printing is accomplished by inking a raised surface, then imposing a sheet of paper against this surface under pressure. There are four general types of presses for doing this. In the rotary presses used in most newspapers, the impression is taken from a curved printing plate which is fastened to a cylinder rotating against a continuous web of paper and pressure is applied by a second impression cylinder.

Telegraph Modern

Letterpress or relief printing is accomplished by inking a raised surface, then imposing a sheet of paper against this surface under pressure. There are four general types of press for doing this. In the rotary presses used in most newspapers, the impression is taken from a curved printing plate which is fastened to a cylinder rotating against a continuous web of paper and pressure is applied **by a second impression cylinder.**

Plantin

Letterpress or relief printing is accomplished by inking a raised surface, then imposing a sheet of paper against this surface under pressure. There are four general types of presses for doing this. In the rotary presses used in most newspapers, the impression is taken from a curved printing plate which is fastened to a cylinder rotating against a continuous web of paper and pressure *is applied by a second impression cylinder.*

Jubilee

Letterpress or relief printing is accomplished by inking a raised surface, then imposing a sheet of paper against this surface under pressure. There are four general types of press for doing this. In the rotary presses used in most newspapers, the impression is taken from a curved printing plate which is fastened to a cylinder rotating against a continuous web of paper and pressure is applied by a second **impression cylinder.**

Times Europa

Letterpress or relief printing is accomplished by inking a raised surface, then imposing a sheet of paper against this surface under pressure. There are four general types of presses for doing this. In the rotary presses used in most newspapers, the impression is taken from a curved printing plate which is fastened to a cylinder rotating against a continuous web of paper and pressure is applied **by a second impression cylinder.**

Paragon

Racing thru the final hours of their lunar voyage, Apollo 12's moon men marveled at a spectacular eclipse of the sun today and briefly fired their jet thrusters to zero in on their splashdown target in the South Pacific.

Opticon

Racing thru the final hours of their lunar voyage, Apollo 12's moon men marveled at a spectacular eclipse of the sun today and briefly fired their jet thrusters to zero in on their splashdown target in the South Pacific.

Textype

Racing thru the final hours of their lunar voyage, Apollo 12's moon men marveled at a spectacular eclipse of the sun today and briefly fired their jet thrusters to zero in on their splashdown target in the South Pacific.

Corona

Racing thru the final hours of their lunar voyage, Apollo 12's moon men marveled at a spectacular eclipse of the sun today and briefly fired their jet thrusters to zero in on their splashdown target in the South Pacific.

Aurora (8½ TTS)

Racing thru the final hours of their lunar voyage, Apollo 12's moon men marveled at a spectacular eclipse of the sun today and briefly fired their jet thrusters to zero in on their splashdown target in the South Pacific.

Olympian

Racing thru the final hours of their lunar voyage, Apollo 12's moon men marveled at a spectacular eclipse of the sun today and briefly fired their jet thrusters to zero in on their splashdown target in the South Pacific.

Ionic

C E G K M R c e g h m p s t w

Ionic is the famous type which led to a revolution in newspaper typography when it was introduced in March 1926, first in the Newark (N.J.)
Evening News in 6½pt and, within 12 months, in 3,000 other newspapers
round the world. It was the first of the Legibility Group produced by
Linotype under the direction of C H Griffith and the first text type
specifically designed for newspapers. An adaptation of an antique face,
Ionic has exceptionally large x-height, short ascenders and descenders,
strong heavy-slab serifs with barely perceptible bracketing. The strokes
are monoline and the characters open and wide, almost square. In
colour, cut, robustness and size, it was a huge improvement on the thin
older moderns which, from the advent of the dry mat after 1900, dis-
integrated so badly that the readability of the newspaper type was at an
all-time low.

The weaknesses
1. The short ascenders hamper readability.
2. The colour is less satisfactory than, say, Corona after letterpress
printing.
3. The uneconomic set-width breeds ugly letterspacing in narrow
measures and costs a newspaper several inches per column compared
with Corona or Times Roman. Ionic in fact requires up to 30 per cent
more room than Corona. There is also a lack of comfort in reading
when set solid because the x-height means, in Morison's phrase, that
the letters stare at the reader. Ideally Ionic should be set with at least
1pt leads between the lines, or the 7pt type should be set on an 8pt body.
This improves readability but at the cost of more space and less colour.
It looks best also at measures over 14 picas: the *Daily Express* (London)
double-column settings in Ionic show it off well (**below right**).

Ionic has, therefore, been falling out of favour—yet it has a basic
virtue in its bold openness. A popular newspaper not excessively concerned with space economy could do worse than Ionic, especially a
version modified to mitigate the other weaknesses.

Manufacturer: Linotype
8pt x-height 0·060 in.
8pt lca (lower-case alphabet length): 127 points

7pt Ionic

Letterpress or relief printing is accomplished by inking a raised surface, then imposing a sheet of paper against this surface under pressure. There are four general types of presses for doing this. In the rotary presses used in most newspapers, the impression is taken from a curved printing plate which is fastened to a cylinder rotating against a continuous web of paper and pressure is applied **by a second impression cylinder.**

7pt on 8pt Ionic

Letterpress or relief printing is accomplished by inking a raised surface, then imposing a sheet of paper against this surface under pressure. There are four general types of presses for doing this. In the rotary presses used in most newspapers, the impression is taken from a curved printing plate which is fastened to a cylinder rotating against a continuous web of paper and pressure is applied **by a second impression cylinder.**

8pt Ionic

Letterpress or relief printing is accomplished by inking a raised surface, then imposing a sheet of paper against this surface under pressure. There are four general types of presses for doing this. In the rotary presses used in most newspapers, the impression is taken from a curved printing plate which is fastened to a cylinder rotating against a continuous web of paper and pressure is *applied by a second impression cylinder.*

8pt on 9pt Ionic

Letterpress or relief printing is accomplished by inking a raised surface, then imposing a sheet of paper against this surface under pressure. There are four general types of presses for doing this. In the rotary presses used in most newspapers, the impression is taken from a curved printing plate which is fastened to a cylinder rotating against a continuous web of paper and pressure is *applied by a second impression cylinder.*

THE currency upheavals since the beginning of the year have brought mixed fortunes to unit trust investors who put their money into funds which specialise in investing in foreign companies, or those British-based enterprises that operate overseas.

Our first Top Twenty table this year is dominated by these specialist unit trusts. It is based on all those which had minimum funds of £1 million at the start of the year.

Excelsior

C E G K M R c e g h m p s t w

A 1931 successor to Ionic, attempting to remedy some of the weaknesses of Ionic. The x-height is quite large but has been reduced below the exceptional one of Ionic so that it does not require leading and consequent loss of space—though leading also improves the legibility of Excelsior. A newspaper can safely set it solid or in 8 on 8½pt. Monotone strokes with even fewer ink traps than the Ionic (*see* the C, a, and e, which are all distinctly open). Strong horizontal serifs, specially designed to withstand repeated stereotyping and high-speed printing with thin inks. But Excelsior has less colour than Ionic and much less than Corona/Royal. Excelsior is little used in Britain—it survived for years at the *News of the World* and *The Sun*—but it is popular in Europe; in North America its small sizes are used by about sixty papers for classified settings.

7pt Excelsior

Letterpress or relief printing is accomplished by inking a raised surface, then imposing a sheet of paper against this surface under pressure. There are four general types of presses for doing this. In the rotary presses used in most newspapers, the impression is taken from a curved printing plate which is fastened to a cylinder rotating against a continuous web of paper and pressure is applied **by a second impression cylinder.**

8pt Excelsior

Letterpress or relief printing is accomplished by inking a raised surface, then imposing a sheet of paper against this surface under pressure. There are four general types of presses for doing this. In the rotary presses used in most newspapers, the impression is taken from a curved printing plate which is fastened to a cylinder rotating against a continuous web of paper and pressure is applied *a second impression cylinder.*

8pt on 9pt Excelsior

Letterpress or relief printing is accomplished by inking a raised surface, then imposing a sheet of paper against this surface under pressure. There are four general types of presses for doing this. In the rotary presses used in most newspapers, the impression is taken from a curved printing plate which is fastened to a cylinder rotating against a continuous web of paper and pressure is applied by *a second impression cylinder.*

Manufacturer: Linotype
8pt x-height 0·0535 in.
8pt lca: 123 points

Paragon, Opticon and Textype

Paragon, Opticon and Textype are developments of Ionic–Excelsior, manufactured in the US only (hence the American spellings below).

Paragon is a lighter version of Excelsior, designed to retain readability in newspapers carrying heavy half-tones and display ads requiring plenty of ink. But then the text type is lost in the page.

Opticon was developed for newspapers using a semi-hard newsprint which permits little spread of ink. It gives the appearance of being old and large. The thickening of Excelsior has taken place on the outer side of the strokes to retain the open bowls. This, however, further increases the set width and diseconomy of the type. It is greedier than Ionic.

Textype is a square face of moderate colour which has nevertheless more economy than the Ionic–Excelsior group. Its alphabet length of 115 points compares with Corona/Royal.

8 Paragon with Paragon Bold—on 9 Pt

Racing thru the final hours of their lunar voyage, Apollo 12's moon men marveled at a spectacular eclipse of the sun today and briefly fired their jet thrusters to zero in on their splashdown target in the South Pacific.

Charles (Pete) Conrad, Jr., Richard F. Gordon, Jr. and Alan L. Bean were in good spirits as their Yankee Clipper streaked toward home on a course that would slam them into the atmosphere 76 miles high at a speed of **24,600 m.p.h.**

8 Opticon with Bold Face No. 2—on 9 Pt

Racing thru the final hours of their lunar voyage, Apollo 12's moon men marveled at a spectacular eclipse of the sun today and briefly fired their jet thrusters to zero in on their splashdown target in the South Pacific.

Charles (Pete) Conrad, Jr., Richard F. Gordon, Jr. and Alan L. Bean were in good spirits as their Yankee Clipper streaked toward home on a course that would slam them into the atmosphere 76 miles high at a speed of **24,600 m.p.h.**

8 Textype with Bold Face No. 2—on 9 Pt

Racing thru the final hours of their lunar voyage, Apollo 12's moon men marveled at a spectacular eclipse of the sun today and briefly fired their jet thrusters to zero in on their splashdown target in the South Pacific.

Charles (Pete) Conrad, Jr., Richard F. Gordon, Jr. and Alan L. Bean were in good spirits as their Yankee Clipper streaked toward home on a course that would slam them into the atmosphere 76 miles high at a **speed of 24,600 m.p.h.**

Manufacturer: Linotype, US only
Paragon x-height: 0·0575 in.
8pt lca: 129 points
Opticon x-height: 0·05575 in.
8pt lca: 130 points
Textype x-height: 0·04925 in.
8pt lca: 115 points

Corona and Royal

C E G K M R c e g h m p s t w

For Corona here, also read Royal (Corona came first in 1941, Royal in 1958, but there is no significant difference). Corona is the most popular face in the United States (used in nearly 400 plants or 45 per cent of the news pages). It has fairly narrow letters of modern stress, with a large x-height, such that 7½pt Royal on an 8pt body still produces a larger printed image than 8pt solid Times Roman. The x-height is smaller than Ionic, but there is better differentiation of the ascenders than Ionic–Excelsior, which helps readability. This means that at a pinch Corona can be set solid—but it is better leaded, as texts are in the country of its origin (the US). Corona/Royal without interlinear white is clotted and, in long passages, fatiguing. The design is more compact than the square Ionics, yielding more words to a column-inch without going to such an extreme in condensation as to become significantly harder to read. That is in ordinary manual setting: it has to be said that the 9pt 8-set Corona used by newspapers served by wire tape in the United States is inferior to the true 9pt, being uncomfortably squashed up. How ironic that Corona with its Ionic pedigree of wide proportions should end up as such a condensed face.

Corona has strong, stubby serifs, open counters, with few ink traps, and stronger colour than Ionic–Excelsior–Paragon or Times. It was the first type in which letters were designed to compensate for the distortions of stereotype shrinkage, and is in many ways a composite of the most desirable features of the Legibility Group. At high speeds and on long runs in letterpress, however, even Corona/Royal can wear thin.

Manufacturers: *Corona*, Linotype; *Royal*, Intertype
8pt x-height: 0·05675 in. (Corona)
                    0·057 in. (Royal)
8pt lca: 118 points (Corona)
            119 points (Royal)

8 Corona with Bold Face No. 2—Set Solid

Racing thru the final hours of their lunar voyage, Apollo 12's moon men marveled at a spectacular eclipse of the sun today and briefly fired their jet thrusters to zero in on their splashdown target in the South Pacific.

Charles (Pete) Conrad, Jr., Richard F. Gordon, Jr. and Alan L. Bean were in good spirits as their Yankee Clipper streaked toward home on a course that would slam them into the atmosphere 76 miles **high at a speed of 24,600 m.p.h.**

9 Solid

Racing thru the final hours of their lunar voyage, Apollo 12's moon men marveled at a spectacular eclipse of the sun today and briefly fired their jet thrusters to zero in on their splashdown target in the South Pacific.

Charles (Pete) Conrad, Jr., Richard F. Gordon, Jr. and Alan L. Bean were in good spirits as their Yankee Clipper streaked toward home on a course that would slam them into the atmosphere 76 miles high at a speed **of 24,600 m.p.h.**

9 on 10 Pt

Racing thru the final hours of their lunar voyage, Apollo 12's moon men marveled at a spectacular eclipse of the sun today and briefly fired their jet thrusters to zero in on their splashdown target in the South Pacific.

Charles (Pete) Conrad, Jr., Richard F. Gordon, Jr. and Alan L. Bean were in good spirits as their Yankee Clipper streaked toward home on a course that would slam them into the atmosphere 76 miles high at a speed **of 24,600 m.p.h.**

8 on 9 Pt

Racing thru the final hours of their lunar voyage, Apollo 12's moon men marveled at a spectacular eclipse of the sun today and briefly fired their jet thrusters to zero in on their splashdown target in the South Pacific.

Charles (Pete) Conrad, Jr., Richard F. Gordon, Jr. and Alan L. Bean were in good spirits as their Yankee Clipper streaked toward home on a course that would slam them into the atmosphere 76 miles **high at a speed of 24,600 m.p.h.**

9 TTS Corona (8 Set) Solid

Racing thru the final hours of their lunar voyage, Apollo 12's moon men marveled at a spectacular eclipse of the sun today and briefly fired their jet thrusters to zero in on their splashdown target in the South Pacific.

Charles (Pete) Conrad, Jr., Richard F. Gordon, Jr. and Alan L. Bean were in good spirits as their Yankee Clipper streaked toward home on a course that would slam them into the atmosphere 76 miles **high at a speed of 24,600 m.p.h.**

9 TTS (8 Set) on 10 Pt

Racing thru the final hours of their lunar voyage, Apollo 12's moon men marveled at a spectacular eclipse of the sun today and briefly fired their jet thrusters to zero in on their splashdown target in the South Pacific.

Charles (Pete) Conrad, Jr., Richard F. Gordon, Jr. and Alan L. Bean were in good spirits as their Yankee Clipper streaked toward home on a course that would slam them into the atmosphere 76 miles **high at a speed of 24,600 m.p.h.**

Imperial

C E G K M R c e g h m p s t w

The coarser monotone blunt serif features of the Ionic group were modified and refined in a sophisticated way in 1954 by Edwin W Shaar to produce Imperial. It is a near monoline face of modern vertical stress, though to avoid monotony the designer introduced transitional characteristics with letter-width proportions leaning towards the classic, and gently sloping serifs.[22] There are open counters and deep crotches to avoid ink trapping. The x-height—bigger than Times—is lower than Corona/Royal and the ascenders have distinction. Its 7pt alphabet length of 108 points is midway between Times (100) and Jubilee (103) and Corona/Royal (111) and its matrix walls are stronger than Times.

Imperial can be set solid much more comfortably than Corona/Royal, but it is seen at its best in the well-printed *New York Times Book Review* section, where the first eight pages are 8½ on 10pt across 13 ems. It has never really caught on in Britain.

7pt on 8pt

Letterpress or relief printing is accomplished by inking a raised surface, then imposing a sheet of paper against this surface under pressure. There are four general types of presses for doing this. In the rotary presses used in most newspapers, the impression is taken from a curved printing plate which is fastened to a cylinder rotating against a continuous web of paper and pressure is applied by a second impression cylinder.

8pt on 9pt

Letterpress or relief printing is accomplished by inking a raised surface, then imposing a sheet of paper against this surface under pressure. There are four general types of presses for doing this. In the rotary presses used in most newspapers, the impression is taken from a curved printing plate which is fastened to a cylinder rotating against a continuous web of paper and pressure is applied *by a second impression cylinder.*

8pt

Letterpress or relief printing is accomplished by inking a raised surface, then imposing a sheet of paper against this surface under pressure. There are four general types of presses for doing this. In the rotary presses used in most newspapers, the impression is taken from a curved printing plate which is fastened to a cylinder rotating against a continuous web of paper and pressure is applied by a second impression cylinder.

Manufacturer: Intertype
8pt x-height: 0·054 in.
8pt lca: 117 points

Ideal

An adaptation of Century, Ideal was designed for the *New York Times* in 1935. Of the other text types displayed here, it is nearest to Excelsior in x-height and openness and squareness of design. In 7pt it is greedy with space, being fractionally less economical even than Ionic and Excelsior, but in 8pt it compares with Royal/Corona. It does not, however, provide their attractive page colour.

7 pt Ideal with bold

Letterpress or relief printing is accomplished by inking a raised surface, then imposing a sheet of paper against this surface under **pressure. There are four general** types of pressure for doing this. In the rotary presses used in most newspapers, the impression is taken from a curved printing plate which is fastened to a cylinder rotating against a continuous web of paper and pressure is applied by a second impression cylinder.

7 pt with bold on 8 pt

Letterpress or relief printing is accomplished by inking a raised surface, then imposing a sheet of paper against this surface under pressure. There are four general **types of presses for doing this.** In the rotary presses used in most newspapers, the impression is taken from a curved printing cylinder rotating against a continuous web of paper and pressure is applied by a second impression cylinder.

8 pt with doric

Letterpress or relief printing is accomplished by inking a raised surface, then imposing a sheet of paper against this surface under pressure. There are four general types of presses for do-**ing this. In the rotary presses** used in most newspapers, the impression is taken from a curved printing plate which is fastened to a cylinder rotating against a continuous web of paper and pressure is applied by a second impression cylinder.

8 pt with doric on 9 pt

Letterpress or relief printing is accomplished by inking a raised surface, then imposing a sheet of paper against this surface under pressure. There are four general types of presses for do-**ing this. In the rotary presses** used in most newspapers, the impression is taken from a curved printing plate which is fastened to a cylinder rotating against a continuous web of paper and pressure is applied by a second impression cylinder.

9 pt with italic

Letterpress or relief printing is accomplished by inking a raised surface, then imposing a sheet of paper against this surface under pressure. There are four general types of presses for doing this. In *the rotary presses used in* most newspapers, the impression is taken from a curved printing plate which is fastened to a cylinder rotating against a continuous web of paper and pressure is applied by a second impression cylinder.

Manufacturer: Intertype
8pt x-height: 0·0525 in.
8pt lca: 119 points

Times New Roman
C E G K M R c e g h m p s t w

This was specially designed for *The Times* of London in 1932. It needs good paper and presswork in letterpress to be at its best, when it is very good indeed, but without these conditions it can easily fail in newspapers. Stanley Morison designed it as a universal type which, in differing weights and sizes, could also provide the design for *The Times* headings and for the small type in classified.[23] At an early stage Morison modified Plantin, making its blunt terminals taper like Perpetua; if it is put alongside Monotype Plantin 110 it is easy to compare the old style diagonal stress and the shorter descenders, and contrast the finer cut, especially in the bracketed serifs, of Times. Weight approaching Ionic was gained by a thickening of the old-style stress in the curves, and the monotony of Ionic was avoided by reducing the weight of the sub-strokes where they join the main stems.[24] These ingenious combinations produce an open readable face which also has an economical word count—as much as 30 per cent more than square Ionic, size for size, which was one of its great attractions for Morison and *The Times*. Times New Roman also offers a reasonable x-height, only fractionally lower than Excelsior so that, as Peggy Lang wrote in 1946, it may indeed never be surpassed either for economy or in psychological appeal. But Times New Roman as designed and Times New Roman in ordinary newspaper production are two different things.

There are two main difficulties. First the close set of Times is achieved at the expense of ultra-thin sidewalls on the matrices which means that they will not stand up so long to the heavy wear of newspaper work.

Secondly, and even more important, Times New Roman without good heavy newsprint (14 lb and upwards), and relatively slow running in the pressroom with time for changes of plates, is not Times New Roman, especially in the ultra-small sizes. The serifs and thin strokes carry insufficient ink or break down altogether under repeated mouldings; ink can be trapped, especially in the eye of the e and the loop of the g, and the E where the top serifs nearly touch, producing an ugly smear. The resulting anaemic text has impelled one of its most distinguished advocates[25] to conclude that it will not survive the decade as a major news-text; and the evidence for that view is strong in letterpress. The *Financial Times* in London switched to Royal in 1970 after twenty-four years of Times; in the United States the face has never caught on. Yet none of the deficiencies so fatal in modern letterpress applies to photoset and offset-printed newspapers. The sidewall weakness does not exist in photosetting, and offset printing retains the colour. Perhaps Times New Roman will make a comeback here. It is still rightly popular as a magazine and book face, particularly in America.

7pt on 8pt Times Roman.

Letterpress or relief printing is accomplished by inking a raised surface, then imposing a sheet of paper against this surface under pressure. There are four general types of presses for doing this. In the rotary presses used in most newspapers, the impression is taken from a curved printing plate which is fastened to a cylinder rotating against a continuous web of paper and pressure is applied by a **second impression cylinder.**

8pt

Letterpress or relief printing is accomplished by inking a raised surface, then imposing a sheet of paper against this surface under pressure. There are four general types of presses for doing this. In the rotary presses used in most newspapers, the impression is taken from a curved printing plate which is fastened to a cylinder rotating against a continuous web of paper and pressure is applied by a second *impression cylinder.*

8pt on 9pt

Letterpress or relief printing is accomplished by inking a raised surface, then imposing a sheet of paper against this surface under pressure. There are four general types of presses for doing this. In the rotary presses used in most newspapers, the impression is taken from a curved printing plate which is fastened to a cylinder rotating against a continuous web of paper and pressure is applied by a second *impression cylinder.*

9pt

Letterpress or relief printing is accomplished by inking a raised surface, then imposing a sheet of paper against this surface under pressure. There are four general types of presses for doing this. In the rotary presses used in most newspapers, the impression is taken from a curved printing plate which is fastened to a cylinder rotating against a continuous web of paper and pressure is applied **by a second impression cylinder.**

9pt on 10pt

Letterpress or relief printing is accomplished by inking a raised surface, then imposing a sheet of paper against this surface under pressure. There are four general types of presses for doing this. In the rotary presses used in most newspapers, the impression is taken from a curved printing plate which is fastened to a cylinder rotating against a continuous web of paper and pressure is applied **by a second impression cylinder.**

Manufacturers: Monotype, Linotype, Intertype
8pt x-height, Linotype version: 0·05325 in.
8pt lca: 109 points

Aurora

C E G K M R c e g h m p s t w

Aurora, produced in 1961 from the same drawings as Corona, is specifically a child of teletypesetting from wire tape. It was created to fill a gap in the TTS wire-circuit range of faces, which was revealed when the standard was changed in 1963 to provide an 8-set face between 8 and 9pt in height. There is a little more weight than in Corona.

It is moderately popular in North America because of the preference for types larger than 8pt and the widespread use of the wire-circuit TTS composition. It is made in one size only, 8½pt, with several combinations, but with a lower-case alphabet length of 118·1 for wire-service transmission. The increase in size at this alphabet length is achieved, as always, by squashing the letters so that they are tall and thin. The basic design is similar to Corona, and the colour is strong monotone, but this maneouvre for TTS makes Aurora less readable than a genuine 8pt Corona. The combinations are Roman with Italic, with Boldface, and with Erbar Bold; and there is also an 8½pt Aurora with Bold, 8·36-set, for 11½-pica columns.

8½ TTS Aurora with Bold Face—Set Solid

Racing thru the final hours of their lunar voyage, Apollo 12's moon men marveled at a spectacular eclipse of the sun today and briefly fired their jet thrusters to zero in on their splashdown target in the South Pacific.

Charles (Pete) Conrad, Jr., Richard F. Gordon, Jr. and Alan L. Bean were in good spirits as their Yankee Clipper streaked toward home on a course that would slam them into the atmosphere 76 miles **high at a speed of 24,600 m.p.h.**

Manufacturer: Linotype, US only
8pt x-height: 0·061 in.
8pt lca: 118 points for the 8-set
123 points for the 8·36-set

Plantin

C E G K M R c e g h m p s t w

Originally introduced as a book face (the present volume is an example), Plantin is widely used in magazines and has some potential for photo-composed web offset newspapers. It is an eminently readable old face, with moderately varied stems, stubby serifs, good ascenders, and generally unobtrusive characters which knit well into words. One attraction is the space economy, when setting is in long paragraphs; it is even better than Times or Jubilee, without looking squashed, and has been used successfully in magazines, including *The Sunday Times* (London) Colour Magazine. Plantin is unfortunately not suitable for letterpress newspapers. First, its profiles are not sharp enough for the rougher processes of reproduction and there are a few ink traps—notably the overlapping stem W and the eye of the e.

Secondly, its attractive space economy, achieved by close-fitting characters, means ultra-thin sidewalls on the matrices and in daily newspaper production these wear out too quickly: it is not a type that will appeal to a newspaper's accountants.

8pt on 9pt Plantin.

Letterpress or relief printing is accomplished by inking a raised surface, then imposing a sheet of paper against this surface under pressure. There are four general types of presses for doing this. In the rotary presses used in most newspapers, the impression is taken from a curved printing plate which is fastened to a cylinder rotating against a continuous web of paper and pressure *is applied by a second impression cylinder.*

Manufacturers: Linotype
and Intertype
8pt x-height: 0·0515 in. (Linotype)
8pt lca: 107 points

Jubilee

C E G K M R c e g h m p s t w

Introduced in 1953, Jubilee was the first original newspaper text face devised in Britain since Times Roman (1932). It is not available in America. It is a livelier face than any of the square Ionic–Excelsior–Corona group. The serifs are firm and blunt, like Excelsior but chamfered at the end to give finish and sharpness. The shading is nearer to the old face contrast of thicks and thins in Times than to the square monotones of Ionic and descendants. The counters are open; note the middle section of w which is without the serifs that can close the openings in high-speed presswork. It has been judged equally satisfactory for reproduction by rotary letterpress or photogravure.[26]

It is economical in set width. Its character count in the normal body sizes is in fact only one or two less than the exceptional Times, and it can be set solid without handicap. By comparison with Corona/Royal it lacks colour, and suffers from a lower x-height than Ionic, Excelsior, Paragon, Corona/Royal, or Times, so that the Jubilee 8pt seems thin and small for the run of newsprint text.

7pt on 8pt Jubilee

Letterpress or relief printing is accomplished by inking a raised surface, then imposing a sheet of paper against this surface under pressure. There are four general types of press for doing this. In the rotary presses used in most newspapers, the impression is taken from a curved printing plate which is fastened to a cylinder rotating against a continuous web of paper and pressure is applied by a **second impression cylinder.**

8pt on 9pt

Letterpress or relief printing is accomplished by inking a raised surface, then imposing a sheet of paper against this surface under pressure. There are four general types of press for doing this. In the rotary presses used in most newspapers, the impression is taken from a curved printing plate which is fastened to a cylinder rotating against a continuous web of paper and pressure is applied by a second **impression cylinder.**

9pt on 10pt

Letterpress or relief printing is accomplished by inking a raised surface, then imposing a sheet of paper against this surface under pressure. There are four general types of presses for doing this. In the rotary presses used in most newspapers, the impression is taken from a curved printing plate which is fastened to a cylinder rotating against a continuous web of paper and pressure is applied *by a second impression cylinder.*

Manufacturer: Linotype
8pt x-height: 0·05225 in.
8pt lca: 113 points

Telegraph Modern

C E G K M R c e g h m p s t w

Introduced in 1968 in the London *Daily Telegraph* as a replacement for Jubilee, Telegraph Modern is an exceptionally crisp text face designed to retain its sharp impression even after the blurring and blunting effects of conventional letterpress processes. It is not available in America.

In part the acceptably clear outlines of Modern are achieved by strong blunt (and intrusive?) serifs which are almost unbracketed: Walter Tracy, the designer, established by photographic enlargements where bits of the serifs of other text types disappeared and took amending action. So, too, with ink traps. In Modern the v-angles of M and W, for instance, are expanded slightly to allow a certain amount of ink fill-in during reproduction without the usual unsightly smear. The face has the angularity of a Modern, with more contrast between thick and thin strokes than in the Ionics, but the vertical stress is modified to provide open bowls and counters. Though the design is different, the proportions are similar to Corona/Royal: in alphabet length it is somewhat less economical than Jubilee, but the loss of lines in a full newspaper column of short paragraphs has been found to be minimal (*see* p.17).

7pt on 8pt Modern

Letterpress or relief printing is accomplished by inking a raised surface, then imposing a sheet of paper against this surface under pressure. There are four general types of press for doing this. In the rotary presses used in most newspapers, the impression is taken from a curved printing plate which is fastened to a cylinder rotating against a continuous web of paper and pressure is applied by a **second impression cylinder.**

8pt on 9pt

Letterpress or relief printing is accomplished by inking a raised surface, then imposing a sheet of paper against this surface under pressure. There are four general types of press for doing this. In the rotary presses used in most newspapers, the impression is taken from a curved printing plate which is fastened to a cylinder rotating against a continuous web of paper and pressure is applied **by a second impression cylinder.**

9pt on 10pt

Letterpress or relief printing is accomplished by inking a raised surface, then imposing a sheet of paper against this surface under pressure. There are four general types of press for doing this. In the rotary presses used in most newspapers, the impression is taken from a curved printing plate which is fastened to a cylinder rotating against a continuous web of paper and pressure is *applied by a second impression cylinder.*

Manufacturer: Linotype
8pt lc x-height: 0·054 in.
8pt lca: 117 points

Times Europa

C E G K M R c e g h m p s t w

This is the new type designed for Times Newspapers in London in 1971 to replace Times Roman at Printing House Square (*The Times, The Times Literary Supplement*, and *The Times Educational* and *Higher Educational Supplements*) and Royal at Gray's Inn Road (*The Sunday Times*). The criteria laid down by a committee[27] have already been mentioned, and the type was designed by Walter Tracy of Linotype. (Another trial type was designed to an idea by Robert Harling, who suggested that the letterforms of Ionic should be reduced to the widths of Corona, the weight increased, with the serifs almost as square cut as in a good egyptian type such as Beton. This provided a bolder face than Europa with very large x-height; but in the end it was judged to be less satisfactory for sustained newspaper reading.)

Times Europa is an original design of clear profiles and great vitality. It has the 'round' effect and some of the oblique stress of the old-style faces, small brackets, and some thick–thin contrast, all of which makes it livelier, especially in the mass, than the 'vertical' monotone Corona/ Royal. It has much more colour than Times Roman and slightly more than Corona/Royal. Europa does not offer the space economy of Times (which is achieved only at the cost of weak sidewalls), but is identical in this respect to the popular Corona/Royal, as the alphabet lengths demonstrate.

In x-height it is between Times, which in 8pt is rather too small, and Corona/Royal, where the large x-height is achieved by abbreviating the ascenders, hence impeding the reader's comfort for sustained reading.

Times Europa is one of the most readable news text-types currently available, and—because a high degree of matrix durability was specified in its design brief—one of the most effective in production terms.

Manufacturer: Linotype (UK)
8pt x-height: 0·555 in.
8pt lca: 1.18 points

7pt Times Europa

Letterpress or relief printing is accomplished by inking a raised surface, then imposing a sheet of paper against this surface under pressure. There are four general types of presses for doing this. In the rotary presses used in most newspapers, the impression is taken from a curved printing plate which is fastened to a cylinder rotating against a continuous web of paper and pressure is applied by a second impression **cylinder.**

7pt on 8pt

Letterpress or relief printing is accomplished by inking a raised surface, then imposing a sheet of paper against this surface under pressure. There are four general types of presses for doing this. In the rotary presses used in most newspapers, the impression is taken from a curved printing plate which is fastened to a cylinder rotating against a continuous web of paper and pressure is applied by a second impression **cylinder.**

8pt

Letterpress or relief printing is accomplished by inking a raised surface, then imposing a sheet of paper against this surface under pressure. There are four general types of presses for doing this. In the rotary presses used in most newspapers, the impression is taken from a curved printing plate which is fastened to a cylinder rotating against a continuous web of paper and pressure is applied **by a second impression cylinder.**

8pt on 9pt

Letterpress or relief printing is accomplished by inking a raised surface, then imposing a sheet of paper against this surface under pressure. There are four general types of presses for doing this. In the rotary presses used in most newspapers, the impression is taken from a curved printing plate which is fastened to a cylinder rotating against a continuous web of paper and pressure is applied **by a second impression cylinder.**

9pt

Letterpress or relief printing is accomplished by inking a raised surface, then imposing a sheet of paper against this surface under pressure. There are four general types of presses used in most newspapers, the impression is taken from a curved printing plate which is fastened to a cylinder rotating against a continuous web of paper and pressure is applied *by a second impression cylinder.*

9pt on 10pt

Letterpress or relief printing is accomplished by inking a raised surface, then imposing a sheet of paper against this surface under pressure. There are four general types of presses used in most newspapers, the impression is taken from a curved printing plate which is fastened to a cylinder rotating against a continuous web of paper and pressure is applied *by a second impression cylinder.*

Olympian

Olympian was specially designed by Matthew Carter at Mergenthaler Linotype to help those North American newspapers seeking a 9pt text face on the 8-set of TTS wire composition. It was designed as a 9pt to be 8-set and the elongation required is less irksome than in other 8-set 9pt faces because of the designer's ingenious exploitation of old-style oblique stress. There is also a regular non-TTS 9pt (lower-case alphabet length 132 points) and a very good bold. Olympian has a large x-height but differs from Aurora in departing from the monotones of Corona/Royal; it has tapered strokes and finer bracketed serifs.

9 TTS Olympian (8 Set)—Solid

Racing thru the final hours of their lunar voyage, Apollo 12's moon men marveled at a spectacular eclipse of the sun today and briefly fired their jet thrusters to zero in on their splashdown target in the South Pacific.

Charles (Pete) Conrad, Jr., Richard F. Gordon, Jr. and Alan L. Bean were in good spirits as their Yankee Clipper streaked toward home on a course that would slam them into the atmosphere 76 miles **high at a speed of 24,600 m.p.h.**

9 TTS Olympian (8 Set)—10 Pt. Body

Racing thru the final hours of their lunar voyage, Apollo 12's moon men marveled at a spectacular eclipse of the sun today and briefly fired their jet thrusters to zero in on their splashdown target in the South Pacific.

Charles (Pete) Conrad, Jr., Richard F. Gordon, Jr. and Alan L. Bean were in good spirits as their Yankee Clipper streaked toward home on a course that would slam them into the atmosphere 76 miles **high at a speed of 24,600 m.p.h.**

9 Olympian Set Solid

Racing thru the final hours of their lunar voyage, Apollo 12's moon men marveled at a spectacular eclipse of the sun today and briefly fired their jet thrusters to zero in on their splashdown target in the South Pacific.

Charles (Pete) Conrad, Jr., Richard F. Gordon, Jr. and Alan L. Bean were in good spirits as their Yankee Clipper streaked toward home on a course that would slam them into the atmosphere 76 miles high at a speed *of 24,600 m.p.h.*

9 on 10 Pt.

Racing thru the final hours of their lunar voyage, Apollo 12's moon men marveled at a spectacular eclipse of the sun today and briefly fired their jet thrusters to zero in on their splashdown target in the South Pacific.

Charles (Pete) Conrad, Jr., Richard F. Gordon, Jr. and Alan L. Bean were in good spirits as their Yankee Clipper streaked toward home on a course that would slam them into the atmosphere 76 miles high at a speed *of 24,600 m.p.h.*

Manufacturer: Mergenthaler Linotype (US)
x-height: 0·063 in.   lca: 129 points

2 The Readability of Newspaper Text

People are inclined to confuse intrinsic legibility with their private aesthetic preference. —BEATRICE WARDE

Despite the giddy optimism of some newspaper designers and editors, there are limits to what text-type settings the human eye can read with comfort. Choosing a suitable news text-type is an infrequent exercise—how many newsmen reading this know the text type of their own newspaper?—but the possibility of exercising an Olympian judgment some day is not the sole or even main reason for studying the varieties. The newsman should know about text types because he should know the strengths and weaknesses of the different varieties and because some appreciation of the implications of designing a single serif will force him to think about making a newspaper wholly readable. The reader has rights. A good text type is one of them. But the readability of newspaper text is also greatly affected by white space, by the style and measure of setting and the size of type.

White Space

Nothing in typography is more neglected at greater cost than the areas of a page which carry no ink. White space is not a mere residue. It is an active force. It marshals type into clear and meaningful units or scatters it like grapeshot. It directs or misdirects our attention. It succeeds most dramatically when it is massed to illuminate headline and picture display. But the correct distribution of white space is also vital in the detail of text setting. Newspaper text type is primarily affected by spacing between the lines of type, and spacing between words or between letters. Here is the correct declension of white space:

Space between letters should be less than space between words.
Space between words should be less than space between lines.
Space between lines should be less than between groups of lines.

Interlinear white
White space is introduced between lines of type to improve readability.

First, the line of type itself may need more illumination. Secondly, white space between lines enables the eye to move more easily from the end of one line to pick up the beginning of the next. It is vital for long lines.

Interlinear white can be obtained by leading—manually inserting metal leads between lines of type—or mechanically by setting the type on a bigger body or slug. Thus a 7pt type can be cast on an 8pt body to give an extra one point of white space between the lines. When the type is set on its own body, it is said to be set 'solid'.

Obviously, if space is desired between the lines of the chosen text face, it is far better in newspaper to obtain it mechanically than by slow leading by hand. However, this does make careful editing on the composing stone more essential. When text does not quite fill a column, the simplest thing is for the comp to lead it out to fill, and this may produce undesirable results when type is already cast on a bigger slug. For instance, if a comp inserts 2pt leads between text type which is already diluted by being set 7 on 8, you end up with 3 points of white between the lines. Given the measure of setting and the type design, this may well be too much white for easy reading—erratic interlinear spacing on a page looks bad, too. To avoid this, the editorial man must cut or reposition stories, or have the spare white concentrated around headings or between paragraphs.

The amount of interlinear white has to be judged by the constant conflicting twin criteria of all newspaper typography—economy and readability. Economy is easily assessed. If a strong face like 8pt Ionic requires 1 or 1½pt leading (and it does) that means one-eighth of the space in a column is sacrificed to white.

Setting 8pt Ionic on the required 9pt body in a 22 in. page means a loss, in depth, of nearly 3 in. per column compared with an 8pt type which is readable when set solid. The newspaper typographer can then consider whether the readability of Ionic is worth losing space in depth by interlinear whiting (and also in width from the squareness of the character). The judgment of just how much, if any, interlinear white a typeface needs depends on three factors: the design of the type, the size, the measure.

The most interlinear white is needed when you have a type with a large x-height, set across a wide measure. A type with a small x-height will not need additional interlinear white, at narrow measure, because by definition, the white is provided in the design itself. The relevance of measure is the ease of the eye's return sweep from the end of one line to the beginning of the next. The eye must be able to do this swiftly and without fractional impediment. In newspaper wide measure—14 ems and above—the eye has a longer return sweep, and if there is insufficient white, facility and time are lost by the reader's trying to ensure that his eye does not swing back to the wrong line.

There is a limit to the amount of interlinear white needed (*see* below), but as a guide one can say a 10pt type with a large x-height set across, say, 17 ems will need 2 or 3pt leads or to be set on a body 2–3 points larger.

With ordinary newspaper setting, say 8pt in 11 ems, the range of judgment is usually between whether to set solid or whether to have interlinear spacing of up to 1½pt; especially on narrower measures, there is a risk not merely of wasting space needlessly, but of actually diluting the typeface too much. Interlinear spacing can change the colour value of the type area from black to grey; excessive interlinear spacing can produce a wishy-washy effect and interrupt the smooth flow of reading.

Cyril Burt's research[1] showed that 8, 9 and 10pt Times New Roman were more legible with 1 and 2pt leading than with 4pt leading. The three settings of 8pt Royal below left illustrate the practical options. The other two have exaggerated interlinear white at this measure.

BRITISH millionaires may be on the endangered species list nowadays, but the World Wildlife Fund have come up with an intriguing holiday package to prevent them dying out completely because of boredom.

BRITISH millionaires may be on the endangered species list nowadays, but the World Wildlife Fund have come up with an intriguing holiday package to prevent them dying out completely because of boredom.

BRITISH millionaires may be on the endangered species list nowadays, but the World Wildlife Fund have come up with an intriguing holiday package to prevent them dying out completely because of boredom.

BRITISH millionaires may be on the endangered species list nowadays, but the World Wildlife Fund have come up with an intriguing holiday package to prevent them dying out completely because of boredom.

BRITISH millionaires may be on the endangered species list nowadays, but the World Wildlife Fund have come up with an intriguing holiday package to prevent them dying out completely because of boredom.

Word- and letter-spacing

Good *word*-spacing is considered by typographers to be not more than one-third of the body em: a thick space or roughly equivalent to the lower-case 't' of the particular face. Good *letter*-spacing in lower-case serif letters is determined principally by the space between the legs of the 'n' and in the counter of 'o' in the design stage half the width is allocated to each side of the letter and visually adjusted; in capitals, 'H' and 'O' are the standards. (In sans serif letters the method of organising the letter-spacing is the same, but the amount is sometimes less because the serifs in serif types act as links between the letters of a word.)

Good spacing is impossible to achieve in newspapers setting lines to relatively narrow measures with lines ranging evenly on the right (*justified* setting, which we discuss later in this chapter). Excess spacing inevitably creeps in, and the excess is inevitably unevenly distributed. Line-casting spacing is essentially variable. Take the setting of this as a justified line in 8pt Corona/Royal at $11\frac{1}{2}$ picas:

French author François Mauriac

When the operator reaches the 's' of François it is clear he cannot set Mauriac on that line and newspapers do not hyphenate a name. The space is therefore spent by expanding the space between the words; the tapering spacebands in the line-casting machine are forced up between the matrices, introducing more and more white, but there is still not a full line. The operator has therefore manually to insert hair spaces between the letters of the word 'author', with this result:

French   a u t h o r   François

Bad spacing is the single worst fault of newspaper setting, and it mars many of the 'modern' newspapers which have computer-assisted setting of narrow-measure text:

TOP   RUSSIAN
Government officials
have been blamed for
the axing of a trip to
Czechoslovakia
planned by Basildon
athletes.

A   PENSIONER
claimed today he had
received poison pen let-
ters   threatening
violence   unless   he
moved out of his home.
But 74-year-old Mr. John
McClelland said: "They just

Letter-spacing destroys words and it is words, whole words rather than letters, that we recognise in efficient reading. Letter-spacing is also time-consuming on conventionally set newspapers since it has to be added by hand. It is a fault most conspicuous on tabloid newspapers setting to narrow measures of 9 picas and such.

The Newspaper Options

What can newspapers concerned with good spacing do? Most fundamentally, they can consider unjustified setting, an alternative we examine in the next section of this chapter. But though ideal spacing is impossible for newspapers committed to justified setting on relatively narrow measures, they can do some things, especially if they control their own machines and are not subject to the vagaries of wire-setting. For example:

(i) They can encourage operators to set tight lines and to hyphenate rather than fill out the line with excess white between words and letters:

(ii) They can equip their line-casting machines with the spaceband which provides initially the thinnest word space consistent with the facility to cast full lines nineteen times out of twenty without hand spacing. This can only be a matter of trial and error.

(iii) They can tell operators that where letter-spacing is required, the spacing should be in a word within the line and never at the beginning of the line.

(iv) They can invest in computers capable of accurately converting perforated primary ('wild') tape into full lines with acceptable hyphenation. The need for hyphenation in the illogical English language means the computer must have a big electronic memory bank; rude computers have let their clients down in the way they split words like therapist, mis-hit and arsenal. But the simpler computers which justify perforated tape without hyphenation only make the word- and letter-spacing worse than it need be.

(v) They can, other things being equal, choose a text type with more characters per line, i.e. with close set-width.

(vi) They can instruct editorial deskmen—as all narrow-column popular papers must—that short words make good setting as well as good English. The English language is fortunate here; it is, for instance, impossible to set Finnish, so long are the words, without gigantic word- and letter-spacing per line.

(vii) And, finally, in fixing their news-text setting measure, newspapers can have due regard to the inevitably bad spacing of narrow measures.

One final qualification should be added, and it is only necessary because of the temptations of photosetting. Composing optically by photosetting, it is easy to squeeze letters together, even to the extent of the serifs connecting one with another. Such gimmicks of compacting became fashionable in the Sixties in advertising and trendy design circles, but there is nothing to be said for compacting text types meant for continuous reading.[2]

Individual letters must be drawn and spaced so that they knit firmly together into words, but they must not lose their individual identity. They must cohere, not adhere.

Setting Styles

The choice in style of setting is between the variations of justified and unjustified. To justify in newspapers and magazines means to set all the lines of type so that the lines range evenly, left and right. Newspapers universally set this way. Each line of type is forced to a uniform length by a combination of frequent hyphenation and variable word- and letter-spacing within the line. But lines can be justified without hyphenation: the space between the words and letters is simply increased to fill out the line. So there are two styles of *justified setting* :

(i) Justified and hyphenated.

(ii) Justified but not hyphenated.

Startling allegations regarding the effect of the breaking of the monsoon over Calcutta on an Indian tailor, aged 34, were made in court when Ali Alendh Singh, of no fixed address, stated to have been found standing drenched in torrential rain on June 15, appeared accused of improper conduct in a public place.

Startling allegations regarding the effect of the breaking of the monsoon over Calcutta on an Indian tailor, aged 34, were made in court when Ali Alendh Singh, of no fixed address, stated to have been found standing drenched in torrential rain on June 15, appeared accused of improper conduct in a public place.

There are three main styles of *unjustified*, or 'ragged right', as it may more frequently be called:

(iii) Unjustified and unhyphenated, which produces a ragged effect on the right. As well as 'ragged right', it is sometimes called 'English line-fall'. Most typewriter work is composed in this way.

> Startling allegations regarding
> the effect of the breaking of the
> monsoon over Calcutta on an
> Indian tailor, aged 34, were made
> in court when Ali Alendh Singh,
> of no fixed address, stated to
> have been found standing
> drenched in torrential rain on
> June 15, appeared accused of
> improper conduct in a public
> place.

(iv) Unjustified but hyphenated. Here, with good setting, the ragged right effect is greatly reduced. There is white space at the end of the line only where words will not hyphenate or where the correct hyphenation still leaves spare space.

> Startling allegations regarding
> the effect of the breaking of the
> monsoon over Calcutta on an In-
> dian tailor, aged 34, were made
> in court when Ali Alendh Singh,
> of no fixed address, stated to
> have been found standing drench-
> ed in torrential rain on June 15,
> appeared accused of improper
> conduct in a public place.

(v) Unjustified as in any of the styles above, but with the white space on the left, producing an uneven left-hand margin and an even right-hand margin; this is, of course 'ragged left'.

> Startling allegations regarding
> the effect of the breaking of the
> monsoon over Calcutta on an
> Indian tailor, aged 34, were made
> in court when Ali Alendh Singh,
> of no fixed address, stated to
> have been found standing
> drenched in torrential rain on
> June 15, appeared accused of
> improper conduct in a public
> place.

(vi) There is also a mad modern variant called zombie composition. Here consistent spacing is maintained between words and letters simply by setting to the margin, irrespective of word sense or syllabification.

This produces go
od word spacing
but does not pro
duce easy reading.

Choosing a style

Four questions should determine any argument about setting style:

1. Is it more readable? 2. Does it save space? 3. Does it save time and materials? 4. Is it acceptable to the reader?

All these four factors must be examined in deciding between the best form of justified setting and the best form of unjustified, but considerations of readability are so strong with four of the styles that they can be eliminated at once.

Zombie composition (vi) destroys words and defies all our patterns of learning and experience.

Ragged left setting (v) may be employed as a variant for a paragraph or two of caption, perhaps to pull it off a messy advertisement in the next column. But it is no use for continuous text. The eye on its quick return sweep needs a fixed point of reference at the left. The varying left-hand margin markedly slows reading efficiency. Beware designers who come bearing text layouts marked 'range right'.

Justified but not hyphenated (ii) persistently produces lines with excess and erratic word- and letter-spacing. This is a greater hindrance to reading than hyphenation; in books, newspapers and magazines readers have become accustomed to reasonable hyphenation. Newspaper hyphenation does sometimes leave a lot to be desired, particularly where a computer is being used to justify type, but corrections can be programmed daily or weekly in the computer's memory and reasonable standards assured.

In unjustified and unhyphenated (iii) the absence of hyphenation increases the ragged effect on the right, which can in excess look odd on a page and irritate the reader.

The choice is therefore between (i) justified and hyphenated setting and (iv) unjustified and hyphenated and this choice requires a rather more detailed examination.

1. Readability

The main disadvantage of justified setting is the wide and inconsistent word- and letter-spacing on narrow measures. This can be a hindrance to quick reading; of course the narrower the measure, the worse the effect. At 18 picas and above in 9pt the average line can absorb any justification spacing without noticeable unevenness. But consistency is also the main weapon of the advocates of justified. The absence of consistent word-spacing is bad, but it is more than offset, it is said, by the gain of consistent line lengths. Justified setting induces regularity of eye movement, line to line, which is comfortable.

Unjustified setting, by this argument, induces fatigue because the ragged line endings confuse the eyes just when they are about to switch attention to the beginning of the following line. There seems to be something in this. An even right-hand margin certainly does signal the end of a line to the reader's peripheral vision better than an irregular margin.

What readership research there is, however, does not support the critics of unjustified text. Fabrizio, Kaplan and Teal report that reading performance was essentially equal for three different right-hand margins (irregular, irregular with printed straight line to guide the eye, and justified).[3] Spencer quotes two experiments which would suggest that the balance is, if anything, in favour of unjustified because the least proficient readers seem able to read competent unjustified setting just a little more quickly.[4]

2. Space

Unjustified setting can use less of the available space. The degree to which this means a significant loss of editorial space depends largely on the skill of the operators. The Dutch evening newspaper *Rotterdamsch Nieuwsblad* began unjustified setting throughout in 1967 and reported that if operators are encouraged to set as many characters as possible on a line, with even word-spacing, and to hyphenate when necessary, there is no loss of editorial space. But it also has to be said that unjustified setting in many attempts can produce exaggerated short lines which are wasteful, notably when hyphenation is discouraged.

3. Production

Unjustified setting has economic advantages arising from simpler line-casting and simpler perforating where tape is used. The saving in manual operating is notable in narrow measure where the operator frequently has to fill the line with hand-placed letter- or word-spacing. The line-casting machine can be fitted with an automatic quadder which automatically fills up any space available at the end of a line.

The gains can be significant. The *Rotterdamsch Nieuwsblad* (**below**) invited the Institute for Time Standards in the Graphic Industry in the Netherlands to do time-and-motion studies in its perforator room. The newspaper was using 8pt type on a measure of 11·5 cicero (5·1 cm). Operators were instructed to get as many characters on a line as possible and to hyphenate when necessary. Lines still short were quadded to fill. The Institute for Time Standards reported that the abolition of justification increased output in the perforator department by 13·5 per cent. These were gains for settings of 29 characters a line; at wider measures the savings progressively diminished but they did not disappear until the measure reached 58 characters to a line.[5]

ROTTERDAMSCH NIEUWSBLAD — WOENSDAG 22 NOVEMBER 1967

Groente-export vangt devaluatie pond zonder paniek op

ROTTERDAM — De devaluatie van het Engelse pond heeft de groenten- en fruitexport geen grote schade berokkend. Dit bleek vandaag uit mededelingen van exporteurs. Voor slechts een grote exportonderneming ligt de zaak slechter. Dit bedrijf zou voor meer dan 20.000 pond vorderingen in Engeland hebben uitstaan. Deze vorderingen verminderde het afgelopen weekeinde ruwweg met 28.000 gulden. Voor vele anderen echter betekent de devaluatie een onverwacht — tijdelijk — voordeeltje.

De meeste bedrijven leveren de Nederlandse tuinbouwprodukten aan hun Engelse afnemers op termijn. Deze bedrijven hadden al bij voorbaat hun ponden laten dekken. Hierdoor zijn leveringen die nog moeten plaatshebben in „zware" ponden betaald.

„Het zal wel een paar weken duren voordat men weer rust op de markt heeft", zei men ons bij de N. J. Mulder N.V. „Voorlopig is bijvoorbeeld de aanvoer van inlandse uien in Engeland groot genoeg voor de eigen consumptie. Tegen de helft van december heeft men hiervoor pas weer import nodig. De concurrentie van Spanje en de Canarische Eilanden is trouwens zeer betrekkelijk. Heel belangrijk is dat Nederland zijn havens het dichtst bij Engeland heeft", meende men.

„We verwachten geen rampzalige gevolgen. De prijs was toch al niet erg hoog en de meeste bedrijven hadden hun ponden gedekt. Tegen het begin van volgend jaar zullen de prijzen zich waarschijnlijk weer op een reëel niveau gestabiliseerd hebben.

Of course the possibility of production savings must in part depend on a particular newspaper's plant and skills. The *Rotterdamsch Nieuwsblad* later abandoned unjustified setting because sharing a computer with an affiliated newspaper offered it even better production gains. The *Denver Post* also abandoned non-justification. The *Post* used a system of partial non-justification, quadding only when justification would have required hand spacing: lines that had enough spacebands between words to fill out the line were allowed to become justified lines. The experiment was successful but the *Post* has since switched to a digital computer which automatically justifies and hyphenates.

4. Reader Reaction

Readers in experiments often fail to notice they are reading unjustified setting.[6] For newspapers the evidence is thin. There are plenty of indications that unjustified setting is acceptable to magazine readers (the British magazine *Car* is set in Univers Light 8 on 9pt unjustified). Only two newspapers seem to have tried unjustified setting for all their text— the *Rotterdamsch Nieuwsblad* and the *Denver Post* mentioned previously —and both are now set justified. The *Denver Post* had 250 comments, mainly critical (though the complaints dried up and were nothing in contrast to the thousands of complaints following their cancellation of a comic strip). Initially, the *Rotterdamsch Nieuwsblad*, out of a circulation of 80,000, had only two readers who protested. They were not, they said, going to read 'poetry'. But the publisher, Dr C H Evers, says[7] that a certain reader irritation persisted even after several months and that was one of the reasons why unjustified was abandoned. The London *Observer*, too, had a chastening experience. It began setting its columnist, Katharine Whitehorn, in unjustified lines 'so that the column will not get typographically lost'. Not wanting to lose Katharine Whitehorn typographically, or any other way, should have been an ambition all men could share, but the *Observer* soon decided to go back to justified setting. Even the better-educated *Observer* readers apparently thought Katharine Whitehorn had been cast into blank verse.

It can be seen that the unjustified controversy is rather more complicated than protagonists suggest. The inherent readability of unjustified may be equal or superior to justified, but, out of the experimental laboratory, enough newspaper readers themselves are conservative to make a change to unjustified questionable. The benefits are not decisive enough. There are production savings but neither these nor the benefits from consistent word-spacing are sufficient to tip the balance against justified for the average newspaper on conventional format. This may change if more magazines and books move to unjustified, conditioning the reader to regard unjustified as normal high-standard printing, rather than the aberration of some jobbing shop. There has been a slow increase in unjustified in magazines, but in books unjustified remains negligible. But if caution is the watchword it should be judicious. It may be that the present limited reader irritation reported with newspaper unjustified would not apply at all to a newspaper of different format basing its whole appeal on innovation. And conventional newspapers can experiment with unjustified for selected areas (in addition to using it to pull text away from crowded areas). When they do they will be helping everyone including themselves if they do so in a controlled way, so that production savings if any can be measured and reader reaction can be noted.

There is too much hunch and rule of thumb in newspaper typography; and certainly too little sharing of experience, even in the United States which is so well served by the ANPA Research Institute. For the moment only one hunch will be offered: that unjustified will make little headway in classified advertising. People paying per line, it can be guessed, will tend to turn nasty at purchasing even the most logical white space.

Size and Measure

The ideal size of type for newspaper and magazine text is defined by a number of special and conflicting factors which we examine later. But, contrary to common assumptions, reading efficiency is not served by each increase in the size of type. William Randolph Hearst used to set his editorials in 14 or 18pt; they were less easy to read than they would have been in 10pt. For the normal eye, the optimum type size for continuous reading is between 9 and 12pt, depending on the x-height, degree of interlinear white and so on. Enlargements beyond that are not helpful because of the way we read. The eye scans the words, it will be recalled, in a series of stops and starts and meaning is absorbed during the stops (fixations). The eye then takes in the words on either side of the focused central point. The type must be big enough to be seen clearly but the bigger the type the fewer words can be absorbed at each fixation: there is an early limit to our peripheral vision. All that William Randolph Hearst accomplished by type enlargement was to force his readers to make more eye movements.

Clearly optimal size and optimal measure are directly related. The larger the type the wider the measure required so that a reasonable number of fixations can take place but the line must not be so wide that the movement of the eye from line to line is difficult.

D G Paterson and M A Tinker, in their study[8] of the influence of line width on eye movements reported:

'One may characterise the oculomotor patterns in reading an excessively short line by saying that the number of fixations is increased, the span of perception decreased, the mean duration of fixations increased, total perception time greatly increased. . . . An excessively long line gives a major difficulty in swinging back to the beginning of successive lines.'

What is a 'short' line and what is a 'long' line is determined within limits by the size of type and the degree of interlinear white. The relationship can easily be demonstrated.

This is 6pt Imperial made by Intertype, each line being set long enough to accommodate about 52 characters, which some consider the optimum measure.

This is 7pt Imperial made by Intertype, each line being set long enough to accommodate about 52 characters, which some consider the optimum measure.

This is 8pt Imperial made by Intertype, each line being set long enough to accommodate about 52 characters, which some consider the optimum measure.

This is 10pt Imperial made by Intertype, each line being set long enough to accommodate about 52 characters, which some consider the optimum measure.

It does not matter for the moment whether the measure of these settings is the best. The important point is the universal one that small types are better served by narrow measures or, put it the other way round, that narrow measures require small types. See what happens when we reverse the principle and set the small type to a wide measure and the larger type to narrow measure.

This is unleaded 5½pt type set to the wide measure of 24 picas, more suitable for the larger type used in the setting above. For continuous reading this length of line at this size of type is difficult, since there is too much in a line and it is also not easy to swing the eye from the end of one unleaded line to the beginning of the next.

This is unleaded 12pt type set across 11½ picas, a measure which would be all right for the smaller type above but makes for inefficient reading at this and other larger sizes.

This is an excessively short line *for the size of type.* It produces, for the type size used, the oculomotor pattern described by Paterson and Tinker of increased fixations and a decreased span of perception. Now look at the setting in 5½pt type; for 5½pt—and the size qualification is vital—the line is excessively long. Even a casual reading of that line in this book should demonstrate Paterson and Tinker's conclusion of the major difficulty created in the eye swinging back to the beginning of successive lines.

Those settings are extremes to demonstrate a principle. It is an elementary principle, and to be precise about the ideal measure for any piece of setting requires considering not only the size of type but its design, the degree of leading and the distribution of white space, and also the nature of the message and audience. Minor variations from any one optimum do not inevitably mean loss of readability. There are tolerances; most of us, for instance, can read 8pt comfortably for short periods if the x-height is large, the colour strong, and the measure and interlinear white are not far from optimum. It is when all constituents of text setting are at the margins of tolerance, or when any one is wildly askew, that reading efficiency is seriously jeopardised. Yet these examples show that even the most elementary principle of the relationship of size and measure is frequently neglected:

This month HARPER'S BAZAAR looks different, feels new. There's a new Fashion Editor, a new Beauty Editor, a new Features Editor, a new Art Director, a new type-face, and a whole clutch of new columnists covering everything from cars and clematis to cognac and the latest gossip in the opera world. **Molly Parkin,** our fashion editor, comes to HARPER'S from *Nova* and the *Sunday Times*

MOLLY PARKIN   JOAN PRICE

where she established a reputation for world with a sort of Welsh gaiety, rather but beautiful old yellow Rolls-Royce, and large oil in the Tate), films and appear- Paris photographer whose work is, as yet, Molly Parkin also visits the space-age salon beachwear, and tells, with photographer takes a size sixteen dress. **Joan Price,** our

fashion second sight. She treats the whole fashion than deep seriousness, arriving to work in a battered ances on *Late Night Line Up.* This month she covers tions, using for the photographs a brilliant young comparatively unknown over here – **Sarah Moon.** of Jean Cacherel, gives a preview of the newest **John Cook,** an encouraging story for anyone who new beauty editor, came to us from *Queen,* where she

has been – apart from a brief time in public relations – since 1948. Recently she opened her own beauty shop – the Face Place – which she finds gives her great insight into the problems women have with make-up every day. This month she analyses the paradox

of modern make-up – more paint to get an unpainted look – at the traditional, satin-cubicle concept of a beauty salon. ures editor, is 24. After Cambridge she went to America for two trip of the States in an old Chevrolet, and was a contributing Tom Wolfe and Gloria Steinem – of *New York* magazine, the becoming compulsive reading for people on both sides of the whisked briefly through the *Vogue* offices, and landed at she prised some extraordinary revelations from Joe Hyman, the lined up other expert contributors like **Margaret Costa**

and lobs a gentle critical grenade **Sally Beauman,** our new features years, did a 50,000 mile round editor – along with people like new weekly which is rapidly Atlantic. Back in England, she HARPER'S BAZAAR. This month millionaire textile tycoon, and (writing on Deep Freezes),

JOHN COOK   SALLY BEAUMAN

HARPER'S: Too wide for the type size, but made even more difficult to read by the inset blocks which provide hurdles for the eye and ambiguities in following the run of the text.

SHE CAN COST UP TO 10s AN HOUR...IF YOU'RE LUCKY

Have we seen the back of Mrs Mop?

HARO

.by PAMELA FOX

THE £5,000-a-year man whose post-Budget comment was that his wife could economise by giving up her 10s.-a-week domestic help little knew the sacrifice he was asking.

Not only is 10s., which would not pay for more than two hours' work, cheap for London. A cleaning lady, once found, is not lightly to be dismissed.

The Mrs Mops are fast disappearing and leaving the dust to settle behind them.

Agency

Many housewives find their Mrs Mop through the grapevine—or turn to one of the agencies which these days employ more men than women.

'Men are more reliable,' one agency told us. (Ouch!)

Nor is your Mrs Mop likely to be unaware of the fact that her services are at a premium.

what jobs she would and would not do—most of the non-starters being essentials like floors and bathroom.

Her minimum: 35s for four hours a week.

The cost – ranging from 4s. to 10s. an hour—for the housewife who needs domestic help is likely to be higher in London than elsewhere.

Even so employment exchanges everywhere are bemoaning the disappearance of the char.

A spokesman for the Aytoun Street, Manchester, exchange said: 'People go to amazing lengths to obtain and keep domestic help.

'We have well over 100 vacancies we just can't fill.'

Vanishing

'A lot of people advertise through local shops and newspapers. But the old char who was prepared to clean is vanishing fast.

'Women these days don't want to clean

they hang on to her. If they don't need her any more they have a dozen friends waiting who do. The 'normal...

Leeds employment

they have to meet her requirements more than half-way. Some drive her to and from home and arrange hours to suit her. We have 67 vacancies at present.'

hours a week ordinary cleaning or about 9s. an hour for a big spring-cleaning job. They also provide party help for 10s. an hour — and window cleaners.

Ryder chars are mainly out of work pop-world people—'Not so many resting actors and actresses now,' says Mr Ryder ruefully.

Your Servant, men only agency, in Half Moon Street, charges 7s. 6d. an hour (minimum four hours) for its cleaners, of which 3s. 6d. goes to the agency.

Fares to and from Baker Street Underground are requested, unless the employer lives in the central Circle Line area.

Most of the Mr Mops are students or evening workers. National Insurance, they say, is paid by the employer who requires the most work.

Insurance

Another agency, Hunt Regina of

a week industrial injury stamp, including 8d. from the employer.

If they work for more than one person, the first of the week pays the 8d.

Housewives do not have to pay SET unless their domestic help works more than eight hours a week for them. If she works between eight and 21 hours, she is treated as a part-time worker. Her employer must pay National Insurance and SET, but can apply for a partial SET refund.

Au pair

Problem Limited, of Grosvenor Gardens, London, S.W.1, also provide home helpers of a wide variety—but only on a temporary basis. Their cleaning rates are 6s. 6d. an hour for three hours minimum, plus time-and-a-half after 6 p.m. and on Sundays.

Another form of temporary help now available is a variation of the au pair systems, devised by International Students' Services, a non-profit organisation.

ISS is looking for 150 English families in or near London to take French girl students for two months during the summer holidays.

SUN: Altogether too narrow, increasing the number and duration of fixation pauses.

Optimum Line-length

We can now take the matter further than merely saying that 'small' type requires 'narrow' measure. The optimum can be expressed in one definition by defining the ideal measure not in absolute terms but in terms of the width taken by the alphabet of a particular typeface and size. To set the alphabet of 12pt type requires a longer line than the alphabet of the same type in 10pt, so the optimum setting for 12pt is that much wider. A type with a wide-set face will require, size for size, a wider optimum measure than a type with a narrow-set face.

Other things being equal, there is general agreement that for solid text setting for continuous reading the optimum line length ranges from around 1½ lower-case alphabet lengths or 39 characters and spaces, to somewhat over two alphabet lengths, i.e. 56 characters. (Interlinear white enables line length to be extended without diminishing readability.) The chief recommendations on line lengths are:

Sir Cyril Burt[9]
In 10pt roman measures shorter than 20 picas or longer than 33 picas diminished ease of reading. He recommends as a guide 50 to 58 lower-case characters and spaces, 10 to 12 words, or 2 to 3 lower-case alphabets.

Herbert Spencer[10]
About 10 to 12 words or 60 to 70 characters.

Paterson and Tinker[11]
Their optimum for 10pt type is somewhat narrower than Burt's: 19–21 picas for 10pt which is just over 1½ alphabet lengths for Intertype Royal (47 characters at 19 picas).

Ed Arnold[12]
Optimum line lower-case alphabet length times 1½; minimum: optimum minus 25 per cent (i.e. 29 characters); maximum: minimum times two (i.e. 58).

Roberts[13]
Not fewer than 47 characters, not more than 75 characters.

These optima can all be expressed in pica measures for any design or size by taking the lower-case alphabet length specified in points in the type catalogues. Assume the ideal is 1½ alphabet lengths. The type specification for Corona says 10pt has a lower-case alphabet length of

138 points. One-and-a-half alphabet lengths is half as much again, and to express the measure in normal terms we convert to pica ems:

10pt Corona Alphabet length: 138 points
138 points × $1\frac{1}{2}$ = 207 points
207 points divided by 12 = 17 pica ems (and 3 points)

Therefore the ideal setting for 10pt Corona by these definitions is 17 pica ems.

And again:

10pt Times Roman alphabet length: 125 points
125 points × $1\frac{1}{2}$ = $187\frac{1}{2}$ points
$187\frac{1}{2}$ points divided by 12 = 15 pica ems (and $7\frac{1}{2}$ points), say 16 pica ems for ideal column measure.

Even taking the lower range of recommended line lengths of around $1\frac{1}{2}$ alphabets, most newspapers in the world have been standardised on measures somewhat narrower than ideal for efficient continuous reading. For instance, a common measure and type is $11\frac{1}{2}$ picas in 7pt. But 7pt Corona/Royal has a lower-case alphabet length of 111 points and therefore an 'ideal' setting nearer 14 picas; 7pt Times Roman has an optimum of $12\frac{1}{2}$ picas. Or put it another way. Forty per cent of American papers were in 1969 using the optimum 9pt size—but 96 per cent of all papers were setting at 11 picas instead of the optimum for 9pt of around 16 picas.[14] The move in the US to a wider column is very slow and small.

Special Newspaper Factors

For a newspaper five special factors must influence the choice of type size and measure for general setting. Size and measure must:

(i) adjust the ideal measure to the special characteristics of newspaper text type and settings;

(ii) match the requirements of page design which basically means the organisation of news in columns;

(iii) be economical in newsprint and setting time. This last factor is especially limiting in North America with many papers on TTS;

(iv) meet the requirements of advertising;

(v) meet the requirements of each newspaper's audience.

(i) The type design and setting

Typographers suggest there is a strong case for reducing the number of words per line,[15] when a type with a large x-height is employed unless there is space for increased leading. Newspapers do use faces with large x-height and have little space for interlinear white, so there is a typographical reason for somewhat reducing what would otherwise be the optimum line-length. The lack of interlinear white in newspapers (for reasons of space economy) does mean that the wider recommended measure of two alphabets is not so appropriate. Where newspapers or magazines do have to exceed the optimum length, there should be compensating interlinear spacing to assist the return eye sweep.

(ii) Columns

The modern newspaper does need columns (*see* Book Five pp. 67–68) to organise the news and express its varying values. Of course column widths are to some extent a function of press cylinder size, web width, plate size and page size, but generally one can say that the more columns to a page the more positions are created for news, and the greater the display permutations. And picture scaling can be more precise when there are eight narrow increments, say, rather than six wider ones. However, the number of columns required for viable display is not infinite, Australian predilections to the contrary. There is a law of diminishing returns for the creation of columns, and there is for increases in type size, and it is evident particularly in the Australian dailies which squash into a broadsheet ten or eleven columns in 8pt type separated by only a 3pt space. The news does not need the display permutation of ten columns: six, seven or eight are plenty. When the ten columns are fully exploited for display there is almost always visual chaos: the column, instead of ordering the news, has begun to be a force for disorder. If there is little to be said for the display potential of the narrower columns, there is nothing at all for the effects of narrow measure on text and headline typography of the broadsheet.

The narrow measure is uncomfortable for continuous reading (a weakness not so important to the popular tabloid presenting stories to be taken in quick gulps). It wastes space and setting time because lines have to be filled out with letter-spacing and word-breaks are prevalent. If type size is reduced, as it should be for the narrow measure, it is being reduced below optimum size. If it is increased, inefficient setting multiplies. The reduction of inter-column spacing which usually accompanies the excessively narrow measures is a further handicap to quick and comfortable reading. The eye is aided by better definition of the measure than a mere 3pt gap between columns. And, finally, the narrow measure provides an inadequate unit count for effective single-measure headlines.

If we do not need ten columns for broadsheet page display, can newspapers manage on as few as five columns, which enables a newspaper, like the *Christian Science Monitor* to produce eminently readable text in 9pt at 16·9 picas, just more than $1\frac{1}{2}$ alphabet lengths of Corona? The answer is probably No. At least it probably is for the ordinary newspaper attempting to present a spectrum of hard news, as I discuss in Book Five. For the moment we can say that for the general broadsheet paper the range of choice in the number of columns is, for page display, either six, seven or eight.

Tabloid size papers have a different problem. Most of them opt for a seven-column page which usually entails a 9-pica column; but again are the news presentation possibilities of a seven-column page so much superior to a six-column page that they compensate for the excessively narrow measures and type sizes produced by squeezing in seven columns? It is exceedingly doubtful.

(iii) Space economy

The need to conserve newsprint presses on newspapers in different degrees, but it presses on all. Newsprint is a high proportion of total costs. Maximum space economy would require a small text size, say 6pt or 7pt unleaded, set across a wide measure, which is a prescription for unreadability. Newspapers seeking maximum space economy consistent with being read at all should therefore think in terms of bigger types, while retaining wide measure. What they almost all do, especially in the US, is think in terms of bigger types in narrow measure, a partial improvement in readability which, if it is consciously justified at all, is justified on the grounds of needing narrower measures for teletypesetting, for advertising or for creating a multi-column page for effective layout.

The space-saving text size of 6pt is too small for general news text; 9pt is ideal, at the appropriate measure. But for a newspaper to go from 7pt to 9pt in an 11-pica measure on a 22-inch column means losing rather more than 150 words—a short news story per column. A text size of 8pt is a good compromise, providing the face has a large x-height and retains good colour, especially if the paper is modelled on 11-pica columns. It is certainly questionable how much of a help it is to substitute 9pt for 8pt, as many American dailies have done, while retaining an 11-pica column. This inevitably means more variable word- and letter-spacing, and more wasteful line breaks. These faults are aggravated when the newspaper is setting perforated wire tape, as so many are in North America. The wire tape is standardised to an alphabet length of 118 on an 11-pica column.

As has been demonstrated earlier, the attempt to use 9pt on an alphabet length suitable for 8pt has produced an uncomfortable bastard type known as 8-set 9pt which has little to say for it beyond the production facility of wire tape.

North American newspapers would be better off with a good 8pt of large x-height and good colour than with the deformed 9pt.

(iv) Advertising

North American newspapers have been standardised since 1963 on a column of 11 picas for display advertising. There is nothing sacrosanct about that sharing of column widths. A newspaper can accept 11-pica advertising and then set news any way it likes. There is inconvenience in this, especially where the advertising is in irregular shapes. But it is not, as we shall demonstrate, impossible, and newspapers which care about the readability of editorial text will not slavishly follow the standards set for advertising. This is a lot more important with the growth of classified advertising which has produced a commercial incentive for narrow classified measures. Much of classified is charged by the line so a reduction in column width represents a real, if disguised, rate increase. Given an elastic demand, that means an increase in revenue; and there is no doubt, too, that a ten-column page of classified seems to have more on it than an eight-column page. Where the classified advertising is in self-contained sections the narrow set of classified need have no influence on editorial measures.

The difficulty arises because classified fluctuates right up to press time in its need for space. It either threatens to spill over on to other pages or to vacate space at the last moment. There is, in either event, a need to reconcile the space vacated or required with the space which can be taken by editorial of a different measure. A half-column of 9-pica classified floats in an 11-pica editorial page; and an 11-pica editorial column will not fit in the gap of a 9-pica column. Many newspapers have solved this problem by reducing the editorial measure so that editorial and classified metal is interchangeable. This creates production flexibility at ruinous cost to readability throughout the whole paper. The *Tampa Tribune* (Florida), for instance, has followed its 9-pica, nine-column, classified format with jerky 9-pica sports editorial in eight-column format (with 1·6 column white!).

It is entirely the wrong solution for newspapers intended for continuous reading; its problems are different. And this brutal 'solution' is not really necessary. In most cases of difficulty, classified and editorial of different measures can be accommodated by one of a number of page-design changes. First, when classified overflows or underfills to any extent it should be made to occupy a self-contained horizontal space. When there is anything over a column invading another page, it should be stretched across the full measure of the page, leaving the top clear for wide-measure editorial.

Similarly when the classified portion of a page is a column light, the classified should be grouped so that editorial gains a column spread horizontally across the top of the page.

Where classified is intruding on to a page with display there are several possibilities. The display advertising can be floated in the excess white provided by the narrow classified measure. Or the classified can simply be floated in white—there will not be so much of it as to be too unsightly. Or a left-hand channel can be created for pre-set metal or bromides giving classified rates and other 'house' advertising information. Or the awkward space can be taken by pre-set house editorial advertisements. When classified falls short by less than a column, the vertical gap can be filled by wide-measure editorial in association with a bastard measure headline or picture or house advertisement.

What all this adds up to is that there is no need for editorial measures to match a narrowing of classified measure. The inhibition created for optimum-measure editorial is rather by display advertising. In many countries the national display advertising is designed by advertising agencies supplying many different newspapers. They therefore work to a common measure and a newspaper which wants to set editorial to a wider measure throughout the paper has limited options.

There would be no difficulty if display advertising consistently occupied full width or half-width of the page, whatever the depth of the display. The trouble arises because display advertising shapes are more erratic than this. A newspaper which decides that for reasons of readability it will go to a wider measure throughout must therefore be prepared to adjust editorial setting from page to page, according to spaces left by display ads made up on an 11- or 11½-pica format. This is a serious, if not insuperable, production hazard. A newspaper which cannot face it has the alternative of trying to convert the rest of the press and advertising to its own new standard, an unpromising piece of proselytising in an industry not noted for charity to competitors.

EXPERIMENTS IN THE US: It is easier in the United States than in many other countries—a limited newspaper experiment in line lengths has taken place there, with about forty newspapers now setting at 12 picas and above—because many American papers are monopolies supported by local advertising.

The American experiment with wide measure should not be exaggerated. In five years there has been a strong move to 9pt but still only a handful of papers are set at 12 picas and above.[16]

The American newspaper can simply notify its local advertisers that it is changing its column standard; and the newspaper itself will be setting a good deal of this display advertising anyway. The problem of moving to a new measure is then reduced to coping with national advertising on a different measure.

The *Louisville Courier Journal*, which has gone to a 14¾-pica column throughout, reports:[17]

> The national advertiser had an option. He could float his prepared copy in our new column size, thus gaining the advantage of added white space. Or he could resize his copy. Most chose to float their ads because—and this is a key point—they could float their copy at less cost than they would have paid under the old rate structure. A bonus, of course, was the white space that served to make their copy jump right off the page. So because of these two considerations, we have had nothing but raves from national advertisers.

The *Christian Science Monitor*, moving to a 16¾-pica column, had national display ads placed in a horizontal configuration. The *Long Island Press* changed from 10 to 15½ picas on 16½ picas and 21·3 on 22 picas to be used in a flexible page of basically five columns, four of them 15½ and one 21¼ picas. How could this be done throughout the paper in the face of ordinary 11-em ads and advertisement variants on 11 ems? The *Press* reports:[18]

> We worked out a basic ad layout—which has now become routine—in which ads are arranged in squared-off blocks rather than haphazard staggered steps. Whenever we can't conveniently square off the ads in 2-column or larger blocks we plug the one-column holes with pre-set editorial matter, legal ads or small house ads. The success of this hinges on the daily conference

between the publications department and the editor in charge of planning the dummy for the next day's paper. . . . The blocking-out of pages into neat, manageable holes has become a painless routine.

Other American newspapers preferring wide measure, but unable to cope with the production of custom-built pages with varying column widths throughout, have opted for wide measure on a few main pages or page one only. Again, there are production problems.

Wide-measure papers cannot use wire tape which is standardised on 11 picas. And newspapers are forced to reset when later news forces existing page one metal inside the paper, or when page one stories have to turn inside. The alternatives then are special continuation pages of similar wide measure or excessive wide space on a standardised page. Some newspapers do overcome these difficulties; some newspapers have tried and gave up, especially smaller papers with limited setting capacity. The *Joliet Herald News* (Illinois) succeeded with a six-column 14-pica format in 10pt for page one, special pages prepared in advance, and on occasions other pages where advertising is in four-column and eight-column widths (a four-column ad in units of 11 picas, i.e. 44 picas becomes a three-column ad in units of 14 picas, i.e. 42 picas).[19]

(v) The audience

The nature of the newspaper and its audience must always be considered in determining the size and measure of setting. Young readers can accommodate to smaller type sizes better than older readers. A serious newspaper aiming at detailed extensive coverage of events must be designed more for ease in continuous reading than a popular tabloid based entirely on titbits of brief news and entertainment. No story in this kind of tabloid is meant to be read for more than a few minutes so the criteria for continuous reading have less force (though one should note that the less proficient readers have more difficulty with the kind of erratic letter- and word-spacing inevitable in excessively narrow measures).

The way these considerations affect a newspaper's design can be demonstrated by the case of the London *Times*. It is a serious paper intended for sustained reading. As such it deserves to be set in 9pt. There had been a research study on the readability of Times Roman, the text type of *The Times*. Christopher Poulton[20] of the Applied Psychology Research Unit, Cambridge University, reported on a type-sizing experiment which highlighted the advantages of normal 9pt. In that experiment with *The Times* it was found that 7 per cent more words could be spotted in a given time when printed in 9pt Times Roman rather than in 8pt: 'Clearly the use of 8pt Times New Roman is not to be recommended'. That conclusion was justified purely on grounds of readability, but *The Times* must give a wide range of news and the 9pt text throughout was consuming a great deal of space. It became obvious at the *Times* that it was failing to give the comprehensive coverage required, because of the pressure on space, especially when compared with the competitive *Daily Telegraph* set in 8pt Modern.

The increasing costs of newsprint, and the tightness of the advertising market, ruled out the possibility of increasing coverage by adding still more pages. So *The Times*, balancing a 7 per cent readability advantage against the loss of news, decided, late in 1970, to reduce the text type on its inside pages to 8pt, retaining 9pt on the front page. The change yielded up to 10,000 words more daily for news. It is clearly not as easy to read as the 9pt and *The Times*, with *The Sunday Times*, began in 1970 to consider the possibility of designing an entirely new face offering much but not all of the economy of 8pt Times with the legibility of $8\frac{1}{2}$ or 9pt. (Times-Europa was the result.)

There were complaints at the reduction in text size but not as many as anticipated; one reason for this is probably that *The Times* had an exceptionally high proportion of young readers.

Of course, a tabloid-size paper carrying longer text meant for continuous reading should be just as concerned as a broadsheet with assisting reading. The serious tabloid *Newsday* rightly sets its 9 on 10pt Century Schoolbook at wider measures (varying from a 19-pica measure giving 59 characters to a 14-pica measure giving 36 characters). The more a text requires continuous reading of any duration, the more the length should approach the optimum.

Summary

The five special factors discussed above do legitimately modify the line length that would be suggested purely by a study of legibility. It is no solution to newspaper typography slavishly to follow the standards appropriate for the very different medium of the book. However, when every allowance has been made, the conclusion must be that the general run of 11-pica newspaper measure is too short and the text type either too small (in Britain) or too distorted (in North America). The degree and manner of an increase in size and measure needs careful thought and adjustment for the five special factors but newspapers should study much more carefully and continuously than they do how they might make their text more readable. Multi-page newspapers in particular have no excuse. Herbert Spencer put the challenge in a wider context:[21]

> The real threat to the survival of the printed word comes not from other, alternative communication, but from the torrent of paper and ink which is today pouring from the presses. No matter how great the author's wisdom or how vital the message or how remarkable the printer's skill, unread print is merely a lot of paper and little ink. The true economics of printing must be measured by how much is read and understood and not by how much is produced.

Small Typefaces

Stock prices, show results, race meetings, and classified advertising almost universally require an exceptionally small body type and of an extremely narrow measure. Both are inimical to easy continuous reading, but both should be accepted. These sections are a service not to the skimmers of text but to the brooders: the impulses which drive a man to ponder the stock prices or the race cards are strong enough to steel him for 5pt type at 8 picas if the 5pt holds even the faintest glimmer of Eldorado.

Ultra-small settings require special care in the choice of type. Because Corona is a good 8pt it does not follow it is good at 5½pt, or good for the nature of the special settings. There are two new essentials for the ultra-small faces. The precision and clarity of the numerals, after printing, must be outstanding. A blurred telephone number or horse's handicap can drive readers to drink. So choosing a small face might just as well begin with studying the numerals;[22] they must be wider-set than the other characters or the normal figures of a fount— nearer to 0·055 in. wide in 5½pt than the normal 0·0043 in. The second special requirement is that the small face must be duplexed with a contrasting face which springs out from the page of results or classified. The reader scanning ten columns for a 1932 ROLLS ROYCE must see it as clearly as that. The contrast of bold with a basic roman fount has proved too weak in small sizes. There are new ultra-small faces which provide the much more serviceable contrast (forget the aesthetics) of mixing a sans with a roman. The initial word in sans is very striking. In North America the preference, especially among the big classified papers, is to set all classified advertising 5½ or 6pt in sans, with bold caps at the beginning.

Despite its popularity it is arguable whether the key initial word springs out as well when it is set in the same sans as the rest of the ad. In the settings which follow, for instance, compare the 5½pt Corona with Doric with the Spartan Book. The advocacy of setting the initial word in caps might seem questionable after the strictures against capitals in this book. But classified is not meant for continuous reading, and, contrary to ordinary text, research here suggests that at the ultra-small sizes, approaching the threshold of legibility, caps are somewhat more easily discriminated than lower-case.[23] This means ordinary caps of the same size as the rest of the word. There is nothing to be said for the former style of setting the initial letter in a drop cap of a larger size. It is time-consuming and it produces too much glitter, especially when the classified ads are each making only two or three lines.

As well as providing better duplexing of ultra-small faces, the type companies are also managing to reduce the point size, for space gains, without appearing to do so. The two latest 4¾pt faces (Maximus and Classad) give 15 lines to the inch but appear as big as the old 5½pt. They are big on body ('The biggest small type so far'), wide-set and have strong colour. They stereotype well. The bowls on such letters as a, b, c, e, g, o, p, q, have been opened out, serifs fractionally shortened and made firmer, ascenders abbreviated, and descenders almost abandoned.

These faces must be attractive to British, Australian and South African newspapers; in North America, where the standard is a 9-pica column, the practice is to choose 5½pt or 5½ on a 5pt body and faces with a lower-case alphabet length of 88 points for wire-tape setting (for stock prices and race meetings, rather than classified, of course). Whether it is the handsomely wide-set Classad and Maximus or the more condensed Corona, newspapers choosing an ultra-small face for classified should always go carefully into the revenue-per-line aspects of choice. If the type produces more lines, is the extra revenue from this from linage advertisers sufficient to offset the loss of volume from the greater use of space? And, of course, on letterpress newspapers ultra-small types in particular should only be judged in the printed page after they have gone through the stereotyping and printing processes.

The main ultra-small faces for specialised settings follow, as specimens mainly from letterpress newspapers. The width of the numerals is given and the lower-case alphabet length.

Name	Size	Fig size	lca	Maker
Adsans with Bold	4¾pt	.054in.	84pts	Linotype

LARGE flat, suitable 3 friends sharing or
family; children welcome. Box 3872.
PLEASANT lge, twin-bedded rm. and small
sitt. rm.; all facilities. Box 3889.
THREE flats, 2 rms., own cooker, water and
use of bath; suit business couple or 2
sharing; 4 gns. each wkly. Including light.
Please write Box 3978.
WELL appointed furn. flatlet, concealed cook-
ing and h. & c., share bath. and toilet;
close trains and buses; 2½ gns. wkly.
Write Box 3934.
WELL FURNISHED 2-rmd. flat for 1 person;
no restrictions; 4 gns. Box 3878.

Name	Size	Fig size	lca	Maker
Bell Gothic	6pt	·0484in.	75pts	Intertype

ANGLIA (Colour): 9.30 London. 10.30 Circus.
11.00 The Doris Day Show. 11.30 London. 1.00
The Champions. 1.50 Weather. 1.55 Farming
Diary. 2.30 The Name of the Game. 3.55 Match
of the Week. 4.45 The Golden Shot. 5.35 Black
Beauty. 6.05 London. 7.55 Film: Walk, Don't
Run, Cary Grant, Samantha Eggar (1966)—
Comedy. 10.00 London. 12.05 A Book for Today.
WESTWARD (Colour): 9.30 London. 10.30 All
Our Yesterdays. 10.55 Gus Honeybun's Birth-

Name	Size	Fig size	lca	Maker
Classad with Doric	4¾pt	·0553	92pts	Intertype

BYFLEET. End 3-storey Span
House, beautiful landscaped estate
(gold medal for design). Private
beach, etc. Spacious through
lounge/diner (25ft.), picture
windows, view of river, wood-
land, 2 dble. bedrms., fitted
cupboards, 1 single bedrm., kitchen, bathrm., cloakrm., utility.
Garage. Walled garden. Fitted
carpets throughout. Warm air
C.H. Near shops. 1 mile station
(30 mins. London). Leasehold
94 yrs. £7.750 o.n.o. Tel.:

Name	Size	Fig size	lca	Maker
Claritas with Bold	4¾pt	·043in.	79pts	Linotype

MANAGING DIRECTOR of an established firm of
Building restorers, decorators, and interior cleaners
is desirous of meeting gentleman who has experience in
this type of work with a view to active Directorship.
Capital required in the region of £1,500.—Box 299.
PROCESS ENGRAVING.—Partnership desired where
technical, organising, managerial ability, and keenness
to work appreciated. State investment reqd.—Box 159.
VACANCY FOR ACTIVE DIRECTOR in manufacturing engineers, agri-horticultural background.
Priority products Home and Export. Nr. London. Capital
for new development under own control. £2,000-£4000.
Write Managing Director, Agro Works, Hartfield, Kent.
SOUND COMMERCIAL undertakings requiring Capital, or Investors seeking active Directorships, invariably contact Commercial Development Co. (Willesden),
Ltd. Write, stating nature of requirement.—Box 138.

Name	Size	Fig size	lca	Maker
Corona with Bold	5½pt	.044in.	94pts	Linotype

LIBRARIAN REQUIRED for busy and progressive Public Relations Company. The successful candidate will be responsible for organising and managing a reference library and for arranging the circulation of trade and technical publications. Box 1471.
ENGINEERS AND DRAUGHTSMEN with coke oven, by-product or coal preparation plant experience in London area. Five-day week. Pension Scheme. Applications in confidence to Managing Director. Box 1570.
WAXED LINEN THREAD, 18/3 cord, ex-Government, at clearance price. Box 1473.

Name	Size	Fig size	lca	Maker
Excelsior	6pt	.048in.	107pts	Linotype

LONDON IS DEPRESSING AT WEEK-ENDS—Why not rent now enchanting small Georgian house in Kent; newly and beautifully furnished, 3 living rooms, 3 double bed rooms with bathrooms; Write Box A.2734, The Times, E.C.4.
KENSINGTON W.14. 3 bed, reception, dining, bath, kitchen, £500 p.a. Box E. 5520, The Times, E.C.4.
MODERN unfurnished flat to let, West Kensington; 4 bed rooms, large double reception room, kitchen, bath; two years more on renewable lease, £650 p.a.
MOST COMFORTABLE FLAT in London—reception, dining room, modern kitchen, bath; select area S.W.10; £12,500 or near offer; 21-year lease.—Write Box E.2994, The Times, E.C.4.
ON BLACKHEATH, S.E.3 — Beautifully converted spacious flat, £400 p.a., exclusive; Write Box E.2896, The Times, E.C.4.

Name	Size	Fig size	lca	Maker
Ionic	5pt	.041in.	84pts	Linotype

AUTO POLISHER and Shampoo Man. Heavy experience. Excellent opportunity for highly reliable man. Good salary, all benefits. Work on late model cars. Town & Country Leasing, division of Bast Chevrolet, 3630 Sunrise Hwy., Seaford. 221-8777.
AUTO PORTER and Lot Man. For new and used car dealer. Must have driver's license. Apply in person: William Pase Inc., 50 W. Jericho Tpke., Huntington Staion.
AUTO PORTER plus polisher and pick-up man. All benefits. 5 day week, salary open. Overtime. Local man preferred. Apply in person. Tyler Lincoln-Mercury, 49 Glen Cove Ave., Glen Cove.
AUTO RADIATOR Repairman. Steady. Experienced only. $4 per hour. (212) PA 7-0554.

Name	Size	Fig size	lca	Maker
Maximus with Doric	4¾pt	.055in.	88pts	Linotype

Name	Size	Fig size	lca	Maker
Royal	5½pt	.0413in.	88pts	Intertype

Name	Size	Fig size	lca	Maker
Spartan	5½pt	.0414in.	88pts	Monotype

Offset and Photoset

Most of the remarks on type design are true for letterpress, or offset, and for papers photographically composed ('photoset' newspapers) or set with hot metal. There is, of course, a distinction between offset printing and photosetting. A newspaper can be made up with hot metal, and printed offset. It can be photographically composed and printed letterpress. Offset and photosetting frequently go together but they should not be taken as being essential to each other. Papers printed web offset have advantages for text printing on newsprint. The offset image in newspapers tends to be sharper and clearer, and, with offset, one need not worry so much about ink traps, given reasonable ink, paper and machining. This means the choice of text type is wider, especially with photosetting combined, than for the conventional letterpress hot-metal newspaper where the type is inevitably debased by stereotyping.

But there are cautions. Offset tends to produce a lighter image than the same face conventionally set, especially where photoset and offset go together. A type with good colour is as essential for offset-photoset newspapers as it is for hot-metal letterpress. Old style faces, in particular, are weakened on coated or calendared surfaces where the ink has no spread; the flimsier the type the more texture needed in the paper.

There are other temptations. Photosetters which work on the point system have a variable film feed of either a half or quarter point, which means the leading can be varied by these tiny increments, and other filmsetters, such as Lumitype, give increments as small as one-fortieth of a millimetre. It is wise to be restrained with this and other facilities. First, leading should be standardised in the run of text type. Second, though it is as easy in photosetting to produce white on black images as the conventional black print on white ground, reading research is conclusive that the normal black print is more than 10 per cent more efficient than white on black. So the long runs of reverse image text should be avoided. (One sees them frequently in magazines and often with a type far too fussy for clear black-to-white reversal.)

3 Newspaper Settings

It is no proof of higher education to describe indents as dated or old fashioned.
—JAN TSCHICHOLD

The newspaper executive should not feel cheated of his creativity if the type family, its basic size and standard measure have already been laid down. He can still do a lot of damage. Setting-styles can be varied between the column rules; bold type and drop letters, and sub-heads, blobs and stars, can all be deployed to create havoc in a page to the satisfaction of the most frustrated executive. Alternatively, if the newspaperman can be reconciled to the less flamboyant aspiration of simply assisting the reader to extract information, all these devices can be unveiled without at the same time offering a prayer for the future of newspapers.

In this chapter we examine the main variants in newspaper setting, the use of vertical white, indentions, rules and ornaments and drop letters, and the way the sub-heading and the paragraph and the intro should be used to help the reader.

Column White and Column Rules

Columns organise the content. To do so effectively, they should be clearly separated. It is difficult to find what you are looking for in a page of a World War I newspaper, either side of the Atlantic, because the headings and type are small but also because the columns are insufficiently distinguished. The white between the columns then was infinitesimal and the dividing rule faint. And here we ought to be clear on our terms. The newspaper custom is to describe the division between columns, not as column white, but as column *rule*. This is confusing. A newspaper described as being on 6pt column rule does not have a thick 6pt rule blackly dividing its printed columns. It will have a fine rule, or a 1pt rule which prints, and this will be centred on a 6pt body. The reference '6pt rule' means only that there is a total of 6 points of white between the columns, and we have no clue about the thickness of the printing surface occupying part of that 6pt gutter. It would help if the terms were used differently—column white for the white and column rule for the printing surface. Or we could borrow the formula used in specifying type in which an oblique stroke distinguishes the appearing size from the body size. Where the term column rule is used, it would then be specified as $\frac{1}{2}$/6pt, meaning a half-point printing surface on a 6pt body.

The newspaper industry's slovenly way of describing column white/rule is a reflection of the way the white between columns is regarded as a left-over, an afterthought, after the column measure has been fixed. Many newspapers in the United States, which obviously care about design in other directions, have been appearing with as little as 3 points of white between 11-pica columns—40 per cent of the North American press has this 3pt column space which makes the page look mean and the reading of it irritating. Contrast the good German spacing and the typical mean US spacing which follows:

utung für das muß das Gezunächst anaaßen in seine aften zerlegen. eltes Tier, für eise, sind die : wahrgenomung als bedeurden, außeroriihre Verarbeiwer entwirrbar. :ier dagegen ist klich von Beiner Kröte ein es Objekt —	Jahres in Zuoz/Schweiz berichtete Professor J.-P. Ewert von der Arbeitsgruppe für Neuro-Ethologie der Gesamthochschule Kassel von neurophysiologischen Versuchen, die seine Arbeitsgruppe über das Beutefang- und Fluchtverhalten der Kröte (Bufo bufo) und die diesen zugeordneten Hirnmechanismen vorgenommen hat. Kröten in einem Glaszylinder wurde ein sich vom weißen Hintergrund abhebendes Stück Karton gezeigt, das sich maschinell um den Zylinder herumbewegte. Dabei löste ein sich bewegendes quadratisches Kartonstückchen immer dann das stärkste Beutefang-	derselben Hirn der Beutefang ronen in der D telhirns (Tect wurde, reagiert verhalten, wei Zwischenhirn (tum) elektrisch gänge im Gehii terschiedlichen grunde liegen, einander erfolg Erkennungsmec Versuche, in c Zwischenhirns tectum —, auf

lley, are perhaps better) area school children ;e of George Washing-)hy was a scout for the al Army and, accord- :tories, took part in just ery important engage- :ing the Revolution in on of the state. ; one of the defenders liddle Fort during the 3rant raid in 1780 and ed with saving it by 1e orders of a cowardly ler who was ready to 1 the valley fort to the	Eventually an elopment developed and Murphy took his bride-to-be to the Middle Fort. The furious father went to the fort but Margaret refused to return home and he could do nothing to enforce his edict inasmuch as Murphy's fellow soldiers were definitely in his corner. In a day or two, Murphy and Margaret were married by a Rev. Johnson of Princetown. The bride, who left her father's home barefooted and with only the clothes she wore, was	Leeds power line. The conference was purpose of s3tting dates sues for a full hearing tentatively scheduled 1 of the State of New Pumped Storate Porjec Mr. Haverly and Weste dents have objected. Mark L. Heller, Weste attorney, accompanied 1 erly to Washington, anc for permission for Wes participate in the sched ing. Federal Power Con representatives offerd

A 3pt gutter is absurd, and one must assume, certainly in the papers obviously conscious of good design, that it is an economy forced on them by the requirements of wire-tape setting. That tends to be standardised on 11-pica columns, come what may. Newspapers which find that this forces them into 3pt column white including rule, should first re-examine the relationship of press cylinder size, web width, plate size and page size, and the economics of a fractional increase in page size. A move to 6pt column white (including rule) would make a remarkable improvement in several hundred American newspapers. Newspapers on 3pt rule which cannot do this and are stuck with 11-pica wire-setting can still do something about column white for special display: we discuss it under Indentions below (p. 92).

There is another trend in North America, and elsewhere to a lesser extent, which is to dispense with column rule entirely in favour of column white. This can work, in certain circumstances, but there is nothing to be ashamed of in column rule. The best division between columns of unrelated material remains a clean straight unbroken rule centred on a larger body. Normally the column rule which prints is a fine, but it can, with effect, be stronger. The London *Sunday Times* found it gained in the organisation of its pages by using an incisive 1pt rule centred on an 8pt body. If the rule is stronger the body should be bigger, giving wider inter-column white. It is not an improvement to substitute a 1pt rule for a fine and retain a 3pt body.

Column white, rather than column rule, can look attractive, but it has two drawbacks. It is less economical in space than column rule. And it loses one useful signal and weakens another. The signal lost is the emphatic organising force of a straight printed line. This is the most effective and economic divider. The signal weakened is white space. If it is used to divide columns, it cannot be used to unite them. A newspaper using column rule has the advantage both ways. It can hold column rule as a divider where the adjacent text is unrelated. It can dispense with column rule and deploy white space as a unifier where, typically, type in the same story is run in adjacent legs in a horizontal layout. The absence of column rule here, in contrast to the rest of the page, helps to knit that story together under its headline.

Column rule is economic because more white is needed where columns are divided only by white. A broadsheet in 11-pica columns which dispenses with printing rules needs at least 10 points of column white, whereas otherwise ½/6pt would suffice. This is a fact which does not seem to be understood by papers dispensing with column rule, not least the growing number of photoset newspapers where column white is preferred because rules have either to be drawn in or stripped in with stick-down material. The effect of skimping on column white is to blur the integrity of the column; it is particularly bad where horizontal lay-out lines up legs of the same story.

;ht ad-
;talked
epping
: more
round
fourth.
Lewis
id up-

shook Leslie somewhat. Lewis' best punch was the uppercut and he put to-gether more combinations than he has in the past.

However, he did not seem to have the zip in his pat-

have it," said the physical fitness instructor at Ent Air Force Base in Colorado Springs. "When you can't do what you want to do you get disgusted — and that's what happened to me. I was deter-

tne
A
lowe
just
endi
rock
Tl
thus

The column measure and column white should always be considered together. Papers on a 9-pica column can manage on 4pt column rule or 6pt column white. Columns wider than 11 picas should carry more than the 6pt rule suggested for 11-pica columns: 14–15–16 pica columns require a pica of vertical white. As for a maximum, a rough guide would be to ensure that column white never exceeded one-fifth the width of column measure. In the example from *The Sun* on page 63, space wasted on excess column white could have been better spent widening the 7-pica setting.

Cut-offs

Another rule which has fallen in disfavour in North America is the cut-off, the rule separating one story from another. The vogue for dispensing with it is worse than that for dispensing with column rule. The absence of a cut-off between stories is a traditional and useful indication to the reader that the two stories are related. Dispensing with cut-offs robs the newspaper of this facility, and generally ends up confusing the reader. If there is no cut-off to direct the eye, or to tie picture to caption and both to the appropriate story, there must be greater care in layout and the considered use of white space to unite and divide. This rarely happens.

The cut-off used to be an elaborate device, an Oxford (thick and thin) rule. All it needs to be is a rule the same weight as the paper's column rule—½pt if the column rule appearing face is ½pt, 1pt if it is 1pt. It can be either full column measure or half-measure centred. There should be ample white either side of the cut-off rule. This is a matter of visual judgment, but with a cut-off centred on a 6pt body there should be at least a further 4 points of white between cut-off and the last text line of the preceding story. Where editorial text has to be divided from advertising, stronger rules should be used—2pt is usually enough, but when editorial text is landscaped over a horizontal spread of classified, then a 6pt, with 6 to 12 points of white either side, is effective.

Introductions or Leads

There is, happily, harmony between the typographical and journalistic requirements of the opening sentence or paragraph of the story—the intro, as it is called in Britain and other countries and the 'lead' (pronounced *leed*) in North America. The intro must be succinct in wording and short in appearance. Many European and Asian newspapers still set intros which are absurdly long for the type size and the degree of interlinear white; dependent clause follows dependent clause, and sentence is piled on sentence, qualification upon qualification, so that the mind reels. We went into this problem in Book One.

Intros which are long typographically are invariably also monuments of impenetrable prose. But no matter how brief or scintillating the sentences are, twenty lines of type or more in an intro cast a forbidding shadow. The eye needs a break before then; and so does the page seen as a whole. Flabby intros crowd too much greyness at the top of a page.

L ANCE .- CORPORAL Robert Craig Shepherd went out on a double celebration — he was about to be married and a friend was going abroad. But he had had too much to drink and when a policeman came to arrest him he spat in his face, it was stated at Darlington Borough Magistrates' Court today when Shepherd (26), of Hill of Minnes, Undy, Aberdeenshire, and serving with the RAMC at Catterick, admitted being drunk and disorderly and stealing a wine glass.

It was stated that when Shepherd was taken to the police station a wine glass was found in his pocket.

After the CO of his unit had described his Army conduct as "exemplary," he was given an absolute discharge.

Newspapers should generally prescribe a maximum number of lines for intros (or alternatively a maximum number of words if the deskmen are enjoined to remember the correlation between type size and line count). The maximum line count prescribed must depend on the type-face, the body on which it is cast, and the column measure. A serious text paper set to an 11-pica measure in Corona/Royal 8 on 8½ should never allow roman intros to exceed 12 lines of type single-column, and no more than 8 in bold. A popular tabloid paper setting 7pt solid in a 9-pica measure should not allow its intros to exceed 8 lines single-column. Where, for some exceptional reason this is to be exceeded, the lines should be 1pt leaded. But if intros at the top of a page should be slimmed to the bone, the marrow should be preserved: a two-line intro is all right on a paragraph filler but it is flimsy on a single-column top in a broad-sheet. It is a question of proportion. Two lines across two columns under, say, a 42pt head, look even thinner than a two-line single-column intro.

No intro across two columns should be less than four lines of 9pt or three of 12pt. At the top of a page, a double-measure intro needs to be 6 to 9 lines in 10pt to provide a shield between its own headline and the headline or advertisement in the intro shoulder. Note that this does not mean longer *sentences*. The lines are measures of type; they can contain full stops.

Intro Type

Because it is thought so important for the intro to do justice to the drama about to unfold, and to snare the reader, it is common practice to set the intro larger than the body size of the newspaper text, and often with a typographical flourish of face and measure. The necessity for this depends on the nature of the newspaper and especially the size of its text, and the position of the story in the page. British popular papers for a time indulged in a frenzy of innovation for each intro: this has lately been abating, and there is a need for restraint. It is hard to see what purpose is served by the variations in the examples **above right.**

Equally there is no doubt that any style of paper set in a basic 7pt should set the intros on any story at the top of a page (a 'top') in some-thing more prominent than 7pt, yet some papers dramatise the drabness of 7pt by juxtaposing it with two-decker headlines handsomely whited. Of course it is far better to set the whole paper in 8pt or even 9pt, and a paper set in 9pt needs no special intro settings for single-columns. Assuming this is not feasible, it is conservative to say that on single-column tops the intro should be in 8pt, and if the resources of the paper or production imperatives limit the size of type throughout to 7 or 8pt,

By BRENDAN KEENAN, of our Political Staff.

MR. WILLIAM CRAIG is now widely expected to break with the Unionist Party in the next few days and launch a new political party based on the United Loyalist Council.

A decision could come at to-night's meeting of the Vanguard council. One Vanguard official said to-day that "quite big decisions" would be taken at the meeting.

There is also a meeting of the Loyalist Association of Workers to-night. This is another constituent of the ULC and its members are known to favour the idea of a new party.

These moves have been in the offing for some time, but the final impetus was given by yesterday's meeting of the Unionist Council.

Vanguard sources see the meeting as a victory for them because, when abstentions are counted, Mr. Brian Faulkner had only a minority vote in favour of further negotiations on the White Paper.

KINGSTONIAN RES. 3, CORINTHIAN CASUALS RES. 3

WITH a fighting rally in the last 30 minutes of the game, Ks Reserves salvaged a Suburban League point against Corinthian Casuals at Richmond Road on Saturday.

Whether their coming to life was the result of the substitution of Mel Catchpole for the injured Jim Honeywood or the realisation that they should atone themselves for their previous defensive mistakes is anybody's guess.

Suffice to say that in the last half-hour they certainly did turn it on, and provided adequate entertainment for supporters who must have considered that the game was already lost.

It was not a case of Ks playing badly for they served up attractive football but as they gave goals to their visitors they became more and more lethargic.

then intros on tops should be 2pt leaded. The largest practicable size for intros on single-column 11-pica tops is 10pt.

One sometimes sees 12pt single-column intros, but the measure is too short for comfortable reading (*see* below) and 12pt at 11-pica breeds too many lines. There is the further production complication that one cannot descend from a 12pt paragraph straight into 7 or 8pt body type, a transition that requires the reader to engage in ocular acrobatics. Instead there must be some shading down in the type sizing—say from 12pt into a paragraph of 10pt and then into 8pt. Dropping from 10pt into 7pt requires only one intermediate setting of 9pt or 8pt. If the 10pt is short it is preferable to drop two sizes straightaway and go into 8pt, which can, if required, be leaded. After an intro in 9pt the setting can reasonably drop to 7pt. These are the effects of the different permutations:

Stout, balding Mr. John Jones, cashier to a firm of textile converters, was missing yesterday from his home in Cemetery Avenue, Openshaw.

12pt Metroblack

Round the corner in Funeral Street, Mr. Henry Brown said he had not seen his blonde, attractive wife, Mamie, since the weekend.

10pt Corona

A director of the firm which employed Mr. Jones said yesterday that the firm's books would have been due for audit next week. Mr. Jones was also treasurer of the local Working Men's Holiday Fund.

8pt Corona

At a flat in Southpool, stout, balding Mr. Arthur Smith said he had never heard of Mr. Jones or of Openshaw. Blonde, attractive Mrs. Dolly Smith said she had never been known as Mamie.

7pt Corona

Stout, balding Mr. John Jones, cashier to a firm of textile converters, was missing yesterday from his home in Cemetery Avenue, Openshaw.

10pt Corona

Round the corner in Funeral Street, Mr. Henry Brown said he had not seen his blonde, attractive wife, Mamie, since the weekend.

8pt Corona

A director of the firm which employed Mr. Jones said yesterday that the firm's books would have been due for audit next week. Mr. Jones was also treasurer of the local Working Men's Holiday Fund.

7pt Corona

Stout, balding Mr. John Jones, cashier to a firm of textile converters, was missing yesterday from his home in Cemetery Avenue, Openshaw.

10pt Corona

Round the corner in Funeral Street, Mr. Henry Brown said he had not seen his blonde, attractive wife, Mamie, since the weekend.

7pt Corona

Stout, balding Mr. John Jones, cashier to a firm of textile converters, was missing yesterday from his home in Cemetery Avenue, Openshaw.

9pt Corona

Round the corner in Funeral Street, Mr. Henry Brown said he had not seen his blonde, attractive wife, Mamie, since the weekend.

7pt Corona

Shading down is suggested for normal tops. Where a top consists of only a few paragraphs, it is better not to shade down but to retain the intro setting size. There is no need on any paper to shade down on single-column stories below the fold; or on short fillers.

Multi-column Intros

Many newspapers find they can manage by keeping all setting single-column. The loss in renouncing multi-column intros is in the possibilities for page design and especially in the display position created in the corner angle or shoulder under double-column setting; the gain is in simplicity and in production. If there is something to be said for double-column intros, there is a lot to be said against still wider intros, happily rare in North America but used all too frequently elsewhere without the proper care. On all multi-column intros the essential correlation between measure, size and readability must be remembered (*see* pp. 60–65) and also the limitations of production. Four-column intros or even three-column are time consuming because line-casting machines have a standard maximum line length of from 30 to 42 picas; over that the line must be set in two parts. But measures even shorter than three-column can be disastrous for reading, as many European and Asian papers demonstrate daily. Even with 1pt leading, 7pt at 23 picas is too small however it is set and wherever the story appears on the page; and 8pt with 1pt leading barely suffices.

7pt on 8pt Jubilee

As I stand bravely in the rush of a 111¾-mile-an-hour Atlantic gale on this crowded 15-square-mile outpost of Britain, South Uist and Benbecula, the wind roars through my desperately bucking typewriter. Today I was the first newspaperman to meet Mr. Mackenzie (Mac) Waggoner, the 47-year-old New York real estate dealer who wants to buy the island.

8pt on 9pt Jubilee

As I stand bravely in the rush of a 111¾-mile-an-hour Atlantic gale on this crowded 15-square-mile outpost of Britain, South Uist and Benbecula, the wind roars through my desperately bucking typewriter. Today I was the first newspaperman to meet Mr. Mackenzie (Mac) Waggoner, the 47-year-old New York real estate dealer who wants to buy the island.

There are two styles of multi-column intro. There is the straightforward multi-column in which every line is set the full measure. Then there is the multi-column leading into narrower setting in which the last few lines of the multi-column intro are set narrower measure in the same size. The 'spilling' slims the multi-column setting when it might otherwise be excessive and it leads the eye unambiguously into the narrower text. What has to be watched is that the amount of narrower setting does not unbalance the wider setting, especially in the larger sizes. And, of course, it is essential that the same size of type is retained during the change of measure. American predilections to the contrary, sentences in the same paragraphs must stay in the same type size, whatever the measure. Only the first of the settings (**above right**) is correct.

When there is extended double-column setting on, say, a page one lead, keep it on the same size after the initial shading down. There is a strong deterrent to reading further when a half-column of 10pt double-measure is succeeded by a half-column of double-measure in 8pt.

On three-column intros, given an 11-pica column, we have to consider introducing a different typeface because many text faces do not run to the sizes required, and the relatively condensed character of most text faces does not show up well at wide measure. A simple increase in the basic text-face size serves well enough for double-column and single-column intros, and where extra emphasis is thought to be required the duplexed boldface is adequate and offers production simplicity. Where this is not enough, never seek emphasis by italic, by underscoring, or, worst of all, by setting the intro in caps, whether bold caps, or roman

10pt Modern intro (good)

The wind roars through my desperately bucking typewriter as
I stand bravely in the rush of a 104½ mile-an-hour Atlantic gale
on this lonely 10-mile-square outpost of the British Empire,
South Uist and Benbecula, to meet 49-year-old, grey-haired,
New York real estate man
Mr. Waggoner ("the Wag")
Mackenzie, who wants to buy
the island.

10pt Modern intro (bad)

The wind roars through my desperately bucking typewriter as
I stand bravely in the rush of a 104½ mile-an-hour Atlantic gale
on this lonely 10-mile-square
outpost of the British Empire, South Uist and Benbecula, to meet 49-year-old, grey-
haired, New York real estate
man Mr. Waggoner ("the
Wag") Mackenzie, who wants
to buy the island.

10pt and 8pt Modern intro (bad)

The wind roars through my desperately bucking typewriter as
I stand bravely in the rush of a 104½ mile-an-hour Atlantic gale
on this lonely 10-mile-square outpost of the British Empire,
South Uist and Benbecula, to meet 49-year-old, grey-haired,
New York real estate man Mr.
Waggoner ("the Wag") Macken-
zie, who wants to buy the island.

caps. A different typeface is to be preferred, and is inevitable in any
intro over three columns.

Three-column (i.e. 34-pica) intros require a minimum size of 10pt,
and 12 or 14pt is better at the top of the page. Intros wider than three-
column should be avoided. If a four-column intro is to be readable, with
easy eye-transfer from line to line, the type size has to be increased to
18pt, which rapidly consumes space and soon becomes slabby. Where it
is necessary for the intro to bridge four columns it should normally be
set in two or three legs; and where, despite the production delays, the
setting has to be across four columns, it is essential that the wordage be

General de Gaulle resigned today as President stitutional referendum. Just under 53 per cent three-line communique from the Elysee Palace, ply: "I am ceasing to exercise my functions as takes effect from midday today."

General de Gaulle resigned tod: after his defeat in the constitu under 53 per cent voted against

kept down, that the new typeface used has a wide face, and that it be reasonably whited. In the examples **above,** the first 18pt setting in Linotype Gothic No. 25 saves space, but it is not as easy to read as the second in Century Extended.

Those are exceptional sizes for what ought to be exceptional measures. For normal multi-column intros the best of the larger serif faces are Century, Century Schoolbook, or Century Bold Extended (both the latter are better at the wider measures) and Caslon Old Face Heavy, all of which mix well with the run of text faces. Rather more distinction is provided by two sans serif faces, Linotype's Helvetica or Intertype's Galaxy, roman or bold, but preferably roman, provided they have at least 2 points of additional interlinear white. But these are the only two machine-set sans faces really suitable for multi-column intros and a standard text face. The popular Metroblack reads nothing like as well as Helvetica Bold; nor does Metrolite, which also lacks sufficient colour. The best of the Metro series is Metromedium, but its relative close-set means that its 14pt can serve for a three-column intro only if the lines are leaded. Vogue, likewise, does not compare. Here is a comparison of 12 on 14pt Helvetica Bold and Metroblack (**right**).

e after his defeat in the con-
gainst his proposed reforms. A
hortly after midnight, said sim-
nt of the Republic. The decision

18pt Condensed
Gothic No. 25 (bad)

President of France
al referendum. Just
roposed reforms.

18pt Century
Bold Extended (good)

12pt Metroblack No. 1 2pt leaded

It can hardly be denied that the assassination of
the whole British Cabinet by Puerto Rican nation-
alists is an exceptional occurrence in the history of
British politics. Not since the Salford by-election of
1872 has there been a comparable outbreak of violence. The motives for the attack remain obscure,
but the theory that those concerned had boarded the
wrong aircraft and so believed they were in Washington can surely be dismissed.

12pt Helvetica Bold 2pt leaded

It can hardly be denied that the assassination of
the whole British Cabinet by Puerto Rican nation-
alists is an exceptional occurrence in the history
of British politics. Not since the Salford by-election
of 1872 has there been a comparable outbreak of
violence. The motives for the attack remain obscure, but the theory that those concerned had
boarded the wrong aircraft and so believed they
were in Washington can surely be dismissed.

A sense of proportion must be cultivated for multi-column intros. Setting two lines across multi-column measure is too thin and it is downright ugly when the second line is short. But setting something like ten lines in 12pt bold double-column is too hefty. And it is absurd to set a multi-column intro across three columns, then across two, for a depth of several inches, and then change to single-column measure for a brief paragraph or two. Changes of multi-column measure in the same intro should be limited unless there is an adequate pillar of single-column text to support the edifice. A delicate balance has to be struck on all multi-column intros between space, economy, readability and weight; and constantly a clear route for the reader's eye must have primacy over pattern. The kind of back-tracking to avoid is shown in the illustration **below**. Two other settings would have been preferable: either to lead the three-column intro into single-column setting in the second or third column, losing its ugly truncated line—a 'widow'—on the way, or to run the second and third pars as double measure in columns 2 and 3.

Planning chief hits at Miltons scheme

HARINGEY'S PLANNING OFFICER, Mr. David Frith, described the neighbourhood improvement schemes run by the council as "very disappointing from a planning point of view" when he spoke to the Highgate Society last Friday.

The Tory-controlled council is running pilot schemes in three neighbourhoods, with the object of encouraging residents to work with the council to improve the areas.

Mr. Frith told the meeting, at the society"s HQ in South Grove: "This was first and foremost an exercise of public participation in planning, but it has been very disappointing from a planning point of view.

the proposed siting objected very strongly," said Mr. Dawson, 47, who lives in Milton Park, "We are now considering another site."

He pointed out that the Miltons area off Archway

Indentions

Vertical white provided by some form of indention is especially necessary when newspapers have standardised on a narrow column rule. A newspaper on 3pt rule, which is not wire-setting, should at least indent the intros. In addition to highlighting an intro, indention can create a special display unit, even for papers setting wire copy; it can pick out significant passages in text; it can relieve the grey of a solid page. The degree of indention and the style and the pattern can be permuted in a score of ways, with varying production costs, but structurally there are six main forms:

1 One-up and bastard setting
2 Ragged right
3 Centred
4 Single indent
5 Reverse
6 Roman

Let us look at these in turn.

1 One-up and bastard

Prospectus Makes 'Interesting' Reading

By AL ALTWEGG
Business Editor

An interesting prospectus came to my desk during the past week. It was for a Dallas-based company called U.S. Bancshares Inc., offering 130,000 shares of common stock to the public at a price of $12.50 a share.

But the thing that caught my eye was the statement on the front of the prospectus that said, in capital letters, "These shares involve a high degree of risk."

So I started reading. And herewith are some excerpts from that prospectus:

"U.S. Bancshares Inc. (USB) was organized by sixteen shareholders for the purpose of becoming a registered bank holding company to be operated in the State of Texas. . . .

"USB was recently formed and has not yet begun operations. There can be no assurance that profitable operations will be conducted. The business in

which USB proposes to engage is highly competitive. After this offering USB will be an insignificant factor in the industry. It anticipates that it will have many competitors most of which are larger, more experienced and have greater resources than USB. . . .

"USB is not presently a bank holding company. In order to become a bank holding company, USB must be able to acquire control of one or more banks and secure the necessary governmental approvals. . . .

"USB does not presently have any understandings, arrangements or agreements for the acquisition or organization of any banks. Therefore there can be no assurance that any banks will be acquired or if any are acquired or organized that they may be acquired on a satisfactory basis to USB. This will create a greater investment risk to potential investors since any banks that may be acquired in the future cannot be identified at this time and their opera-

tions examined by prospective investors.

"Further, there is no assurance that USB will be successful in becoming a bank holding company or if it does that its operations will be profitable.

"In the event USB is unable to qualify as a registered bank holding company within two years from the date of this prospectus, management of USB will call a meeting of the shareholders of USB for the specific purpose of determining USB's future. There is no provision to refund the proceeds of this offering in the event USB does not become a bank holding company. . . .

"USB's current revenues are insufficient to meet its current operating expenses and there is no assurance that such revenues will be increased. . . .

"There can be no assurance that operating revenue will increase sufficiently to offset reduction of USB's working capital, which will be depleted in approximately 34 months if the present

rate of income is not increased.

"Such operating expenditures are principally of such character that they are unrecoverable. Accordingly, investors undertake a risk of losing all of their investment if USB is not successful in becoming a bank holding company.

"USB presently has only two full time employees, neither of which are experienced in the management of bank holding companies. . . .

"The underwriter, Gallagher, Knight & Co., Incorporated, is a recent entrant into the investment banking business. To date it has not underwritten any offering. . . .

"There can be no assurance that additional financing may not be required in the near future. Such financing may not be available, and, if it is, may not be available on reasonable terms. Lack of adequate, reasonable financing could have a materially adverse effect on USB's operations and future growth. . .

"There is no present market for USB's common stock and no assurance that an established market will develop as a result of this offering. . . .

"A suit is pending to enjoin USB from using its corporate name in connection with its proposed bank holding company activities. . . .

"Net proceeds to USB from this offering will be approximately $1,384,500, after deduction of the estimated expenses of the offering. . . .Even though USB estimates that upon completion of this offering it will have sufficient assets to acquire approximately three banks, since USB has no understandings, arrangements or agreements for acquisitions or formations of subsidiary banks, there can be no assurance that USB will be able to acquire any banks with the proceeds of this offering."

There is, of course, much more in the 37-page prospectus. But then who reads prospectuses?

Business & FINANCE   Sunday, February 4, 1973   15 B

The Dallas Morning News

Truhill Airline Booms

Air Freighters Doesn't Have to Advertise

By PATRICIA HARMON

When Joe Truhill was a youngster, he and 14 friends bought a small plane. Then they built an airstrip. (They lived in a small town that didn't have one.) Then they decided to learn to fly.

Now, some 25 years and several hundred thousand flying hours later, Truhill owns Air Freighters Internation-

Freighters is an unscheduled airline, and, so keep it from competing with scheduled ones, it is not allowed to advertise.

"We don't have to advertise, really," said Truhill. "We have contracts for certain runs which no scheduled airline could make. For instance, we carry automotive parts from Ford Motor Co. in

the war. After a short time running a small airplane sales and rental business in Deming, New Mexico, he was back in the Air Force to instruct pilots for Korea. He was a flight commander at the training base.

In 1958, Truhill started a business in Dallas called Air Service Inc. at Addison Airport. He sold, leased and maintained heavy aircraft and also provided

Amtrak Says Slow Orders Slow Trains

KANSAS CITY, Mo. (UPI)—Track and traffic problems on the Penn Central railroad tracks east of St. Louis were blamed by an Amtrak spokesman for giving the Kansas City-New York passenger train run the second-worst on-time record in the Amtrak system.

The spokesman said the passenger

This indention is different from the others in that it is not provided on the lines of type. It is provided by stretching five legs of type across six columns, or six legs across seven columns, and so on, the 'unused' column being spent on white space between the legs of type. The device, called one-up display in North America, is not to be confused with bastard setting. In bastard setting, type is set at an eye-catching irregular measure, usually wider, with appropriate white in the gutter. The essence of one-up display is that the type is set at single-column measure. *The Dallas Morning News* (**above**) runs five columns at the top across a six-column measure.

PURPOSES: One-up display is especially useful for North American newspapers condemned to 3pt column rule or less by the exigencies of wire-tape setting. Though the copy is still set 11 picas by wire tape, the newspaper can create special display units by running the single-column measures across an extra column. The extra white emphasises the news item featured in this way, so it is excellent for wide horizontal units at the top or foot of the page. These units can give even greater effect if the type is enclosed within either a full or sideless box (sometimes misleadingly called a 'cut-off'). The full box with rules down four edges takes time to create in hot metal; the sideless box merely requires a strong rule top and bottom.

The real display power of the white lies in its contrast with the greyer areas of tighter spacing, so one-up should be used sparingly. There are a great many variants—one across two for a short sideless box in the middle of a page; two across three; three across four; and so on. And it is of course possible to go two-up for special panels or sideless boxes, four columns of single-column measure across a six-column space. But this can produce too much gutter white. Anything over three picas of column white begins to divide 11-pica setting like a canyon.

MECHANICS: There is no special marking for the copy though, if the text is to be run horizontally, longer paragraphs help. It is in spending the extra increments of white space that the craft lies. Let us assume we have a six-column space at the foot of the page on a newspaper setting 11 picas with 3pt column rule. This is a width of 66 picas plus 1·25 picas of column rule, making a total of 67·25 picas. If we have only to accommodate five legs of type in that area, i.e. 55 picas, we have 12·25 picas over for column white. This gives us just over two picas for each gutter of white. That fraction over is small enough here not to matter, but it is as well if all these calculations are not made at the last minute in the composing room. The newspaper intending to use multiples of one-up display at all frequently (or bastard measure) should work out and specify a regular division of the way the white gained is to be spent. The layout sheet can then be marked with the appropriate code or specification: '5 across 6, 2·5 picas left, then 2-pica gutters' and so on.

2 Ragged right

The lines are ragged right (see p. 55) but there are first-line two styles—paragraphed and unparagraphed. The paragraphed version indents the first line of each par in the usual way one em of the body size, but, except in long runs of text, paragraphs should be avoided in unjustified setting. The unparagraphed version, in which each line is flush left, helps to make the left a clearer pivot of the design.

PURPOSES: Whatever the disadvantages of ragged right or 'unjustified' for complete standard text, it is useful as a variant. It can emphasise a piece of text (such as an announcement by the newspaper); it can avoid the monotonous squared-up effect when text is aligned over an advertisement of the same measure; and it can relieve an overcrowded section of the page. Ragged right is especially useful where text would otherwise run unpleasantly into an adjoining headline, text, half-tone or advertisement. Ragged right setting here pulls the lines of type away from the adjoining material by leaving varying white space on the right, and it puts its own emphasis on the left. Ragged right is, by its nature, asymmetric setting with the left-hand margin as the main structural axis of the design. The left-hand margin should therefore be somewhat wider than usual—every line indented an extra mutton(em) or nut(en) so that the left margin can act 'as a buttress and counterbalance to the text'.[1]

lacunae—who, for example, was the hapless individual assigned to telephone LBJ and break the news that he, an incumbent President, was not wanted at the National Convention of his own party?

It explores some fascinating subplots, such as the one in which Richard Goodwin attempted to engineer a surrealist alliance at the 11th hour in Chicago between McCarthy and that suave Southern mandarin, Governor John Connally of Texas.

But lacking a single author it tends to sprawl and wander.

It is overstuffed with facts and in places the writing flags. The smart-Alec device of printing wry extracts from Camus, Little Lord Fauntleroy, Brecht, Machiavelli and Dean Inge as chapter headings adds nothing to an understanding of American politics.

The finest passages of the book are those depicting the poisoned idyll of the American South and analysing the dark forces which move behind such breeders of racial tumult as George Wallace and Strom Thurmond. I credit these to the individual expertise of Godfrey Hodgson, who has made a special study of Southern politics.

Mr. Nixon, at least, will have

ADVENTURES BEFORE FIFTY. Denys Val Baker. John Baker, 45s. Things happen to Denys Val Baker and his family—from floods to shipwreck, and other minor disasters in Cornwall and similar fraught places. But you cannot keep a writer from writing: hence this happy tale of a century of mishaps.

SERMONS IN SOLITARY CONFINEMENT. Richard Wurmbrand. Hodder, 21s. To keep himself whole, a Protestant pastor incarcerated by Communists in Rumania for three ghastly underground years, preached sermons to himself in the silent, terrible nights. Here, now, they are. Christians will see, anew, the courage of their church in this man; others will, if they are honest, admire the power of his spirit.

WILDE
Balance restored.

THE WIT OF OSCAR WILDE. Frewin, 18s. Some of the Wit series have been pretty unfunny:

joyed exceptional pre-publication publicity. It is said to have taken ten years to write: the chairman of the publishers writes comparing it to Dickens: Release, BBC2's Arts programme, featured it: advance sales have already, it is claimed, set new records for a first novel. Lucky author!

Is it then so very exceptional? I don't find it so. It is a long patient haul through the life of Dublin, seen largely from the underside, from 1907-1914. These were years in which the city was crippled and finally paralysed by a series of devastating strikes, organised by the union leader, James Larkin.

In a conventional form and in conventional language, Mr. Plunkett follows the fortunes of a handful of characters selected to show the effect of the strikes on a typical cross-section of the population.

From among the workers there is Fitz, foreman at the Foundry, and his wife Mary, who was earlier in service: they are a nice respectable hardworking couple whose loyalty to their fellow workers will eventually (as we

MECHANICS: The markings for the unparagraphed unjustified setting are 'Set left, ragged right'; or, 'Set left, unjustified right'.

Even though you omit the paragraph marks on the copy it is wiser to insure with the positive instruction: 'Note no par indent.'

In addition to the verbal instruction, draw a wavy line down the right-hand margin, a useful visual reminder to the operator that the right-hand margin is ragged.

3 Centred indent

her instructors round the bend.

She is good at gear changes, expert at three-point turns and finds hill starts no problem.

But she just can't get the hang of going round corners. Somehow she always seems to go off course.

So now she is retiring from driving—after 120 fruitless lessons.

In eight years on and off the road Mrs. Ryan, of

THE town was delighted when Mr. Knicker married his girl.

For farmworker Krelis Knicker had been courting Jannet since 1945.

Finally, they decided to get married quietly at the register office at their town of Oldebroek, Holland.

But the town found out. Eight hundred people and the town band were waiting to congratulate the Knickers when they arrived home.

killed by the baby lurking in its mum's pouch.

Seventeen - year - old Stephen Higgings was shooting with friends 100 miles south of Sydney when they bagged the female kangaroo.

Stephen, a student, walked up to the carcass with his rifle at the ready.

Suddenly the baby jumped out at him, the gun went off, and Stephen fell dying with a bullet through his head.

Justified setting with each line indented at both ends. The indention is usually either:

(a) An em of the body size of the type, specified as 'em each side' or '1 + 1'. With 8pt body type an em each side produces 8 points of white in each margin.

(b) An en of the body size, specified as 'en each side' or 'nut each side' or '½ and ½'. An en indent in 8pt type produces 4 points of white in each margin.

Of course, justified copy can be marked for any dimension of indention. A pica indent each side is sometimes seen in an 11-em column, though it is not attractive. It reduces the set matter to the excessively narrow measure of 9 picas, and the vertical white from the pica indent is out of proportion. The indention must relate to the column width. A wider indention than an em is appropriate on wider measures: in a 21½-pica measure set in a double-column panel for instance, a pica each side would be right.

PURPOSES: Centred indent is a versatile tool of text typography. The white concentrates attention on an intro; a significant quotation; a caption; or a list of names; and centred indent is not restricted to highlighting a few paragraphs. A long single-column can be set centred indent throughout to provide a vigorous vertical element on a cramped page. Where text set with centred indent is adjacent to the headline, the executive must watch for its effect on the style of headline setting. It looks ugly when the headline is poised over a gutter of white, and this is most likely to happen with centred indent when the newspaper style is to set headings left. The answer is to indent the headline as well as the text so that text and headline line up at the left.

Centred indent is essential to a panel. The type must be kept clear of the rule. The fancier the rule and the wider the setting, the bigger the white indent must be. Centred indent can be wasted. There is no point in adding white to both margins when the text occupies the first column or the last. The page margins add sufficient white at the extremes then. The centred indent should run as a clean swathe between grey areas of type.

MECHANICS: Copy in 8pt single-column to be indented one em each side is specified: '8 × 1 em each side'; or '8 × 1 indented 1 and 1'.

In addition draw a vertical line down each margin with the numeral 1 at the side. This is a constant reminder to the operator. For the nut indent mark copy: '8 × 1 NES'; or '8 × 1, $\frac{1}{2}$ and $\frac{1}{2}$'

Draw a vertical line in the margin and the numeral $\frac{1}{2}$.

PANEL MECHANICS: There are two extra steps:

1. Always draw a plan for a panel, showing dimensions, the placing of headline and copy, and the nature of the border required.

2. Calculate the set-measure. Say the standard setting is $11\frac{1}{2}$ picas and that the panel is a solid 6pt rule. The space available for type, therefore, is not $11\frac{1}{2}$ picas but $11\frac{1}{2}$ picas minus 2 × 6 points, i.e. $10\frac{1}{2}$ picas. Therefore the copy is marked to be set: '$10\frac{1}{2}$ ems nut each side in panel 6pt border—see plan'. The left-hand result **below** is wrong, the right-hand one correct.

Editorials which perennially hold a fair balance between opposing arguments are sure to be read by fewer and fewer people. The leader-writer who will not come off the fence is boring and useless. There are plenty of times, of course, when he is so baffled that even from Mount Olympus he cannot make up his mind. Then there is justification for a tentative, discursive leader. The rest of the time, however, the leader should argue a case, illustrate it with facts, and come to a conclusion. The leader should lead.

Editorials which perennially hold a fair balance between opposing arguments are sure to be read by fewer and fewer people. The leader-writer who will not come off the fence is boring and useless. There are plenty of times, of course, when he is so baffled that even from Mount Olympus he cannot make up his mind. Then there is justification for a tentative, discursive leader. The rest of the time, however, the leader should argue a case, illustrate it with· facts, and come to a conclusion. The leader should lead.

4 Single indent

strator. Use of the centre would be shared between the polytechnic and local organisations.

The report must be approved by the arts council and the polytechnic governors before it is submitted to Kingston Council, possibly next month.

The working party says the centre would be more easily

tive party's economic research department before winning the Sutton and Cheam seat in 1954.

He held several key posts in Government and Opposition and was once tipped as Britain's first minister for Ulster.

Messages of sympathy have been sent to Lady Sharples and the couple's four children

The text is indented at either the left or right margin—but not at both sides.

PURPOSES: The left indent is more useful because one begins reading from the left. It can add white to an intro or a bold paragraph, but its most general use is when type is being run in several legs. On a page with narrow column rules, a left indent enables column white to displace a series of bitty surface rules. In these short depths column rules are often untidily cut, and unlike ordinary column rules, are not dividing separate stories. If the column rule is 6pt on an 11-pica column, a nut indent provides sufficient white, since the nut indent is repeated in the adjoining leg of type. Where the squared-up story begins in column 1, adjacent to the page margin, the text is set nut right. The right indention should not be used on intros, especially on multi-measure intros leading to single column. This is the unhappy effect produced:

THE "give-away" to surtax payers in the Budget had created a new political situation among workers, Mr Wedgwood Benn, Opposition spokesman on trade and industry, said in the Commons last night.

This explained much of the current industrial unrest and the Government's only answer had been to wheel out the Lord Chancellor, Lord Hailsham, "like Big Bertha," to make a speech about patriotism.

The civil servants, gas workers and hospital workers were demanding no more than justice, he said.

Mr Patrick Jenkin, Chief Secretary, Treasury, opening the last day of the Budget debate, rejected criticism of Government spending by the all-party Select Committee on Expenditure as "misconceived."

ments over the next three years meant surtax payers got a tax-free loan and paid it off in devalued currency.

If the ordinary income-tax payer overpaid through P A Y E he was making an interest free loan to the Exchequer. The surtax payer alone was being allowed to pay up to four years late without paying interest on the loan he received from the Exchequer.

Roy Jenkins

Tories blamed for 'impasse'

Mr ROY JENKINS (Lab., Stechford) said the Government now faced a borrowing requirement of £4,423 million in the year now beginning, as against a surplus of £600 million in 1969/70. This was most extraordinary for a party which for six years in Opposition had spent its time moaning about public expenditure.

The falseness of the Government's election manifesto had led them to an economic impasse. "Ever since they have been without compass and belief, ready to follow any deceiving chink of light which might seem to offer them a way out."

MECHANICS: Mark the copy 'nut left' or 'half left', and draw a straight line down the left margin with a large numeral $\frac{1}{2}$.

5 Reverse indent

EGGS may cost five pence each by the end of the year.

The bob-an-egg price tag was predicted yesterday by the boss of Britain's biggest egg-packing and marketing organisation.

Mr Gordon Lounsbach, egg manager for the Co-operative Wholesale Society, claims that first signs of the rise are already creeping in.

Large white eggs are expected to cost 30p to 32p a dozen in the next few days—two pence up on last week.

This reverses the normal pattern in which the first line of a paragraph is indented and the rest of the text set full measure. With reverse indent, the first line is set full out and it is the rest of the text which is indented. An alternative specification is 'hanging indent' or 'o and 1', since the first line hangs over the white indentions of the succeeding lines.

PURPOSES: Reverse indent is more limited than centred indent. It is such a bizarre variation that it should be used sparingly—one area of reverse indent is enough to a page. Secondly, unlike centred indent, it cannot be used in one paragraph to distinguish an intro. It looks like a setting error. It has to be employed in several paragraphs at a time, so that the rhythm of the style can be established. Reverse indent on text of two or three paragraphs looks absurd; it has no time to show its paces. For the same reason reverse indent needs frequent paragraph marks. Paragraphs should be no more than eight lines: over-paragraphing is worth risking to escape the disconcerting effect of a few full-measure first lines poised over vertiginous chasms of white. Finally, reverse indent is best in self-contained single legs. It does not show up well when doubled up in two or more legs. Inevitably then indented lines are turned to the top of a column, leaving the first full line behind. This is ugly and the purpose of the indention is lost.

Reverse indent, then, is for occasional text of some length, preferably sandwiched in one column between regular text; for single-column captions; for highlighting a section of single-column text; and for enumeration (*see* below).

MECHANICS: There are two variations of reverse indent. The straightforward reverse indent seems unbalanced and the superior form re-

> FOUR GIRLS have been suspended from an exclusive convent school after a police probe into pot smoking.
> The girls, all aged 14, were alleged to have lit up a marijuana cigarette
> Now school governors will decide if the girls, close friends who are all in the fourth form, can re-
>
> In the garden he said he saw a " vast " queue of people aged mainly between 17 and 25.
> They were going into the surgery and bypassing the waiting room.
> Mr Gaber alleged that he saw a similar queue when he visited the surgery again later.
> He also said that the doctor gave him prescriptions

dresses this by adding a nut of white space at the right. The effect thus produced (**above right**) is to be preferred.

Every folio should be marked with the words 'reverse indent' and in addition the numerals 'o + 1' added. This means the first line has no indent and the others carry 1-em indentions. The first line of each paragraph, which is to be set full out, is marked with a reverse paragraph mark, i.e. *a bracket open at the left*. The superior style of reverse indent is marked on copy: 'Reverse indent left, nut right'.

Copy should be marked with the numerals 'o + 1' on each page, with a straight line down the right-hand margin and a numeral ½ in the white space.

Reverse indent setting in standard text should be separated from other paragraphs by 3 points of white; and each paragraph within the reverse indent section should have 1 point of white.

6 Roman indent

In sections to be distinguished by Roman indent the first line of the paragraph is indented 2 ems and subsidiary lines are indented 1 em. This shifts the paragraph to the right and lines up the subsidiary lines with the paragraph openings of unindented text. The style is also called '2 and 1' because of the indentions of 2 ems and 1 em.

PURPOSES: For distinguishing in a restrained way roman or bold paragraphs of enumeration (*see* below).

MECHANICS: Mark the copy 'Indent 2 + 1'.

The Roman indent section should be separated from standard text by 3 points of white. Each paragraph of Roman indent has an additional 1 point of interlinear white. Roman indent is rarely used in double-column; when it is, the indention remains 2 + 1. Doubling the indention to 4 + 2, which is sometimes done, produces a zigzag of lines at the left, four indentions in all, which makes the soberest feel giddy.

Enumerations

The settings below indicate the different ways in which the copy editor
can highlight enumeration occurring in text:

> The purpose of this statement is
> threefold :
> 1. To set forth the facts about
> my own relationship to the Water-
> gate matter.
> 2. To place in some perspective
> some of the more sensational, and
> inaccurate, of the charges that have
> filled the headlines in recent days,
> and also some of the matters that
> are currently being discussed in
> Senate testimony and elsewhere.
> 3. To draw the distinction be-
> tween national security operations
> and the Watergate case. To put

1. Normal paragraphing: the copy is broken into paragraphs, one for
each numbered section. The first line is indented 1 em of the body size,
just like a normal paragraph opening, with the figure, preferably in bold,
either full out (as in this paragraph) or itself indented.

2. Roman indent: the first line of each numbered section is indented
2 ems. The other lines are indented 1 em.

3. Reverse indent: the first line bearing the numeral in roman or bold is
set full out and others indented so that the numeral hangs in white. All
three are thus simple variations on ordinary text. Now elaboration sets in:

> These were:
> 1 The Stans Fund—an amount
> which fluctuated between
> $800,000 and $1.3 million in
> cash kept in a safe in the office
> 2 The Haldeman Fund—$350,000
> reportedly transferred by
> Creep to the White House
> chief of staff
> 3 The Kalmbach Fund—an esti-
> mated $500,000 from un-
> disclosed contributors in 1971
> and 1972.

4. Reverse indent with big numeral: the numeral has been introduced
to hang in the white of the reverse indent.

Three important factors
indicate that the M.P.s are
now engaged in the most
significant campaign of its
kind since hanging was
abolished in 1965.

1 It is being supported by
some politicians who have
voted against hanging in the
past.

2 It is led by senior Tory
b a c k b e n c h e r s highly
respected on both sides of the
House for their moderate views.

3 And it is coming at a time
when there is near world-
wide reappraisal of the issue.

5. Drop letter: standard text but with a large numeral introduced as a two-line drop letter. Subsequent lines 'cover' the drop—which is the reverse of style 4 above, where the lines deliberately leave the numeral in white. The two-line drop numeral is produced by marking the numeral two-line drop but specifying fount and point size. Check whether the numeral in the type specified is a full titling cap (i.e. without beard) or whether the size has to be increased. To cover two lines of 8pt requires 24pt in ordinary caps of the commoner display faces.

THE AIM : To tackle five
p r o b l e m s which have
become more and more
acute in recent years.

1 Providing a richer leisure
life for everyone ;

2 Improving opportunities
for people to change
careers later in life ;

3 To counter the impact
of shorter working hours
and earlier retirement on
society ;

6. White numeral on black background introduced as a drop letter in standard text.

7. White-on-black numerals introduced in reverse indent.

Paragraphs

For the newspaper the paragraph is primarily a typographical, not a literary, device. This may seem a philistine attitude. Is violence to be done to the language and to thought for the sake of the mere mechanics of typography? No, it need not be; but it has to be recognised that purity of literary style is an empty thing if the reader has already been lost. And that loss is a certainty if we attempt in mass-circulation papers to retain paragraph breaks strictly for new ideas, new subjects, new speakers. Breaks then come too infrequently to relieve the eye in the expanses of small grey newspaper type. The paragraph in the newspaper still serves to indicate where new thoughts, subjects, and speakers begin, but in addition paragraph breaks are introduced for the purely typographical reason of providing white space as refreshment to the traveller.

It has to be admitted also that a narrower self-interest creeps into the matter. Shorter paragraphs help the newspaper in its production. Ten men can set ten short paragraphs on separate folios ('takes') simultaneously—a great boon when deadlines are close. When a section of text does not fit the page space allocated and something has to be cut, it is easier to cut when the paragraphs are short.

If the dispensable sentence or word is in the middle of a paragraph, deleting it means resetting the whole paragraph. With well-paragraphed stories, properly edited, it is a simpler matter to cut the end two lines of a paragraph or drop a whole paragraph.

That said, how frequently should newspaper text be marked for paragraphing? The answer is that the newspaper paragraph is a function of four separate forces: (i) Literary meaning, which is closely related to the kind of newspaper and its audience; (ii) type family; (iii) type size; and (iv) the set-measure. But nothing in what follows should suggest that all paragraphs must be the same length. There should be variety, for the sake of avoiding monotony and for the lively appearance of the page, but the variety should be within certain set limits.

(i) Meaning

There is common ground between newspapers that a new speaker always needs a new paragraph:

Mr Smith: Have you stopped beating your wife?

Jones: Yes, I mean No.
The witness hesitated and then protested that he thought the question was unfair.

Mr Smith: Well, I'll put it to you another way. Have you ever beaten your wife?

Further than this, it can safely be said that the reader of a serious newspaper can more nearly be served by the literary paragraph. He is divined to be made of more durable stuff than the tabloid's snapper-up of unconsidered trifles, and the content of the serious paper more lends itself to the literary paragraph. It generally offers a more connected narrative, and less a series of episodes, so that paragraphs of fifteen lines are tolerable. But in the more popular paper there is such a succession of separate thoughts that even literary sense calls for paragraphs as frequent as every half-dozen lines.

(ii) Type family

The harder the type is to read, the more frequently the paragraphs must break. There should be more paragraph breaks for the wider typeface than for the narrower, since the wider face will create longer slabs of type. Ionic needs more breaks than Corona/Royal or Times Roman, because a given number of words set in Ionic takes more space and looks slabbier sooner.

This qualification about the equal legibility of types is important in North America. Here there are the ravages of wire-tape setting and the abuses of photosetting to consider. (They use such things as a width-compressing lens to squeeze already-compact faces like Aurora.) For these reasons too many North American newspapers have text too condensed for comfort, and the basic unreadability of these compact faces overrides my general suggestion that narrower-set faces need less paragraphing. Newspapers with difficult-to-read text should give the reader a chance by paragraphing more frequently.

(iii) Type size

The eye needs more rests in reading small type. Therefore, the smaller the type, the more frequently must the paragraphs break. Papers set in 7pt solid must paragraph more often than papers set the same measure in 9pt. It is true that, just looking at the page, the 9pt paragraphs will tend to heaviness, but the normal 9pt is sufficiently easier to read than 7pt that the reader does not need as many pick-me-ups of paragraph white. The answer to the apparent heaviness of the longer 9pt paragraphs is deliberately to seek more variety in paragraph breaks. Provided the sense is retained, a few short paragraphs (and well placed sub-headings) can do a lot to break up the apparent visual monotony of a long-paragraphed page.

(iv) Measure

The narrower the measure the more frequent must be the paragraph breaks. A tabloid like the London *Sun*, shown **below** in contrast with *The Times*, must make paragraphs and sentences virtually synonymous:

BRITISH RAIL got tough with their rebel train drivers yesterday.

In future men who refuse to take trains out will lose mileage payments—up to £2 a day.

But the men will still get their basic rates of pay. The move brought an immediate protest from the men's union secretary, Mr Ray Buckton.

"It's a very unwise decision — provocative attitudes could mean worse disruption," he said. The union has already promised increasing chaos over the next 10 days.

British Rail has toughened its attitude to its 29,000 train drivers who are operating a militant campaign of strikes and non-cooperation. From today it will pay only basic wages, without bonuses of any kind, to drivers who refuse " unreasonably " to take a train out. The present basic for drivers is £30.75.

Drivers who fail to earn their bonuses will lose up to £2 a day on suburban routes ; mainline drivers, of whom only a handful are operating the non-cooperation policy to any extent, could lose up to £5 a day.

Mr Ray Buckton, general

Three or four sentences soon begin to suggest a paragraph of epic proportions. Curiously, the obverse lesson—that wide measure should have less frequent paragraphing—is constantly forgotten.

Short paragraphs in wide measure provide too many breaks; they interrupt whatever thought there is, waste space, and look hideous. Here is an example from the *Christian Science Monitor* where the paragraphs are so fragmented that reading is impeded:

Inside the lobby of the large London department store half-a-dozen baby prams complete with infants stood in a neat row against a wall.

It was a busy Saturday morning, and customers streamed in and out, past the carriages.

The babies' mothers were nowhere in sight.

The only explanation was that the mothers were inside, shopping.

As an American I couldn't remember ever seeing the same thing in my own country. Certainly not in comparable New York.

This injunction to restrain the impulse to paragraph on wide measure is especially important when a wide measure is being squared up across several columns; and in this situation it has force also for normal 11-pica measure. The turns of type from column to column will provide some eye-relief; frequent paragraphing here will only give the compositor the difficult task of avoiding turning short 'widow' lines to the top of a column.

If in doubt about paragraphing, always try to visualise how the text will look in the page. If it is in danger of appearing long—and by that I mean anything in news pages over fifteen lines—a new paragraph should start even at the risk of cleaving some celebrity's thought-structure.

Mere mechanical breaking of paragraphs must be avoided. Variety, as in all newspaper make-up, is helpful. A mixture of medium, short, and long paragraphs is required, related both to the meaning of the message and to its typography.

LEADING: Paragraph breaks provide their own white space because last lines are rarely full measure, and a new paragraph should start with an indent of one em of the body size. There is a new fashion of abandoning the indent showing, as Jan Tschichold put it,[2] that the typographers responsible attach greater importance to a deadly even appearance than they attach to function; and that they either do not or cannot read.

An additional 1pt lead does no harm between paragraphs, but it is easy to lead too much between paragraphs and spoil the flow of a story. This is one failing in the *Minneapolis Tribune* whose 1970 redesign— handsome on the whole—was arranged so that all text type, including paragraph spacing, could be set by computer. The spacing here badly interrupts the narrative.

By Dan Wascoe Jr.
Staff Writer

It may be too late for the city of Minneapolis to participate in building Hennepin County's proposed civic center, county officials said Thursday.

City Council President Richard Erdall told the Council yesterday morning that it should decide quickly whether to join the county in building the $45-million, twin-towered structure.

But plans may have gone too far and a leasing arrangement may be the only option remaining for the city, said county officials. They agreed that a joint city-county project would be the most economical arrangement if quick agreement could be reached on details.

Erdall said in an interview later, "I personally doubt if we'd be interested in a lease arrangement" because of the "constraints" it would involve.

The civic center, now planned for the two blocks south of the present City Hall-County Courthouse, is scheduled

should face during the next two years.

He said the space needs of city government now and in "the next quarter of a century ... can best be met by joining with Hennepin County in the civic-center building."

If the city participates, Erdall said, more floors would have to be added to the 17 stories now planned. The county has specified that the building be designed to accommodate an additional six floors.

If the city chooses not to participate, he said, "then I think it is incumbent upon this Council to deal with the question of how we solve the city's space needs without participation in the civic center.

"Obviously, there are some possible answers, but I do not feel that we can let the matter rest in hopes that some future Council will address itself to this question," he said.

The city now is leasing 200,000 square feet on the private market at $350,000 annually, he said.

If there is this amount of space going spare, it is better used for an extra sub-heading (or, if the type is of large x-height and set solid, it is better judiciously distributed between lines if it can be done evenly).

4 Sub-headings

Common sense is a prized national characteristic, but we make sparing use of it in design, and we take an arrogant delight in our blindness to matters of style. —JAMES SUTTON

It may seem a simple matter to recommend the sub-heading as a relief to the reader in a column of text, yet this humble device has a curious way of arousing passion. There are newspaper designers today who regard it as a gimmick, a confession of design failure, just as the Victorian critics of the 'New Journalism' regarded it as a frivolous intrusion in an eight-column Budget speech. Perhaps the feeling of revulsion had something to do with the cross-head's first appearance in England—the words 'Confession, Execution, and Dissection,' in a grisly Sunday newspaper report (*The Weekly Dispatch*, August 17, 1828), of the murder of Maria Marten in the Red Barn. At any rate the reader of the London morning newspaper had never seen a cross-head until W T Stead introduced it in the *Pall Mall Gazette* in 1881. Stead's cross-heads, only slowly copied by the dailies (1888 for the *Morning Post*, 1890 for *The Times*), were too thin, being light roman caps of the text face, but in every other way they are an excellent example for the modern newspaper. They were simple; they were centred with reasonable white at either end; they were leaded top and bottom in just the right proportions; they were placed where they could illuminate text, and they made sense. If these precedents are followed, the sub-heading deserves to survive.

Cross-heads and Side-heads

The term 'sub-heading' is the general name for any small headline inserted in a run of text. There are two basic styles: the cross-head, which is set centred on the text below, and the side-head which is set flush left, lining up with the left-hand edge of the text. Sub-heads set right pop up from time to time (some Dutch and Spanish papers use them) but right-hand setting of text or head is a freak.

There is no reason why a newspaper should not use both cross-heads and side-heads provided two principles are observed: they rarely are. The principles are that the balance of the sub-head should relate to the balance of the text, and the style should be constant within each text unit. On standard full-measure text either side-head or cross-head may be used, but text set with centred indent or indented left should have cross-heads rather than side-heads. A side-head on centred indent text can so easily project into the white margin, spoiling the effect of the indention. A cross-head, by contrast, emphasises the symmetry of the design.

The difficulty with side-heads on left-indented text is that they look untidy unless the side-head is indented to the same degree as the text. This is not easily achieved. To mark a 10pt side-head 'nut indent left' certainly will *not* make it line up with 7pt nut indent text. The 10pt nut indent represents half the space occupied by a 10pt em. That is clearly more than half the space occupied by a 7pt em. Therefore marking a 10pt side-head 'nut indent left' will ensure it ends up fractionally but noticeably to right of the indented text.

Nor can precision be achieved by marking the side-head with the indention appropriate to the text. This is because of the way line-casting machines work. A nut of 10pt Royal, in practice, is $5\frac{1}{2}$ points rather than 5, and the nut of 7pt Royal is 4, not $3\frac{1}{2}$.

Theoretically, then, one should mark the 10pt side-head with the instruction 'Indent 4 points left', so that the indention would equal the indention of 7pt type. However, an operator on a line-casting machine cannot produce this fine gradation of spacing. In a 10pt fount, which has a $5\frac{1}{2}$pt nut, the operator can indent one em (11 points); a nut ($5\frac{1}{2}$ points); a thick ($2\frac{3}{4}$ points); and a nut and thin ($8\frac{3}{4}$ points). Thus in reality the newspaper can have that 10pt side-head on 7pt text indented too much ($5\frac{1}{2}$ points) or too little ($2\frac{3}{4}$ points).

It is better to stick to cross-heads for left-indented text. With reverse indent, however, there is no problem, since the first line is full out, nor is there any with text set ragged right. On both of these, in fact, side-heads are to be preferred since they emphasise the asymmetry.

Constancy of style means that the deskman should not switch from side-heads to cross-heads in the same text, unless side-head and cross-head fulfil entirely different roles. If they are mere breakers of text *either* side-head *or* cross-head should be used, but not both together. However, there are occasions with long text when the sense calls for division into sections and then sub-sections and even sub-sub-sections. It is then not merely permissible to use both, but essential if the reader is to be presented with a concise dissection of content. On these occasions the cross-head and side-head need to be differentiated by more than setting style.

The sub-heading for the section should be set larger and bolder than the sub-heading for the sub-section; and that distinction must be maintained throughout. It matters not at all whether side-head or cross-head is the style chosen for the main section headings so long as the signal is constant. For instance, a President's review of a country's affairs might have side-heads in an 18pt gothic for major topics (Europe, Crime, Trade, The Cities) with the text in these sections broken by 12pt roman cross-heads for sub-sections or for typographical relief (Offer on Berlin, Gold Pledge, 'Intolerable'). A newspaper with limited resources, which has only the duplexed bold of body text for sub-headings, can change the emphasis between section and sub-section headings by allocating two lines of caps to the side-head and one line of lower-case to the cross-heads.

With these two qualifications we can now discuss the function and form of the sub-heading, either side-head or cross-head.

The function

Like the function of the paragraph, the function of the sub-head is a compromise between content and typography, with the claims of typography stronger. There is, as we have just seen, an important area in which side-head and cross-head work together to categorise content. In such long texts the communication of meaning would be confused if the criteria for the sub-head became solely typographical. Part of the judgment of the executive in choosing categories for special presentation is to ensure from the start that these also lead to sufficient breaks in the grey of text, in other words that the category breaks incidentally provide their own typographical relief.

Other than instances like this, however, the dominant criterion for the sub-head is typographical. The executive will try to use the sub-head to distinguish subject from subject, speaker from speaker, but the overriding concern must be to provide horizontal breaks in the text for comfort in reading. This will often mean introducing a sub-head where there is no literary justification for it, and even sometimes omitting a sub-head where there is literary justification. The sub-head must first serve as an illuminator of the text.

How often this needs to be done depends on the size of text type; the typeface; the width of the column; and the page plan. A story 12 in. long set in 7pt across 11 picas may need two sub-heads—but only if it is run straight down a column. If it is run in four legs, each of 3 in., sub-heads would be an intrusion and the text executive should specify on copy that sub-heads are not required.

As with paragraphing, you have to judge by visualising the text. If it is a handsome 9pt, well set and with good vertical white, schemed on a page with many half-tone and display breaks, it may be possible entirely to dispense with sub-heads. Too many sub-heads are certainly as bad as unrelieved text; the popular tabloid habit of throwing the reader a typographical crutch every two paragraphs is less a mark of charity than of irritating condenscension. And there are places where, whatever the demands of typography, the text should not be interrupted by a sub-head, eg, in mid-sentence, mid-paragraph, or after a colon:

management shake up was followed by a big cut back in staff. About 4.000 men were made redundant.

And yesterday other workers spoke of their apprehension that more redundancies were on the way.

Said one man who has worked for B.S.A. for 10 years:

Sacrifice

"We have learnt to live with crises, but we have all been working flat out to get the company back on its feet."

Frequency

If one is still pressed to put a figure on sub-head frequency, one could say that a small sub-head every four inches or so is not out of place in a broadsheet news page. If this looks right, one can also say that the first sub-head should be separated from the first line of text by rather more than this. Sub-heads too close to the top are as absurd as over one paragraph at the bottom. Stories which turn from one column to another often catapult sub-heads too high and too near the headline, and in production one must watch also for sub-heads in adjacent columns lining up side by side. One of the subheads should be moved, checking always that in its new position it is still covered by the text below.

The words

This brings us to the writing of sub-heads. The facility with which sub-heads can be moved on the stone or at the paste-up stage depends on the point in the succeeding text on which it is written. The sub-head should never be written on a point in the first succeeding paragraph (still less should it repeat a phrase in the first line). This advice is contrary to the traditional rule for writing sub-heads, which is based apparently on the fear that the reader will be round for his money back if the promise of the sub-head is not immediately fulfilled. The risk must be braved. The 'first paragraph' practice is an infuriating impediment in production. It means that the awkward sub-head can only be moved upwards, since moving it down a par removes its textual support, and involves rewriting, new setting, and lost time. No, write the sub-head on a point in the second or third paragraph below so that it becomes mobile in both directions in the column.

Writing a news sub-head is different from writing a news headline. Sub-heads with pretensions to be headlines are windy fellows:

INQUIRY IS URGED BY
CHAIRMAN ON DELAY

Quite adequate here, literally and typographically, was:

INQUIRY URGED

The news sub-head, unlike the headline, has no need to be an abbreviated sentence summing up the salient news point below. It is too brief for that, though it must be fair and non-libellous, and quotes must be in quotes. It is primarily a typographical device. If the sub-head writer agonises over which is the most crucial of several important points he will waste time and produce too many words. Something different should be attempted—the selection of two or three words which combine sense with pungency. Sub-heads may not be read like text, but there is nothing to be said for long words, abstractions, single words which mean nothing, or gobbledegook even if it is faithfully reproduced gobbledegook:

ATTITUDINISATION	**REMARKABLE**
GOA	**INCENTIVES-BASED**
ENSUING SUCCESS	**UNCONDITIONAL**
REGULATED	**CONSTITUTION**

The sub-head words should be short, specific, and, if possible, suggest action or the tone of the text. That sub-head 'GOA' should have been 'GOA "A BLUNDER",' 'REMARKABLE' could have been '2-HOUR SPEECH'. These sub-heads have the right sense of direction:

HE MAY SHOOT   HECKLING

WIFE'S NOTES   100 DESERTIONS

ORDER FOR COSTS   OFFER TO RESIGN

QUICK PUNCHING   SCHOOL CLOSED

It is occasionally possible, and quite effective, to link sub-heads by a theme:

THE JOKE

THE JUROR

THE JUDGE

McNamara goes
cool on bombing

Johnson goes
cool on Clifford

Wilson gets hot
on the hot line

Text Face, Display Face or Fancy

For ordinary news the sub-head should be one line, and once the style is decided it must be maintained. The European practice of letting sub-heads come up erratically at one, two or even three lines is sloppy. The simplest style, though not the most effective, is one line of the body text of the paper, but in a bold lower-case or bold caps (and without a full point at the end). Where bold lower-case is used elsewhere in the paper, generally in occasional bold paragraphs, the sub-heads should be distinguished by bold caps. The extra black of the caps always helps to give some substance to the text size sub-head.

> the freeze began at an annual rate of 28 per cent, complained Mr. Meacher. He demanded an immediate increase in family allowances.
>
> **RUSSIAN HARVEST**
> Replying, t h e Prime Minister insisted that an increase in family allowances would not be a solution to the problem of the lower

In hot-metal production the text size sub-head has the attraction that it can be set on the same machine as text (matrices being duplexed with either bold or italic) and offers a good unit count. When it is properly deployed, though that is rare, it just about suffices as a text break. It is generally misused (*see* spacing section below), especially by North American papers: they should study the wording and the whiting of the text size sub-heads in the *International Herald Tribune*. White space or more frequent paragraphing are better than badly executed text size sub-heads.

Sub-heads larger than text size are preferable, but they should then be used less frequently than text size sub-heads. They, too, should generally be single lines, and in these larger sizes they should be lower-case of regular weight. The basic choice in larger-than-text sub-heads is whether to employ the type(s) used in the headline display of the paper, or to seek a contrast by importing a sans into a serif paper and vice versa, or by enlisting one of the ultra-heavy faces. Matching sub-heads are preferable in straight news.

This is not much of a restriction. It is sometimes said that using the display face for sub-heads risks confusing the reader between sub-heads and news-heads on fillers. That is really an alibi from deskbound fidgets who, in the British popular newspapers, have debased the sub-head with unsuitable type mixes and fancy ornamentation. It is doubtful if anyone notices when the styles of news fillers and sub-heads are identical, but there is in any event a range of variation, even within one face, let alone within one family. The sub-heads **below** in 14pt Century Bold show some of the range. They are not, to be sure, equally satisfactory. The best are the simple lower-case sub-heads without frills (the fashionable boxed sub-head, in particular, is a fussy ornament not worth the effort). However, the settings do show some of the possibilities there are in one size and one face without raiding the fancy rule department. That should, anyway, be out of bounds to news.

Jury's 16 hours

16 HOURS

16 HOURS

Jury's 16 hours

Jury's 16 hours

Jury out for
16 hours
---

16 hours

THE JURY
Out for 4 days

THE JURY
Out for 4 days

THE JURY
Out for 4 days

Underscoring, if acceptable at all, needs care. The rule should hug the typeface and its weight should be roughly that of the face.

Papers setting headlines in sans should confine themselves to sans sub-heads. Serif display types produce weak sub-heads in a sans-dressed paper, though for features the ultra-heavy letters, used judiciously, can bring relief to the bare monotones of the sans. If a serif paper does hanker after sans for news sub-heads, then the choice is rather similar to the choice for intros. Linotype's outstanding Helvetica and Intertype's Galaxy are excellent machine set sub-heads in 12pt and below, and since they can be used for intros they are the best choice. Above 12pt, Linotype Gothic Condensed No. 25 or Erbar Bold is better than Linotype's Metroblack (which kills the text in the papers where it is used as a 14pt sub-head) or Intertype's Sans Serif No. 2, though the condensed faces are bad on multi-column sub-heads.

From Ludlow, for page leads and exceptional sub-heads, there is the

Helvetica Bold

JURY'S 16 HOURS

Record Gothic Bold

JURY'S 16 HOURS

Helvetica

JURY'S 16 HOURS

Tempo Heavy Condensed

JURY'S 16 HOURS

Galaxy Bold

JURY'S 16 HOURS

Erbar Bold Condensed

JURY'S 16 HOURS

Pabst

JURY'S 16 HOURS

Galaxy

JURY'S 16 HOURS

Poster Bodoni

JURY'S 16 HOURS

Condensed Gothic No 25

JURY'S 16 HOURS

Cameo

JURY'S 16 HOURS

well-mannered Record Gothic Bold Medium Extended, and Tempo Heavy Condensed Italic (not the Roman). The ultra-heavy faces should not be considered for news (except perhaps in an occasional page-one treatment on a popular tabloid), but for colour in features Linotype's Pabst and Ludlow Black have punch and verve in the smaller sizes; and there are also Poster Bodoni (Linotype), Bodoni Modern (Intertype), Ludlow Tempo Black Condensed Italic, and Ludlow's shadow letter, Cameo. Always give these faces plenty of white and never embroider them with fancy rules.

Size and Spacing
The size must relate to the text size (never smaller), the amount of text, the column measure, and the sub-head typeface. The blacker the face and the larger the x-height, the smaller the point size required: 12pt

Helvetica Bold easily does the work of 14pt Bodoni. Generally speaking, standard news text set in 8pt across 11 picas is served well enough by sub-heads in 12pt boldface or sans, provided they are not too frequent. On very long runs of text, up to a broadsheet column, fewer but larger sub-heads are more effective; on long runs of 7pt, sub-heads in 14pt; and 18pt on long runs of 8 or 9pt.

Sizing does not present much difficulty anywhere (some oversizing on English dailies, undersizing in North America), but newspapers all over the world go haywire over the spacing of sub-heads. The commonest fault is squeezing the sub-head into the text without white anywhere. Cross-heads and side-heads are both written too full, and then the text is brought in like a vice top and bottom. The exigencies of production never excuse this. It is better to throw out the sub-head altogether, because once the sub-head is squeezed in this way it has lost typographical justification. More than that, it is impeding readability, because it is taking paragraph white from the text.

The campaign to save the sub-head must begin with editorial executives ensuring that the wording is shy of full measure. Sub-heads in 11½ picas should occupy no more than 7½, whether side-heads or cross-heads (two-line side-heads look best short–long or two equal lines; two-line cross-heads should always be long–short). Adequate horizontal spacing should be laid down for the composing room and disturbed only on editorial instruction. Here it is:

7–8–9pt text sub-heads in 11 picas: 6 points above, 3 below.

10–12pt, 11 picas: 8 points above, 4 below.

18pt, 11 picas: 10 points above, 5 below.

18–24pt, double-column: 12 points above, 6 below.

Note that the spacing below the sub-head is less. This is to tie it to the text to which it refers. The standard American practice of floating the sub-head equally in white is wrong, though papers using Bodoni sub-heads must watch the Bodoni descenders in the larger sizes.

The only occasion when sub-heading top spacing can safely be reduced is when the last line of the preceding paragraph is less than half measure and the sub-head also is short. Then 3 points may be taken off the top spacing. If in doubt, err on the side of white. There are a few papers using too much white—notably some of the newer photoset papers—but their sin is not mortal.

5 Other Text-breakers

In most examples the visual effect is disturbing, in a few, deplorably ugly, and in every case it would have been better to avoid initials altogether in favour of a simple opening. —RAYMOND ROBERTS

Newspaper text is broken for four reasons: to classify content, to provide eye-rests, to relieve the appearance of the page, and to emphasise a particular passage. The best basic way to achieve any or all of these aims is to use sub-headings, numerals, paragraphs, illustrations, and changes in setting-style, especially those which introduce vertical white in the ways described earlier. Where text is extremely long—say there are four columns of a document or speech—the deskman's first task is intellectual rather than typographic. He has to study the text to see if the formal divisions in the original text dissect it enough for the lay reader for comprehension. The sub-headings in an official document are often insufficient or inexplicit; in a speech there is generally no formal division.

Once the deskman has decided what is roughly the best way to dissect the content of the long text, he must then see how this fits the requirements of the page and the need to avoid over-long runs of text. The ideal dissection, intellectually, may need some adjustment to avoid a boring layout; and, conversely, the layout requirements may have to be relaxed a little. It is no good insisting on a dividing sub-head every six inches if this kills the logic of the whole classification system. This balance between intellectual and typographic requirements is not easy to achieve. Newspapers in developed countries err on the side of sacrificing content to display; newspapers in Asia abandon the reader in a fog of grey text.

Quite often the ideal balance cannot be achieved by keeping the text single-column. Wide measure eats up the text more quickly and lends itself to large sub-headings (breaker or divider heads). Often, too, it is better to avoid running text straight down several 22-in. columns of a page. Text can be doubled up in short self-contained units under double-column dividers, or tripled up. Americans call this system Canadian wrap. Big consecutive numerals in each of the sub-divisions help the reader along; reverse blocks are effective, too.

There is a range of other devices for breaking text, some useful, some gimcrack gimmicks devised by bored copy editors for the torment of typographers. This section discusses some of them.

Initial Caps

The first letter in each of these settings is a display inital cap. In the first setting the cap is dropped below the line of the text and is known as a dropped (or 'drop') cap or letter; in the second the display initial rises above the line of text and is known as a rising cap:

SINCE numerology is concerned with the numbers in your life, it obviously places great stress on your date of birth.

In the blackness of the night, flying into Kuwait is a psychedelic spectacular. Below flicker the huge

In both these instances the device is decorative. Newspapers borrowed the drop cap from books and use it to emphasise the start of a story and provide a spark of colour on a text page. The rising cap has rarely been used in news; in features it is used as a dramatic typographical break. The drop cap used in news stories has generally been equal to two or three lines of the text type—a two-line or three-line drop—but there is nothing to stop a newspaper having drop caps of four, six or ten lines; nothing, except of course a sense of proportion, and of fitness for purpose. Indeed the modern news page is capable of being so different from the book that there is really no justification for even two-line drop letters on news stories. They are an anachronism, they waste production time, and are anyway rarely executed effectively.

Features are another matter. There the ceremonial initial cap, dropped or raised, is one decorative device that can economically bring visual colour and differentiate parts of the narrative. The initial cap here is best deployed infrequently but with a large bang. Small initial caps in a large area of continuous text are overwhelmed; they look fussy. A four- or six-line drop letter in a strong fount is preferable; with roman type a gothic sans can legitimately provide the punch, but a serif drop letter rarely looks well with sans serif text.

Newspapers and magazines using initial caps, and especially drop letters, have important details to get right. They rarely succeed, hence the distaste among typographers for newspaper drop letters. Look for a moment at this drop letter in a British tabloid:

B **B C television is to kill off " The New-comers " —the twice-a-week television serial which has run for nearly three years.**

The initial cap in this example is in Bodoni and it looks effete against the black sans of the text: drop letters should have some typographical relation to the text and/or the newspaper's display dress. The use of compact sans drop letters to accompany serif text is often much more acceptable. Too many newspaper drop letters are mere accidents or whims—old display letters or letters which blur the character of the text or headline dress (as, for instance, Cheltenham drops in a Century paper). The safest course is for drops to be bold roman caps of the headline dress of the paper. Always study the colour value of the drop letter: it is meant to provide emphasis. Against bold text a light initial is wasted.

A second defect of newspaper drop letters is that too often they do not fit. They are meant to be a two-line drop—which is the right size for a news column—but the initial cap does not cover two lines of text:

AMERICA'S big four motor manufacturers said yesterday they could not meet the Government's

It is left floating in white. Instead of being an integral part of the text, the drop letter is detached. The rule is that the foot of the initial letter should be aligned with the base of the x-height of the last text line against which it fits. Here is an example where that defect is aggravated by another:

PROMOTIONS have been announced for two well-known members of the Wigan branch in top-level editorial changes at The Wigan Observer, award-win-

The drop letter here does not cover the text—and, in addition, the second line of text is allowed to wander away from the initial cap. The drop letter again fails to be an integral part of the text. Compare the effect of a correctly sized and aligned drop letter:

C HANCELLOR Anthony Barber made a last-minute bid yesterday to stop building societies putting up home loan interest rates today.

The spacing problem of the second line is something a newspaper executive should raise with the printer. Inadequate sizing is often the fault of editorial. It is insufficiently understood that a 24pt capital letter does not provide cover for two lines of 12pt type (unless it is specifically a titling letter with virtually no beard). The capital letter in the ordinary fount is *not* twice the size of the text letter; it is less, how much less depending on the design of the type. Bodoni, of small x-height has a notoriously small cap and a 24pt Bodoni cap provides cover for only two lines of 8pt type, since the face depth of 24pt Bodoni Bold caps is about 17 points. (24pt Century Bold on the other hand suffices for two lines of 9pt type.) No, to cover two lines of 12pt intro type would require either a 24pt titling cap, or something like 36pt in Century Bold or Franklin Gothic.

Attention should also be paid to the style of the first word. If an initial drop cap is followed by letters in lower-case there may be

S eit Jahren wird in der Bundesrepublik über die Abtreibung diskutiert. Sprecher aller im Bundestag vertrete-

ascenders to protrude nastily above the cap letter. This risk is small in newspapers, given the compression of text type, but it is the understandable justification for the printing convention that following an initial drop in the first word or phrase (particularly names in full) should be set in ordinary caps of the text fount, as in the top example.

But if the first word is to be set harmoniously in caps, it is important, in narrow newspaper columns, that the capital letters should not turn on a second line. Because of such awkwardness some offices abandon the caps style and specify lower-case letters to follow an initial cap. If this is the style, however, it should be noted that it is no answer to the problem of the protruding ascender, to have the top of the initial cap aligned with the top of the ascender.

Opening quotation marks are a nuisance with drop letters, and should be avoided.

The First Words

Below are six simple ways of beginning ordinary newspaper text. The abandonment of the drop letter is justified, but typographically some modest signal of the start of the text is probably helpful to the reader and certainly to the maker-up trying to identify type or film. Most American newspapers prefer the first style here, beginning in caps with the place-name and agency, and sometimes a dateline, too, even for domestic stories. This style has the distinct editorial advantage of identifying

> **WOUNDED KNEE, S.D.,** March
> **9** (AP).—The Justice Department
> said today that the government

the source of the story for the reader, and it is set quickly on the same machines as the following text. Typographically its snag is that long place-names plus datelines or agency credits produce an awkward first line or two.

NEVER BEFORE IN AMERICAN history has the intellect and conceptual view of the world of one man, who was neither in an elected

GASMEN are now deciding by ballot whether to end their strike, which caused

BRITAIN'S "anti-porn brigade," is to hold its first "summit meeting" in London soon to launch a unified attack on "increasing permissiveness."

Factory supervisor James Bell of Dagenham, Essex, was awarded £7,000 agreed damages in the High Court yesterday for the loss of his

Chief Gatsha Buthelezi, the Zulu leader, warned businessmen and trade unionists in Johannesburg today that a

The other five styles are all set without trouble on the same machine as text. The second style of initial caps on a full line is simple and effective for newspapers; the third of caps for the first word or phrase is preferable and makes for easier setting; the fourth with a bold first word can be an irritant when spotted frequently over a page; and the fifth is the very barest indication possible of the start of the text—the line full out without paragraph indention. The sixth style of setting the first line with a paragraph indention does not provide an opening signal and the indention itself has no logical justification.

Whichever style is preferred, it should be used consistently. All the settings, other than the first, imply that the dateline and agency accreditation, if any, are set elsewhere. A common practice is to run the agency's name on the end of the last line, but this either limits stone-cutting or risks the loss of the agency credit. There is a lot to be said for setting by-line, dateline and agency credit, if any, all self-contained at the top of the text. The simplest style is to do this in bold, or bold and light, of the text face and centred on the text:

> **By JOHN BULLOCH**
> **in Ankara**
> **A**LL political parties in Turkey were meeting last night to decide whom

Source lines on multi-column stories will normally require to be set larger than bold of the text face (or possibly in a different face). They should certainly not be much smaller than the text of the intro: an 8pt by-line on a 14pt intro looks absurd. Provided there is reasonable white at either end, most multi-column source lines are best centred on one line:

> **From HENRY MILLER : Salisbury, March 14**
>
> The hearing of a second   The Minister of State for appeal by Mr Peter Niesewand African Affairs, Lady Tweeds-

Popular British newspapers have gone in for all sorts of fancy work around source lines, with underscoring and panelling and even panelling broken at the centre in top and bottom rules. It is all quite unnecessary.

Bold Paragraphs

The Americans call this a bold graf. There was a time when hardly a British daily or provincial had not succumbed to this typographical eczema; and it is recommended by the leading American designer Edmund C Arnold in his *Modern Newspaper Design*. Arnold urges that a story 6 inches long should have one bold graf, and one every 4 inches thereafter to provide 'typographic colour at places where the content just doesn't warrant emphasis', and says that 55 per cent of American editors in a 1968 NEA survey reported using bold this way. I think we should always pause twice when we concede that a typographic emphasis is not justified by content. Typography should serve content and not the other way round.

The traditional bold paragraph has devalued itself because it has been rarely anything other than a decoration. Of course the fear is that the uncommitted reader who has to traverse three or four inches of type unstimulated by shots of bold will drift off before the last paragraph. It is a poor comment on content.

Where bold is still used as a stimulant in the run of text (or where it is genuinely used to emphasise important paragraphs), there are four essentials:

(i) The bold intruder should have 2 points of white before and after.

(ii) The bold should be sandwiched between paragraphs of roman—it ought not to be next to a bold sub-heading or italic or intro, or at the end of a story.

(iii) The bold should never be underscored.

(iv) The bold should be infrequent—one paragraph in ten—and it should be brief. Anything over eight lines is too much.

**Before it came, Satur-
days were a torment.
The climax of his normal
working week was pur-
poseless.**

**"People think I've
made a killing from a
golden handshake," he
says. "So far, as money
goes, we're having to
draw in while things are
sorted out.**

**"I was only thinking
when I was running this
morning that in Decem-
ber life was as bare as
the trees. Now the buds
are forming.**

There is another different use for bold which can be commended: the first paragraph of a sub-section of a long story. It should be separated from the preceding roman by at least a pica of white.

Of course, breaks in the text like these can also be provided with roman type—a pica of white preceding a new paragraph set simply with initial roman caps, flush left (as on p. 121).

Key Words

Some stories lend themselves to a sequence of paragraphs where the narrative is assisted by emphasising the opening words of the paragraph, rather than the entire paragraph. It may be a time sequence, or a subject division. These initial signals can be set in bold lower-case, italic, roman or italic caps, or bold roman caps. The strong variant of bold roman caps should be used only when there are several lines of text between each sub-section, and the line with the bold caps should be preceded in every instance by 2 points of white. Note the disadvantage of not doing so, over 'Rumbelows' here:

Customers wanting to buy other items will be advised by branch managers whether they will make a saving by waiting until after April 1 when VAT is officially introduced.

BOOTS the Chemists slashed prices on 300 products from to-day. Staff stayed until late last night to work out the price cuts and estimate a £2,000,000 saving for customers.

They will continue to cut prices daily so that by VAT-day a total of 20,000 lines will be reduced.

RUMBELOWS, one of the largest electrical retailers in the country with 300 branches, have also introduced immediate VAT savings on goods that are subject to the 25 per cent high rate of purchase tax.

For example an automatic washing machine with a pre-budget price of £124·95 today costs £114·85.

But prices of items subject to low-rate purchase tax at 11½ per cent which will go up in April remain the same price until the end of the month.

WOOLWORTH'S, Britain's largest sweets retailer, welcomed the VAT relief on confectionery, ice-cream, crisps and soft drinks.

Italics

Italics have not been abused as much as bold. The best use of an italic paragraph is to distinguish genuinely different sections of text, as in a question-and-answer interview, or a specialist's series of brief comments on sections of a statement; or a preface to a news story; or simply to emphasise individual words. It is better for these purposes than the more obtrusive bold. Like bold, italic pars should be differentiated in the text by linear white. Extended setting in italic should be avoided, because italic is harder to read, and italic and bold should not be mixed in the same setting because most newspaper setting machines are not equipped for that combination.

It is mere megalomania to elaborate the italic variant by setting it in reverse indent or underscoring it:

Living-pods may be tomorrow's houses. Architect Sir Hugh Casson is planning one for a household exhibition this spring, and American-based architects David Greene and Michael Webb have already published their predictions about living-pods.

Corbusier's definition of the house has, I am afraid, been made démodé. Greene, making his apologies to the master, says in an issue of Architectural Design, "The house is an appliance for carrying with you. . . ." Illustrations of the living-pod—an idea which constantly recurs in architectural daydreams — shows inflatable sleep mats, automatic body-cleaning equipment and temperate zone climate machinery. They look, and sound, like working models of the womb. Not inappropriately or, for that matter, perhaps, not so futuristically after all. Messrs Webb and Greene say you don't need to know what next year's materials will do for you to dream up next year's architectural modes, but it is impossible to imagine any designs for this new year, or for the year 2000, without an increasing use of plastics.

Blobs and Stars

Instead of picking out the opening word, a paragraph or sequence of pars can be distinguished by a type ornament. The back of any printing catalogue will show the range—everything from the ace of spades to Father Christmas. Here are some of the simpler geometrical decorations:

The C B I warned t h a t the code would—

● Deter investment by many major firms;

● Force some industries into financial losses because they could n o t increase prices to match rising costs;

● Undermine Britain's competitive position in export markets.

The Government's view is that to show any favour to the C B I at this stage

OPERA has gone full frontal. Blonde Carol Neblett, in the lead role of a New York production, sings faultlessly as she takes a

■ FROM a 7½-year-old boy comes this recipe for what he calls "health lollies." Make up straw-

★ HARRY CORBETT and Sooty have made few appearances on B B C since they were dropped in 1968

Any decorations, even as simple as this, should be used only with the utmost restraint in newspaper text columns, and that means in features as well as in news. They should be spent like gold sovereigns. Once a decoration has been decided on for several paragraphs it should be retained: don't mix the cocktails. The simpler the decoration, the better: an outline or black circle or quad (square) is better than a star or diamond. All the column breakers look better, too, when they are separated from each other by text.

Rules and Borders

The use of rules and borders in breaking text is limited. Sub-headings can be enclosed within rules (which should approximate in thickness to the thickness of the letter strokes), or alternatively, text can be broken by rules without sub-heads. When this device is chosen, it is essential to do it whole-heartedly with a thick rule, not less than 4pt. These are effective:

ness. They should now broadcast these points for public digestion.—*C. W. Judd, 98 Park Road, W.4.*

CHEER, cheer, cheer for Milton Shulman! Whenever I read letters protesting about programmes not being fit for family entertainment viewing at peak times I want to throw up. Who do these morons think they are who want not only these but programmes at ALL times to fit

A subscription costs £1 a year for four issues. 18 Victoria Park Square, London E2.

INITIALS are gaining ground. They don't have to be CD, or YSL, or V; they can even be your own. But they must be big and flashy, none of that hiding discreetly

Printers' catalogues offer a heady variety of rules and borders. First, a selection of rules, then of borders for panels:

¹₄ point center face	¹⁄ point x ¹⁄ point—2 point space
1 point center face	
2 point center face	2 point x 2 point—2 point space
3 point center face	2 point x 1 point—2 point space
6 point center face	4 point x ¹⁄ point—1 point space

♦♦♦♦♦♦♦♦♦♦♦♦♦♦♦♦♦♦♦♦♦♦♦♦♦♦♦ ♦
A2219—6 x 6 points

ooooooooooooooooooooooooooo o
A2229—6 x 6 points

□□□□□□□□□□□□□□□□□□□□□□□□□□□□□ □
A2232—6 x 6 points

|||||||||||||||||||||||||||||||||||||||||||||||||||||| ||
A2234—6 x 6 points

▶▶▶▶▶▶▶▶▶▶▶▶▶▶▶▶▶▶▶▶▶▶▶▶▶▶ ▶
A2949—6 x 6 points

Folio rules are generally run at the top of a page to underscore or to accommodate the paper's title, date and page number, though this information can be given without a rule.

Some newspapers run the title, date and page number sideways down the gutter, to provide a clean top. That has attractions, but not at the expense of setting the page number sideways (as in *Women's Wear Daily*, New York). This number is something the reader must be enabled to pick out instantly. *Newsday*, more effectively, sets the title and date at the foot of each page.

The folio rule, where provided, can run the length of the title, etc., or across the full page. The full page cut-off is the tradition in English quality newspapers; popular papers and American papers prefer the open top. White space is certainly better than a hairline cut-off across the top of the page. If a cut-off is used it must be decisive—a 2pt, or even a 4pt—or a thick-and-thin double rule. It then provides colour and a foil for the white space around the headings. At least 18 points of white should intervene between the folio rule and the headlines.

Bold simplicity is the best criterion, too, for borders, for sideless boxes and for panels. In fact, the plainer rules illustrated above are better for newspaper news-page panels than the more exotic borders shown. The single 3pt rule or the double-fine border provides a satisfactory panel for other than the very jazzy newspapers. The column value of the text should be studied and the weight of rule selected exactly to balance the text or to contrast clearly with it. It is essential in all panels, of course, to see that the corners are snugly mitred: the awkwardness of achieving this is a good reason for preferring sideless boxes, with decorative rules top and bottom of indented text.

Illustrations

Illustrations already accompanying a story can, of course, be placed at strategic positions in a long run of text, but in addition special column-breakers can be devised for some stories. A story on a take-over battle for a large manufacturing organisation, for instance, could be broken with shallow single-column pictures, without captions, of their brand names. Or drawings can be commissioned. These drawings broke the text in a long article on gardening:

plantings are positively rustic. However, the working-class garden (see below) retains traces of the Victorian manner.

big business, and the membership of most specialist societies is rising, with the Alpine Garden Society particularly active.

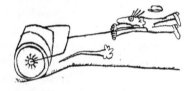

The stockbroker's suburban garden, though large and the best kept of all modern gardens, is not so much a garden as a display space for garden

The tool - shed is well-equipped. According to the Contimart Gardening Survey, 18 per cent. of houses with

George Gambol, forced to mow on the hottest Saturday afternoon, secretly loathes his garden

At its best, the small suburban garden is exquisitely tidy. Edges are well-trimmed

6 Information Settings

The classified ads (and stock market quotations) are the bedrock of the press. Should an alternative source of easy access to such diverse daily information be found, the press will fold. —MARSHALL MCLUHAN

To a large number of its readers a newspaper is less a mirror of the world than a mosaic of clues to one small mystery or another. For one man the clues are in the price-earnings ratio of Ford Motors compared to Shell Oil and Woolworth; for another they are in the weight of Lester Piggott's horse in the 3.30 race; for another they are in the home run score of Robinson, chasing Carew up the individual batting league. Newspapers tend to take for granted such staples as stock prices, race meetings and sports results. The types and the setting styles are rarely given a second thought; in many a local newspaper there is no setting style at all for that plague and benefice, the local produce show. It is left to the deskman's inspiration of the moment to decide how to indicate second prizewinners in the long results in the flower arrangement competition, sub-section for newly weds, in the category for junior farmers of the 54th country fair. He scatters bold, italic, doric, italic caps, stars and blobs to distinguish categories, winners and places, and wastes space. He sows confusion. He ends up using the same signal for the baby show and the best pig contest, and finds that there is no space for two categories won with distinction by the publisher's wife.

Style and types must be laid down for every staple of information setting. This is not a matter of a moment. Each category is a different problem, requiring different styles, different measures, different type. The style must be laid down in the minutest detail to maximise economy of space and ease of reference. No choice at all must be left to the deskman, for it will eat up the time he needs to check figures and mark copy clearly; and it will inevitably introduce a jarring inconsistency.

In specifying styles for information setting, there is more to consider than the best typeface (*see* pp. 73–77). The typecasters offer choices in styles of numerals, fractions and leaders (the dots or dashes which lead the eye across a tabulated column). The basic choice in numerals is between old style and modern. Old style numerals have both ascenders and descenders and line up optically with lower-case letters and small capitals. Modern numerals are lining capitals, aligning with capitals only. For any setting requiring a lot of numerals, modern numerals are better, and reasonably wide modern numerals are best. There are also vertical figure matrices for narrow settings.

It is always worth spending time with the catalogues and with trial settings. Some basic suggestions for style setters follow as comments on newspaper examples.

THE Law Society announces that the following candidates were successful in Part 2 'of the Qualifying Examination held from Feb. 10-13. There were 2,911 entries and 1,790 were successful.

An asterisk shows that a distinction was obtained. The numbers indicate the sections passed:

The key is: 1, Conveyancing; 2, Accounts; 3, Revenue Law; 4, Equity and Succession: 5, Commercial Law; 6, Company Law and Partnership; 7, Family Law; 8, Local Government Law; 9, Magisterial Law.

Candidates were required to sit only one of the three sections 7, 8 and 9.

SECOND CLASS HONOURS
(in alphabetical order)

Cadwallader, Cherry E., LL.B., 1, 2, 3, 4*, 5*, 6*, 7; Child, A. A., 1, 2, 3, 4, 5*, 6*, 8; Coles, A. R., 1*, 2, 3, 4*, 5, 6*, 7; Colville, C. A., 1, 2, 3, 4*, 5, 6, 7; Craig, R. D., 1, 2, 3, 4* 5* 6, 7; Davies, J. W., 1*, 2, 3, 4* 5, 6*, 8*; Edwards, M. D., 1, 2, 3* 4, 5, 6*, 7; Foster, R. G. S., 1, 2, 3, 4, 5* 6* 7; Gillibrand, R. M. N., 1, 2, 3, 4, 5*, 6*, 7; Haggie T. J., 1, 2, 3, 4, 5, 6*, 7; Hayes, J. W., 1*, 2, 3, 4, 5, 6, 7; Haywood, D. G., 1, 2, 3*, 4, 5*, 6*, 7*; Holman, R. C., 1, 2, 3*, 4, 5, 6, 7; Krupnik, A. M., 1, 2, 3*, 4, 5, 6, 7*; McCarry, A. J., 1, 2, 3*, 4*, 5*, 6, 7*; Miles, P. J., 1, 2, 3*, 4*, 5*, 6, 7*; Miller, D. J., 1, 2, 3, 4*, 5, 6, 7; Morton, K. J., 1*, 2, 3, 4, 5, 6, 8; Nightingale, Janet T., 1, 2, 3, 4, 5, 6, 7; Parkinson, A. J., 1*, 2, 3, 4, 5*, 6, 7; Parsloe, J., 1, 2, 3, 4, 5*, 6, 8*; Ridley G. M., 1, 2, 3, 4, 5*, 6*, 7; Rodwell, G., 1*, 2, 3, 4, 5, 6*, 7; Smith, R. W., 1, 2, 3, 4*, 5*, 6, 7; Walters, C. J., 1*, 2, 3, 4*, 5*, 6, 7; Whysall, W. F., 1*, 2, 3, 4*, 5, 6, 7*.

Passed (Wholly or in Part)
(in alphabetical order)

Abenson, E. S., 1, 2, 6, 7; Ackroyd, P. W., 1, 2, 4, 5, 6, 7; Adam, R. D. I., 3, 4; Adams, D. W., 1*, 3, 4, 5, 6, 7; Addington-Smith, N., 5, 6, 7; Agar, Jane C., 2; Aldridge, Alison L., 2; Alexander, A. L., 2, 3, 5; Alexander, B. J., 1, 2, 3, 4, 5, 6, 7; Allcock, R. C., 1, 2, 3, 4, 5, 6, 7; Allen, A. P. C., 1*, 2, 3, 4, 5, 6*, 7; Allen J. R., 1, 2, 5;

I

The Law Society announces the following candidates were successful in Part Two of the qualifying examination held on February 10, 11, 12 and 13, 1969.

An asterisk shows distinction was obtained, and the numbers are those of the sections passed. The key is: —1, conveyancing; 2, accounts; 3, revenue law; 4, equity and succession; 5, commercial law; 6, company law and partnership; 7, family law; 8, local government law; 9, magisterial law.

FIRST CLASS HONOURS.—None.
SECOND CLASS HONOURS.—Cherry E. Cadwallader, LL.B, London, 1234*5*6*7; A. A. Child, LL.B. London, 12345*6*8; A. R. Coles, 1*234*56*7; C. A. (The Hon.) Colville, B.A., Oxon, 1234*567; R. D. Craig, LL.B. London, 1234*5*67; J. W. Davies, B.A., LL.B. Cantab., 1*23*1*56*8*; M. D. Edwards, LL.B. Newcastle, 123*456*7*; R. G. S. Foster, LL.B. Southampton, 1*345*6*7; R. M. N. Gillibrand, B.A. Cantab., 12345*6*7; T. J. Haggie, B.A. Cantab., 12345*6*7; J. W. Hayes, LL.B. Manchester, 1*234567; D. G. Haywood, LL.B. Manchester, 123*4*5*6*7*; R. C. Holman B.A Cantab., 123*4567; A. M. Krupnik, B.A. Cantab., 123*4567.

A. J. McCarry, LL.B. London, 123*45*67*; P. J. Miles, LL.B. London, 123*4*5*67*; D. J. Miller, LL.B. London, 123*4*567; K. J. Morton, LL.B. Exeter, 1*234568; Janet T. Nightingale, B.Sc. London, 1*2345*67; J. Parkinson, LL.B. Southampton, 1*23456*7; J. Parsloe, M.A. Oxon., 1*234*567; B. A. Price, B.A. Oxon., 1234*567; G. M. Ridley, B.A. Cantab., 123*45*6*7; G. Rodwell, 1*23456*7; R. W Smith, B.A. Oxon., 12345*67; C. J. Walters, 1*234*5*67; W. F. Whysall, B.A. Cantab., 1*234*567*.

PASSED (WHOLLY OR IN PART).—E. S. Abenson, 167; P. W. Ackroyd, 124567; R. D. I. Adam, 34; D. W. Adams, 1*34567; N. Addington-Smith, 567; Jane C. Agar, 2; Alison L. Aldridge, 2; A. L. Alexander, 235; B. J. Alexander, 1234567; R. C. Allcock, 1234567; A. P. C. Allen, 1*23456*7; J. R. Allen, 125;

2

Simple sparseness is the essence of good information setting. Punctuation should be limited to what is vital. There is no need here for full points in such abbreviations as m.p.h. or p.m.—mph and pm will do. Spacing should not be traditional. It should be controlled so that white is collected where it aids ease of reference. Fussy punctuation and spacing takes time, and space, and when carried to pedantic extremes can actually make the small settings harder to read. There is a vivid illustration of this in the way the London *Daily Telegraph* (**1, opposite**) and the London *Times* (**2**) reported the Law Society examination results. Each successful name is accompanied by a figure to indicate which of the special papers the candidate has passed, and an asterisk, for a distinction. The *Telegraph* had the benefit of the excellent Linotype Maximus, but it set the results with word spacing between each numeral and also, for some reason, between a candidate's initials. In type this produced rivers of white running through the page and the information on each candidate, straggling from line to line, was harder to absorb at a glance. The cumulative effect of this misplaced penchant for white space was that the results which took 3½ columns in the *Times* took 4½ in the *Telegraph*.

At 11.30 am — B. F.
Guyatt v R. F. Guyatt; N. A.
Searcey v D. Searcey; E. G.
Kerr v A. M. Kerr; C. J.
Dein v N. J. Dein. McDonald
co-resp; T. N. Pratt v W. G.
Pratt; L. A. Wills v J. N.
Wills; S. A. Wood v J. F.
Wood.
2 pm — L. F. Davis v F. H.
Davis; R. A. Boughton v J.
Boughton; J. L. Hartmann v
L. Hartmann; R. L. Harrison
v D. P. Harrison. Cooper co-
resp; K. W. Holz v L. Holz;
A. J. Livingstone v H. E.
Livingstone. Gregory co-resp;
I. L. Henshaw v R. L.
Henshaw, Midgley co-resp; T.
J. Kopec v F. Kopec; M. I. I.
Edwards v A. A. Edwards; J.
M. Berrill v D. L. Berrill.
Mr Justice Nagle. No 18
Court, 10 am—L. M. George v
C. A. George (part heard);
V. M. Tanner v M. Tanner,
McMahon co-resp (part
heard); W. Bernstein v E.
Bernstein; M. C. M. Younger
v C. R. Younger; L. J. Reilly
v B. P Reilly; F. Barker v
V. D. Barker; V. Graves v **3**

Similarly in (**3**) **above**. This is a list of court cases in *The Australian*. The unnecessary full point plus space after each person's initial wastes space dreadfully to no good effect.

HARBOUR COURT (B.
McClune) 8.7 1; COMING
ALONG (R. Quinton) 8.5 2;
GEMSONG (M. Gnech) 8.1 3.
1¼ len, 2½ len. 54 2-5. Off
12.40.
First trained by T.
Ramsey, second by M. F.
Anderson, third by S. Behn.
TAB Nos: 5, 10, 12.
Course Tote and A.C.T.
TAB: Win 90c; place 60c, 50c,
$5.10.
NSW TAB (for 25c): Win **4**

These race results from *The Australian* (**4**) are a mess because of the succession of run-on caps settings, and also because the information has not been organised properly. Here each race result carries a second paragraph saying 'Winner trained by so and so, second by so and so and third by so and so'. A repeating pattern of words like this is almost always a symptom of waste. The results in *The Australian* would be easier to read—and would take less space—if the first three horses each began a new line, full out, with the training information on the same line there where it belongs:

Harbour Court (B McClune, trainer T Ramsey) 8:7
Coming Along (R Quinton, trainer M Anderson) 8:5

In the 9-pica measure and type of *The Australian* that style of setting would take six lines instead of a total of nine or three lines across 18 picas. If the horse's name were in bold lower-case the brackets could be dropped for simplicity, with succeeding names in roman.

MIDGET (10-11)
50 Dash — James Harris, NWS, 6.5; 100
Dash — James Harris, NWS, 12.1; 220
Dash — John Reilly, RP, 28.9; 440 Run —
Robert Carter, RP 1:08.4; 660 Run —
George Coakley, RP, 1:51.6; 440 Relay —
Richmond Perrine, 66.0; Long jump —
James Harris, NWS, 14-8; High Jump —
John McCarthy, NWS, 3-10; Shot Put (6
lb.) — Jack Zigelsky, Unattached, 28-2¾. **5**

Results run-on are less easy to follow than separate-line results, but of course run-on results can save a lot of space when each result is much less than a line long or just a bit more than a line long. The decision to run-on should not be automatic. There are occasions when the nature of the information is such that run-ons save little or no space. A typical example (**5**) is the *Miami Herald's* setting of junior athletics results where the information in each case is so nearly a line-long that each result could have begun more clearly a separate line. Note and avoid the un-economic dashes here with space either side. This is another instance of punctuation getting in the way of information.

The measure must fit the message. No city would dream of running-on the names in a telephone directory, or of having the lines too short to accommodate the names and numbers. There are sections of news-paper setting which call for single-line comparisons for the reader's convenience. Race cards and stock market prices are the most important. Horses and shares must have a line to themselves so that the reader can find what he wants and at a glance compare line for line, prices and pedigrees. The information in each line will be comparable so the lines will come out about the same length. Allowing these items to turn from one line to another is bad because it does not facilitate the reader's need for quick, accurate comparisons, and it wastes space. This happens with

---

1.15 TWO-YEAR-OLD HANDICAP
1st div, 5f

1—117	Golden Coaster	7	9 0
2—291	The Catcher 1 (inc 4lb pen)	8	6
3—	Boy Armagh 8 ..	8	0
4—	Dal Winsor 16 ..	8	0.
5—301	Dimiri 2	8	0
6—	French Tone 4	8	0.
7—	Great Response 14	8	0
8—	Master Magic 5	8	0
9—	Nimbool 11	8	0
10—	Romany Rise 13	8	0
11—	Scholar 9	8	0
12—	High Spirits 6	7	12
13— 9	Lumaraz 15	7	12
14— 00	Night Craze 10	7	12
15— 7	Royal Blend 3	7	12
16— C	Spearset 12	7	12

Emergencies

17— 00	Bengali Sar	7	10
18—003	Iconium	7	10

The Catcher 1, Dimiri 2, Golden Coaster 3.

6

PRIX RADIS ROSE

(20.000 F, 2.000 m)

1. Cupid Man 310 (J. Taillard) à M. J. Puerari .... **G. 7,2C**
   P. 3,0C
2. Roscof 307 (Y. Saint-Martin) .... P. 2,2C
3. Fato 305 (R. Couteleau) .... P. 8,00
4. Golden Girl 316.
   N'a pas couru : Mayab 301.

Jumelé : 14,70.
1 l. 1/2, 1 l. 1/2, ene.
Durée : 2′ 22″.

7

SECOND—One mile. Pace. Conditioned. Purse $1,000.

PP	Horse	Priver	PO
2	Franciscan	(Hansen)	9-5
3	Sea Tac Chief	(Conroy)	5-2
4	Commander Lad	(Olds)	7-2
5	Dante Hanover	(Bailey)	6-1
1	Diamond Princess	(Perkins)	6-1
6	Texas Freight	(Thompson)	12-1

FRANCISCAN—First, second last two.
SEA TAC CHIEF—Rough customer here.
COMMANDER LAD—Didn't repeat early victory.

8

4.15—HOLLYBUSH NOVICES' CHASE. 2 miles. Winner £340. (5 runners.)

1	1211-F1 ERRING BURN G. Richards 7-12-1 (D, F)	R. Barry 31●
4	004404 COLDSTREAM Kilmany 7-11-8 (O/T)	S. Hayhurst 28
5	240U20- DULCIANA Jordon 7-11-6 (O/T)	NON-RUNNER
7	0412F0 MOUNT KELLY C. Bell 7-11-8	M. Barnes —
11	300000 GOOD REASON Gillem 5-11-0 (SF)	M. Dickinson —
12	03B3U LAUDER HA' Oliver 5-11-0	C. Tinkler 30

FORECAST : ERRING BURN, LAUDER HA'.
Betting Forecast.—11-10 Erring Burn, 7-2 Good Reason, 5 Lauder Ha', 8 Coldstream,

9

---

the race cards (6) and (7) which are from *The Australian*, at 9 picas, and *Le Figaro* at 10·5 picas. Compare the neatly tabulated race card in (8) from the *Sacramento Bee* and, better still, the runners in (9) from the London *Daily Mirror*, set to the measure required. Bastard setting, provided it is regular, can be fitted into smooth production routines.

Three different standards of league tables are shown **below**. The type used in (**10**) is a narrow face which enables the paper, the London *Observer*, to give twelve columns of statistics for each team. But the narrow numerals in 4¾ Claritas are not clear. In the second example, (**11**), the *Sunday Express* has set the tables in the marvellously clear 6pt Helvetica (Linotype)—but the wider numerals in Helvetica take so much space that the *Express* has had to dispense with two of the columns of numerals (the differentiation between goals scored at home and away). To give the information in the clarity needed requires the bastard setting of (**12**) where the *News of the World* sets tables in Adsans at 14 picas.

10

		HOME					AWAY				
	P.	W.	D.	L.	F.A. Gls	W.	D.	L.	F.A. Gls	P.
Leeds	17	7	1	0	17 5	4	4	1	11 6	27
Tottnhm	17	6	1	1	16 4	4	4	1	13 6	25
Arsenal	17	7	2	0	24 3	3	3	2	10 12	25
Chelsea	17	3	4	1	13 12	4	3	2	10 8	21
Wolves	17	5	1	2	17 14	4	2	3	17 19	21
Man C	16	4	4	0	15 5	3	2	3	6 9	20
C Palace	17	5	2	2	12 7	2	4	2	7 7	20
Liverpl	16	5	3	0	14 2	1	4	3	3 5	19
So'ton	17	5	2	1	12 3	1	3	5	9 13	17
Stoke	17	5	4	0	17 3	0	3	5	7 20	17
Everton	17	4	3	1	13 7	2	2	5	10 19	17
Coventry	17	4	1	3	9 7	2	3	4	6 10	16
Man Utd	17	3	4	2	10 7	2	2	4	9 16	16
Newcastle	17	2	5	1	7 6	3	1	5	10 15	16
WBA	17	5	3	1	17 9	0	2	6	11 25	15
Ipswich	17	5	2	2	16 8	0	2	6	1 10	14
Huddsfld	17	3	4	2	9 6	1	2	5	7 17	14
West Hm	17	2	5	2	14 14	0	4	4	8 14	13
Derby	17	3	2	4	11 11	1	3	4	8 14	13
Nottm F	17	3	2	3	13 9	0	4	5	1 13	12
Blackpl	17	1	3	4	9 14	1	1	7	6 19	8
Burnley	17	1	2	6	8 16	0	2	6	2 16	6

11

		Home			Away			Goals		
	P	W	D	L	W	D	L	F	A	Pts
Leeds	16	6	1	0	4	4	1	25	10	25
Arsenal	16	7	1	0	3	3	2	33	14	24
Tottenhm	16	6	1	1	3	4	1	27	10	23
Chelsea	16	3	4	0	4	3	2	23	18	21
Wolves	16	5	1	2	4	1	3	31	30	20
Man City	15	4	3	0	3	2	3	20	13	19
C. Palace	16	5	2	2	2	3	2	18	13	19
Liverpool	15	5	2	0	1	4	3	17	7	18
Sthamptn	16	5	2	1	1	3	4	21	15	17
Stoke	16	5	3	0	0	3	5	23	22	16
Everton	16	4	3	1	2	1	5	22	25	16
Coventry	16	4	1	3	2	2	4	15	17	15
Newcstle	16	2	4	1	3	1	5	17	21	15
Man Utd	16	3	4	2	1	2	4	17	22	14
Ipswich	16	5	2	2	0	1	6	17	18	13
Wst Brom	16	4	3	1	0	2	6	27	34	13
West Hm	16	2	4	2	0	4	4	19	25	12
Derby	16	3	2	4	1	2	4	18	24	12
Nottm F	16	3	2	2	0	4	5	13	20	12
Huddsfld	16	3	4	2	0	2	5	13	21	12
Blckpool	16	1	3	4	1	1	6	14	30	8
Burnley	16	1	2	5	0	2	6	8	29	6

12

		HOME			Goals		AWAY			Goals		
	P	W	D	L	F	A	W	D	L	F	A	Pts
Leeds	15	6	1	0	14	4	4	3	1	10	5	..24
Arsenal	15	7	1	0	23	2	2	3	2	9	12	..22
Tottenhm	15	5	1	1	12	4	3	4	1	11	6	..21
Man City	14	4	3	0	14	4	3	2	2	5	7	...19
Chelsea	15	3	4	0	13	10	3	3	2	9	8	..19
C Palace	15	5	1	2	11	6	2	3	2	6	6	..18
Wolves	15	4	1	2	15	13	4	1	3	14	16	..18
Liverpool	14	5	2	0	14	2	1	3	3	3	5	...17
Sthampton	15	4	2	1	10	3	1	3	4	9	12	...15
Stoke	15	5	3	0	16	2	0	2	5	5	18	...15
Newcstle	15	2	4	1	7	6	3	1	4	10	13	...15
Everton	15	3	3	1	12	7	2	1	5	9	18	...14
Coventry	15	3	1	3	7	6	2	2	4	6	10	...13
WBA	15	4	3	1	16	9	0	2	5	10	23	...13
Man Utd	15	3	3	2	8	5	1	2	4	7	15	...13
W Ham	15	2	4	2	11	11	0	4	3	7	12	...12
Nottm F	15	3	2	2	12	7	0	4	4	1	12	...12
Hudrsfld	15	3	4	1	9	5	0	2	5	4	15	...12
Ipswich	15	4	2	2	14	7	0	1	6	1	10	...11
Derby	15	3	1	4	11	11	1	2	4	7	13	...11
Blackpool	15	1	3	3	9	13	1	1	6	5	16	... 8
Burnley	15	1	2	5	6	13	0	2	5	2	12	... 6

7 The Mechanics of Text Editing

It is the belief now, as it was in the days of Moxon, the first English writer on the technics of printing, that it is the duty of the printer to supplement the negligences of the writer. —THEODORE LOW DE VINNE

This is good copy—cleanly typed, in double spacing with plenty of margins, on one side of a folio. For text typesetting, composing rooms normally prefer to work from a small slip of paper about 8 in. wide and 6 in. deep, which fits neatly on the setting position on the machine. Copy taken down by telephone often comes on bigger quarto sheets—to save the typist changing paper—and it depends on local conditions whether deskmen are required to cut this into two pieces before editing.

P1/2   14CB lc

Evans News Agency   July 1 17.21 PB

A new lion figurehead will be unveiled today on the
Sail Training Association's 300-ton schooner, the
Sir Winston Churchill — replacing her original red-
and-gold lion figurehead, torn from her bows in a
North Sea gale last November.

                              end

The copy on the folio here is self-contained. No sentence or paragraph is split between folios or ever should be: that sloppy habit wastes time in the composing room and increases the chances of error. If the typesetters are busy the overseer gives out copy a folio at a time to different operators and 'split' copy means that he must spend time pasting the two sections together. The 'end' typed on the copy is another must: otherwise nobody has any way of knowing whether there is more copy to come. The top left 'Evans News Agency' is the agency supplying the copy and the rest means it was phoned on July 1 at 17.21 hours and taken down by copytaker PB. The mark 'P1/2 14CB lc' is an instruction to the deskman that this story is for page 1, second edition, headed in 14pt Century Bold lower-case.

Evnas NewsA&ency   Julyl 17221 PB

a new loin firugehead wlbe unveeiiled todya on the Sail

trainign asssociations 3801ton schooner the Sr Winston

Churchhill-replacing her øxxxxigkximxoriginal red and

gold lion figurøissonsoehead torn frm her bow s ina North

Sea glae las Novmebr.end

All too often copy is presented to the desk like this. Time is wasted and tempers are tested by a variety of sloppy reporting room practices; if only the culprits appreciated how it sours the copydesk approach to their masterpice. The efficient way to present copy is admirably set out in these rules compiled for the staff of *The Times* of London by a working party:

1. Put your name and the date at the top of the first sheet.

2. Leave at least a third of the first sheet blank before starting your story. This is to allow room for instructions to the sub-editor and the printer to be clearly marked.

3. Leave at least $1\frac{1}{2}$-inch margin on the left-hand side and 1 inch on the right-hand side of all pages of copy. Leave at least 2 inches clear space at top and bottom of each page.

4. Each page should start and end with a paragraph. In particular avoid turning a few words to the top of the next sheet. Never type off the edge or bottom of a page.

5. Spacing should be equal to three times the height of the type-face on your machine. Single spacing is absolutely barred. Spacing between paragraphs should be twice that between lines. An average length for a paragraph is 35 words. Sentences generally should not exceed 20 words (25 for an opening sentence).

6. If you make a mistake in typing or spelling, type the word again. In no circumstances type or write a letter or figure on top of another. Always read through your copy before handing it in; if you find an error, correct it above the line.

7. If you have to write in a word or phrase please write it legibly, preferably in ink. A lot of time is wasted by sub-editors and compositors in trying to decipher a cramped, often faint, scrawl.

8. Make sure that your typewriter is properly maintained. Clogged letters are often ambiguous, particularly hollow ones such as c, e and o. If these letters punch holes in the paper get them adjusted. Copy that resembles a pianola-roll is not only difficult to read but may lead to a pen or pencil catching in a hole and tearing the page. Replace your ribbon as soon as it gets faint.

9. Leave underscoring, paragraph indents and all other typographical markings to the sub-editor. Wrong underscoring and paragraph marks are messy to obliterate.

10. Make sure that all pages of copy are properly catchlined, numbered and in the right order. Put 'MF' at the bottom of each page before the last, which should be marked 'End'.

11. Avoid abbreviations; they often save no time and little space and can be ambiguous.

12. After 'today', 'yesterday' and 'tomorrow' put the name of the day in brackets. After 'not' put 'repeat NOT' in brackets.

13. In manuscript copy write all proper names in legible block capitals every time they appear.

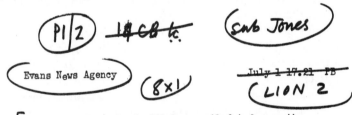

[A new lion figurehead will be unveiled today on the

Sail Training Association's 300-ton schooner, the

Sir Winston Churchill, replacing her original red-

and-gold lion figurehead, torn from her bows in a

North Sea gale last November.

Here is our original folio of phoned copy marked for setting. Some marks have been circled, some crossed out. Neither will be set, but the distinction is this: what nobody needs to see any more is crossed out, but essential service messages are circled. The 'P1/2' is not obscured because the printer needs it to assess the urgency of the copy. The news agency is circled because the accounts department needs to read it to make payment. But '14CB lc' can be crossed out because that headline will be written off on a separate folio. The new markings are:

$$8 \times 1 \qquad \text{Sub Jones} \qquad \text{LION 2}$$

whose meanings are as follows:

8 × 1: Set the copy in 8pt of the newspaper's text fount across one column. There is no need to specify the name of the face or to say it is in roman (though such marks would, of course, be needed in magazines or where there is no established type or measure). The rule in newspaper setting is to specify the unusual and otherwise to keep the copy clean. The fewer the marks, the easier setting.

Sub Jones: The name of the text editor (sub in Britain, copyreader in America) editing the copy. Some offices do not bother, but this can save time when there is a printer's or proof-reader's query, and it cuts down on the whodunit work when there is an editorial inquest.

LION 2: This is the vital catchline or slug, devised from the opening phrase. The operator setting the text sets the catchline Lion 2 and then the text metal can be identified and married with the headline which is set separately from a folio marked LION 1. We discuss the catchline further with the headline.

The other marks on the edited copy are symbols for paragraphing and capitalisation, which we need to study in detail (pp. 141–143).

All this is simple enough, but there is a special caution for even the clearest telephoned copy: beware of mishearings, especially in descriptive writing or review notices where more unfamiliar language is used. Keep asking 'Does it make sense? Does it flow, is this the way this writer would put it?' No text editor should ever pass anything which raises a doubt. He should be able to answer for every word in the copy.

Headline and Catchline

Every headline is written on a separate folio. This is because only a few very small headlines, if any at all, can be set by the machine which sets text. If there are two decks, use two folios numbered 1 and 1½. The headline must be written clearly—in caps if necessary—and the letters which need capitalisation should be double ticked. If the headline is to be set the normal style of the newspaper (whether centred or set left) there is no need to mark the copy with these instructions: but always mark style-breaking headlines both with the words and the symbol. The mark on the folio **above right** is the British mark for set-left heads.

(PI/2)　　　　　　(LION 1)

(14 CBcrk x 1 set left)

] Pride of Lion
  =

The edition page mark goes in the top left corner and the catchline in
the top right. Some offices do not number headline catchlines, but
numbering clearly identifies the sequence and number of decks, which
can be helpful in multi-deck stories.

LION I is the headline catchline here: and it is good practice to make a
note of your daily catchlines. The text editor invents the catchline, and
there are four guidelines: relevance, particularity, brevity, fluency.
By fluency I mean easy to say. It is simpler for the stone editor to ask the
overseer for a story catchlined BUG than for one catchlined BACILLUS.
Brevity means one word, or one intelligible part of a word, for speed in
writing and setting, but two short words are occasionally justified if
necessary to meet the twin criteria of relevance and particularity. Hair-
raising things can happen if the catchlines do not indissolubly marry
copy and type. Catchlines such as COURT, CRASH, DEATH, STRIKE are
relevant enough on such stories—but they are not particular. There
may be several stories running from the courts, say, with the risk of
getting folios and headlines muddled. The catchline must be specific
enough to give some clue what the court story is about, which means
seizing on a relevant particular. A word in the intro is usually best (KISS,
MEAL, BEDROOM, etc.), or a name in the story if it is not common: the
names of people in public life are to be avoided because they can pop up
in several contexts in any day. Wit should be confined; the man assemb-
ling the story may be slow to see the joke, and blue catchlines have been
known to slip through into the page without the management collapsing
helpless with laughter. Newspaper terms such as Kill, Hold, Dead, Must,
Bold, which might be misread as instructions, should never be used as
catchlines.

NEWS—1

Pride of lion

1 — D. SMITH — 1

A new lion figurehead will be unveiled today on the Sail Training Association's 300-ton schooner, the Sir Winston Churchill—replacing her original red-and-gold lion figurehead, torn from her bows in a North Sea gale last November.

Smoked-out future

— HOWE —30— —0—

Cigarette smoking may lead to male infertility, a Melbourne doctor has claimed, Dr Michael Briggs, of the Alfred Hospital, ʼing in the Medic⸱ ⸱⸱alia ⸱ʼ

The proof

This is the proof of the same story which comes back to the deskman. The text and headline have been assembled correctly on a galley— a metal tray slightly longer than a column. The slug, NEWS 1, identifies the galley. On big newspapers each proof will carry a bold slug identifying the galley by such descriptions as NEWS 5, FEATURES 7, BUSINESS 8, WOMEN 4. The other setting above the text (Smith) identifies the operator.

At this stage the news executive simply reads through the proof, if he has time, to see that headline and text are correctly married and handwriting has not been misread. Small typographical errors (called 'typos' or 'literals') he leaves to the proof-reading department.

The only occasion for the deskman's correcting a typo is when it is an error in a name: it is worth double insurance to get names right: then he should be quite sure that resetting does not compound some other error. Some offices prefer such proofs to go to the readers' department to avoid the risk of double setting. Otherwise the deskman makes corrections in the proof margin using the correct signs (*see* pp. 141 *et seq.*) and sends the proof to the composing room. It is emphatically not right to phone the production executive on the stone with corrections. He should be warned of big changes near edition time or when serious errors require a page to be held, but the production man on the stone is not a corrector of proofs (*see* pp. 166 *et seq.*).

After the proof, there is the published edition. The deskman should again read through everything he has edited. Something may have gone wrong between proof and publishing. It is the deskman's responsibility to ensure accuracy and intelligibility from copy to print.

Copy-editing Marks

We now turn to a detailed examination of the correct symbols for extensive copy editing. Newspaper practice varies from the more scrupulous methods of book production (which usually are offered as instruction), and also between newspapers. What follows shows most of the marks a deskman customarily uses:

This mark indicates that the first line is to be set full out, and the underlinings indicate that the first two words are to be in CAPS. (These letters, however, are not to be set in caps, and so are lightly struck through with an oblique stroke.)

To begin a new par, with an indent, the first mark is reversed. Make insertions, as well as corrections, above and between words with a caret mark ( ). Close up words with "hooks" above and below; separate incorrectly joined words with a firm stroke; combine the two to take out an extra letter. Clean up overtypings even when they look obvious. On very dirty copy (which you should try to avoid) illegible dubious words should be written out and ringed in the margin. dubious

[Sometimes letters need to be transposed, and so
words do. If complicated are they, number them, or
~~write out again them~~ *write them out again.*

[Should you delete in error (and the words are
still legible), put dots under ~~the reinstated words~~ (stet)
and write "stet" above or alongside them. When you
cross out several lines of copy also draw a line
to carry the typesetter's eye from the end of one
section of clear text to the start of the next.
~~cross out several lines of copy also draw a line
to carry the typesetter's eye from the end of one
section of clear text to start of next.~~ You use
the same device to run on paragraphs.

Some are too short as written to stand
by themselves.

Equally you can start a new paragraph,
with the proper mark, in the middle of a line.
Write in NP (new par) for emphasis. [Underline
words to be set in *bold* or *italic*, but also write in
which you want: house styles vary. To ~~change~~ *change* either

to roman circle the word and write Rom above or
alongside. If you underline in error take it out
this way. Circles are useful. Round an abbrev they
mean set in full, and round figs, eg 10, they mean
spell out (ie, ten). But if there is any room for
doubt, as with initials (eg CPO for Chief Petty
Officer) spell it out yourself. 100 is bad for
beginning a sentence, but in mid-sentence there is no
need to write Two Hundred, Acacia Avenue; in this case
the circle will tell the setter to use figures. A
circle round a comma changes it to a period. Don't
forget to mark copy "mf", more follows; or "mtc",
more to come - indicating a likely pause in the flow
of copy; or "mfl", more follows later, meaning that
the pause will be a long one, so the copy so far
may as well be pulled and corrected; or "end", with
or without the gatemark # , which means the same.

Abbreviations in Copy

Three wks aftr completg a 12-mth-ban f drvg

w too much alcohol in his blood, a 50-yr-old

cclr ctted t same offence, a mags' crt ws

told yesty.

This is an example of copy with abbreviations, which are used in large or small measure by copytakers, reporters and deskmen and accepted, in small or large measure, by news and typesetting departments. It is hoped that from this copy the composing room will produce:

> Three weeks after completing a 12-month-ban for driving with too much alcohol in his blood, a 50-year-old councillor committed the same offence, a magistrates' court was told yesterday.

The commonest abbreviations are contractions of suffixes: -g for -ing (jokg); -mt for -ment (punishmt); -n for -ion (junctn); -ce for -ance (acceptce). But not all these deserve to be encouraged. Indeed, abbreviations make casting-off so much more difficult that many offices will prefer to do without them. The purpose of the abbreviations is speed. Any abbreviation which causes a doubt in the typesetters' or proofreaders' minds or anything which risks an error of spelling or meaning, should not be countenanced. For instance, the contraction -ce for -ance inevitably produces mis-spellings because of the possibility of ending with -ence.

It is not good enough to pass maintence for maintenance and be annoyed when a busy operator sets it maintenence; and it is easy to slip into using -ce wrongly (i.e. dependce instead of dependence). The same applies to the familiar thr for their or there. It is easily mis-spelled. The contraction -n for -ion is all right provided the words are familiar (collisn passes but not transfusn. It may cause, confusn). The best contraction is undoubtedly -g for -ing: stealg, housg, swimg, eatg, jokg, smokg, laughg, denyg, overtakg, passg, waitg, standg, boatg, votg. But even here beware of the further contraction which is sometimes seen: bldg—building or bleeding; dvg—driving or diving.

Some offices, like *The Times* above, ban abbreviations altogether, which is perhaps prudent, but since the habit widely persists, here is a list of abbreviations that seem commonly understood:

abbrevn	abbreviation	f	for
abt	about	fm	from
acct	account	Fri	Friday
ad, adv, or advt	advertisement		
aftn	afternoon	gd	good
agn	again	gnl	general
agst	against	govt	government
amg	among	gt	great
amt	amount		
		hd	had
bec	because	hvg	having
bn	been		
btwn	between	impt	important
brd	board	indvl	individual
		lge	large
cclr	councillor	ltr	letter
cd	could		
chm	chairman	mkt	market
confce	conference	mng	morning
crt	court	Mon	Monday
cttee	committee	mtg	meeting
decd	deceased	necy	necessary
def	defendant	nr	near
dffce	difference	nt	not
dffct	difficult	nthg	nothing
dgr	danger		
		o	of
esp	especially	objn	objection
evg	evening	offcl	official

oppy	opportunity	t	the
othr	other	thks	thanks
		tho	though
pdce	produce	thru	through
plse	please	Thurs	Thursday
pol	police	tt	that
psble	possible	Tues	Tuesday
rfce	reference		
rlwy	railway	w	with
		wd	would
Sat	Saturday	Wed	Wednesday
sbjt	subject	wh	which
schl	school	whr	where
sd	said	wr	were
sgst	suggest	ws	was
shd	should		
Sun	Sunday	yesty	yesterday
svl	several	yr	year

Copy Editing in Practice

Opposite is typical telephoned copy which requires substantive editing. The copy is typed, with copytakers' abbreviations, on two quarto sheets. This is the first sheet and you note that in mid-sentence it runs over on to the next folio. In all it is a full account of the Minister's speech during a critical railway strike, with direct quotes, but it is loosely written and the intro is wrong. The intro starts with a subsidiary clause, which is always a debilitating influence, and this is a monster piece of debilitation of 38 words. The news should be in the first clause, and it should be the main clause. Here the most pungent expression, 'Cutting their own throats', is not even in the first paragraph-sentence.

The black pencil lines in the margin indicate what the news executive thinks is the news point. When receiving copy to edit always read through it first and note marks like this in the margin (which may be on the third or fourth folio). They are not meant to inhibit the judgment of the text editor but they are good general guidance on how the executive sees the story.

Aberystwyth Agency   Phoned July 1   JT

At t end o a rousg speech on Labr Govt policies wh she

sd wr designed to remould t economic life o t country

irrespective o t many difficys involved and t grumbles o

those who disliked change, t Minister o Transport, Mrs

Barbara Castle, speakg at Aberystwyth yesty (Sat) expressed

hr disappointment tt t Stratford rail strike hd nt bn

settled.

She appealed to t 5,000 rlwymen concerned in t Stratford

strike to realise tt by their stand they wr in dgr o

wreckg t new deal for t rlways and in fact o "cutting

their own throats.

Sir Stanley Raymond had made a supreme effort in t

discussions to meet t objections put up by t unions. He ws

so confident o t potential at Stratford he ws willg if t

strike ws called off to issue immediate orders to double t

rlwy-operated space and thereby create further jobs f

rlwymen.   She sd this ws not a case of men losg jobs.

"Stratford means more jobs". T minister sd Stratford ws

a first class example of new ways o going after new   mf

SET & HOLD FOR RELEASE

Aberystwyth Agency   Phoned July 1   JT

~~at t end o a rousg speech on Labr Govt policies wh she~~
~~sd wr designed to remould t economic life o t country~~
~~irrespective o t many difficys involved and t grumbles o~~
~~those who disliked change,~~ t Minister o Transport, Mrs
Barbara Castle, ~~speakg~~ at Aberystwyth yesty (Sat) ~~expressed~~
hr disappointment tt t Stratford ~~rail~~ strike hd nt bn
settled.

She appealed to t 5,000 rlwymen ~~concerned in t~~ Stratford
strike to realise tt ~~by their stand~~ they wr in dgr o
wreckg t new deal for t rlways and ~~in fact o~~ "cutting
their own throats.

~~Sir Stanley Raymond had made a supreme effort in t~~
~~discussions to meet t objections put up by t unions.~~ He ws
so confident o ~~t~~ potential at Stratford ~~he ws willg~~ if t
strike ws called off to issue immediate orders to double t
rlwy-operated space and thereby create further jobs f
rlwymen. ~~She sd~~ this ws not a case of men losg jobs.
"Stratford means more jobs". T minister sd Stratford ws
a first class example of new ways o going after new   mf

Foul copy

It has been reasonably well edited for meaning, but text marking has been done in the slovenly way which sends head printers prematurely to convalescent homes. Even if the operator can set accurately from this kind of copy, he will inevitably set it slowly. In detail this is what is wrong with the copy marking here:

Bad handwriting: It is the biggest single delayer of setting. Cultivate a big, bold open style of handwriting.

The executive marked the story 'Set and Hold for Release', presumably since the report was written from a handout and the Minister had still actually to deliver the speech. Important house instructions like this should be set and appear at the top of the galley, or the story stands a good chance of appearing prematurely in print. To make sure these words are set, the instruction must be plain: SET CATCH–HOLD FOR RELEASE. And it must *not* be ringed. If it is ringed it is not set.

Lines at the top of the page have been left carelessly unringed. Does the text editor want them set? Probably not, the typesetter assumes, but he should not have to pause.

Line 5: No clear idea where copy begins.

Line 5: No paragraph mark and no instruction to set full out either.

Line 6: It isn't enough to link *at Aberystwyth yesty* to the second paragraph *appealed* by link line. The remaining lines of the first paragraph should also be crossed out.

Line 9: Is the stet cancelled and *by their stand* out? If so there should be a link line from *that* to *they.*

Line 11: Where do the quotes end?

Line 11: New material and corrections should never be written sideways.

Line 18: To transpose the phrase *Stratford means more jobs* is difficult on this copy. But it should at least have the correct ringed instructions in the margin, TRS, and not the unringed 'Move up please' given here. No editorial person could complain if the copy here were set: She said Move up please.

Line 19: The copy has been allowed to spill over to the next folio in mid-sentence.

And are we still in 10pt × 2? There has been no type marking and no change of folio for a smaller type-size.

Some general rules emerge. Here is another list drawn up by *The Times* working party:

1. Copy should have as few marks on it as possible. They should all be clear, legible and unambiguous. Never write on top of copy; always make your emendations above the line or in the margin. It is unnecessary to circle punctuation marks or standard contractions except in special circumstances; a page with rings all over it is distracting to the eye and difficult to read.

2. If letters have been transposed write the correct version above the line; an S-shaped squiggle round the offending letter means that the compositor has to waste time working out what the word ought to be.

3. Be careful with run-on lines on either side of an excision or deletion; they are often carelessly done and go through 'good' copy, making it look as though it had been struck out.

4. Never obliterate original copy; a single, light line is quite sufficient and enables the revise and chief sub-editors to make sure that your emendation is correct. This is in the sub-editor's own interest.

5. Be careful with letters that may be confused; write clearly, especially in headlines. 'Change' and 'charge', 'more' and 'move', 'casual' and 'causal' are common examples of words that are often mis-set because of bad writing; other letters are 'e' and 'l'; 'b' and 'h'; 'm', 'n', 'r' and 'v'; 't' and 'l'.

6. If a passage has been heavily subbed it is usually better to rewrite it; this saves time in the long run. Always stick the original copy on the back of the rewritten version; it is your safeguard.

Opposite is the same copy correctly handled by a combination of editing on copy, paste-up and writing off, the three basic techniques of copy editing which need matching to copy requirements to produce the quickest and clearest result. The basic mistake with the previous effort was the attempt to edit on copy, without using scissors and paste. It was essential to cut the raw copy into more viable editing units, and paste these on separate folios of copy paper. This has now been done, and for two reasons:

1. Two sizes of type should never be marked on the same folio because in most offices different sizes have to be set on different machines. The 10pt has therefore been separated from the rest.

2. All that survives from the first paragraph is 'Mrs Barbara Castle, Minister of Transport, speaking at Aberystwyth,' and this information is quickly written out.

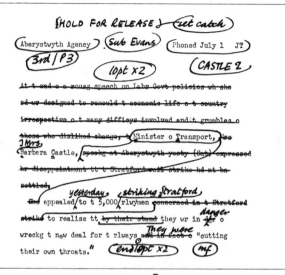

{HOLD FOR RELEASE} *cut catch*

(Aberystwyth Agency) (*Sub Evans*) (Phoned July 1 JT)

(*3rd / P3*) (*10pt ×2*) (*CASTLE 2*)

~~At t end o a mousg speech on Labr Govt policies wh she~~
~~sd wr designed to remould t economic life o t country~~
~~irrespective o t many difficys involved and t grumbles o~~
~~those who disliked change, t~~ (Minister o Transport, ~~Mrs~~
] Mrs
~~Barbara~~ Castle, ~~speakg at Aberystwyth yesty (Sat) expressed~~
~~hr disappointment tt t Stratford rwll strike hd nt bn~~
~~settled.~~
~~She~~ appealed *yesterday,* /to t 5,000/ rlwymen ~~concerned in t Stratford~~ *striking Stratford,*
~~strike~~ to realise tt ~~by their stand~~ they wr in ~~fr~~ o *danger*
wreckg t new deal for t rlways ~~and in fact o~~ *They were* "cutting
their own throats." (*end 10pt ×2*) (*mf*)

(*8pt ×1*) (*CASTLE 3*)

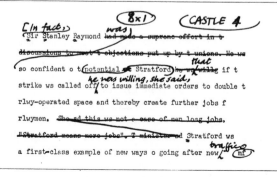

[Speaking at Aberystwyth, she
said that the strike was a
"bitter disappointment". This was
not a case of men losing
jobs. "Stratford means more jobs."

(*mf*)

[*In fact,* (*8pt ×1*) (*CASTLE 4*)
was)
~~Sir~~ Stanley Raymond ~~had made a supreme effort in t~~
~~discussions to meet t objections put up by t unions. He ws~~ *that*
so confident o t (potential ~~of~~ Stratford) ~~he wd willg~~ if t
he was willing, she said,
strike ws called off /to issue immediate orders to double t
rlwy-operated space and thereby create further jobs f
rlwymen. ~~She sd this ws not a case of men losg jobs.~~
~~"Stratford means more jobs". T minister sd~~ Stratford ws
a first-class example of new ways o going after new / *traffic* (*mf*)

The second paragraph of raw copy, which now, as edited, forms the intro, has been pasted on a separate folio (because of the 10pt instruction). The difficult transposition 'This was not a case of men losing jobs' has been dealt with by the third method of copy editing—writing off. The point has been handwritten on a separate folio (together with the location of Mrs Castle's speech), and deleted from the third folio. Finally, the spill-over to another folio has been avoided by transposing the missing words from the following folio. The 'mf' at the end of the folio is a clear indication that more follows.

Cable Copy

Opposite is a section of cable message from Hongkong. It looks something like copy from one of the news agencies (*see* below), being printed in capitals. It is a great pity that so many teleprinters are standardised on capitals, but there is some belated move to the more legible style of all-lower-case. This kind of cable copy has not been through any agency's headquarters. It therefore needs more thorough editing and it also needs checking with especial care for names and for any accidental distortion of meaning in transmission. Not all the symbols at the top of cable copy are of daily concern but the relevant ones should be understood.

The top four lines are the cable company's routing instructions and codes. If anything has to be queried with the cable company the message will be identified by reference to the middle two lines.

The first editorial line—HONGKONG 276 29 2123 PAGE 1/50—translates:

HONGKONG:	Station of origin.
276:	Total number of words in the message.
29:	Date of the month.
2123:	The first two figures give the hour according to the 24-hour clock, and the last figure the nearest minute. This message was dispatched at 9.23 pm.
PAGE 1/50:	To one folio of teletype copy there will be 50 words.

The line THOMSONEWS LONDON PS4 is the telegraphic address of *The Sunday Times*. The first line of copy opens with a repeat of the time-group and refers to a message numbered 271 from *The Sunday Times* Foreign Manager (McCormick). If this typescript was for McCormick's personal attention it would be slugged PRO MC-CORMICK.

OSEAGRAM 27 LN

PTX170 CPS GHD266 CD13394

GBPS CP HXHK 276

HONGKONG 276/274 29 2123 PAGE1/50

PRESS THOMSONEWS LONDON PS4

29213 MCCORMICKS 271 Q WANG EN HYPHEN MAO COMMA THE NON HYPHEN
MAOIST MILITARY AND PARTY BOSS OF CHINAS WILD NORTHWESTERN
PROVINCE OF SINKIANG COMMA HAS AGREED TO KEEP HIS HANDS OFF
CHINAS KEY NUCLEAR INSTALLATIONS COMMA IN AUTHORITATIVE
JUDGMENT HERE PARA IT IS BELIEVED THAT AN UNOFFICIAL
COL PS4 29213 27191

P2

QUOTE TRUCE UNQUOTE HAS BEEN ARRANGED BETWEEN WANG AND HIS
EIGHT DIVISIONS AND MOSLEM SUPPORTERS COMMA ON THE ONE HAND
COMMA AND CHAIRMAN MAO AND MARSHAL LIN PIAO
AND THEIR QUOTE CULTURAL UNQUOTE REVOLUTIONARIES COMMA
ON THE OTHER PARA NEITHER MAO NOR LIN PIAO HAS BEEN ABLE
TO SUBDUE WANG

P3

COMMA AYE FORMER HUNANESE PEASANT WITH LONG PARTY EXPERIENCE
WHO WAS PERSONALLY SELECTED IN NINETEEN FIFTYFIVE BY MAO
HIMSELF FOR THE SINKIANG POST PARA LANCHOW COMMA ON THE YELLOW
RIVER AND THE OLD SILK ROAD TO SAMARKAND COMMA HAS BEEN
THE HEART OF CHINAS
NUCLEAR EFFORT COMMA BUT BRACKET AS

P4

REPORTED IN THE SUNDAY TIMES JULY TWENTYFOURTH NINETEEN SIXTYSIX
UNBRACKET AYE NEW NUCLEAR BASE WAS ESTABLISHED ON LAKE TSINGHAI

The cable copy is shown edited, without substantive changes. Cable copy spills out from the teleprinter in long rolls of copy. The first thing to do is cut the paper into manageable folios, taking care to number through correctly and not to spill sentences between folios. If there is a great deal of substantive editing it is always quicker in the end to have everything retyped. The service messages have been cut off and the author's name transposed to the top. For the rest the editing operation here consists of mechanical editing—translating the punctuation symbols, punctiliously employing the ticks which indicate the few places where capitalisation is to be retained and checking for accuracy and office style. There is rather more to that than there sounds, because foreign copy is full of nasty traps. It would have been an elementary error, but it has been done, to headline the gentleman in the cable as Mao, but of course he is not the world-famous Mao. In fact he is not a Mao at all because in Chinese names the family name comes first—Wang here. Chiang Kai-shek is Chiang not Kai-shek in headlines or second references; and note the punctuation, which is initial caps for the first and second names and a hyphenated lower-case for the third name.

Other Far East countries (such as Korea) also usually put the surname first, but many Burmese and Indonesians have only one name: U as in U Thant or U Nu is a courtesy title meaning Uncle, and Thakin means master. These should be used in the first reference but in the second reference it is Mr Nu or Premier Nu, Secretary-General Thant, or Mr Thant. There is a great deal to be said for that title Mr. Some newspapers go to elaborate lengths to call Germans Herr and Spaniards Señor and Portuguese Senhor, and others, genuflecting to the days when French was the language of diplomacy, call all foreigners M for Monsieur, hence M Kosygin. Executives should follow the office style book, but it is more logical and simple in English-language newspapers to call all foreigners Mr, Mrs or Miss, etc. Much more important than the sham gentility of referring to Mlle Bardot is to get all foreign names correctly spelled and punctuated. For people consult *Who's Who* (and foreign equivalents), *International Who's Who, Statesman's Year Book,* and *World Biography*. For places *The Times Atlas* has an excellent gazetteer. If in difficulty check with the international news agency supplying the paper. You might also want to re-read Chapter 8 in Book One of this series as it deals with accuracy and house style.

The main difference between this cable copy and agency copy is that punctuation marks are spelled out here and the author's name comes as a signature at the end of the message.

[BY RICHARD HUGHES]

~~£9213 MCCORMICKS 271~~ WANG En-mao, ~~EN HYMEN MAO COMMA~~ THE NON-
MAOIST MILITARY AND PARTY BOSS OF CHINA'S WILD NORTHWESTERN
PROVINCE OF SINKIANG, ~~COMMA~~ HAS AGREED TO KEEP HIS HANDS OFF
CHINA'S KEY NUCLEAR INSTALLATIONS, ~~COMMA~~ IN AUTHORITATIVE
JUDGMENT HERE. NP IT IS BELIEVED THAT AN UNOFFICIAL

~~COL PS4 £9213 27191~~

~~P2~~

~~QUOTE~~ "TRUCE" ~~UNQUOTE~~ HAS BEEN ARRANGED BETWEEN WANG AND HIS
EIGHT DIVISIONS AND MOSLEM SUPPORTERS, ~~COMMA~~ ON THE ONE HAND,
~~COMMA~~ AND CHAIRMAN MAO AND MARSHAL LIN PIAO
AND THEIR ~~QUOTE~~ "CULTURAL" ~~UNQUOTE~~ REVOLUTIONARIES, ~~COMMA~~
ON THE OTHER. NP NEITHER MAO NOR LIN PIAO HAS BEEN ABLE
TO SUBDUE WANG,

~~P3~~

~~COMMA~~ a FORMER HUNANESE PEASANT WITH LONG PARTY EXPERIENCE
WHO WAS PERSONALLY SELECTED IN (NINETEEN FIFTYFIVE) BY MAO
HIMSELF FOR THE SINKIANG POST. NP LANCHOW, ~~COMMA~~ ON THE YELLOW
RIVER AND THE OLD SILK ROAD TO SAMARKAND, ~~COMMA~~ HAS BEEN
THE HEART OF CHINA'S
NUCLEAR EFFORT, ~~COMMA~~ BUT ~~BRACKET~~ AS

~~P4~~

REPORTED IN THE SUNDAY TIMES on JULY 24, 1966) ~~TWENTYFOURTH NINETEEN SIXTYSIX~~
~~UNBRACKET~~ a NEW NUCLEAR BASE WAS ESTABLISHED ON LAKE TSINGHAI

Agency Copy

ANTI-CHINESE DEMONSTRATION

RANGOON, BURMA, JULY 1 (AP)-ABOUT 800 UNIVERSITY STUDENTS LAST
NIGHT STAGD AN ANTI-CHINESE DEMONSTRATION IN MANDALAY AND
POLICE USED TEAR GAS AND FIRE HOSES TO DISPERSE THM.

A REPORT FROM MANDALAY SAID POLICE DETAINED 112 STUDENTS WHO
ORGANISED THE DEMONSTRATION. AUTHORITIES IMMEDIATLY BANNED
ALL DEMONSTRATIONS, ASSEMBLIES, SPECHES AND OTHER PROVOCATIVE
ACTIVITIES.-AP

RLH0501BSTJUL1

PAC EV.   22-TIP.

THE COLLIERY TIP, LOOMING ABOVE THE VILLAGE, SPLIT
ALMOST IN HALF WITH CONTINUOUS WATER POURING DOWN FROM THE
MOUNTAIN. IT SLID DOWN TO THE SCHOOL, WHICH WAS COMPLETELY
BURIED, AND ON TO THE HOUSES.

GUSHES OF WATER LIKE A RIVER RUN THROUGH THE STREETS
OF THE MOUNTAINSIDE VILLAGE AND INTO THE HOUSES.

GLAMORGAN POLICE KEPT THE 20 MILE ROAD TO CARDIFF AND
THE EIGHT MILE ROAD TO MERTHYR CLEAR FOR AMBULANCES.

THE NATIONAL COAL BOARD SENT THEIR RESCUE TEAMS TO THE
SCENE, TOGETHER WITH EXCAVATORS TO REMOVE THE DEBRIS.
MF 1258 AJ 21/10/66

Now let us look at ordinary agency copy. It is always flagged by its source: Reuter, AP (Associated Press) and UPI (United Press International) are the three main international agencies. The top left corner may carry an identity number for reference. A time and date appear at the foot of each folio: the AP folio here, for instance, ends

RLH0501BSTJUL1

This means the operator's initials are RLH and he sent the message at 0501 British Summer Time on July 1. The copy these agencies supply by teleprinter to newspapers, still sometimes called wire copy, has fewer symbols than cable copy because it has already been edited; prefixes they carry are mainly indications of the urgency of the message (*see* pp. 180–181). When starting in an office always ask the teleprinter department to explain the current symbols of agency copy. Executives on British newspapers have a great deal to do with the Press Association which supplies domestic news and should be thoroughly familiar with its system of priorities and routing copy.

Provincial newspapers—morning, evening and Sunday—are supplied over a network of telegraph lines known as the Provincial Teleprinter system or 'Creed'. These are the PA copy markings:

PA: To London only, not to Provincials

PACEV: Identical report to London and Provincial evenings

PACMO: Identical report to London and Provincial mornings

PAC: Identical report to London and Provincial evenings and mornings.

PACEV (Creed only): To Provincial evenings only, not to London.

PACMO (Creed only): To Provincial mornings only, not to London.

PAC (Creed only): To Provincial evenings and Provincial mornings —not to London.

On all agency copy, domestic and foreign, there will occasionally be a)8, 3 9! !8&743' which means there will occasionally be a

LINE OF FIGURES

On each bar of a teleprinter there are a capital letter together with a punctuation mark or figure: the machine shifts for points or figures instead of for capitals as a typewriter does. Sometimes a machine jams and the message continues in code. If it is only for a line it should be decoded as follows:

−	?	:	$	3	!	&	£	8	'	(	)	.	,	9
A	B	C	D	E	F	G	H	I	J	K	L	M	N	O

0	1	4	'	5	7	;	2	/	6	"
P	Q	R	S	T	U	V	W	X	Y	Z

This is a line of garbled copy decoded:

043'8$3,5   ,−''34   2−4,3$ 5£3   8'4−3)8'
PRESIDENT   NASSER   WARNED   THE   ISRAELIS

Of course any extended section of garbled copy should be referred back to the agency.

Casting Off

The deskman has to be able to estimate the space that copy will fill when it is set up in type. He has to do this by estimating or counting the number of characters—letters, figures, or spaces—in the copy. This is called 'casting off'. By being able to cast off accurately from copy a deskman can say: (*a*) how many column-inches of a newspaper a given amount of copy will fill; or (*b*) how much copy is needed to fill a certain amount of space in the paper. He can therefore know how much a piece of copy needs to be cut, or how much needs to be added to it, to fit the space allocated.

Under-estimating the length produces wasted setting, with hurried cuts in production. Over-estimating produces empty holes in the page plan. Under-estimating is the commoner fault, especially when a deskman is new to editing for narrow-column tabloid pages.

Experience with a proper system of casting off will enable a deskman to cast off merely by running his eye down the typescript, but arithmetic is the foundation of the art. And the arithmetic's basic unit must be the character, not the word or the line. When the character count is known it is simple enough to cast off the copy for any type or measure. So we begin by determining how to count characters.

Counting characters

Life would be simpler if newspaper offices had typewriters and tele-printers whose characters were the same size; if there were no abbreviations in copy; and if a standard-size copy-paper were used marked with a marginal word-count. Most teleprinter and typewriter copy uses 12pt or pica characters; some have the smaller 10pt (Elite). Let us concentrate on the 12pt machines. They produce 10 characters to a span of one-inch typing. In the normal width of typed and teleprinted copy of six inches to a line there are therefore 60 characters. So we can count the lines of the copy and multiply to produce the total number of characters. A small complication is that copy is interspersed with many shorter and a few longer lines. For *rough* casting off these can all be counted as full and a rough deduction made at the end.

For more accurate casting off, first decide what shall be regarded as the basic full line (say, 5 in. or 6 in. wide). Lightly rule a line down the copy at this point. Some characters will fall to the right, in excess of a full line; some will fall to the left as short. All these odd characters can be added to the total produced by the full lines. Counting the odd characters can be made easier by marking a piece of card with a scale of both sizes of typewriting characters. Place this card along the base of the short or long lines of the typescript and the number of characters in each odd line is given at once.

Translation into type

How much space given copy will occupy depends on (1) the design of newspaper typeface; (2) its size and (3) the measure. Linotype,[1] Intertype,[2] and Monotype[3] publish character-count or copy-fitting tables. I include in the appendices a conversion table supplied by Linotype. Here, for instance, is the character count for 8pt Royal at different measures compared with Times Roman:

(picas)	9	10	11	12	13	14	15	16	17	18	19
8pt Royal	24	27	30	33	36	39	42	45	48	51	54
8pt Times	27	30	34	37	41	44	47	51	54	57	61

Character-counts can also be deduced from alphabet lengths which are always given in the manufacturers' specimen books and pamphlets. Any type with an alphabet length specified as 100 points gives 36 characters in an 11-pica column. If alphabet lengths or character-count tables are not readily available (as they are not, for instance, for some Indian language papers) the characters in 20 lines should be counted and the total divided by 20 for an average per line.

Let us take the character-count table and cast off typescript into type and type area into typescript.

How much type will the copy make?

Take a folio of copy in pica typewriter or teleprinter, with ten lines about six inches long (ie, about the norm for this kind of copy).

(i) Pica typing or teleprinter produces 10 characters including spaces to an inch.

$$6 \times 10 = 60 \text{ characters}$$

(ii) Count the lines of the typed copy. Count short lines as full lines because short lines will also occur in typesetting.

$$10 \text{ lines of copy} \times 60 \text{ characters} = 600 \text{ characters}$$

(iii) Consult the character-count chart for the typeface, size and measure: 8pt Times Roman at 11 picas. It says 34 type characters of Times can be set in 11 picas. Therefore divide the 600 to derive the number of lines of type:

$$34 \text{ into } 600 = 17 \text{ lines plus } 22 \text{ characters over,}$$
$$\text{say } 18 \text{ lines of type}$$

(iv) 18 lines of 8pt = 144 points = 2 in.

TABLOID SETTING: How many lines will 600 characters produce when set in Ionic across 9 picas?

(i) The character-count table says 20 Ionic characters fit 8pt at 9 picas.

20 into 600 = 30 lines of type

(ii) 30 lines of 8pt = 240 points = $3\frac{1}{4}$ in.

Note, however, that the narrower the measure the harder it is to be accurate in casting off, because narrow measures entail distorting word- and letter-spacing. On a tabloid, therefore, err on the generous side.

How much copy will the space hold?

(i) Assume there is a 10 in. space, 11 picas wide.

(ii) In 8pt, nine lines of type occupy one inch ($8 \times 9 = 72$ points). Therefore 10 in. will contain 90 lines.

(iii) Consult the unit-count chart. In 8pt Royal the type character count for 11 picas is 30.

(iv) In 10 in. of 8pt Royal, therefore, there is space for 90 lines × 30 characters to yield a total character count of 2,700.

(v) Divide by six to put this into words—it being generally agreed that the average word has five letters, with one added for the space following each word.

2,700 divided by 6 = 450

(vi) The 10 in. space will hold 450 words of copy.

What typeface and size will fit?

There is a third use for the character-count table. It can help us to determine which typeface at which size will most precisely fit a pre-determined measure. For instance, if the same copy had to be squeezed into 2 in. of a 9-pica column, without cutting the story, what face and size would do that?

(i) In 8pt we can have no more than 18 lines.

(ii) 18 lines for 600 characters = 33 characters to a line.

(iii) Consult the character-count table for a typeface which yields 33 characters at 9 picas. In 8pt there is only one on our table: Vogue Bold Condensed, with a character count of 35. So the tabloid story would go easily into 2 in. in 8pt Vogue Condensed.

But this typeface may be undesirable or simply not available. Then the type size has to go down to 7pt.

(i) In 7pt we can have 21 lines in the 2-in. space.

(ii) 21 lines for 600 characters = 28 characters to a line (and 12 over), so say 29 characters a line.

(iii) Consult the chart. In 7pt, Times Roman has 29 characters per 9-pica line. So the tabloid story would go into 2 in. in 7pt Times Roman.

Word count

When working with one main text face, simplify casting off by relating wordage directly to column-inches. Most of the trouble with casting off by word-counting comes because somebody once said 'A thousand words to a column', and the guide has been followed despite changes in standard type size, typeface and measure. As a matter of fact, in 8pt, Times Roman is one of the few faces which will enable 1,000 words to be set in a 20 in. column of 11 picas. This is what you should do to draw up a word-inch table for any face:

(i) In 8pt of any typeface, one inch of type set solid contains nine lines.

(ii) How many words will nine lines of type contain? Consult the unit character count for the appropriate typeface and measure.

(iii) At 11 picas 8pt Royal gives 30 type characters to a line, which is five words to a line.

(iv) Nine lines at five words to each line = 45 words to 9 lines = 45 words to one inch.

This means 450 words will occupy 10 in. of an 11-pica column in 8pt Royal. And, of course, the system works both ways. A 20-in. column in 8pt Royal at 11 picas holds 900 words.

Estimate wordage by remembering the character-count. If the typing or agency copy is in 12pt and is 6 in. wide, it gives 60 characters to a line so there are 6 words to a line of typing. Or if the typing is 10pt Elite and 6 in. wide, each line gives 72 characters so there are 12 words to a line of typing.

Here is a typical word-inch table drawn up for a newspaper using Royal at different sizes and measures (eg, 43 words per inch in 8pt at $11\frac{1}{2}$ pica ems, 53 at 13 ems, and so on):

ems	8pt	9pt	words	inches
$11\frac{1}{2}$	43	35	200	$4\frac{3}{4}$
13	53	40	350	8
$15\frac{1}{2}$	62	53	500	$11\frac{3}{4}$
$17\frac{1}{2}$	65	55	750	$17\frac{1}{2}$

Handwritten copy

We can deal with handwritten copy as follows:

(i) Establish the average number of words per line by counting the words in 12 to 20 lines.

(ii) Multiply the average number of words by the number of lines on each page. This gives the average number of words per page.

(iii) If calculating on the character-count system, translate the words into characters by multiplying by six (five characters to a word plus one for each word space).

Irregular shapes

When type is to be set to follow the lines of an irregular shape, the deskman will have to supply the printer with a proof of the irregular shape. In newspapers the lengths of these irregular settings are so short and rare that there is no need to go into details of the casting-off variations required. The key to it is finding the equivalent *regular* type area and then compensating. For instance, to set type in a circle—(ugh!)—a square is drawn round the circle. The width of the square is taken as the calculating measure, but only three-fourths of the depth of the square is measured. These and the more sophisticated adjustments required for special work are well set out in two publications—by Caspar Mitchell[4] and Charles Fyffe[5]. Fyffe is especially good on irregular shapes.

Measured setting

Multi-column copy is sometimes marked to be set for a specified depth. For instance:

12pt Bold 4 in. across two col into single col *or*

10pt Roman 2 in. across three col into 2 in. of 9pt across two col into single col *or*

14pt Helvetica $3\frac{1}{2}$ in. across 17 picas into 2 in. Royal across 14 ems into single col

The deskman has the responsibility for ensuring that there is sufficient copy for the required depths and sizes, and for clear marking, and should always aim to supply all the measured copy together. The measured setting instructions should be written out in full at the top of the first folio. On subsequent folios, the marking should be:

Measure setting. See Folio 1 then into 8pt × 1

This should be continued for as long as the copy editor estimates the measured setting will run. When the measured setting is brief, say requiring only two folios, mark the copy normally from folio 3.

8 Work on the Stone

Journalists do not understand type. Consult the craftsman who knows.
—LORD NORTHCLIFFE

As deadline time approaches in the printing department, comps crowd round the page forme like surgeons round an operating table. One pair of hands is slipping in late headline type. Another is cutting column rule. Another is jamming in last and extra last corrections. In a moment one of the comps will call out 'Four lines over on de Gaulle' and the editorial man watching all this will quickly mark a four-line cut on proof. The make-up comp—nobody calls him a compositor—is as nimble fingered as a surgeon. Indeed in photo-composition he slices the bromide film strips with a scalpel; he is expected, in emergency, to cut out a line or even a letter and strip in an indistinguishable correction. In letterpress he has not merely deftly to identify and excise metal lines, but to do it by reading words upside down (though still from left to right). The editorial man works facing the comp, so everything for him is the right way up but has to be read from right to left.

In photo-composition production both comp and editorial man see the page as it will be on publication. This is a major facility, but the responsibilities are the same for the editorial production executive in letterpress and photo-composition. The task is to see that the original editorial ideas are successfully translated into finished pages, accurately and to a strict time-schedule. The following detailing of the skills required to do this will be based, for convenience, on a letterpress operation, but the editorial executive in a photo-composition office will appreciate their relevance and a few special techniques for photo-composition production will be outlined at the end.

Scope of the Job

The editorial executive in charge at the production stage is called a stone sub in Britain and a production or works editor in North America. The 'stone' part of the title comes from the days when the galleys of type and their headlines were assembled into a page on a long flat surface topped with marble.

The marble has been replaced with a thick plate of cast-iron, but the 'stone' survives. Its width just accommodates the depth of the newspaper page, and it is usually long enough for a series of pages to be assembled at one time. When a page is complete, the forme is slid on to a metal trolley of the same height and taken to the stereotyping department. Sometimes, for speed, a page is assembled on one of these trolleys.

The comp and the stone editor stand facing each other over the stone. The editorial man should never attempt to work from the comps' side. Comps like to have their side of the stone to themselves. Between comp and stone editor is the chase, the metal frame in which the type is deployed according to the editorial page plan. (When complete it is known as a forme.) In an ideal world everything would fit into place in the exact space allotted to it, and in magazine work where production is from paste-ups of proofs the comp can indeed manage by himself and editorial has time to check his work from page proofs. By its nature newspaper work means change with speed, and a variety of tasks devolve on the stone editor. He must:

1. Check that the comp is following the editorial plan.
2. Cut stories that fall too long.
3. Fill any 'holes' that appear.
4. Adjust the page design for any emergency such as a new story or a story which develops unexpected length and must be allowed to run.
5. Check the reasons for delays in the arrival of type or blocks and take corrective action.
6. Check galley proofs and page proofs for literal and setting accuracy.

All these tasks have to be carried out for each page, and at any one time a stone editor may be looking after half-a-dozen pages all going to press within fifteen minutes of each other. He has to concentrate his energies. He has to be decisive. Some newspapers, conscious of the vital role of the stone editor, seek to improve production by allocating more editorial men to the stone. There is a very early limit to the value of this. A separate stone editor is an advantage for specialised pages, such as sport and business, and an extra editorial eye helps in checking page proofs, but two stone editors on, say, six news pages easily get in each other's way, both physically and in the risk of duplicating work; better that they should have three pages each.

In any event one man should be clearly in charge, and every effort made to keep the stone clear of other editorial men not precisely charged with production responsibilities. Comps do not like crowded stones, for the very good reason that the extra bodies simply get in the way. The newspaper aiming at efficient production on the stone should do two things. First, it must provide the stone editor with a messenger whose task is to supply him with the right proofs for the right pages, and to carry corrections and copy to the printer's desk. Second, it must lay down that the stone editor has a limited function and is not the editorial sweeper-up of minor mistakes and alterations. Too few offices define the role of the stone editor with precision, and the ambiguities reap inaccuracies (and injustices to individuals). Obviously if the stone editor spots a mistake he should do something about it. Preferably, if he has time, he should report it to the copydesk so that there is no danger of a correction sent direct from the editorial floor crossing with one given out on the stone.

It is particularly important to warn editorial where an obvious error is going to be corrected in text whose setting plan has misfired—where, for example, the error is in double-column setting which is having to be reset in part to single-column because it is over-long. The role of sweeper-up, though, should be resisted. Copy editors must be forbidden from phoning alterations and corrections to a stone editor for him to carry out. Near edition time it is prudent to warn a stone editor that there is an alteration, but the alteration should never be made at second hand. Chief subs themselves and layout men should also restrict their calls on the stone editor. When a complicated change of make-up is required they should send for the plan and do the alteration in their own hand. The stone editor then needs to be told—but he must be allowed to concentrate on those jobs that only he can do.

The Routine

The equipment a stone editor needs includes: type rule or gauge; schedule showing times pages are due off the stone; ballpoint pen for marking proofs (pencil is no use for damp proofs); a pad of blank copy paper; and a metal spring clip for holding together the galley proofs he will accumulate (in well-organised offices he may even have a row of spikes on which to hang them). The work should begin with a consultation with the executive who plans the pages. The stone editor should gain an idea at this stage not merely of layouts completed, but also of the thinking behind page design and content. He should ask what problems are to be anticipated, and especially if there is anything which is likely to be delayed.

Once in the printing department, the first step is to arrange a proper supply of galley proofs. The stone editor should insist on two proofs of everything, and three on a running story. Too often does a stone editor find himself without a proof to work on because by the time he reaches a page an impatient comp or overseer (or worse, trespassing editorial colleague) has used the one and only proof to mark something for resetting, and the stone editor must wait for this to come back while trying to remember what he needed the proof for in the first place.

It saves a great deal of his time, particularly on first edition when there is a crush of pages to get away, if he can arrange to have his proofs distributed for him to his various pages. If there is no editorial messenger to do so, the most satisfactory alternative is to get the random to put the stone editor's proofs with the metal so that they are distributed automatically as each stonehand collects his galleys.

Proofs

There are basically two kinds of proof: uncorrected and corrected. Some offices supply only corrected proofs; in others, especially busy evening papers, the earlier, uncorrected proof will be supplied as well. The practice is full of pitfalls, and the first caution is to distinguish corrected from uncorrected proofs. Usually the uncorrected proof still carries at intervals the name of the operator who has set that section. For efficient stone work every galley proof should be slugged with certain information:

1. A galley number, for quick identification of metal on the random (or of film bromides); i.e. News 27, Women, Sport 12, and so on.

2. Page and edition.

3. A clear sign whether that galley proof completes the particular story or not. A long story may run to three or four galleys, and there is a risk of galleys being overlooked unless a clear end sign is agreed. Usually the completion of a story on a galley is signified by a half-rule.

4. The setting instructions, whenever these are non-standard.

An editor who gives out corrections on a proof must know the exact type-size and measure of the setting, and it is no use guessing and producing wasted resetting. Even the most practised eye has difficulty distinguishing 8pt solid from 8 on $8\frac{1}{2}$, or $11\frac{1}{2}$ from 11 picas. On a galley proof without column rules there is no way of knowing, even taking a type gauge to the proof, whether the setting is 9pt across 11 picas nut each side or 9pt across 11 picas, one em indent on the left. The visible measure is 10 picas in both instances, but no proof can show if there is an indent and where it occurs.

Where a large variety of measure plays a part in display (as in a popular tabloid, for instance) *every* galley should be flagged at the top with its setting (9pt News × 11 and so on)—even the standard galley. Any variation in the story should of course be flagged as well. Layouts to the stone should also indicate special setting, though as an additional safeguard, not as an alternative.

If by mischance the setting is not marked anywhere and the stone editor suspects it is not standard setting, he should, before marking a proof, inspect the metal. He should not measure it—that is the comp's job, and if necessary he should be asked to do it. It will not help the stone editor to measure his own proof if there is a hidden indent. If the office does not slug galleys with the setting, then the stone editor must point out the folly of leaving him to guess.

Know your proofs

Let us assume now that the stone editor has the right supply of properly marked proofs. What does he do with them? Read and read and read. A stone editor who knows the contents of his proofs is nearly home—yet I have seen many who buzz busily from page to page offering their services while their proofs go unread. They mistake activity for action. When they are eventually asked to make a series of cuts they hunt for the right proofs and laboriously read each one, while the page is delayed. The good stone editor reads as many proofs and as much of each one as he can. This is what he should look at:

HEADLINES: Is this the headline intended for this story? If not, tell the overseer: it is his job to locate the correct headline. If the headline is properly assigned, is it set properly? If it has been squeezed in without adequate space between the words, change the wording to make it fit, taking care that the meaning is the same. If it is out of character with the paper's typographical style, check back with the layout. If the head is correctly assigned and correctly set, is it supported by the text?

SUB-HEADS: Are these the right ones—and are they in the right place in the text?

DOUBLES: Different editorial departments sometimes work on the same story without realising it. And sometimes stories are set twice (a failure to kill metal during a rejig or an accidental oversight by the copy-taster, usually committed with filler paragraphs). Report editorial doubles to the executive in charge and meanwhile hold both.

TEXT: Examine for verbal and typographical errors. Small setting errors should be left at this stage to the proof readers, though they can be ringed so that later the stone editor can check that they have all been caught. Transposed lines should be correctly located and marked in readiness. These are the kinds of marks the stone sub should be making basically at this stage for his own guidance:

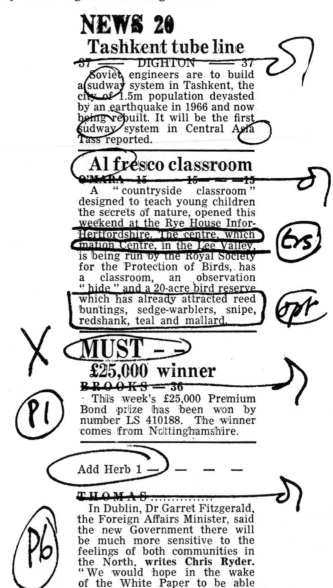

NEWS 20
Tashkent tube line
37 ——— DIGHTON ——— 37

Soviet engineers are to build a subway system in Tashkent, the city of 1.5m population devasted by an earthquake in 1966 and now being rebuilt. It will be the first subway system in Central Asia Tass reported.

Al fresco classroom
O'MARA — 15 ——— 15 ——— 15

A "countryside classroom" designed to teach young children the secrets of nature, opened this weekend at the Rye House Infor-Hertfordshire. The centre, which mation Centre, in the Lee Valley, is being run by the Royal Society for the Protection of Birds, has a classroom, an observation "hide" and a 20-acre bird reserve which has already attracted reed buntings, sedge-warblers, snipe, redshank, teal and mallard.

MUST - -
£25,000 winner
BROOKS — 36

This week's £25,000 Premium Bond prize has been won by number LS 410188. The winner comes from Nottinghamshire.

Add Herb 1 —

THOMAS

In Dublin, Dr Garret Fitzgerald, the Foreign Affairs Minister, said the new Government there will be much more sensitive to the feelings of both communities in the North, **writes Chris Ryder.** "We would hope in the wake of the White Paper to be able

Suspected factual errors should be reported back to editorial on the constant understanding that the copy editor will check and correct. This operation is facilitated if the galley proof is slugged, as it should be, with the name of the copy editor. Suspected errors of setting should be checked against the slug at the top of the galley and the page layout and again notified to the copy editor for correction. Near edition time the stone editor will have to correct setting and factual errors, but when there is a reasonable time to deadline he should be reluctant to give out proofs for correction. He can make a mark in the margin to remind himself to check later that the required correction has been done by proof readers or editorial, but at this stage he should not attempt to do their work for them. If he does duplicate their work, setting time is certainly wasted and there is the risk of a more serious complication—the curse of the crossed proof. It can go like this:

The stone editor reads this three-line intro:

> Britain's Ambassador in Metro-
> land, Mr Jonquil Mackenzie, flew
> to London yesterday for talks

He knows that the name is properly McKenzie, and unwisely alters and sends out the proof for resetting. Meanwhile, the readers have discovered that the word 'new' has been omitted, and the lines are reset:

> Britain's new Ambassador in
> Metroland, Mr Jonquil Mackenzie,
> flew to London yesterday for

Now the stone editor's reset line arrives:

> land, Mr Jonquil McKenzie, flew

and is hurriedly dropped in. The lines now read:

> Britain's new Ambassador in
> land, Mr Jonquil McKenzie, flew
> flew to London yesterday for

Over a long run of type, such confusion is disastrous.

Making Up Pages

The stone editor working in letterpress soon learns to see everything in reverse. The extreme right of the printed page is the extreme left of the metal chase facing the stone editor from his side of the stone. The knack to acquire is to count the columns from right to left: column 1 remains column 1, column 2 remains column 2, and so on, both on the stone and in the printed page. The comp is actually counting from left to right—but you are both identifying columns by the same number.

Armed with the galley proofs of the stories in the page, the stone editor should quickly familiarise himself with the layout and check that it is being correctly followed by the stonehand and that it looks like working. Particular care is needed with blocks. When the block arrives compare it with the original photograph and the edition and page scheduled on the original, and with the caption. Wrong blocks on wrong captions are more frequent than they should be. If setting intended to fill a prescribed special area is falling short or long, tell the overseer. If a story is obviously going to require not merely cutting but slaughtering, tell the executives planning the pages: they may decide to switch the story to another page, or, if time does not permit, to cut now and restore on a later edition—in which case it helps to be able to tell the stonehand to save the cut matter with this in view.

It may be possible for the stone editor, being closer to the job, to see that heavy cutting can be avoided by switching a story position within one page. Again the executives should be told. If the change is agreed, do two things: tell the comp and mark the layout boldly. If you fail to mark the layout, and are away for a few minutes, he may be relieved by another stonehand who will start to follow the old layout.

When cuts are obviously required, it is easier for the stonehand to do them on the galley before the metal is arranged in the page. The stone editor should ask the stonehand to measure the type and the space available. Similarly, the stone editor should try to place adds and inserts before the type is put into the page. Anything the stone editor can do to help the stonehand saves time.

Since it is the stone editor's duty to see that the page is off the stone on time, he should be on edge about delays. If the text is there, but not the headline, check whether the headline is waiting on the random, or whether one was written. If the text is missing or short, ask the overseer to check what is happening on the random or the copydesk. In some offices the stone editor is permitted himself to check with the random.

It may be that there is a galley of type on the random awaiting an end paragraph. Nearing edition time the stone editor will normally be encouraged to use his own initiative to close the story and have the type already set delivered to the page. When a page is in danger of being delayed by late blocks, find how long they will be and notify the copydesk. It may be decided to make a line block more quickly as a tone for first editions, or to switch a block from another page, or go to press without a block. Don't wait. Do something!

Time-conscious executives give the man on the stone wide discretion on the other snags which hold up a page. He should have the freedom to fill small holes in the page by switching metal or film from one unfinished page to another nearly complete. This may mean a deviation from the page layouts, but it is justified to get one page away, provided there are no local-editioning implications. If news metal or film is short. columns falling fractionally short can be completed by leading-out or sub-heads, and for bigger holes the stone editor should have proofs of material already set—house announcements of variable size should always be available. Of course genuine news fillers are preferable, but the stone editor must be the final arbiter.

This is one of the most under-rated jobs in any newspaper office. The stone editor should take as much care with this selection as the page executives have taken in the selection of tops. A good device for avoiding trivial fillers in key positions is to have the people 'upstairs' mark what they consider to be the best fillers in such a way that the random can collect them together on a 'star fillers' galley. The stone editor then has half his fillers job done for him. If he is hard pressed, and has an intelligent stonehand at call, he can order any fillers required to be selected by the stonehand from the 'star' galley. This will require a quick check on the page by the stone editor once they are in, and a closer look when the page is proofed. Never leave it to the stonehand if there is not going to be time to proof the page.

Cutting Stories

Most of the stone editor's time is spent on excision and amputation, cutting back metal or film so that the page approximates to the layout. The rigour with which the stone editor is expected to enforce the layout varies from office to office. Some newspapers prepare layouts detailed down to the last 14pt filler paragraph and expect the stone editor to follow the blueprint. Others give the stone editor discretion. Some do not plan a page beyond indicating the positioning of main stories, and expect the stone editor to squeeze in as much more as he can.

The deskman who is inexperienced at stone cutting can spill a lot of blood. Bad cuts hold up production, spoil the sense of text and mar the appearance of the page. Good cutting begins by being aware of the possibilities. The choices are:

(i) *Leave out one or more sub-headings.* Judge whether this produces too great a run of unbroken text. Are the adjacent columns well broken with heads or are they, too, unbroken text? If the adjacent columns are lively, sub-heads may be dropped.

(ii) *Reduce the headline display.* This does not mean having the headline reset smaller—that is rarely worth the effort in time for the space saved, and can easily spoil a page's appearance. Sometimes, however, a line of a headline or an overline can be left out altogether without spoiling the appearance or sense. For instance, faced with the alternative of a difficult text cut one line could be dropped:

Six fight	**Six fight**
800ft down	**to free**
to free	**trapped youth**
trapped youth	

(iii) *Reduce the space in the headline or in the sub-heads.* This should only be done when the reduction in spacing improves page appearance, and then it should be done anyway. It is too easy, in particular, to reduce sub-heading space and destroy the effect of the sub-head. It is always better to remove the sub-head than to jam it in tight (*see* pp. 00–00).

(iv) *Reduce the space between paragraphs and between lines.* Sometimes stories are prematurely and excessively leaded out, and the comp should be asked to 'strip' them. Avoid reducing the leading when it is part of the design for an intro at the top of a page.

(v) *Take out a secondary block.*

(vi) *Cut the text.* The dangers are cuts that leave headline or sub-head unsupported; create new setting; spoil the flow of the text; take out qualification and balance essential to the story (especially in court stories); and confuse the comp. The alert stone editor anticipates requests for cuts and, in his preliminary reading of the proofs, will have noted safe optional cuts. Otherwise, when asked to cut—

usually the number of lines will be specified—read the whole story through and then the headline and sub-head so that these are at the front of your mind. Resist the temptation to save a few seconds by reading only the last few paragraphs in the hope that they will provide an easy way out. Often they do, but they can also answer one of those essential 'who? what? where? when?' questions.

"They are old customers and friends who have been calling to say goodbye," explained 72-year-old Mr. Fred Reed, who retired on Saturday after working at the shop for 58 years. The shop will now close, ~~and it is understood that the premises will be sold.~~

~~"It is rather a sad day," said Fred, "but~~ I don't ~~really~~ think I could ~~put up with~~ VAT — decimalisation was bad ~~enough—still I am not really sorry to go.~~

"I am the last of the old Market Plain tradesmen," he said. "Most of the others I grew up with are dead now, and the place has changed completely."

HUDDLE

Once the site of Lowestoft Market, the Plain used to be a busy little centre, backed by a huddle of narrow streets. Now the Plain is a car park, the streets have gone and a tower block of flats has taken their place.

The little shop still has the old-fashioned air of a craftsman's workshop — indeed it has changed little over the half-century. Fred, on his last day at the shop, was still cutting out leather by hand, as he did when he started in the trade as a boy ~~of 12.~~

A bachelor, Fred said: "I have no fancy retirement plans like taking up gardening, or fishing, or getting a car. At my time of life there is no point in making too many plans. That's not being pessimistic, it is being sensible. As long as I am able to keep my good health I shall be a rich man."

Aim for a straight clean cut which will not involve any resetting. These cuts avoid resetting because they are at the end of lines or are whole paragraphs. Mark decisively and show the proof to the comp. Never dither over the proof with a pen. A stone editor needs the stone-hand's co-operation and confidence, and he is certainly not going to get it if he gives the impression of not being able to make up his mind. If a cut looks like being difficult to make, take the proof away from the page where you are working and do it quietly, away from the comp and the page. When you cut a line, of course, you may also remove a full-point; if a comma remains, the comp can chip this to a full stop if you draw it to his attention.

> Already Blake is going into the installation business, supplying local authorities and organisation with package planning kits for indoor sports centres, with every sort of detail including where the trampoline will go. " Teaching and sales are no different," says Blake. "You are selling ideas." He certainly knows what he's talking about. When he went to London University on a health education course he acquired a diploma and sold his alma mater a trampoline as well. Now the former gym teacher earns rather more than the Director of Education for a large city.

It is sometimes possible to cut a slice from the middle of a paragraph, yet avoid resetting. The occasions for this are infrequent and the result somewhat untidy, but stone editors should be aware of the possibility when time is pressing. In this instance, the stone editor can ask the comp to cut the line 'Now the former . . .' into the shortened line 'Blake' so that the line appears to run on. Alternatively the line 'Now . . .' can be left as it is, as an exaggerated paragraph opening.

Sometimes it is impossible to cut on the stone without resetting. But the stone is not the place to re-edit the text. The resetting should not be to save words; it should be to facilitate smooth cuts of whole lines.

If there has to be resetting, try to confine it to one type size. If the intro is 10pt dropping to 8 and 7, and there is a cut in each size requiring some setting, then obviously the total reset will have to be split between three machines.

Where this cannot be avoided, flag each part of the proof bearing reset instructions with the page and edition so that the printers know exactly where to take the new lines. With a reset involving a long paragraph, read that paragraph to the end for mistakes that may be obvious to the editorial eye but not to the operator, or there may be a danger of the cut proof crossing with a reader's proof.

If you must reset, then make up your mind firmly that it is going to be reset no matter how unpopular it makes you with the printing over-seer. Look for an easier way out and he will never hesitate to bother you with similar requests. Always be willing to listen to his advice, or that of the stonehand, but never let any doubt arise about who is ultimately responsible.

The stone editor should learn to read type backwards. It is a great help in a last-minute rush if the editorial man can point out to a busy stonehand the location of the lines to be cut. Take the paragraph openings as signposts in finding your way through the type. The routine is:

Identify the story in the page; identify the paragraph; identify the line. The verbal guidance for the stonehand might be: 'Second leg, second par, end it at full point on fourth line'.

But always accompany the words with that clearly marked proof. And never, ever, try to rush the stonehand.

Page Proofs

When a page is proofed, check it at once, however pressing the calls to go to another page. It is surprising how the most glaring mistakes only become obvious when seen in page proof. Ideally every line should be read on a page, but in a busy office one man will not often have time to do that. Here, however, is a minimum checklist for every page proof:

1. Has it the right date and page number? The printing overseer will normally check that, but it is an insurance to skim it.

2. Are the right heads on the right stories? Check every one.

3. Are there any doubles?

4. Does the caption marry the picture? Some offices allow page proofs to be pulled before the block has been placed, and they do it at real peril. Insist on comparing block, photograph, and caption before passing the page. If the caption gives five names, are there five people? Are the sexes correctly described?

5. Do the text turns from one column to another (and from one page to another) read on correctly?

6. Run your eye down every column of type looking for the tell-tale signs of error—'paragraphs' that begin with a full line or end with a full line but no full point, or quotes that open but do not close. Paragraphs that begin and end with indention white spaces are more likely to be free of error.

7. Read the text which arrived late or where late corrections went in, looking for transposed lines, typographical errors, catchlines, and doubled lines produced by the stonehand putting in the new correction without discarding the old line.

8. Are there any unhappy editorial juxtapositions—headlines which were harmless in proof but read on embarrassingly across adjacent columns?

9. Are there any unhappy editorial–advertising juxtapositions, such as a story about a hijacking on top of an airline ad?

10. Is the spacing around headlines correct?

This may seem a long list, but with practice a stone editor can check all these points in six or seven minutes. Tell the overseer what corrections are required so that he can expedite them. If there is new setting, time is saved if the stone editor indicates to the stonehand where the waiting page will be affected.

Bad errors discovered after the letterpress page has been passed into the foundry (or the filmset page into the camera room) may require a remaking of the plate or film. When this has to be done, give the order quickly and decisively. Some errors in letterpress can be caught by having the matrix knocked to remove a line or a letter.

9 The Running Story

There is in the sound archives a memorable recording from a radio commentator in the United States at the arrival of the Hindenburg airship in New York in May, 1937. He is talking slowly, filling in time. 'It's starting to rain again. . . . The rain had splashed up a bit. . . .'

And then it happens: 'The back motors of the ship are holding this, er, just enough to keep it . . . It's bursting into flames! Get out of the way! Get this started! Get this started! Oh, it's crashing, it's crashing terrible. Oh, my. Get out of the way, please. It's burning, oh my, all the folks. It's a terrible blaze. This is the worst, the worst catastrophe in the world. . . . Oh twenty, oh four or five hundred feet in the sky, smoke and flames and the plane is crashing to the ground. Oh, the humanity and all the passengers. It's, Oh, it's, Oh . . . I can't talk, ladies and gentlemen.'

The broadcaster broke down in sobs, but when you hear the recording, with all its crackled confusions, it still conveys across the years the horror and emotion of a major disaster. These are the moments which test any medium of communication—to record history in the instant that it happens. The newspaper cannot match the emotional immediacy of radio; but when a major news story breaks during press time, the newspaper must attempt almost instant communication, and it must do it with the accuracy required of the printed word and throughout with coherency. The words of the Hindenburg broadcaster, even in print all these years later, give some idea of the opportunities and the obstacles for the newspaper. There is the vividness of the eyewitness account; and the confusion. There is the certainty that the airship has caught fire; and the unresolved hope that people might have escaped. There is the open shock of the disaster and the burgeoning anxiety of why it happened. There is the large event, visible and terrible; and there are the names of the individual tragedies.

A major disaster which breaks in press time and develops is called a 'running' story. It is the supreme test of a deskman's skill. The running story is most frequently bad news, but there are golf championships and budgets where taxes go down, and these, too, may be running stories. Kennedy's cliffhanger defeat of Nixon was a running story and so was the fall of Khruschev. The birth of quins was a running story, and so was the first man on the moon. When you come to edit a major running story like any of these, you will feel almost as much a part of the event as the Hindenburg broadcaster. For a start there is the sheer impact of the event, even when it has been developing towards a climax—a staccato message usually on the teleprinters: FLASH, it says, MAN ON MOON. There is a series of short messages, often contradictory, illuminating only one aspect perhaps, leaving the rest in darkness, and then there is the flood of everyone talking at once. Scores and even hundreds of folios of teleprinter copy pour in on every aspect of the story.

It must all be read, assessed, edited and presented, and be re-read, and re-assessed and re-edited as the story changes so that through a succession of editions the newspaper is presenting a coherent, accurate, and up-to-the-minute narrative without repetition and in time to catch the 4.20 train to Crewe and the 5.30 to Birmingham.

To succeed in handling a running story of any dimension the deskman must be able determinedly to set priorities for editing attention, which must be based on keen news judgment. He must be able to unravel three or four strands of a story and work on them as separate parts until he is ready to knit them into the right pattern. He must be able quickly to sift the ten key facts for an intro from five thousand words. The wise deskman handling a running story is realistic enough to know that meeting the deadline with five minutes to spare is more important than a bothersome jerkiness of style; but he is craftsman enough still to be polishing the story after four or five editions.

Of course, newspapers can opt out from this difficult task. There are newspapers which simply print everything they receive on a running story, all the contradictions and all the developments, helter-skelter, without attempting to relate the later information to the earlier and often publishing contradictory information under the same headline. This practice may save on sub-editors but it is hard on readers and newsprint. It confuses the one and devours the other.

The first running story any deskman handles is a formidable, nightmarish undertaking. You will make mistakes. But you will make fewer next time and you will learn to relish the prospect of a difficult running story if you think through the principles of the operation and master the techniques. There are many and they will be set out in this chapter in a full-scale exercise. But right at the beginning, before we plunge in, there are certain essential preliminary points.

First, accuracy. The temptation in handling a running story is to assume that since the current is flowing one way it will continue to do so.

Many a skyscraper of a story has been built on such a shaky assumption only to collapse at the topping-out ceremony.

Running stories change bewilderingly. Be suspicious of uncorroborated statements especially from untrained observers or people without responsibility. Even then, never jump to a conclusion: go as far as the facts go but not an inch further.

Secondly, control. Try to keep calm even when all about you is copy and more copy and the loudest clock you have ever heard. Try to keep mental track of all the eddies of the story and physical control of the mass of paper. Be decisive with the spike.

The practical difficulties in a running story can be listed summarily: first organising the mass of material into a chronological narrative. In a running story, time is always out of joint and you never receive copy in the right sequence. Secondly, knowing how to cope with late information or a correction when you have sent all the copy to the composing room and closed the story. Thirdly, writing an intro and headline after you have rushed all the copy for setting. The commonest mistakes are falling behind the flow of copy; the different one of failing to change the emphasis of the report as the facts themselves change; editing similar material twice without quite realising it so that substantially the same information is repeated in the story. And, of course, misnumbering the folios and writing in too much of a hurry so that everyone has to waste time having it deciphered.

These immediate practical points should be made:

1. Envisage every long running story as splitting into sections. What these are depends on the story—but even the mental act of dividing the story orders the editing priorities for you and makes the whole prospect less daunting.

2. Build every running story on the single paragraph on a single folio. All stories are built in units. The single paragraph of two or three sentences is the best unit for a running story because it is a unit of information of near maximum mobility. (The sentence has the highest mobility.) I mean by this that two or three sentences on the same topic on a single folio can be relatively easily positioned in the narrative. Where the folio, on the contrary, contains three or four paragraphs, you cannot easily interleave that folio where you would like, especially where the paragraphs retail slightly different aspects of the story. One paragraph on the folio may marry well with one section of the narrative and another paragraph on the same folio would be entirely out of place in the narrative as you conceive it.

3. Never run a sentence from one folio to another.

4. Keep the copy as clean as possible—because the setting operator like you is working at speed.

5. Note and check the numbering of every folio before you let it leave your hand.

Let us take a genuine developing story, second by second, with all its cross-currents and confusions. This will illustrate the opportunities and pitfalls of the rapidly changing running story and also the mechanics of coping with new facts in the story in time for various editions. If you have four or five hours to the edition it is easy to collect the copy in its numbered folios and edit a coherent narrative. The real skill is in doing this as you go along, feeding the composing room with every paragraph of copy, working without a proof, and, of course, without any idea of the twists and turns the story might take.

You should first be quite clear about the markings on agency copy (in addition to those mentioned in Chapter 7). Routine news messages will be headed by the name of the agency and the catchline of the story:

PAC
1 Colour

This is a routine message in the Press Association Creed service. It is the first folio of a story about colour television. The next story will be headed PAC 2 Colour. Later if the story develops a long sub-section, it will be sent with a different catchline. Imagine there is a lot of comment on the colour TV announcement. To help the deskman it would be differentiated:

PAC A1 Colour (Reaction)

With more urgent stories a second mark will appear at the top of the agency copy next to the agency name—words like Snap, Rush, Flash. This indicates that the copy has a certain priority in transmission: and it will invariably merit similar priority at the receiving end.

PAC Rushfull 47 Plane

This is a full version of a message previously sent as a Rush—a folio abbreviated for speed. It is the 47th folio of a story about a plane. Here are the Press Association's priority markings:

FLASH: Top priority marking. It is reserved for such events as the death of a Prime Minister or first news of a major disaster.

RUSH: Next in a descending scale. PA would rush the death of a Minister, a train crash which looked like developing into a major story. The 'full' of such a story would be marked

RUSHFULL: the RUSH would be in telegraphic style with subsidiary details deleted for speed.

SNAP: The lowest form of priority marking. Used for the death of an MP or other well-known personality, also the results of court cases, to release embargoed copy and on several other occasions when speed is essential. The 'full' of a SNAP is marked SNAPFULL.

A LEAD: A new 'top' to a running story. Several leads might be done, for instance, for a rail disaster. A LEAD to Press Association is what a 'rejig' is to a newspaper.

For this exercise we will use the PA messages of an air crash, with their original timings and content. The timings fall between evening and morning newspapers. We will assume, however, that you have to edit this story for a continuous series of editions: this call for continuous editing is more demanding, and, I hope, will make the exercise more illuminating.

The same exercise could have been done with Associated Press, Reuter, United Press, or any other agency. The actual PA messages will be used, just as the newspapers would have received the news.

The story starts with a FLASH, and thereafter runs for seven hours with various degrees of priority, and in several sub-sections. Handling this story for several editions of a newspaper, you have to deal with it as it comes. You cannot afford the luxury of waiting until a complete accurate narrative is in hand. For first editions you cannot be very choosy: speed, simplicity, and accuracy are the criteria. Polish can come later. You have to edit the story folio by folio, just as the agency sends it, and you have to set it like that.

When you send it to the composing room, brief folio by brief folio, the composing room desk will be able to give it out to many different setting operators, one folio for one operator at a time. Hence the supreme necessity of correct numbering of folios. Because of the old practice of the operator coming to the composing room desk to take his copy for setting, the editorial department will be requested to send the copy in reasonably short 'takes'. (In the middle of a court case or a big fight this can be frustrating for the printers: only the operator who sets the last paragraph or the page comp know who has won.)

The PA folios are given throughout in caps, as they were sent by teleprinter. Handwriting superimposed on the copy is my editing.

Rather than repeat every folio, first as it was received and then with editing marks, many folios are given once only with the editing marks superimposed on the original. You should be clear what is original and what is editing: anything in handwriting is editing. I give you the editing marks to show how the copy should be handled for clarity and also how the story should be linked as it runs. Between each folio I give a commentary on the way it should be handled. Clearly if you were handling this story you would not go through this apparently laborious process of ratiocination. You have no time to debate various courses of action. I do it for you here to underline the principles in the handling of a running story.

The PA, like other agencies, gives the time of each message on each folio, usually at the foot of the folio. To illustrate the sequence of messages more clearly I will transpose the time to above each one.

For the sake of simplicity I assume throughout that you keep pace with the flow of messages so that when the folio is slugged 1730 hours you are indeed reading and editing that folio at 5.30 p.m. In a real situation there would not be this synchronisation. You would be minutes behind, depending on the volume of messages, your speed in reacting and editing, and the promptitude of the wire room.

This is a point for purists; it does not affect the exercise—and don't despair if in the first running story you handle you find you are behind the copy flow. Stick firmly to priorities, guided by the PA markings, and work steadily on.

The best way to grasp the exercise is to read through the whole chapter once quickly without pausing, and then do it a second time imagining you are at the receiving end of the flow of messages. Note the detailed editing and handling and see where you think my treatment might have been improved. Then set different edition times, and therefore different editing criteria, and do the exercise again yourself. (If you type out all the original PA copy and put it into time order, you can have a real practice. Set an alarm clock for the deadlines so you are not tempted to overrun.)

We begin with the first edition treatment. Be clear about the terms we will use:

The *folios* are the PA folios.

The *takes* are the form in which these folios are available to the composing room for setting.

When you *send* the copy, you are sending it to the composing room for setting.

When you *close* the story, you are ending the run of setting at that point.

Spiking the copy means discarding it but not destroying it. (Never just throw it away in a watepaper basket: you never know how or when you may need previously discarded copy.)

Letting the copy *run* means not worrying about the length of the story: you are not casting off to a prescribed length.

Rejigging means making a complete new story by rearranging the order of existing type and new matter.

First Editions

The first news of the crash is received like this:

1645

RUSH 1 - PLANE

    A BOAC BOEING 71XXXX 707 REOXXXX REPORTED TO

HAVE CRASHED NEAR MAIN RUNWAY LONDON AIRPORT

Your first instruction is to have this news set in the Stop Press—to 'fudge' or 'box' it. Keep the original copy and write off on separate paper the headline and the urgent point of hard news, shedding every word you can in telegraphic style (some newspapers have special copy in 'grid' form, to make sure that the character count is right for setting a line at a time):

FUDGE

BOEING CRASH
AT LONDON

BOAC Boeing 707 reported
Crashed London Airport

Clear your desk for action. If this message is confirmed you are in for a flood of copy. Get two new spikes, and a notepad—one spike for discards from the running story, one for proofs. The notepad is for two purposes: firstly to check your numbering of the copy as you send the takes, one at a time, to the composing room. However quickly and brilliantly you sub the text of a big running story, you will fail miserably if you misnumber the folios. There is no simpler way to waste time in confusion and delay in the composing room.

Secondly, the notepad is for writing down key points in the story for headline and intro purposes. Accept the PA catchline of plane, write PLANE at the left-hand side of the notepad and underneath enter the folio numbers as you dispatch them. You now have instructions from the newsdesk executive:

Rush every line of the text double-column 10pt bold.

Stop sending copy at 5 p.m.

Headline streamer is two lines. (Work out the unit count quickly—14 to each line.)

Don't wait for more copy, edit that first sheet and let it go. Mark it MFL—more follows later.

P1 Splash

RUSH 1 — (PLANE) 1

(10pt bold x 2 cols)

(Rush)

was

A BOAC BOEING ~~TILTED~~ 707 ~~RECENTLY~~ REPORTED TO
the
HAVE CRASHED NEAR MAIN RUNWAY, LONDON AIRPORT, this afternoon.

(MFL)

1646

RUSH 2 PLANE

NO FURTHER DETAILS IMMEDIATELY AVAILABLE

Spike this. It is not worth putting into print. But it helps because it is your signal that there is to be a delay in the copy. This is the time to write the headline. If nothing else comes in the next fourteen minutes before deadline you can still go to press on headline and first take:

JET CRASHES AT
LONDON AIRPORT

But wait a minute. The crash has not been confirmed. It may turn out
to be a false alarm. The big bold streamer asserting the crash as a fact
may then look rather silly. There is nothing for it but to write:

JET CRASHES AT
LONDON—REPORT

But you have a few minutes in hand yet. Hold on to the headline to
see if the story is confirmed or there is news of passengers. Obviously
you must not hold on to it too near the 5 p.m. deadline.

16 55

FLASH 3 PLANE (2 and 3 PLANE) (10pt bold x2)

[A BOARD OF TRADE SPOKESMAN SAID the LONDON-TO-ZURICH
PLANE CRASHED at the END OF the RUNWAY AFTER TAKEOFF.

This confirms the story. The headline you are holding is now too
cautious. Make it 'JET CRASHES AT LONDON AIRPORT'—and
let it go without fail. You cannot wait any longer for more details.

Now note how the catchline has been changed. Since we spiked
PLANE 2 we could renumber this folio as PLANE 2 but this would mean
that all the later takes would need renumbering. To call this folio
'PLANE 2 AND 3' means we are still conveniently on PA numbering.
Enter numbers 2 and 3 on your notepad under PLANE.

16 57

FLASH 4 PLANE

SPEEDBIRD 707 FLIGHT FROM LONDON TO ZURICH CRASHED

AT END OF RUNWAY IMMEDIATELY AFTER TAKEOFF THIS

AFTERNOON, SAID BOAD OXXXXXXXX BOARD OF TRADE.

'Speedbird' is radio code for BOAC: but the copy carries no new
information, so spike it. Never let such discards clutter your desk.

16 59

~~PA~~

~~FLASH~~ 5- PLANE   *(4 and)*   *(copt bold x2)*

the airline

[A BRITISH AIRPORTS AUTHORITY SPOKESMAN SAID/ BOEING/
a   *emergency*
SENT OUT/ "MAYDAY"/ SIGNAL TWO MINUTES AFTER TAKE-OFF
3.27 to say *its*
AT ~~15 27~~ THAT/ PORT WING WAS ON FIRE. *(end)*

You should close up on this folio, marked PLANE 4 and 5, because by
the time you have received, edited and dispatched it you have reached
the 5 p.m. deadline. But now a second later come another two takes.
What do you do?

17 00

FLASH 6 PLANE

IT LANDED ON CROSS RUNWAY IN FRONT OF QUEENS

BUILDING AND WAS COMPLELTLY DESTROYED ON THE GROUND

BY FIRE.

---

17 00

FLASH 7 PLANE

THERE WERE 131 PASSENGERS ON BOARD BUT THE AIRPORT

AUTHORITY HAD NO (NO) NWSXXXXXX NEWS OF THEM.

You have closed the story but it is so near deadline and this is such
useful information that you should send these takes—one at a time,
quickly. When you have done that, not before, tell the man on the stone,
who can decide whether to wait for one or both and allow space in the
forme accordingly.

~~FLASH 6—PLANE.~~ *(10pt bld x 2)* *(1 add Plane)*
[The plane   a   the
  /~~It~~ LANDED ON/CROSS RUNWAY IN FRONT OF/ QUEENS
                                                      the
BUILDING AND WAS COMPLETELY DESTROYED ON/ GROUND BY
²
FIRE.   *end add 1*

~~FLASH 7—PLAND.~~ *(2 add Plane)* *(10pt Bold x 2)*
  e   the Airports Authority
[THRE WERE 131 PASSENGERS ON BOARD, BUT/~~B.A.A.~~ HAD NO
= ∧
~~(NO) NES XXXXXX~~ NEWS OF THEM.
~~M.F.L.~~   *end add 2*

Since the machines will be running for another 15–20 minutes on your original Stop Press, add to the Stop Press: 'Plane destroyed by fire on ground, no news 131 passengers.' (On any story of this size, the senior executive should by this time have assigned another deskman to feed the box from carbon copies of the flashes.)

Your notepad now says:

PLANE
1
2 + 3
4 + 5   Port wing fire
Add 1
   2   Destroyed
                 131 aboard

Cross out the numbers under PLANE because you will begin again for the next edition. For this you are given another deadline—5.30—in the hope that by then you will have some news of the passengers. The first task is to obtain two or three proofs of what you have had set. If they do not arrive send for them. Immediately put one proof on a spike for future reference. This is what is now in type (for convenience here, all the examples of matter in type are shown in 9pt single-column):

FIRST EDITION PROOF

A BOAC BOEING 707 was reported to have crashed near the main runway, London Airport, this afternoon.

A Board of Trade spokesman said the London-to-Zurich plane crashed at the end of the runway after take-off.

A British Airports Authority spokesman said the Boeing airliner sent out a 'Mayday' emergency signal two minutes after take-off at 3.27 to say that its port wing was on fire.

The plane landed on a cross runway in front of the Queens Building and was completely destroyed on the ground by fire.

There were 131 passengers on board but the Airports Authority had no news of them.

Second Edition

Your shape for the page is still the same. Clearly the story in the page is now overtaken and needs a new intro and headline, even if no more news comes. It seems that 131 people have died in the burning plane: but it would be wrong to take this as a hard fact and announce their deaths. Never jump to conclusions in a running disaster story. The most you can say at this stage is something like:

↑A BOAC Boeing 707 jetliner crashed at
London's Heathrow Airport yesterday afternoon
with 131 passengers on board ⊙ It was
completely destroyed on the ground by
fire ⊙ There was no news of the passengers ⊙

You should begin writing an intro like that and recasting the main deck of headline. You also now have a second deck to write, though leave that for the moment for a possible later detail.

Now a new factor enters your work. The Press Association itself at **1705** begins to send a new version of the story, catchlined RUSHFULL, which means you are to receive a fuller, edited version of the story. The news points in the Flashes have been taken from this fuller version and sent baldly for speed. So you now have three elements to knit together:

1 **The proof** of existing metal based on flashes
2 **More Flashes** updating the story to the last minute
3 **Rushfull:** a fuller version with more detail and edited to make a coherent narrative.

If another edition pressed within five minutes it would be best to stay on the Flashes, spending the time adding these to your existing story, amending the proof text and writing a new head. In this way you have the very latest information in the page, even if in a rough-and-ready fashion. However, since you have until 5.30 p.m., the technique now is to regard the Rushfulls as the basic copy. You edit these, interpolate what you can save from the first edition metal, and keep the Flashes at one side in case the Rushfull falls too far behind them.

By **1707** there are no more Flashes but there is a second Rushfull:

1705

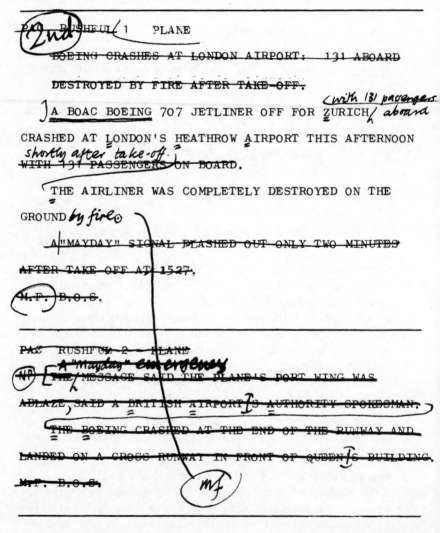

Some of this information is already in type. If you can use the type cleanly, you save setting time. Therefore you process the Rushfulls as above and take in the proof of existing metal in this way:

A BOAC BOEING 707 jetliner off for Zurich with 131 passengers aboard crashed at London's Heathrow Airport this afternoon shortly after take-off. The airliner was completely destroyed on the ground by fire.

The editing has brought the people nearer the beginning; made it clear it was an accident near take-off—and that the trouble was fire.

We delete the rest and pick up that information on the proof of existing metal.

IN TYPE-kt *2 Plane*

~~A BOAC BOEING 707 was reported~~ to have crashed near the main runway, London Airport, this afternoon.

~~A Board of Trade spokesman said he London-to-Zurich plane crashed at the end of the runway after take-off.~~

A British Airports Authority spokesman said the Boeing airliner sent out a 'Mayday' emergency signal two minutes after take-off at 3.27 to say that its port wing was on fire.

The plane landed on a cross runway in front of the Queens Building ~~and was completely destroyed on the ground by fire.~~

There were ~~131~~ passengers on board ~~but the Airports Authority had no news of them.~~

In a rejig, the marked proof(s) must account for all the metal from the first edition.

~~PAG~~ ~~RUSHFUL~~ (3 PLANE)

[AT ~~1700~~ ~~HOURS~~, 5 pm the BRITISH AIR~~WAYS~~ ports AUTHORITY HAD NO FURTHER INFORMATION ABOUT THE PASSENGERS.

M.F. // ~~B.O.S.~~

Edit and send.

17 09

FLASH - 8 PLANE

AIRCRAFT WAS BOUND FOR SYDNEY AUSTRALIA AND AUCKLAND

NEW ZEAXXXX ZEALAND.

Put on one side in case not covered in the Rushfulls.

RUSHFUL 4 PLANE

  A B.A.A. SPOKESMAN SAID THAT THE AIRCRAFT A BOAC

70& - BA 172 - WAS BOUND FOR SYDNEY AND AUCKLAND VIA

ZURICH. IT TOOK OFF AT 16.27

Can now spike Flash 8. The intro, you recall, said the plane was going
to Zürich. Presumably Zürich is a first stop. More significantly, the time
does not square: is it 16 27 or 15 27 as we have said earlier?

17 14

PAC RUSHFUL 8 — PLANE 4

[ALMOST IMMEDIATELY AFTER TAKE-OFF THE PLANE'S

PILOT, CAPTAIN CHARLES TAYLOR, RADIOED THAT HE HAD AN

ENGINE ON FIRE AND THAT HE WAS RETURNING, SAID A BOAC

SPOKESMAN.

[THE AIRCRAFT DID NOT COMPLETE A CIRCUIT OF THE

FIELD, THE SPOKESMAN ADDED, IT WAS COMING *came down* DOWN ON

RUNWAY 05.)

"IMMEDIATELY AFTER TOUCHDOWN THE PLANE CRASHED AND

BURST INTO FLAMES."

M.F. B.O.S.

---

17 14

FLASH 9

A BOARD OF TRADE SPOKESMAN SAID AA XXXXAIRCRAFT

BECAME AIRBORNE AT 1527, THEN AN ENGINE FELL OUT

17 15

FLASH 10

AIRCRAFT MADE LEFT TURN AND WAS CLEARED FOR

EMERGENCY LANDING. WHEN IT LANDED IT WAS ALREADY

ON FIRE. WING FELL OFF.

Hold for the 'full', which you hope will arrive soon.

17 16

PAC   RUSH INSERTION: MEM TO CSE:

    IN RUSHFULL 1 PLANE (TIMED 1705) PLEASE READ

"... OFF FOR ZURICH, EN ROUTE FOR SYDNEY,

AUSTRALIA, AND AUCKLAND, NEW ZEALAND," THUS INSERTING

"EN ROUTE FOR SYDNEY, AUSTRALIA, AND AUCKLAND, NEW

ZEALAND."

END B.O.S.

Leave until the next edition. The point has been covered. Corrections like this are a real problem on running stories. If you have a proof, make them on the proof. In this instance, you would not have a proof. If the correction is important, the best course is to send the message to the stone editor, who will have a proof before you do.

1717

PAC RUSHFULT 6 PLANE. 5

[A BOARD OF TRADE SPOKESMAN SAID THAT THE PLANE'S
ENGINE FELL OUT WHEN IT BECAME AIRBORNE AT 1527.
[THE *air* LINER EXECUTED A LEFT TURN AND WAS CLEARED
FOR AN EMERGENCY LANDING. WHEN IT CRASHED THREE
MINUTES AFTER TAKEOFF IT WAS ALREADY ON FIRE. THE
fire BLAZE GAINED IN INTENSITY AND THE WING FELL OFF.)
EMERGENCY SERVICES RUSHED TO THE SCENE. *crash* ©
M.F.N. B.O.S.

Edit and send—and spike the Flashes held as precaution.

1722

FLASH 12

SPOKESMAN FOR LONDON FIRE BRIGADE SAID HE HAD HEARD
A NUMBER OF PEOPLE SURVIVED.

1723

FLASH 13

SPOKESMAN FOR FIRE BRIGADE SAID HE HAD NO CONFIRMATION
THIS WAS SO.

This is a difficult one. The possibility of survivors is the vital missing
element in the story. Given the second Flash here, there is a need for
caution. But the information is so important it should none the less be

given a higher position in the story than it would have if you merely added this to the end of what you have already sent. What you should do is paste these two flashes together, and then send them as one INSERT, taking care to note 'A INSERT (survivors)' on your separate pad.

[A SPOKESMAN FOR LONDON FIRE BRIGADE *(A insert Plane)* SAID HE HAD HEARD

A NUMBER OF PEOPLE SURVIVED ⊢ *though he had no,*

~~SPOKESMAN FOR THE FIRE BRIGADE SAID HE HAD NO~~

CONFIRMATION ~~OF THIS WAS SO~~ *(end A insert)*

1725

PAC   RUSHFULL 7 PLANE.

LONDON FIRE BRIGADE SENT EIGHT APPLIANCES TO THE

CRASH AND THEY ASSISTED THE AIRPORT BRIGADES.

A LONDON FIRE BRIGADE SPOKESMAN SAID HE HAD HEARD

A NUMBER OF PEOPLE SURVIVED THE CRASH BUT HE HAD NO

CONFIRMATION THAT THIS WAS CORRECT.

M.F. B.O.S.

With five minutes only to go to deadline put on one side to deal with any further Flashes on survivors.

1725

~~FLASH 14 PLANE~~   *(B insert Plane)*

[A ~~EYE~~ WITNESS SAID HE SAW PEOPLE "RUNNING AND

JUMPING" OFF *the* PLANE ☉   *(end B insert)*

Edit as shown and send as: B INSERT PLANE.

17 26

~~FLASH 15 PLANE~~ *(C inset Plane)*

[It was ESTIMATED THAT ABOUT 50 PEOPLE JUMPED OUT SECONDS

AFTER PLANE CRASHED *(end C insert)*

Rush as: C INSERT PLANE.

17 26

PAC   RUSHFULL B1 PLANE (PREVIOUS)

   PREVIOUS AIR CRASHES

   LAST TWO BOAC CRASHES IN WHICH THERE WER FATALITIES

WERE ON MARCH 5 1966 WHEN A BOEING 707 CRASHED AT

TOKYO KILLING 113 PASSENGERS AND CREW OF 11, AND ON

JUNE 24, 1956 AT KANO, NIGERIA, WHEN AN ARGONAUT

CRASHED ON TAKE OFF KILLING 29 PASSENGERS AND THREE

CREWE.

M.F.L.B.O.$.

In the middle of the Rush items about the possibility of survivors, there is no time to deal with this. Put it firmly on one side.

17 26

~~FLASH 16~~ *(6 Plane)*

BLACK SMOKE WAS POURING FROM THE AIRCRAFT AS IT CAME

DOWN

To send this as an Insert might simply be confusing. Add to end of story: 6 PLANE. You could end the running story here but there are a few minutes left so you mark it, hopefully, MF.

17 29

PAC   RUSHFULL A1 PLANE (BOAC)

    BOAC BOUGHT FIFTEEN 707S.

    THE GOVERNMENT AGREED TO BOAC'S PURCHASE OF

FIFTEEN 707 AIRLINERS POWERED BY ROLLS ROYCE CONWAY

JET ENGINES, IN 1956.

    MR. GERAR D'ERLANGER, BOAC'S CHAIRMAN SAID THEN:

"THE ACQUISITION BY BOAC OF LARGE, HIGH SPEED AND

LONG RANGE TURBO JET AIRLINERS IS IMPERATIVE IF THE

CORPORATION IS TO SECURE ITS COMPETITIVE POSITION ON

WORLD ROUTES ESPECIALLY ACROSS THE NORTH ATLANTIC

FROM 1960 ONWARDS."

    IN 1960 IT WAS ANNOUNCED THERE WOULD BE MAJOR

MODIFICATIONS TO THE BOEINGS ON ORDER.

M.F. B.O.S.

Don't read beyond the first paragraph if you can help it. Put on one side for the next edition. With one minute to go send note to desk that last take sent (PLANE 6) is the end of the story. At PLANE 6 it will then be moved from the random to the page forme.

But you have not finished yet:

17 30

FLASH 17

    POSSIBLY 70 ESCAPED ACCORDING TO LONDON FIRE

BRIGADE MESSAGE

This is the hardest news yet on survivors. It is too late to incorporate it in the intro. It could be sent up as an Insert paragraph but it is hard to see it reading well anywhere in the running story you have sent. Given the deadline the best course is to send it as a Late Flash (U.S., Bulletin) —a bold paragraph to be set immediately before the intro to the story. This does not make for a smooth opening but it puts the latest news right at the front. First, send up a Late Flash.

(P1 lead PLANE)

LATE FLASH : Possibly 70 passengers escaped, said London Fire Brigade.

Note that if you are editing on a paper which uses drop caps in the intro, you should not use drop caps on the Late Flash. Let it stand distinctly for what it is—a rushed sentence. Next, warn the desk that you have sent:

A Late Flash for the intro.
Three Inserts on the same point for the body of the story.

The editor on the stone can place these when he has a proof or you can go on the stone and place them yourself. Send a substitute second deck of headline should the stone editor decide there is time for it, marking it 'substitute second deck'.

This is now the situation just before going to press. The running story and the Inserts have been proofed separately. The Inserts lie on the stone waiting the stone editor's instruction on placing them.

LATE FLASH: Possibly 70 escaped, said London Fire Brigade.

INSERT A PLANE
A spokesman for London Fire Brigade said he had heard a number of people survived—though he had no confirmation.

INSERT B PLANE
A witness said he saw people 'running and jumping' off the plane.

INSERT C PLANES
It was estimated that about 50 people jumped out seconds after the plane crashed.

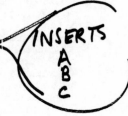

2nd IN TYPE

Late flash

INSERTS A B C

A BOAC BOEING 707 jetliner off for Zurich with 131 passengers aboard crashed at London's Heathrow Airport this afternoon shortly after take-off. The airliner was completely destroyed on the ground by fire.

A British Airports Authority spokesman said the Boeing airliner sent out a 'Mayday' emergency signal two minutes after take-off at 3.27 to say that its port wing was on fire.

The plane landed on a cross runway in front of the Queens Building.

At 5 p.m. the British Airports Authority had no further information about the passengers.

Almost immediately after take-off the plane's pilot, Captain Charles Taylor, radioed that he had an engine on fire and that he was returning, said a BOAC spokesman.

The aircraft did not complete a circuit of the field, the spokesman added. It came down on Runway 05. 'Immediately after touchdown the plane crashed and burst into flames.'

A Board of Trade spokesman said the plane's engine fell out when it became airborne. The airliner executed a left turn and was cleared for an emergency landing. When it crashed three minutes after take-off it was already on fire. The fire gained in intensity and the wing fell off. Emergency services rushed to the crash.

Black smoke was pouring from the aircraft as it came down.

SECOND EDITION PROOF

LATE FLASH: Possibly 70 escaped, said London Fire Brigade.

A BOAC BOEING 707 jetliner off for Zurich with 131 passengers aboard crashed at London's Heathrow Airport this afternoon shortly after take-off. The airliner was completely destroyed on the ground by fire.

A spokesman for London Fire Brigade said he had heard a number of people survived—though he had no confirmation.

A witness said he saw people 'running and jumping' off the plane.

It was estimated that about 50 people jumped out seconds after the plane crashed.

A British Airports Authority spokesman said the Boeing airliner sent out a 'Mayday' emergency signal two minutes after take-off at 3.27 to say that its port wing was on fire.

The plane landed on a cross runway in front of the Queens Building.

At 5 p.m. the British Airports Authority had no further information about the passengers.

Almost immediately after take-off the plane's pilot, Captain Charles Taylor, radioed that he had an engine on fire and that he was returning, said a BOAC spokesman.

The aircraft did not complete a circuit of the field, the spokesman added. It came down on Runway 05. 'Immediately after touchdown the plane crashed and burst into flames.'

A Board of Trade spokesman said the plane's engine fell out when it became airborne. The airliner executed a left turn and was cleared for an emergency landing. When it crashed three minutes after take-off it was already on fire. The fire gained in intensity and the wing fell off. Emergency services rushed to the crash.

Black smoke was pouring from the aircraft as it came down.

The Inserts A, B, C have been effectively placed—all together, in this instance, after the intro. Given a few seconds longer, the story would have been improved by two transpositions which make the narrative flow better and bring the more important news higher up:

Transpose the paragraph 'At 5 p.m. . . . .' to become paragraph 3.

Transpose the paragraph 'The plane landed . . .' to the end.

That discussion was on the basis of a 5.30 deadline. Assume a deadline of 5.40 and the handling of Flash 17 with the news of 70 passengers must be different. You should be able to send this substitute intro:

POSSIBLY 70 ESCAPED when a BOAC Boeing 707 jetliner off for Zurich crashed shortly after take-off at London Heathrow Airport this afternoon with 131 passengers on board.

The stone editor will kill the standing intro and use this paragraph instead, with, of course, all the other paragraphs following.

Third Edition

Your instructions for third edition are as follows:

1. Let it run. Copy deadline 6.30.

2. Do separate story on Boeing safety record and previous big air disasters when these come from agency or staff. This should be six to eight paragraphs. (Normally at this stage the desk will assign such secondary background stories to other deskmen, but let us assume you have to cope yourself.)

You have an hour to go before your copy deadline. You have a second edition proof and by now three unused folios of background information. You should anticipate an increasing flow of copy as more reporters arrive at the airport and the authorities begin to discover what has happened. Therefore it would be wise to clear away now any of the debris of the second edition.

The unused folios plus another which arrived at 5.30 are given below, left clear so that you may consider how you would deal with them quickly. Don't waste time on such background fillers. Speed is the thing.

17 26

PAC   RUSHFULL B1 PLANE (PREVIOUS)

    PREVIOUS AIR CRASHES

    LAST TWO BOAC CRASHES IN WHICH THERE WER

FATALITIES WERE ON MARCH 5 1966 WHEN A BOEING 707

CRASHED AT TOKYO KILLING 113 PASSENGERS AND CREW OF

11, AND ON JUNE 24, 1956 AT KANO,NIGERIA, WHEN AN

ARGONAUT CRASHED ON TAKE OFF KILLING 29 PASSENGERS

AND THREE CREW.

N.F.L. B.O.S.

A better start than Rushfull A1 PLANE (p.197).Make this SAFE 1 and follow with sharply edited folios from A1 and A2 PLANE:

1729

PAC   RUSHFULL A1 PLANE (BOAC)

BOAC BOUGHT FIFTEEN 707S.

THE GOVERNMENT AGREED TO BOAC'S PURCHASE OF

FIFTEEN 707 AIRLINERS POWERED BY ROLLS ROYCE CONWAY

JET ENGINES, IN 1956.

MR. GERAR D'ERLANGER, BOAC'S CHAIRMAN SAID THEN:

"THE ACQUISITION BY BOAC OFLARGE, HIGH SPEED AND LONG

RANGE TURBO JET AIRLINERS IM IMPERATIVE IF THE

CORPORATION ISTO SECURE ITS COMPETITIVE POSITION ON

WORLD ROUTES ESPECIALLY ACROSS THE NORTH ATLANTIC FROM

1960 ONWARDS."

IN 1960 IT WAS ANNOUNCED THERE WOULD BE MAJOR

MODIFICATIONS TO THE BOEINGS ON ORDER.

M.F. B.O.S.

1730

PAC   RUSHFULL A2 PLANE (BOAC)

AMONG THE MODIFICATIONS WAS A 35 INCH ADDITION

TO THE TAIL FIN AND ALTERATIONS TO THE FLYING CONTROLS.

THESE FOLLOWED TESTS ON THE AIRCRAFT BY THE

BRITISH AIR REGISTRATION BOARD. THEN, NINETY 707'S

HAD ALREADY BEEN DELIVERED TO VARIOUS AIRLINES.

M.F. B.O.S.

Close this story now, write the headline (113 died last time) and dispatch it to the composing room. Take note on your pad of the headline wording and the catchline SAFE. Closing the story means the random will deliver it straight away to the stone without waiting for additional material. Any add paragraphs can then be taken direct to the page.

With an hour to edition time, and a short weak story in type, the normal composing room will be able to set a long new story comfortably, if it is sent in short takes. There is, therefore, little mechanical advantage in trying to retain the second edition metal, so the best course is to regard it as expendable. Warn the composing room—directly by note, marked proof, or through a desk executive—that an entirely new story is coming, but that they should hold the second edition story: you can then lift paragraphs if you wish. Your second-edition proof goes on your proof spike, and you are ready to begin the new story. The mistake inexperienced men often make at this stage is to begin at the beginning— to attempt an intro on incomplete information. An hour is a long time in a running story. Never underestimate how much the emphasis can change in fifteen minutes. Nor, of course, should you sit back until sufficient copy has piled up in front of you to suggest an intro. Straight away you go back to the first edition practice, which is to edit a folio at a time, getting into type as much narrative detail of the crash as you can.

Leave all the intro setting for the moment, and set the body of the story, imagining that it will follow immediately on the latest news points. As you dispatch this copy make careful note on your notepad of the key points so that you can write the intro and headlines without requiring a galley proof. The first folio of your single-column material should be catchlined PLANE I and clearly marked:

INTRO TO COME—set catch
NEW PLANE STORY

After 5.30, the first folio from PA arrives as follows:

1736

PAC RUSHFULL.

PLANE (1-LEAD).

AUSTRALIA-BOUND JET CRASHES ON FIRE.

SOME PASSENGERS LEAP CLEAR.

SEVENTY MAY HAVE ESCAPED.

A BOAC BOEING JETLINER BOUND FOR SYDNEY AND AUCKLAND WITH 131 PASSENGERS ABOARD CRASHED ON FIRE AT HEATHROW AIRPORT LONDON TODAY.

AN EYE WITNESS SAID HE SAW ABOUT 50 PEOPLE JUMP OUT OF THE PLANE SECONDS AFTER IT CRASHED. "THEY WERE RUNNING AND JUMPING" FROM THE AIRCRAFT, HE SAID.

POSSIBLY SEVENTY ESCAPED, ACCORDING TO A LONDON FIRE BRIGADE MESSAGE.

ONLY MINUTES AFTER TAKE-OFF, THE ENGINE OF THE AIRLINER - BOUND FOR SYDNEY AND ACUKLAND - FELL OFF.

- M.F.

This is a helpful PA service. They have combined the information so far into a new 'top' for the story—but don't send this as the intro. It has arrived too early for your timings.

Put this on one side, safely under a paperweight, as material for your delayed intro. You will note that the new lead folio is marked 'MF' so, with luck, the PA subs may do the work for you, though you do not know when their second folio will come.

If you have time, cut the new lead folio into its four paragraphs and paste each paragraph separately on copy paper. I suggest this for several reasons. First, if you do have to use the PA new lead you may have to ensure that there is a separate folio for each style of setting. Secondly, having a sentence or paragraph to a folio means you can more easily insert later material, again on separate folios, with careful re-numbering.

17 38

PAC RUSHFULL 8-PLANE.

DRAMATIC MESSAGES.

DRAMATIC MESSAGES OF RESCUE OPERATIONS WERE

FLASHED TO LONDON FIRE BRIGADE HEADQUARTERS IN LONDON

"BOEING 707 BROKEN BACK ON LANDING.....ABOUT TWO-

THIRDS OF AIRCRAFT INVOLVED IN FIRE.....PASSENGER

CASUALTIES BEING RECOVERED FROM TAIL.....POSSIBLE

70 ESCAPED AFTER CRASH LANDING.....SEARCH OF FUSILAGE

FOR FURTHER CASUALTIES IN PROGRESS USING BREATHING

APPARATUS.....".

M.F.

A good folio for beginning the single-column narrative at the end of the intro. If set unchanged it would begin a little abruptly immediately after the intro. In all running stories, you need to write in some linking phrase for smooth transition and to indicate that the detailed narrative has now begun. The commonest linking phrases are 'Earlier . . .' or 'The first news of the accident/triumph came . . . when . . .' This folio PLANE 8 we edit as follows and dispatch it for setting at once:

~~PAG RUSHFL~~ (INTRO T/C) -PLANE. / (set catch) NEW PLANE STORY 3rd

~~DRAMATIC MESSAGES.~~

All afternoon , DRAMATIC MESSAGES OF RESCUE OPERATIONS WERE

FLASHED TO LONDON FIRE BRIGADE HEADQUARTERS, ~~IN LONDON,~~ _and hope increased for survivors..._

"BOEING 707 BROKEN BACK ON LANDING.....ABOUT TWO-

THIRDS OF AIRCRAFT INVOLVED IN FIRE.....PASSENGER

CASUALTIES BEING RECOVERED FROM TAIL.....POSSIBLE

70 ESCAPED AFTER CRASH LANDING.....SEARCH OF FUSELAGE

FOR FURTHER CASUALTIES IN PROGRESS USING BREATHING

APPARATUS.....".

~~M.F.1738 APRIL 8th R.JR~~

1739

PA FLASH 18 PLANE

AIRPORT EYEWITNESS SAID TWO THIRDS OF PLANE

APPEARED TO BE INTACT WITH THE TAIL END STILL

STICKING UP

M F L

This is so much an indication of the possibility of survivors that it should be retained under the paperweight with the intro section. If you have cut the copy for this section into paragraphs, slip it in as a separate paragraph four.

1740

PAC RUSHFULL 9 PLANE

A SPOKESMAN FOR AUSTRALIA HOUSE SAID THE
PASSENGERS INCLUDED 24 PEOPLE MIGRATING TO
AUSTRALIA.

THEY INCLUDED A HUSBAND AND WIFE AND SIX CHILDREN
AGED FIVE TO FOURTEEN (INCLUDING TWINS): A MAN AND
WIFE WITH TWO CHILDREN, NINE AND 17: MAN AND WIFE
AND TWO CHILDREN, FIVE AND SEVEN: AND WIFE AND THREE
CHILDREN BETWEEN FOUR AND NINE: TWO SINGLE MEN, AGED
22, AND 26, AND A CLERGYMAN AND HIS WIFE, AGED 64 AND
60.

"WE DO NOT (REPEAT NOT) KNOW WHAT HAS HAPPENED TO
THEM" HE SAID, "BUT THEY WERE ALL ON THE PLANE".

- M.F.

This would fall unhappily as the second paragraph of the narrative you are attempting. In the next fifty minutes you can hope for rather more precise information on passengers. Spike it. But the next folio is just what you want, providing dramatic detail to buttress the intro and reading on well from your first folio. Edit it as shown and retain for a minute or two to see if there is more of this eye witness to close the quotes.

1743

PAC RUSHFULL 10-PLANE.

MR JIMMY SHAND, HEAD OF SHAND NEWS AND PRESS
SERVICES AT HEATHROW, WAS AN EYE-WITNESS.
HE SAID "WE ARE ALMOST ON TOP OF THE CRASH SCENE. WE
ARE ABOUT 300 YARDS FROM THE RUNWAY AND WE HEARD A
TERIFFIC NOISE DUE TO ANOTHER PLANE OVERSHOOTING THE
RUNWAY BECAUSE, WE WERE TOLD, THE BOEING WAS IN TROUBLE

"WE WATCHED THIS ONE GO BY AND THE STAFF AND I WENT
BACK INTO OUR OFFICE. THEN, JUST A FRACTION LATER,
THERE WAS A TERRIFIC BANG.
-M.F.

PAC RUSHFULL 10-PLANE.2

[MR JIMMY SHAND, HEAD OF SHAND NEWS AND PRESS
SERVICES AT HEATHROW, WAS AN EYE-WITNESS.
HE SAID "WE ARE ALMOST ON TOP OF THE CRASH SCENE, "he said "WE
ARE ABOUT 300 YARDS FROM THE RUNWAY AND WE HEARD A
TERIFFIC NOISE DUE TO ANOTHER PLANE OVERSHOOTING THE
RUNWAY BECAUSE, WE WERE TOLD, THE BOEING WAS IN TROUBLE

["WE WATCHED THIS ONE GO BY AND THE STAFF AND I WENT
BACK INTO OUR OFFICE. THEN, JUST A FRACTION LATER,
THERE WAS A TERRIFFIC BANG.
- M.F.

17 44

PA FLASH 19 PLANE

    BOAC SPOKESMAN SAID "WE KNOW THERE ARE SOME

SURVIVORS"

M F

Retain for intro.

17 45

PA FLASH 20 PLANE

    SPOKESMAN SAID "WE HXXXXXX "WE HAVE NOT HAD ANY

REPORTS OF FATALITIES"

MF

Retain for intro.

At the same time you receive the following Rushfull, giving the first names (and supplementing the vague PLANE 9 which you have spiked). These names would not read well as the third paragraph of your main narrative—which is, remember, suspended in quotes at the moment. But this is essential information. You cannot put it on one side. You must keep copy flowing. One of two things should happen. On hearing that you have the first names, the chief sub should give you (or another colleague) a type and headline shape for a separate story on names. Alternatively, you should use your own initiative, and send the names as a separate single-column story: a separate story on names can easily be placed when it is set in maneouverable single-column.

This folio then needs a new catchline—NAMES is the best—so you edit and send with a single headline 'Emigrants on Board', which cannot be superseded. Note that you should delete the figure 24: there are not 24 on this sheet and we cannot be sure the others will come in time to support the figure.

1745

AAAAAAAAUUUUUUUU
PAC RUSHFULL.

1-PLANE (NAMES).

THE FOLLOWING NAMES OF 24 MIGRANTS ON CRASHED PLANE

WERE ISSUED BY AUSTRALIA HOUSE, LONDON, TONIGHT:

FORSYTH, THOMAS, 22, 95, BELLEVUE CRESCENT, BELLSHILL,

LANARKSHIRE, SCOTLAND.

WALSH, PETER F., 26, 41, TUNNEL ROAD, EDGEHILL,

LIVERPOOL.

WILFRID HEMM, 64, AND GLADYS HEMM, 60, THE VICARAGE,

BRANSCOMBE, SEATON, DEVON.

BRIAN H.M. COOPER, 31, AND HIS WIFE SHIRLEY, 30, AND

CHILDREN KEVIN, 9, JACQUELINE 8, ANDREW, 4, OF 150

WATERHOUSE LANE, MILLBROOKE, SOUTHAMPTON.

FREDERICK J. PRAGNELL, 29, AND HIS WIFE VERA, 28,

CHILDREN STEVEN (7) AND DAWN (5), OF 33, HEARNS

ROAD, ST.MARY CRAY, KENT.

- M.F.

Remember to write the catchline NAMES I on your notepad. You now have three catchlines and three running stories; the main one catchlined PLANE, with folio 2 waiting to go; the background, catchlined SAFE, which your pad shows you is closed; and now NAMES I.

17 45

PAC RUSHFULL

A.3 PLANE (BOAC)

PRICE PHILIP PILOTED A BOAC BOEING 707 OVER THE IRISH CHANNEL IN 1961, ON A TRIP TO VISIT PILOTS TRAINING ON THE AIRCRAFT.

BOAC GROUNDED SIX 707S IN APRIL 1966 FOR CHECK ON "HAIRLINE CRACKS" IN A TAIL COMPONENT.

IN 1967 THE AIRLINE SAID THAT ITS FLEET OF 707S WAS UNDERGOING MODIFICATIONS - THE FITTING OF A COMPLETELY REDISIGNED "FINE TERMINAL FITTING" AND A NEW BULKHEAD TO WHICH THIS WAS ATTACHED.

MFL SF

Send the material on 707s as an Add to your existing story 'SAFE' (the Prince Philip point is irrelevant).

17 46

PAC RUSHFULL

B.2 PLANE (PREVIOUS)

THE MOST RECENT BIG AIR CRASH IN OR NEAR BRITAIN WAS THAT OF THE AER LINGUS VISCOUNT INTO THE IRISH SEA LAST MONTH, WHEN 61 PEOPLE LOST THEIR LIVES.

IN NOVEMBER LAST YEAR, AN IBERIAN AIRLINES CARAVELLE CAME DOWN AT FERNHURST (SUSSEX) AND 30 PASSENGERS AND SEVEN CREW WERE KILLED.

A BEA COMET 4 AIRLINER CRASHED INTO THE
MEDITERRANEAN 170 MILES WEST OF NICOSIA LAST OCTOBER.
FIFTY NINE PEOPLE AND SEVEN CREW DIED.
MF SF

You can send this as ADD SAFE 2. True, it is not really the same story but it will fit in there for the moment as background information.

1747

~~PAC RUSHFULL 11~~ (PLANE. 3)

["WE DASHED OUT OF THE OFFICE AGAIN AND SAW THE
BOEING ON THE MAIN RUNWAY. IT APPEARED TO BE TAXIING, ~~BUT WE HAD NO IDEA WHERE IT HAD COME FROM.~~

"~~IT IS~~ ALMOST IN THE CENTRE OF THE AIRPORT, AND
ALMOST 500 OR 600 YARDS FROM THE MAIN BUILDINGS IN THE
CENTRAL AREA. ~~THE PLANE IS FACING NORTH EAST.~~

THERE WAS A TERRIFIC PALL OF BLACK SMOKE AND
FLAMES COMING FROM THE AIRCRAFT. TWO-THIRDS OF ~~THE~~ *it*
~~PLANE~~ APPEAR*ed* TO BE INTACT, WITH THE TAIL-END STILL
STICKING UP.)

"BUT WHERE THE GALLEY IS APPEAR*ed* TO HAVE ~~BEEN~~
BURNT OUT." ~~IT HAS NOT TIPPED OVER.~~

(—M.F.)

This is clearly the continuation of the Shand eye-witness account, four minutes after the first folio of it, which you are holding as PLANE 2. Release PLANE 2 now that it is clear the quotes continue and edit this

new folio, as shown, as PLANE 3. Should you hold on to PLANE 3 and see
if the interview continues? Rather than do that a second time, with the
clock ticking on, and only two folios away, you should release PLANE 3—
but close the quotes. Then if they resume you can write in an attributive
linking phrase, 'Mr Shand went on . . .'

1747

PAC RUSHFULL

B.3 PLANE (PREVIOUS)

NINETY-EIGHT PEOPLE DIED IN SEPTEMBER 1966, WHEN

A BRITANNIA AIRLINER CRASHED AT LJUBLJANA AIRPORT,

YUGOSLAVIA.

ON JUNE 3 AST YEAR, A DC4 SKYMASTER OWNED BY AIR

FERRY, LTD., CRASHED IN THE PYRENEES AND 88 PEOPLE

WERE KILLED.

THE NEXT DAY A DC 4 ARGONAUT OWNED BY BRITISH

MIDLAND AIRWAYS CRASHED AT STOCKPORT, CHESHIRE, KILL-

ING 72.

A B.E.A. VAGUARD CRASHED AT HEATHROW AIRPORT,

LONDON, IN OCEOBER, 1965, WHEN THE CREW OF SIX AND

30 PASSENGERS WERE KILLED.

END SF

Edit and send as ADD SAFE 3.

1748

PAC RUSHFULL

PLANE (2-LEAD)

THE PLANE CRASHED ON A CROSS RUNWAY IN FRONT OF QUEENS BUILDING. AN EYEWITNESS SAID TWO THIRDS OF THE PLANE APPEARED TO BE INTACT AFTER IT HIT THE GROUND.

ALMOST IMMEDIATELY AFTER TAKE-OFF THE PILOT, CAPTAIN CHARLES TAYLOR, RADIOED THAT HE HAD AN ENGINE ON FIRE AND WAS RETURNING.

THE LINER EXECUTED A LEFT TURN AND IMMEDIATELY ON TOUCH DOWN CRASHED AND BURST INTO FLAMES.

M.F.L. RJW

Hold with intro section.

1749

PA FLASH 21 PLANE

CONFIRMED PLANE TOOK OFF AT 16.27 HOURS BRITISH STANDARD TIME (15.27) GREENWICH MEANTIME)

M F L

Hold for intro section.

1749

PAC RUSHFULL

C2-PLANE (NAMES).

JOHN MOLINEAUX (39), AND HIS WIFE LILIAN (39) AND
CHILDREN IRENE (17), JOHN (9), OF 53, DAWES STREET,
WALWORTH, SE 17.

DONALD HAY (38), AND HIS WIFE PATRICIA (33) AND
CHILDREN TREVOR (14), DIANE (13), KEVIN (10) AND
TWINS LORRAINE AND CHERYL (5), OF 12, OSBORNE ROAD,
WARSASH, HANTS.

ALL THESE WERE BOUND FOR PERTH, WESTERN AUSTRALIA.

(END AUSTRALIA HOUSE LIST).

- M.F.L.

Add to your separate names story. A check on the notepad will show you that you have sent one folio, so this is NAMES 2. Since it says 'End Australia House List', it is well to mark the copy closed at NAMES 2, so that the type is made available on the stone. Any further information on names can be sent as Add matter.

1751

~~HPAC RUSHFULL 12~~ (PLANE. 4)

[Mr Shand continued :-

"WE HEARD AT LEAST FOUR DISTINCT BANGS WHICH
COULD HAVE BEEN SOME OF THE PETROL GOING UP, AND
THEN WE SAW A LOT OF PEOPLE GETTING OUT.

"THEY WERE JUMPING FROM THE PLANE AND RUNNING
QUICKLY AWAY. IT WAS ONLY SECONDS AFTER IT HAD COME
DOWN, ~~SAID MR SHAND.~~

["WE ESTIMATE THAT AT LEAST 50 ~~PEOPLE~~ GOT OUT AND
PERHAPS ~~THE FIGURE WAS~~ as many AS ~~HIGH AS~~ 70 others might,

"~~I WOULD STRESS THAT OTHERS MAY~~ ALSO HAVE GOT OUT,
BUT THE SMOKE PREVENTED US FROM KEEPING A CONTINUAL
WATCH.

"~~AT THIS MOMENT (17.25)~~ WHITE SMOKE ~~IS NOW~~ came COMING
FROM THE TAIL END OF THE PLANE WHICH ~~IS~~ was SURROUNDED BY
FIRE ENGINES.

"~~IT HAS BEEN SAID THERE IS AN ENGINE MISSING, BUT
WE CAN'T SEE ANYTHING FROM HERE.~~ ["THERE SEEMS ed A GOOD
CHANCE THAT THE PILOT AND CREW WERE SAFE BECAUSE THE
NOSE APPEARS ed TO BE PERFECTLY INTACT.

—M.F.

1752

PAC RUSHFULL

PLANE (3-LEAD)

    THE LINER, CALL SIGN WHISKY ECHO, TOOK OFF AT

1627 FROM THE AIRPORTS MAIN RUNWAY. A BOAC SPOKESMAN

SAID:- "WE KNOW THERE ARE SOME SURVIVORS, WE HAVE

NOT HAD ANY REPORTS OF FATALITIES."

END LEAD.

RJW

1752

~~PAC RUSHFULL 13~~ PLANE. **5**

    ["AT THE SAME TIME AS WE SAW THE BLACK SMOKE WHEN

IT FIRST CRASHED, WE SAW QUITE A LOT OF FLAMES, BUT

THESE DID NOT APPEAR TO BE ANYWHERE NEAR AS GREAT AS

THE SMOKE. THERE WERE FLAMES COMING FROM THE TAIL

END".

~~(END SHAND)~~.

M.F.

These three folios reach your desk together. PLANE 3 LEAD is the
final PA intro folio which you put with the other waiting intro material.
Rushfulls 12 and 13 end the eye witness you are running. These should
be sent one at a time single-column—but remember you have to
reintroduce Mr Shand. You closed the quotes on PLANE 3, so edit the
two Rushfulls and send them for setting.

17 53

PAC RUSHFULL 14-PLANE.

A BOAC SPOKESMAN SAID LATER (17.42): "WE KNOW THER~~E~~
ARE SOME SURVIVORS. WE HAVE NOT (REPEAT NOT) HAD ANY
REPORTS OF FATALITIES".

- M.F.

Hold for intro.

17 55

~~PAC RUSHFULL 15~~ PLANE. 6

[A BOARD OF TRADE SPOKESMAN LATER: *said* ~~STATED:~~

"A BOAC SPEEDBIRD BOUND FOR ZURICH DEVELOPED SOME
FORM OF TROUBLE IMMEDIATELY AFTER TAKE-OFF AT 1~~5~~. 27 *(3)*
AND A PORT ENGINE THEN FELL OUT.

THE AIRCRAFT EXECUTED A LEFT HAND TURN AND WAS
CLEARED FOR AN EMERGENCY LANDING.

["WHEN IT LANDED AT 1~~5~~.30 *(3)* IT WAS ALREADY ON FIRE.
THE FIRE GAINED IN INTENSITY AND THE WING FELL OFF.
THE AIRCRAFT CAME TO A STOP AND THE EMERGENCY SERVICES
WHICH HAD ALREADY BEEN CALLED OUT BEGAN TO DEAL WITH
THE FIRE".

 - M.F. L.

This is PLANE 6 in the narrative. It is a good place for a cross-head
('Wing fell off'), marking a natural break after five folios. Edit and send.
Cross-heads are often a matter of house-style: I have not written them
all in here—but where they are used they must be written off separately.

17 56

~~PAC RUSHFULL 16~~ PLANE. 7

[ALL AVAILABLE RAC PATROLS IN THE AREA WERE

DRAFTED TO LONDON AIRPORT ~~TONIGHT~~ AFTER POLICE

APPEALED FOR HELP TO CONTROL TRAFFIC ~~NEAR THE SCENE~~

~~OF THE CRASH.~~

MAIN ROADS IN THE AREA WERE JAMMED WITH RESCUE

VEHICLES, HOME GOING MOTORISTS AND SIGHTSEERS.

- M.F.

Edit as PLANE 7 and send.

17 57

PAC RUSHFULL 17-PLANE.

BOAC CONFIRMED THE PLANE TOOK-OFF AT 16.27 HOURS

BRITISH STANDARD TIME.

- M.F.

This does not fit smoothly into the narrative flow. Can you remember what time take-off was stated as being in the previous Board of Trade statement? If you are editing in a rush it is quite probable that you will not have made a mental note of this time point. The best course with this time statement is to put it with the intro copy for checking there and later when you have a proof.

1801

PA FLASH 22 (PLANE *8*)

[An AIRPORT SPOKESMAN SAID The WRECKAGE OF the ENGINE FELL IN
THORPE AND OTHERS PARTS fell IN WRAYSBURY, NEAR WINDSOR.

Edit it and send as PLANE 8—there seem to be enough points on survivors for the intro section.

1802

PA FLASH 23 PLANE.

LONDON FIRE BRIGADE SPOKESMAN SAID 78 PASSENGERS

ESCAPED FROM WRECKAGE.

Here at last is a hard statement on the numbers who have escaped. It is for the intro, of course, now. But wait a few more minutes before settling on the intro.

1804

PA FLASH 24 PLANE

FIRE BRIGADE SAID THREE BODIES RECOVERED.

SEARCH CONTINUING.

Hold for the intro.

1804

PAC.
RUSH CORRECTION.
IN PAGE 12-PLANE IN FIRST PARA "COULD HAVE BEEN
SOME OF THE FUEL GOING UP". THIS SUBSTITUTES "FUEL"
FOR "PETROL" ASSENT.
- END CORRECTION

Not a really vital correction. Put it to one side until you have a proof.

1807

PA FLASH 25 PLANE

BOAC SPOKESMAN SAID T BELIEVED OVER 100 SURVIVORS

M.F

Astonishing! Here is the key point for the intro. Should you now begin to pull it all together? A deskman at this stage faces a difficult judgment. To delay much more may risk skimping the writing of the intro. But at the moment the Flash is tentative—and you have still to close the running story which is at PLANE 8. As you hesitate, two more folios arrive:

1807

PAC RUSHFULL 18-PLANE.

AT 1800 HOURS LONDON FIRE BRIGADE STATED THERE WAS

A COMPLEMENT OF 115 PASSENGERS ON THE PLANE.

OF THEM, 78 HAD ESCAPED. THREE BODIES HAD BEEN

RECOVERED. SEARCH WAS CONTINUING.

- M.F.

1808

PA FLASH 26 PLANE

EMPHASISED THIS FIGURE WAS NOT OFFICIAL.

M F

Quickly spike anything which has been overtaken. Break off here and review your intro material (the earlier folios you put under a paper-weight), repeated overleaf:

PAC   RUSHFULL.

PLANE (1-LEAD).

AUSTRALIA - BOUND JET CRASHES ON FIRE.

SOME PASSENGERS LEAP CLEAR.

SEVENTY MAY HAVE ESCAPED.

A BOAC BOEING JETLINER BOUND FOR SYDNEY AND AUCKLAND WITH 131 PASSENGERS ABOARD CRASHED ON FIRE AT HEATHROW AIRPORT LONDON TODAY.

AN EYE WITNESS SAID HE SAW ABOUT 50 PEOPLE JUMP OUT OF THE PLANE SECONDS AFTER IT CRASHED. "THEY WERE RUNNING AND JUMPING" FROM THE AIRCRAFT, HE SAID.

POSSIBLY SEVENTY ESCAPED, ACCORDING TO A LONDON FIRE BRIGADE MESSAGE.

ONLY MINUTES AFTER TAKE-OFF, THE ENGINE OF THE AIRLINER - BOUND FOR SYDNEY AND AUCKLAND - FELL OFF. - M.F.

PAC RUSHFULL

PLANE (2-LEAD)

THE PLANE CRASHED ON A CROSS RUNWAY IN FRONT OF
QUEENS BUILDING. AN EYEWITNESS SAID TWO THIRDS OF
THE PLANE APPEARED TO BE INTACT AFTER IT HIT THE
GROUND.

ALMOST IMMEDIATELY AFTER TAKE-OFF THE PILOT,
CAPTAIN CHARLES TAYLOR, RADIOED THAT HE HAD AN ENGINE
ON FIRE AND WAS RETURNING.

THE LINER EXECUTED A LEFT TURN AND IMMEDIATELY
ON TOUCH DOWN CRASHED AND BURST INTO FLAMES.

M.F.L.

PAC RUSHFULL.

PLANE 3 LEAD)

THE LINER, CALL SIGN WHISKY ECHO, TOOK OFF AT
1627 FROM THE AIRPORTS MAIN RUNWAY. A BOAC SPOKESMAN
SAID:- "WE KNOW THERE ARE SOME SURVIVORS, WE HAVE NOT
HAD ANY REPORTS OF FATALITIES."

END LEAD.

PA FLASH 18 PLANE

    AIRPORT EYEWITNESS SAID TWOTHIRDS OF PLANE APPEARED TO BE INTACT WITH THE TAIL END STILL STICKING UP.

M F L

Covered in PA New Lead. Spike it.

PA FLASH 19 PLANE

    BOAC SPOKESMAN SAID "WE KNOW THERE ARE SOME SURVIVORS"

M.F.

Spike it, overtaken.

PA FLASH 20 PLANE

    SPOKESMAN SAID "WE HXXXXX "WE HAVE NOT HAD ANY REPORTS OF FATALITIES"

MF

Spike it, overtaken by Rushfull 18.

PA FLASH 21 PLANE

    CONFIRMED PLANE TOOK OFF AT 16.27 HOURS BRITISH STANDARD TIME (15.27 GREENWICH MEANTIME)

M F L

Write in qualification 'British Standard Time' on New Lead 3, then spike this.

PAC RUSHFULL 14-PLANE

A BOAC SPOKESMAN SAID LATER (17.42): "WE KNOW
THERE ARE SOME SURVIVORS. WE HAVE NOT (REPEAT NOT)
HAD ANY REPORTS OF FATALITIES."

Spike, already covered.

PAC RUSHFULL 17-PLANE.

BOAC CONFIRMED THE PLANE TOOK-OFF AT 16.27 HOURS
BRITISH STANDARD TIME.
- M.F.

Spike it, time confusion cleared up earlier.

PA FLASH 23 PLANE.

LONDON FIRE BRIGADE SPOKESMAN SAID 78 PASSENGERS
ESCAPED FROM WRECKAGE.

Spike—both covered by the last Rushfull 18 PLANE.

While you have been skimming these folios and spiking, three other folios arrive:

1810

PA FLASH 27 PLANE

    BOAC SPOKESMAN IN LONDON SAID TENTATIVELY

ESTABLISHED 103 SURVIVORS.

M F

PA FLASH 28 PLANE

    ALL CREW ESCAPED

M F

PA FLASH 29 PLANE

    126 WERE ON BOARD INCLUDING 11 CREW

M F L

You must lose no more time. The news point is no longer the crash itself but the escape of so many people from a burning plane. Let the arriving folios wait as you write out the intro. Ignore Rushfulls but keep one eye open for Flashes which might change the figures. You put the intro together, using what you can of the existing folios pasted on copy paper—leaving the existing words where they read properly. On the first lead folio, cut off below the first paragraph, retain the rest, and edit the first section as follows:

~~PLANE (1-LEAD).~~ *(Plane intro 1)*

~~AUSTRALIA-BOUND JET CRASHES ON FIRE.~~

~~SOME PASSENGERS LEAP CLEAR.~~

~~SEVENTY MAY HAVE ESCAPED.~~

[MORE THAN 100 passengers are believed to have escaped from ~~A~~ BOAC BOEING JETLINER BOUND FOR SYDNEY AND AUCKLAND ~~WITH 131 PASSENGERS ABOARD~~ *which* CRASHED ON FIRE AT HEATHROW AIRPORT, LONDON, ~~TODAY~~ *yesterday.*

PA FLASH 29 PLANE [There were,

126 ~~WERE~~ ON BOARD INCLUDING 11 CREW *who,*

~~M F L~~

~~PA FLASH 28 PLANE~~

ALL ~~CREW~~ ESCAPED o *A.*

~~M F~~

~~PA FLASH 27 PLANE~~

BOAC SPOKESMAN IN LONDON SAID ~~TENTATIVELY~~ *it was thought there were*

~~ESTABLISHED~~ 103 SURVIVORS.

~~M F~~

~~PA FLASH 24 PLANE~~

London

[FIRE BRIGADE SAID THREE BODIES *had been* RECOVERED.

~~SEARCH CONTINUING.~~

M F ~~L~~

18 14

PAC RUSHFULL 20-PLANE.
 A HEATHROW AIRPORT SPOKESMAN SAID TONIGHT:
"WRECKAGE OF THE PORT OUTER ENGINE FELL IN THORPE
AND OTHER PARTS IN WRAYSBURY (BUCKS) FOUR MILES SOUTH
EAST OF WINDSOR.
 "THE AIRCRAFT LANDED ON RUNWAY 05R AT 1631 HOURS
AND CAME TO A HALT ON BLOCK 49 DUE EAST OF THE QUEEN'S
BUILDING WITH THE PORT WING ON FIRE. SUBSEQUENTLY THE
FIRE SPREAD TO THE WHOLE AIRCRAFT.
 - M.F.

 Adds precise details to earlier information. Not worth sending since
it would involve repetition—but worth holding for next edition.
18 15

~~PAC RUSHFULL 21 PLANE~~.   (Plane 9)

[THE ARRIVAL AND DEPARTURE RATE AT THE AIRPORT ~~IS~~
  2 *was*
~~AT PRESENT~~ GREATLY REDUCED OWING TO THE TOTAL

INVOLVEMENT OF RESCUE SERVICES, ~~SAID THE AIRPORT~~

~~SPOKESMAN.~~

 (M.F.)

 Send as PLANE 9.
18 15

~~PA FLASH 30 PLANE~~   (Plane intro 2)
 [*According to an*
  2 AIRPORT POLICE SPOKESMAN ~~SAID~~ THREE WOMEN ,

ONE MAN AND A CHILD DIED.

Run this on as part of INTRO 2 and pick up now whatever accurate is left of the PA Lead:

[AN ~~EYE~~ WITNESS SAID HE SAW ABOUT 50 PEOPLE JUMP OUT OF THE PLANE SECONDS AFTER IT CRASHED. "THEY WERE RUNNING AND JUMPING" FROM THE AIRCRAFT, HE SAID.

~~POSSIBLY SEVENTY ESCAPED, ACCORDING TO A LONDON FIRE BRIGADE MESSAGE.~~

ONLY MINUTES AFTER TAKE-OFF, THE ENGINE OF THE AIRLINER ~~BOUND FOR SYDNEY AND AUCKLAND~~ FELL OFF.

M.P.

~~PAC RUSHFULL~~

~~PLANE (2~~LEAD)

THE PLANE CRASHED ON A CROSS RUNWAY IN FRONT OF QUEENS BUILDING. ~~AN EYEWITNESS SAID~~ TWO THIRDS OF THE PLANE APPEARED TO BE INTACT AFTER IT HIT THE GROUND.

[ALMOST IMMEDIATELY AFTER TAKE-OFF THE PILOT, CAPTAIN CHARLES TAYLOR, RADIOED THAT HE HAD AN ENGINE ON FIRE AND WAS RETURNING.

THE LINER EXECUTED A LEFT TURN AND IMMEDIATELY ON TOUCH-DOWN CRASHED AND BURST INTO FLAMES. *The plane, call sign Whisky Echo, took off at 4.27* M.P.L. *from the main runway.* (end intro)

Intro complete, scan quickly the second edition proof you retained (see p. 200). Nothing to be salvaged in that: it has been overtaken completely. Send it to the composing room marked KILL SECOND EDITION MATTER.

Send INTRO 2. Hold INTRO 1 for a moment in case there is any official figure on the number of survivors and deaths.

1811

PAC RUSHFULL 19-PLANE.

SHORTLY AFTER 1800 HOURS A BOAC SPOKESMAN SAID:

"WE UNDERSTAND THERE ARE A LOT OF SURVIVORS.

IT IS BELIEVED THAT THERE ARE OVER 100".

HE EMPHASISED THAT THIS FIGURE WAS NOT (REPEAT

NOT) OFFICIAL AS YET.

- M.F.

Spike it.

1815

PAC RUSHFULL 22-PLANE.

A SPOKESMAN AT B.O.A.C.'S HEADQUARTERS IN LONDON

SAID TONIGHT IT HAD BEEN TENTATIVELY ESTABLISHED THAT

OF 126 PEOPLE ON BOARD THE 707, INCLUDING 11 CREWE,

THERE HAD BEEN 103 SURVIVORS.

ALL THE CREW HAD ESCAPED.

- M.F.

Spike it.

18 16

PA FLASH 31 PLANE

    BOAC SAID "WE KNOW THERE ARE 103 SURVIVORS BUT WE
CANNOT ACCOUNT FOR ANYONE ELSE"

M F L

Spike it.

18 16

PAC RUSHFULL 23-PLANE.

    AN AIRPORT POLICE SPOKESMAN SAID THREE WOMEN,
ONE MAN, AND A CHILD PASSENGER, DIED IN THE CRASH.

– M.F.

Spike it—duplication.

18 22

PAC RUSHFULL 24-PLANE

    BOAC SAID TONIGHT THERE WERE 103 SURVIVORS.

    A SPOKESMAN SAID: "THE AIRCRAFT WAS OPERATING
FLIGHT BA 712 TO SYDNEY. IT WAS OFF BLOCKS (ON THE
MOVE) AT 16:15 HOURS AND AIRBORNE AT 16:27 HOURS,
CARRYING 115 PASSENGERS AND 11 CREWE.

    "IMMEDIATELY AFTER TAKE-OFF THE COMMANDER
RADIOED HE HAD AN ENGINE ON FIRE AND WAS RETURNING
IMMEDIATELY, BUT HE HAD NOT FINISHED A COMPLETE

CIRCUIT WHEN HE CAME DOWN ON RUNWAY 05.

"IMMEDIATELY AFTER TOUCH-DOWN THE PLANE CRASHED

AND BURST INTO FLAMES.

"WE KNOW THERE ARE 103 SURVIVORS, BUT WE CANNOT

ACCOUNT FOR ANYONE ELSE. THE CHAIRMAN AND VICE-

CHAIRMAN OF BOAC ARE ON THE SCENE".

- M.F.

Make INTRO 1 firm on 103 survivors, i.e. change to:
More than 100 passengers are known to have escaped etc. . . .
A BOAC spokesman in London said there were 103 survivors.
Now release INTRO 1. The running story is still open at PLANE 9,
with eight minutes to deadline.

You can fillet two bits of information from Rushfull 24. Delete all
except the following and send to the composing room as PLANE 10.
Close the story there and write the headlines. Other matter can go as
Adds, if time allows.

PAG RUSHFULL 24-PLANE.   *Plane 10*

[A BOAC, SAID TONIGHT THERE WERE 103 SURVIVORS.

A SPOKESMAN SAID THE AIRCRAFT WAS OPERATING
number was BA)
FLIGHT 712 TO SYDNEY. IT WAS OFF BLOCKS (ON THE

MOVE) AT 16:15 HOURS AND AIRBORNE AT 16:27 HOURS,

AND BURST INTO FLAMES.

"WE KNOW THERE ARE 103 SURVIVORS, BUT WE CANNOT

ACCOUNT FOR ANYONE ELSE. THE CHAIRMAN AND VICE-
                    went o
CHAIRMAN OF BOAC ARE/ON THE SCENE".

M.F.   *end Plane*

1830

PAC RUSHFULL 25 PLANE.

THE CAPTAIN OF THE BOEING WAS CAPTAIN CHARLES

TAYLOR.

MANY OF THE SURVIVORS WERE BROUGHT BACK TO THE

AIRPORT'S TERMINAL AREA BY A B.O.A.C. COACH.

SOME WERE BEING TREATED IN ONE OF THE AIRPORT'S

MEDICAL CENTRES AND PASSENGERS WHO WERE UNHURT

WERE ESCORTED TO A PRIVATE V.I.P. LOUNGE.

M.F. B.O.S.

Too late and not worth rushing. Hold for next edition, and enjoy reading a third-edition proof with your intro superimposed on the earlier copy.

THIRD EDITION PROOF

MORE THAN 100 passengers are known to have escaped from a BOAC Boeing jetliner bound for Sydney and Auckland which crashed on fire at Heathrow Airport, London, yesterday.

There were 126 on board including 11 crew who all escaped. A BOAC spokesman in London said there were 103 survivors. London Fire Brigade said three bodies had been recovered.

According to an airport police spokesman three women, one man and a child died.

A witness said he saw about 50 people jump out of the plane seconds after it crashed. 'They were running and jumping from the aircraft', he said. Only minutes after take-off, the engine of the airliner fell off. The plane crashed on a cross runway in front of Queens Building. Two-thirds of the plane appeared to be intact after it hit the ground.

Almost immediately after take-off the pilot, Captain Charles Taylor, radioed that he had an engine on fire and was returning. The liner executed a left turn and immediately on touch-down crashed and burst into flames. The plane, call sign Whisky Echo, too off at 4.27 from the main runway.

All afternoon dramatic messages of rescue operations were flashed to London Fire Brigade headquarters, and hope increased for survivors. . . .

'Boeing 707 broken back on landing...about two-thirds of aircraft involved in fire...passenger casualties being recovered from tail...possible 70 escaped after crash landing . . . search of fuselage for further casualties in progress using breathing apparatus. . . .'

Mr. Jimmy Shand, head of Shand

News and Press Services at Heathrow, was an eye-witness. 'We were almost on top of the crash scene', he said. 'We were about 300 yards from the runway and heard a terrific noise due to another plane overshooting the runway because, we were told, the Boeing was in trouble.

'We went back into the office. Then, just a fraction later, there was a terrific bang.

'We dashed out of the office again and saw the Boeing on the main runway. It appeared to be taxi-ing, almost in the centre of the airport, and almost 500 or 600 yards from the main buildings in the central area. There was a terrific pall of black smoke and flames coming from the aircraft. Two-thirds of it appeared to be intact, with the tail-end still sticking up. But where the galley is appeared to have burnt out'.

Mr. Shand continued: 'We heard at least four distinct bangs which would have been some of the petrol going up, and then we saw a lot of people getting out. They were jumping from the plane and running quickly away. It was only seconds after it had come down.

'We estimated that at least 50 got out and perhaps as many as 70 others might also have got out, but the smoke prevented us from keeping a continual watch. White smoke came from the tail end of the plane which was surrounded by fire engines.

'There seemed a good chance that the pilot and crew were safe because the nose appeared to be perfectly intact.

'At the same time as we saw the black smoke when it first crashed, we saw quite a lot of flames, but these did not appear to be anywhere near as great as the smoke. There were flames coming from the tail end.'

A Board of Trade spokesman said later: 'A BOAC Speedbird bound for Zurich developed some form of trouble immediately after take-off at 3.27 and a port engine then fell out. The aircraft executed a left-hand turn and was cleared for an emergency landing.

'When it landed at 3.30 it was already on fire. The fire gained in intensity and the wing fell off. The aircraft came to a stop and the emergency services which had already been called out began to deal with the fire.'

All available RAC patrols in the area were drafted to London Airport after police appealed for help to control traffic. Main roads in the area were jammed with rescue vehicles, homegoing motorists and sightseers.

An airport spokesman said the wreckage of the engine fell in Thorpe and other parts fell in Wraysbury, near Windsor.

The arrival and departure rate at the airport was greatly reduced owing to the total involvement of rescue services.

A BOAC spokesman said the flight number was BA 712. The chairman and vice-chairman of BOAC went to the scene.

You will notice the two versions of the time. Correct the proof to 4.27 and 4.30, and send it. There may be time. Also you have completed a new story without using any of your second-edition matter: so it can now safely be killed.

Fourth Edition

You will have noticed that the news focus of the story has changed within two hours. At first it was the crash itself, then the fears for the numbers killed, and now the emphasis must be on the astonishing escape of 100 or more people from a burning plane. You begin to ask yourself the natural questions: What happened to the plane? How did the pilot manage to land on fire and without an engine? Why should an airliner catch fire? Editing the story for a morning newspaper, you will be aware that the television and radio news will have announced the crash, and probably the numbers who escaped, by the time the evening is over. You still have to give that news, but now you are hoping to build up a narrative answering all the questions in the detailed way where the written word, more economical in the consumer's time, scores over the spoken word. The executive in charge of the story will be organising photographs, and you should yourself suggest any diagrams which will help to make it all more comprehensible.

Your next edition is two hours ahead, at 8.30 p.m. You are at the stage in a running story where you seek a polished and accurate splash and will not be content with the abrupt and raw recording of the latest PA Flash.

You can afford to let a few folios accumulate so that you can judge which way the story is going and decide on the structure of your splash. Clearly you cannot enjoy this luxury too long: if you let too great a volume of copy accumulate you will be too submerged to deal effectively with the later folios. But certainly for the next half-hour or so—depending on the copy flow—you can read what comes, spike some of it, and see how you can marry the rest with the third edition story.

First obtain proofs of the third-edition story and send any corrections to the composing room. Retain a set of proofs and as the evening progresses we will see how and in what way we can use the type.

At this stage, having established that it is possible to handle the lead and two subsidiary background stories, I think we can also assume that the desk executive has decided to assign another sub-editor to these.

On a major running story on an evening paper, you will have two or three colleagues working at your side, perhaps with a separate man also to sort the copy for you. Each of you will take a distinct part of the story, with distinct catchlines, and the intro will be written by yet another man working with carbon copies or reading over your shoulder. In that kind of team effort, the principles are exactly the same as I have set out earlier—keep the copy moving, note your catchlines and key points, and don't panic.

Discarding the background folios, then, the copy flows to you as shown here.

18 44

PAC RUSHFULL 27 PLANE

AS THE 707 WAS PASSING OVER THE VILLAGE OF THORPE (SURREY) FIVE MILES FROM HEATHROW, ONE OF ITS ENGINES FELL AND DROPPED INTO A GRAVEL PIT.

AN EYEWITNESS, MR. IAN MCDONALD, 29, A TOWN-PLANNING ASSISTANT, OF MANSFIELD PLACE, ASCOT (BERKS) SAID: "I WAS ON A SITE NEAR A GRAVEL PIT IN GREEN LANE, THORPE, WHEN I HEARD THE 707 GO OVER.

"AS I LOOKED UP I SAW FLAMES POURING OUT OF THE INBOARD PORT ENGINE.

"THE PLANE CIRCLED ROUND AND, WHETHER BY ACCIDENT OR BY DESIGN, THE ENGINE FELL OFF AND WENT SMACK INTO THE CENTRE OF THE WATER IN THE PIT.

"FORTUNATELY NO ONE WAS AROUND AS THE ENGINE HIT THE WATER. I WAS ABOUT 200 YARDS AWAY.

"HAD THE ENGINE FALLEN SECONDS LATER, IT WOULD PROBABLY HAVE HIT THE SHOPPING CENTRE OF STAINES (MIDDLESEX). FLAMES WERE STILL POURING FROM THE AIRCRAFT AS IT PASSED OVER THE TOWN."

M.F. B.O.S.

---

18 45

PAC   RUSHFULL 26 PLANE

SIR GILES GUTHRIE, B.O.A.C. CHAIRMAN, IN A
STATEMENT TONIGHT SAID: "BOAC DEEPLY REGRETS THE
ACCIDENT WHICH HAS OCCURED TO ONE OF ITS BOEING
AIRCRAFT TODAY AND EXPRESSES ITS SYMPATHY TO
RELATIVES AND FRIENDS OF THE CASUALTIES.

"IT IS A MATTER OF GREAT CREDIT TO EVERYONE
CONCERNED THAT THERE HAVE BEEN SO MANY SURVIVORS.
EVERY EFFORT WILL BE MADE TO ESTABLISH THE CAUSE OF
THE ACCIDENT."

A BOAC SPOKESMAN ADDED THAT THE UNOFFICIAL
FIGURE SO FAR FOR PEOPLE CERTIFIED DEAD WAS FIVE
(REPEAT FIVE).

M.F. B.O.S.

---

18 46

PAC MO   RUSHFULL PLANE (1- SECOND LEAD)

103 ESCAPE AS JET CRASHES ON FIRE.

PILOT TURNS BACK AFTER ENGINE DROPS OFF

CREW SAFE: FIVE PASSENGERS KNOWN DEAD.

MORE THAN 100 PEOPLE WERE ALIVE TONIGHT AFTER
THEIR AUSTRALIA-BOUND JETLINER CRASHED AND BURST
INTO FLAMES ONLY FOUR MINUTES AFTER TAKE-OFF AT

LONDON'S HEATHROW AIRPORT.

FIVE PEOPLE ARE KNOWN TO HAVE DIED - THREE
WOMEN, ONE MAN AND ONE CHILD.

A BOAC SPOKESMAN SAID: "WE KNOW THERE ARE 103
SURVIVORS, BUT WE CANNOT ACCOUNT FOR ANYONE ELSE."
IT WAS UNDERSTOOD THERE WERE 126 PEOPLE ON BOARD,
INCLUDING 11 CREWE.

ALL THE CREW ESCAPED, SAID THE SPOKESMAN.

THE PLANE, FLIGHT 712 TOOK OFF AT 1627 HOURS AND
FOUR MINUTES LATER CAME DOWN IN A PALL OF SMOKE,
CRASHING INTO FLAMES ON A CROSS RUNWAY IN FRONT OF
QUEEN'S BUILDING.

MEM TO CSE: HERE PLEASE PICKUP FROM "PLANE, ONE
LEAD" SECOND PARA, READING:-

"AN EYE WITNESS SAID" ETC.

END LEAD   B.O.S.

1847

PAC   RUSHFULL 28 PLANE

AMONG THE 115 PASSENGERS ON THE BOEING WERE MR.
AND MRS. STANLEY THORPE, ON THEIR WAY TO PERTH,
AUSTRALIA TO SEE THEIR SON WHO WAS BADLY INJURED IN
A CAR CRASH AND HAD BEEN UNCONSCIOUS FOR TWO WEEKS.
M.F. B.O.S.

1848

PAC RUSHFULL 29 PLANE.

A BRITISH AIRPORTS AUTHORITY SPOKESMAN SAID
TONIGHT A SUBSTANTIAL NUMBER OF FLIGHTS HAD BEEN
DIVERTED TO GATWICK CAUSING SOME DELAYS TO PASSENGERS.
BUT THE SITUATION WAS BACK TO NORMAL WITHIN TWO HOURS.
M.F. B.OMS.

1851

PAC FLASH 32 PLANE.

SPOKESMAN FOR AMBULANCE SERVICE SAID "WE REMOVED
25 CASUALTIES TO HILLINGDON HOSPITAL SEVEN WERE TAKEN
TO ASHFORD HOSPITAL BY PRIVATE CAR."

M F L

1851

PAC RUSHFULL D1 PLANE (SURVIVORS)

MARK WYNTER, THE POP STAR, WAS ON THE AIRCRAFT,
FLYING TO AUSTRALIA TO BE MARRIED.

"WE KNOW HE WAS ON THE AIRCRAFT AND WE KNOW HE IS
ALRIGHT," SAID HIS AGENT, MR IAN BEVAN, TONIGHT.

"HE WAS FLYING THERE TO BE MARRIED ON APRIL 19.
HE IS MARRYING AN AUSTRALIAN GIRL, JANEECE CORLASS,
OF MELBOURNE."

MR. BEVAN SAID HE UNDERSTOOD BOAC WERE DRIVING
MR WYNTER AND OTHER SURVIVORS BACK INTO LONDON.

MR. WYNTER'S FIRST BIG SONG "HIT" WAS "VENUS IN
BLUE JEANS," WHICH CAM OUT SVERAL YEARS AGO.

M.F. B.O.S.

1852

PAC   RUSHFULL 30 PLANE.

THE CRASH COINCIDED WITH HOWARD BOUND AIRPORT
TRAFFIC. AMBULANCES AND FIRE ENGINES HAD TO FIGHT
THEIR WAY DOWN A NARROW CENTRE LANE TO GET THROUGH.

M.F. B.O.S.

1855

PAC   FLASH 33 PLANE

NORMAL SERVICES RESUMED AT HEATHROW AT 18.30
HOURS.

M F L

1856

PAC   RUSHFULL 31 PLANE

A LONDON AMBULANCE SERVICE SPOKESMAN SAID TONIGHT:
"WE REMOVED 25 CASUALTIES TO HILLINGDON HOSPITAL,
(MIDDLESEX) AND FOUR DEAD TO HILLINGDON. SEVEN

CASUALTIES WERE TAKEN TO ASHFORD HOSPITAL (MIDDLESEX)
BY PRIVATE CAR."

ABOUT 25 AMBULANCES WERE SENT TO THE CRASH, HE
ADDED.

M.F. B.O.S.

---

18 56

PAC   RUSHFULL 32 PLANE.

NORMAL SERVICES WERE RESUMED AT HEATHROW AIRPORT
AT 18.30 HRS.

M.F. B.O.S.

---

19 06

PAC   RUSHFULL E 1 PLANE (SCENE)

CRASH SMOKE SEEN 10 MILES AWAY

FROM PRESS ASSOCIATION STAFF REPORTER.

LONDON AIRPORT, HEATHROW. THE SCENE WAS MARKED
BY A PALL OF SMOKE WHICH COULD BE SEEN CLEARLY OVER
10 MILES AWAY AT EALING (MIDDLESEX) AND BRENTFORD.

AIRCRAFT WERE STILL COMING INTO LAND AND TAKING
OFF AS RESCUERS WORKED AMONG THE DEBRIS ON RUNWAY
05 RIGHT.

A MEMBER OF THE AIRPORT FIRE BRIGADE STAFF SAID:
"SHE TOOK OFF ON A FLIGHT FOR AUSTRALIA.

"NO SOONER WAS SHE AIRBORNE WHEN A SMALL FIRE
BROKE OUT IN THE INNER PORT ENGINE. SHE SWUNG ROUND
AND CAME IN AGAIN PASSED THE QUEEN'S BUILDING.

"SHE WAS WELL ALIGHT BY NOW AND FINALLY CAME DOWN
OPPOSITE BRITISH EAGEL HANGERS. THERE WERE A SERIES
OF EXPLOSIONS AND WE WENT STRAIGHT OUT THERE."
M.F. B.O.S.

1907

PAC   FLASH 34 PLANE
AT B.O.A.C. LONDON H.Q. SPOKESMAN SAID THAT IN
ADDITION TO 11 CREW THERE HAD ALSO BEEN A
POSITIONING" CREW ABOARD - BEING TAKEN TO FOREIGN
AIRPORT TO MAN ANOTHER B.O.A.C. AIRCRAFT.
M.F. B.O.S.

1908

PAC   FLASH 35 PLANE.

SPOKESMAN SAID THIS HAD LED TO SOME DIFFICULTIES
IN ESTABLISHING IDENTITIES OF DEAD PEOPLE AND
SURVIVORS.
B.O.S.

1911

PAC   RUSHFULL E2 PLANE (SCENE)

THE PORT WING WAS COMPLETELY DESTROYED AND THE
FIRE HAD SPREAD TO FUSELAGE AND TAIL SECTIONS.

BROKEN DEBRIS COVERED THE RUNWAY AS FIREMEN
SHOWERED WHITE FOAM ON TO THE AIRCRAFT'S STILL
SMOULDERING INTERIOR.

THE FRAME STOOD OUT LIKE A SKELETON.

OTHER FIREMEN CARRIED ARMFULS OF DEBRIS FROM
THE WRECKAGE.   THEY BROUGHT OUT BURNT CASES, CHARRED
SUMMER DRESSES BELONGING TO THE WOMEN PASSENGERS,
AND ONE RECOVEREDA BABY'S BATH TUB.

THE REV. STEPHEN BLOOD, VICAR OF ST. HILDAS
CHURCH, ASHFORD, FIVE MILES FROM HEATHROW, STOOD
AMONG THE RESCUERS.   HIS SHOES COVERED WITH WHITE
FIRE-FIGHTING FOAM.

"I WAS GARDENING WHEN I SAW THE AIRCRAFT" HE SAID
"IT WAS LOW AND ONE ENGINE WAS ALIGHT.

"I WENT UPSTAIRS TO GET A BETTER LOOK, WENT BACK
DOWN PUT THE MOWER AWAY AND DROVE TO THE AIRPORT
FOLLOWING THE AIRCRAFT AS BEST I COULD.

1914

PAC   RUSHFULL 33 PLANE.

AT B.O.A.C. LONDON H.Q. A SPOKESMAN SAID TONIGHT
THAT THE AIRCRAFT WENT INTO OPERATION IN THE SUMMER
OF 1962. IT WAS THEN A NEW AIRCRAFT.

HE ADDED THAT IN ADDITION TO THE AIRLINER'S 11
CREW THERE HAD ALSO BEEN A "POSITIONING" CREW ABOARD -
BEING TAKEN TO A FOREIGN AIRPORT TO MAN ANOTHER B.O.A.C
AIRCRAFT.

M.F. B.O.S.

1914

PAC   RUSHFULL 34 PLANE.

THE SPOKESMAN ADDED THAT THIS HAD LED TO SOME
DIFFICULTIES IN ESTABLISHING IDENTITIES OF THE
DEAD PEOPLE AND SURVIVORS.

M.F. B.O.S.

1915

R PAC RUSHFULL   E3 PLANE (SCENE)

"I SAID A PRAYER THAT THE PASSENGERS WOULD BE
ALL RIGHT. WHEN I GOT HERE SOME HAD ALREADY GOT
OUT OF THE AIRCRAFT AND WERE RUNNING TO AMBULANCES.

"THEY SEEMED TO BE BADLY SHOCKED AND SOME HAD
BROKEN ANKLES. I BELIEVE MANY WERE KILLED BUT DID
NOT SEE ANYTHING OF THEM.

"I BELIEVE THAT AMONG THE CASUALTIES WAS A WOMEN
AND THREE OR FOUR SMALL CHILDREN".

TWO OTHER EYE WITNESSES WERE MR. HENRY JONES,
OF STRATFORD ROAD, HAYES (MIDDLESEX) AND MR. RONALD
REVELL, OXFORD COURT, HANWORTH (MIDDLESEX) K.L.M.
DUTY CREW.

MR. JONES SAID "I WAS ON STAND 58 ADJOINING THE
RUNWAY WHEN THE AIRCRAFT CAME IN ITS ENGINE WAS IN
FLAMES. WHEN IT CAME DOWN AND STOPPED THE FIRE
ENGINES WERE ABOUT 200 YAD BEHIND. THEN THE AIRCRAFT
BLEW UP.

"BLACK SMOKE AND FLAME WAS EVERYWHERE. I DID
NOT SEE ANYBODY GET OUT. THEY MUST HAVE COME DOWN
THE CUTE ON THE OTHER SIDE OF THE AIRCRAFT".

MF BH

1916

PAC RUSHFULL E4-PLANE (SCENE)

MR. REVELL SAID "I WAS ON THE OTHER SIDE OF THE
AIRCRAFT PICKING UP SOME FREIGHT. AFTER IT HAD
LANDED THE ENGINE WENT AND I SAW PEOPLE RUNNING
AWAY FROM THE AIRCRAFT.

"THEY MUST HAVE USED THE EMERGENCY DOORS. ABOUT
20 OR 30 GOT AWAY AND SCATTERED ACROSS THE RUNWAY,
RUNNING TOWARDS THE BRITISH EAGLE BUILDING."

MFL BH

Surveying this copy and your third edition proof (pp. 233–4) several conclusions emerge. First, the emphasis of the existing lead is correct—only five known dead from a burning plane is remarkable. Secondly, it seems that in the next ninety minutes you can expect a strong run of good copy describing the crash scene. Thirdly, there is some prospect also of receiving copy on survivors—PA has started a separate category on this and, though the copy on DI PLANE (SURVIVORS) is poor at the moment, it does indicate the possibility of survivors being interviewed. Fourthly, in the third edition story we failed to do justice to the drama of an engine dropping from the airliner.

All this will flash through your mind—and so will the immediate problem: in what order and in what manner should you use the unset copy you have and the third-edition type?

With a major running story it always helps to imagine the story breaking up into sections. It helps to sort the copy and it helps to fix priorities more clearly. The agency catchlining is some indication of possible sections, but my experience is that you are best served by rather more sectionalisation than the agency normally gives. This division of the story into several sections is something you do mentally; it is not a formal matter and it must not imprison you in an inflexible treatment of the copy.

In the present story I envisage five sections at the moment:

(i) Intro with the crash news, the number of survivors and dead.

(ii) Survivors' accounts.

(iii) Ground eye-witness accounts of what happened at the airport.

(iv) Ground eye-witness accounts of what happened to the engine.

(v) Formalities, such as Rushfull 26 (the Guthrie statement) and 29 (news of traffic movements), etc.

Section (i) is too important to work on at this stage: it would be premature to do so. Therefore we put on one side any material for the intro: PLANE I Second Lead, Flash 32. We also put on one side the copy from Section (v) because it is least important and does not of itself make a coherent narrative, i.e. Rushfull 26, 28, 29, 30, Flash 33, and Rushfulls 32, 33, 34.

This leaves sections (ii), (iii), (iv). We have nothing worth editing in section (ii), but we can process copy in section (iii) and (iv) and it does knit together. For simplicity and speed, the technique then is to begin editing and dispatching all the copy in sections (iii) and (iv) under a new catchline WITNESS. At a later stage, you will close this and ask for a proof. You will then marry the newly set WITNESS type with the type held over from the third edition. As you send the WITNESS copy keep a careful note of the numbering under the notepad heading WITNESS and of any key phrases or points worth alluding to in the intro. Correct numbering is so vital I must re-emphasise it. Your check on numbering is easier if you can synchronise your own numbering with the agency numbering. Sometimes the agency copy does come out of number sequence, and if you are not careful you can create a dreadful mix-up. Keep in sequence with agency as long as you reasonably can.

So with ninety minutes to edition time, we continue the flow to the composing room by editing as follows:

4th — with PLANE   *WITNESS 1*

IN TYPE 3rd — LIFT

All afternoon dramatic messages of rescue operations were flashed to London Fire Brigade headquarters, and hope increased for survivors....

'Boeing 707 broken back on landing... about two-thirds of aircraft involved in fire... passenger casualties being recovered from tail... possible 70 escaped after crash landing ... search of fuselage for further casualties in progress using breathing apparatus. . . .'

mf

~~PAC RUSHFULL E 1 PLANE (SCENE)~~ *with PLANE* (*Witness*)
~~CRASH SMOKE SEEN 10 MILES AWAY.~~

~~FROM PRESS ASSOCIATION STAFF REPORTER.~~

~~LONDON AIRPORT, HEATHROW,~~ THE *crash* SCENE WAS MARKED BY A PALL OF SMOKE WHICH COULD BE SEEN CLEARLY OVER 10 MILES AWAY AT EALING (MIDDLESEX) AND BRENTFORD.

AIRCRAFT WERE STILL COMING INTO LAND AND TAKING OFF AS RESCUERS WORKED AMONG THE DEBRIS ON RUNWAY 05 RIGHT.

A MEMBER OF THE AIRPORT FIRE BRIGADE STAFF SAID: "SHE ~~TOOK OFF ON A FLIGHT FOR AUSTRALIA.~~

"~~NO SOONER WAS SHE AIRBORNE WHEN A SMALL FIRE BROKE OUT IN THE INNER PORT ENGINE. SHE SWUNG ROUND AND CAME IN AGAIN PASSED THE QUEEN'S BUILDING.~~

"~~SHE~~ WAS WELL ALIGHT ~~BY NOW AND FINALLY~~ *when she* CAME DOWN *and there was a* ~~OPPOSITE BRITISH EAGLE~~ HANGERS. ~~THERE WERE A~~ SERIES OF EXPLOSIONS ~~AND WE WENT STRAIGHT OUT THERE."~~

~~M.F. B.O.S.~~

~~PAC RUSHFULL E2 PLANE (SCENE)~~

THE PORT WING WAS ~~COMPLETELY~~ DESTROYED AND THE FIRE HAD SPREAD TO FUSELAGE AND TAIL SECTIONS. *my*

NOTE FOR INTRO: Pall of smoke visible 10 miles away.

BROKEN DEBRIS COVERED THE RUNWAY AS FIREMEN *witness 3*

SHOWERED WHITE FOAM ON TO THE AIRCRAFT'S STILL

SMOULDERING INTERIOR.

THE FRAME STOOD OUT LIKE A SKELETON.

OTHER FIREMEN CARRIED ARMFULS OF DEBRIS FROM

THE WRECKAGE. THEY BROUGHT OUT BURNT CASES, CHARRED

SUMMER DRESSES BELONGING TO THE WOMEN PASSENGERS,

AND ~~ONE~~ RECOVERED A BABY'S BATH TUB. *mf*

THE REV. STEPHEN BLOOD, VICAR OF ST. HILDA'S, ~~CHURCH~~ *witness 4*

ASHFORD, FIVE MILES FROM HEATHROW, STOOD AMONG THE

RESCUERS. ~~HIS SHOES COVERED WITH WHITE FIRE-~~

~~FIGHTING FOAM.~~

~~"I WAS GARDENING WHEN I SAW THE AIRCRAFT" HE~~

~~SAID", IT WAS LOW AND ONE ENGINE WAS ALIGHT.~~

~~"I WENT UPSTAIRS TO GET A BETTER LOOK, WENT BACK~~

~~DOWN PUT THE MOWER AWAY AND DROVE TO THE AIRPORT~~

~~FOLLOWING THE AIRCRAFT AS BEST I COULD.~~

~~R DAC RUSHFULL   E3 PLANE (SCENE)~~

"I SAID A PRAYER THAT THE PASSENGERS WOULD BE

ALL RIGHT. ~~WHEN I GOT HERE~~ SOME ~~HAD ALREADY GOT~~

~~OUT OF THE AIRCRAFT AND~~ WERE RUNNING TO AMBULANCES.

THEY SEEMED TO BE BADLY SHOCKED" *mf*

~~TWO OTHER EYE WITNESSES WERE~~ [MR. HENY JONES, OF ~~STRATFORD ROAD~~, HAYES, ~~MIDDLESEX~~, AND MR. RONALD REVELL, ~~OXFORD COURT~~, *of* HANWORTH, ~~MIDDLESEX~~, ~~K.L.M.~~ *also* ~~DUTY CREW.~~ *described what happened.*

~~MR. JONES SAID~~ "I WAS ON STAND 58 ADJOINING THE ~~RUNWAY~~ WHEN THE AIRCRAFT CAME IN, ITS ENGINE WAS IN FLAMES, *said Mr Jones.* "WHEN IT CAME DOWN AND STOPPED THE FIRE ENGINES WERE ABOUT 200 *yds* ~~YARD~~ BEHIND. THEN THE AIRCRAFT BLEW UP.

BLACK SMOKE AND FLAME WAS EVERYWHERE." ~~I DID NOT SEE ANYBODY GET OUT. THEY MUST HAVE COME DOWN THE CUTE ON THE OTHER SIDE OF THE AIRCRAFT."~~

(MF) ~~BH~~

---

19 16

~~R PAC RUSHFULL   E4 PLANE (SCENE)~~   (witness 6)

[MR. REVELL SAID: ~~"I WAS ON THE OTHER SIDE OF THE AIRCRAFT PICKING UP SOME FREIGHT.~~ "AFTER IT HAD LANDED THE ENGINE WENT AND I SAW PEOPLE RUNNING AWAY ~~FROM THE AIRCRAFT.~~

THEY MUST HAVE USED THE EMERGENCY DOORS. ABOUT 20 OR 30 ~~GOT AWAY AND~~ SCATTERED ACROSS THE RUNWAY" ~~RUNNING TOWARDS THE BRITISH EAGLE BUILDING."~~

(MF) ~~BH~~

Dual attributions should always be avoided in running stories. Hence the separate attributions written in for Jones and Revell. This means these paragraphs are now self-contained and one can be deleted if necessary.

~~PAC RUSHFULL 27 PLANE~~ *witness 7*

[*The blazing engine fell away,*
AS THE 707 WAS PASSING OVER THE VILLAGE OF

THORPE (SURREY), FIVE MILES FROM HEATHROW, ~~ONE OF~~

~~ITS ENGINES FELL AND DROPPED INTO A GRAVEL PIT.~~

~~AN EYEWITNESS,~~ MR. IAN MCDONALD, ~~29, A TOWN~~

~~PLANNING ASSISTANT, OF MANSFIELD PLACE, ASCOT~~

~~(BERKS)~~ SAID: ~~"I WAS ON A SITE NEAR A GRAVEL PIT~~

~~IN GREEN LANE, THORPE, WHEN I HEAD THE 707 GO OVER.~~

"AS I LOOKED UP I SAW FLAMES POURING OUT OF THE

INBOARD PORT ENGINE.

THE PLANE CIRCLED ROUND AND, ~~WHETHER BY~~

~~ACCIDENT OR BY DESIGN,~~ THE ENGINE FELL OFF AND

WENT SMACK INTO THE CENTRE OF THE WATER IN THE

~~PIT.~~ *gravel pit in Green Lane, Thorpe.*

~~"FORTUNATELY NO ONE WAS AROUND AS THE ENGINE~~

~~HIT THE WATER. I WAS ABOUT 200 YARDS AWAY.~~

["HAD THE ENGINE FALLEN SECONDS LATER, IT WOULD

PROBABLY HAVE HIT THE SHOPPING CENTRE OF STAINES

(MIDDLESEX). FLAMES WERE STILL POURING FROM THE

AIRCRAFT AS IT PASSED OVER THE TOWN."

M.F ~~B.O.S.~~

NOTE FOR INTRO: Engine fell in gravel pit five miles away. Editing change here is because at this point the reader will have read the intro and will know the engine dropped off into a gravel pit.

It will clearly be later than 7.18 when you come to read the next folio, but let us stick to the timings and continue processing the copy piece by piece.

1918

PAC   RUSHFULL 35 PLANE.

AN ASHFORD HOSPITAL SPOKESMAN SAID TONIGHT

NINE CASUALTIES FROM THE 707 HAD BEEN BROUGHT TO

THE HOSPITAL.

TWO HAD BEEN ADMITED, TWO WERE AWAITING THE

RESULTS OF X-RAYS, AND FIVE HAD BEEN TREATED FOR

MINOR CUTS AND DISCHARGED.

THE TWO ADMITTED WERE

"NOT SERIOUSLY HURT1, HE SAID.

M.F. B.O.S.

Transfer to the intro section of folios and retain. The next folio continues the story:

1921

~~PAC RUSHPULL B5 PLANE (SCENE)~~ (witness 8)

[Another airport witness,]

~~/~~ MR. BERT WATTS, ~~25,~~ OF ~~LONDON ROAD,~~ ASHFORD, SAID:

~~"I HEARD A POPPING AND BAGING NOISE.~~

~~"ONE ENGINE WAS ABLAZE, THERE WERE FLAMES~~

~~LEAPING EVERYWHERE.~~

"I SAW IT LAND ALL RIGHT, THEN I HEARD THE PILOT
PUT ON THE REVERSE THRUST TO TRY AND SLOW HER DOWN.
THERE WAS A BANG AND IT BURST INTO FLAMES.

"I SAW PEOPLE PUSH OPEN THE EMERGENCY HATCH AND
RUN ACROSS THE WING. WITHIN MINUTES THE WHOLE
CENTRE OF THE PLANE WAS ALIGHT AND THE TAIL PLANE."

M.F. ~~B.O.S.~~

1922

~~PAC RUSHPULL 36 PLANE (SCENE)~~ (witness 9)

"THERE WAS NO PANIC, ALTHOUGH PEOPLE MOVED VERY
QUICKLY FROM THE PLANE. MANY OF THEM FLOPPED DOWN
ON THE GRASS. THEY SEEMED SHOCKED AND SHATTERED.
I SAW CHILDRENS PUSH CHAIRS LYING AMONG THE CHARRED
WRECKAGE. THERE WAS A CHILD'S DOLL IN ONE OF THE
PUSHCHAIRS."

M.F. ~~B.O.S.~~

Look again at the copy subbed on the previous page as WITNESS 9. You would expect Rushfull E6 PLANE (SCENE) to follow Rushful E5 PLANE (SCENE). Of course the mistake could be in using the slug line (SCENE)—but it is more likely to be in a numeral than a word. You just have to assume that 36 should be E6. Send (via your own wire room) a quick note to PA naming your paper and saying:

RUSHFULL 36 PLANE (SCENE) seems misnumbered.
Please confirm should be E6 PLANE (SCENE)

In the meantime it is best to act on your assumption and edit the folio under your WITNESS catchline. The next folio you see is Rushfull 36, so it looks as if you were right to assume the previous Rushfull 36 was a mistake:

1924

PAC   RUSHFULL 36 PLANE.

ACCORDING TO REPORTS, AN ENGINE OF THE BOEING CAUGHT FIRE AT 2,000 FEET ABOVE THE THAMES AND THE PILOT TURNED BACK TO HEATHROW.

AN EYE WITNESS SAID: "THE AIRLINER WAS INTACT AS IT CAME INTO LAND BUT AS IT HIT THE GROUND IT BURST INTO FLAMES.

"THE ESCAPE CHUTE OPENED TO LET OUT ESCAPING PASSENGERS BUT THE AIRCRAFT WAS QUICLY ENGULFED IN FLAMES."

M.F. B.O.S.

1925

PAC   RUSHFULL 37 PLANE.

MR K. FOREMAN, OF EASTLEIGH END COTTAGE, THORPE, WHO WORKS FOR MARCO'S SAND AND BALLAST

PITS, SAID: "MY COTTAGE IS ONLY A FEW YARDS FROM
THE SPOT WHERE THE ENGINE SPLASHED INTO THE WATER.
MY SEVEN-YEAR-OLD SONE, PHILIP, WAS PLAYING IN THE
GARDEN.

"SEVERAL OF OUR EMPLOYEES WERE WORKING WITHIN
100 YARDS OF WHERE THE ENGINE FELL, "ADDED MR
FOREMAN.

M.F. B.O.S.

Spike these. They add nothing new.

1930

PAC   RUSHFULL   38-PLANE

A BOAC LONDON HQ SPOKESMAN SAID THAT TWO OR
THREE OF THE SURVIVORS, WHO LIVED BEAR THE AIRPORT,
HAD BEEN TAKEN HOME BY CAR.   THEIR NAMES AND
ADDRESSES WERE NOT YET AVAILABLE.

HE SAID THE AIRCRAFT WAS BOUND FROM LONDON TO
SYDNEY. VIA ZURICH, TBL AVIV, TEHERAN, BOMBAY,
SINGAPORE AND PERTH.

IT HAD TAKEN OFF AT 16:27 HOURS - 12 MINUTES
LATE.   THIS DELAY HAD POSSIBLY BEEN CAUSED BY
TRAFFIC CONTROL HOLD-UPS.

MF BH

Spike, nothing worthwhile.

1932

PAC RUSHFULL 39-PLANE.

ALMOST IMMEDIATELY AFTER TAKING OFF FROM RUNWAY
24 RIGHT, THE CAPTAIN HAD RADIOED THAT AN ENGINE
WAS ON FIRE AND THAT HE WAS RETURNING TO LAND, SAID
THE SPOKESMAN.

HE DID A HALF CIRCUIT AND CAME IN ON RUNWAY 05.

THE AIRLINER APPEARED TO TOUCH DOWN AND CRASH
AT THE SAME TIME. IT BURST INTO FLAMES SIMULTANEOUSLY.
MF BH

Hold for intro.

1941

~~PAC RUSHFULL 40 PLANE.~~ (witness 10

[A witness at the gravel pit,,

MR ANTHONY D'MARCO, ~~OF THE FIRM MARCO LTD, SAND
AND BALLAST MERCHANTS~~, SAID: "I WATCHED THE PLANE THE
WHOLE TIME IT WAS IN DIFFICULTY AND I HAVE NOTHING BUT
ADMIRATION FOR THE WAY THE PILOT HANDLED IT.)

IT WAS ONLY ABOUT 200 YARDS IN THE AIR AND I
SAW THE WING WAS ON FIRE—A TREMENDOUS ORANGE GLOW,
LOOKING MUCH MORE THAN IT REALLY WAS BECAUSE IT WAS
REFLECTED IN THE SHINING METAL OF THE FUSELAGE.

THE PLANE WAS ALMOST OVERHEAD WHEN THE ENGINE
FELL."

M.F. ~~P.O.S.~~

NOTE FOR INTRO: Pilot skill. The interview is not closed on copy, so it may continue. Close the quotes and note the name so that you can reintroduce it if there is indeed more. So you write on your pad 'Pilot skill—d'Marco, Witness 10'.

1945

PAC RUSHFULL   E8 PLANE (SCENE)

    CANON WILFRID HENN, 64, WAS ON THE PLANE WITH HIS WIFE, GEORGINA, O GO TO A PARISH IN WEST AUSTRALIA, AFTER SIX YEARS AS VICAR AT BRANSCOMBE SEATON, DEVON.

    "WE WERE SITTING ON THE STARBOARD SIDE JUST LEVEL WITH THE WINGS WHEN WE SAW FLAMES COMING OUT OF THE PORTSIDE ENGINE," HE SAID.

    "THE WING BEGAN TO BURN AND A STEWARD CAME UP THE AISLE TELLING TO PUT OUR HEADS DOWN ON OUR LAPS.

    "HE SAID THERE WAS NO NEED TO WORRY. WE FELT THE AIRCRAFT COMING DOWN, BUT IT WAS A MARVELLOUS LANDING," HE SAID.

MF BH

READ MUTILATION..."TELLING US TO PUT OUR HEADS DOWN" ETC.

    An important folio. It is the first interview with a survivor. But where is E7 SCENE? Put E8 on one side to see if E7 arrives—and also because the first survivor interview is too good to put at the end of the long eye-witness material you are having set. As you put E8 PLANE on one side another Rushfull PLANE arrives. It is the conclusion of the interview with the gravel pit witness. Check your notepad—the name was d'Marco. Edit this folio accordingly and close the section so that you can have an early proof of the witness section for a rejig.

1945

~~PAC. RUSHFULL 41 PLANE.~~

[Mr d'Marco said the engine

~~IT~~ SPLASHED INTO THE WATER IN THE GRAVEL PIT.) — witness 11

~~ABOUT 100 YARDS FROM WHERE I WAS SUPERVISING THE~~

~~BUILDING OF A BAILEY BRIDGE.~~

"I WAS TENSED UP, THINKING OF THE EMOTIONS THE PILOT MUST HAVE BEEN GOING THROUGH.

"WHEN THE ENGINE FELL, THE PLANE TILTED FROM SIDE TO SIDE AND ROCKED, BUT THE PILOT KEPT IT ON COURSE, KEPT IT IN A STRAIGHT LINE FOR LONDON AIRPORT.

"HE MADE A VERY STEADY DESCENT. HE TOOK THE BLAZING PLANE BEAUTIFULLY INTO LONDON AIRPORT ABOUT FOUR MILES AWAY.

"IT DROPPED OUT OF VIEW. THEN I SAW A COLUMN OF BLACK SMOKE RISE ABOUT 100 FEET ~~INTO THE AIR.~~

"BEING SO NEAR TO LONDON AIRPORT WE ARE QUITE FAMILIAR WITH THE TAKE-OFF AND LANDING OF AIRCRAFT. HE TOOK THIS CRIPPLED MACHINE DOWN BEAUTIFULLY."

~~M.P. B.O.S.~~   end witness

As you edit WITNESS 11, note how much stronger is the story of the pilot's skill—the plane 'rocked', but he took it down 'beautifully'.

You now have setting a good three-quarters of a column of eye-witness material, plus whatever you salvage from the third edition. For

the intro you have no further confirmation of the number of survivors ·
or dead, but you have one or two colourful eye-witness phrases and the
praise for the pilot which has just been reinforced in E8 SCENE by a
survivor. Survivor quotes are good for the intro, but if there is one
survivor interview there will be others. You must open a section
catchlined SURVIVOR and start sending that as soon as E7 has arrived
(just as you did with WITNESS). The survivor section will clearly precede
the witness section. There is plenty to do while you wait a moment for
E7 before dealing with E8:

1945

PAC   RUSHFULL D2 PLANE (SURVIVORS)

    LATER, MR. WYNTER'S AGENT SAID THAT THE POP STAR

HAD BEEN AT HILLINGDON HOSPITAL FOR TREATMENT.

    "HIS INJURIES ARE NOT (REPEAT NOT) TOO SERIOUS

BUT WE BELIEVE THAT THEY CONSIST OF SPRAINS ABOUT

THE FEET," HE SAID.

M.F.L. B.O.S.

This refers to Rushfull D1 (SURVIVORS) you have put on one side
earlier—about Mark Wynter the pop star. Spike this but use the
information in editing the earlier folio as the start of your SURVIVOR
section.

1851

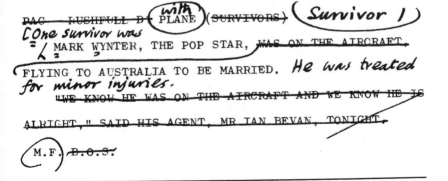

Here now is the missing folio E7 (SCENE). Send it as SURVIVOR 2 noting the information 'no panic' for the intro and also the 'marvellous landing' phrase from E8 which you now send as SURVIVOR 3.

1947

~~PAC   RUSHFULL E7 PLANE (SCENE)~~   *(Survivor 2)*

[TWO MIDDLE-AGED SISTERS *on the Boeing,* DOROTHY AND HELENA TAYLOR, OF MILL HILL, LONDON, *said* ~~WERE ON THE BOEING ON THEIR WAY TO TEHRAN.~~

THEY HEARD A SLIGHT BANG AND SOME ONE SAID THERE WAS A FIRE.   "THERE WAS NO PANIC AT ALL". ~~THEY SAID.~~

(M.F.) ~~B.O.S.~~

~~PAC   RUSHFULL   E8 PLANE (SCENE)~~   *(Survivor 3)*

[*Another survivor,*] CANON WILFIRD HENN, 64, ~~WAS ON THE PLANE WITH HIS WIFE, GEORGINA, O GO TO A PARISH IN WEST AUSTRALIA, AFTER SIX YEARS AS~~ *formerly* VICAR AT BRANSCOMBE, SEATON, DEVON, *said he and his wife,*

~~"WE WERE~~ SITTING ON THE STARBOARD SIDE JUST LEVEL WITH THE WINGS, ~~WHEN WE~~ SAW FLAMES COMING OUT OF THE PORTSIDE ENGINE, ~~HE SAID.~~

⌜"THE WING BEGAN TO BURN AND A STEWARD CAME UP
THE AISLE TELLING/TO PUT OUR HEADS/ON OUR LAPS.

⌜"HE SAID THERE WAS NO NEED TO WORRY. WE FELT
THE AIRCRAFT COMING DOWN, BUT IT WAS A MARVELLOUS
LANDING." ~~HE SAID.~~

(MF) ~~BH~~

~~READ MUTILATION..."TELLING US TO PUT OUR HEADS DOWN"
ETC.~~

1949

~~PAC RUSHFULL E9 PLANE (SCENE)~~ (Survivor 4

⌜THE CANON ADDED: "THERE WAS NO PANIC, ONE OR TWO
CHILDREN WERE CRYING THAT WAS ALL.)

"THERE WERE ONE OR TWO SMALL EXPLOSIONS AFTER WE
GOT DOWN. MY WIFE AND I SLID DOWN AN ESCAPE CHUTE
AND WERE TOLD TO GET AWAY FROM THE PLANE BEFORE IT
EXPLODED."

(MF) ~~BH~~

NUMBERING NOTE: When you write note '4' under the SURVIVOR
section on your pad put in brackets PA E9 SCENE so that you have some
check on the PA sequence.

1951

PAC   RUSHFULL   42-PLANE.

A BOAC SPOKESMAN SAID THAT THE BOEING'S PILOT CAPT. CHARLES TAYLOR, 47, A NEW ZEALANDER, JOINED BOAC IN 1947.

EDUCATED IN HIS HOME TOWN OF AUCKLAND, AND THEN AT HAMILTON TECHNICAL COLLEGE, HAMILTON N.Z.

HE WAS WITH THE RAF DURING THE WAR AS A DOMINION ENTRY RAF APPRENTICE. IN 1941 HE WAS A PILOT IN COASTAL COMMAND.

IN 1954 CAPT. TAYLOR COMMANDED THE AIRCRAFT CARRYING THE QUEEN AND PRINCE PHILIP FROM ADEN TO ENTEBBE AND FROM ENTEBBE TO TOBRUK.

MF BH

Hold for intro or lead section since you now see that the skill of the pilot is one of the main points of the news.

1955

PAC   RUSHFULL E 10 PLANE (SCENE)

A MAN WHO SAW IT ALL FROM THE FIRST FLICKER OF FLAME TO THE GREAT FLASH AND PALL OF SMOKE SAID TONIGHT "IT WAS THE MOST FANTASTIC THING I HAVE EVER SEEN."

MR. BERNARD KEITH WAS IN HIS GARDEN AT EGHAM, SURREY, WHEN HE HEARD THE ILL-FATED BOEING ROAR OFF FROM HEATHROW.

"I LOOKED UP AND THE FIRST THING I NOTICED WAS
THE SUN SHINING ON THE BRIGHT SILVER OF THE AIRCRAFT.
SUDDENTLY THERE WAS A BRILLIANT RED STREAK ON THE
INBOARD ENGINE - JUST AS IF AN ARTIST HAD SPLASHED IT
WITH A PAINTBRUSH. THE AIRLINER SEEMED TO BE ABOUT
3,000 FEET UP AND WAS JUST COMING TO EGHAM HILL.
M.F. B.O.S.

Ideal for your WITNESS section—but don't send it as an Add. Wait till you get a proof and hold this meantime. There is plenty to do headlining SURVIVOR section copy and thinking about the intro.

1959

PAC   RUSHFULL   E13 PLANE (SCENE)
"AFTER THE SECOND EXPLOSION THE FIRE SEEMED TO
SPREAD THROUGH THE FUSELAGE TOWARDS THE COCKPIT. WE
SAW PEOPLE JUMPING OUT OF THE FRONT EXIT."
MF BH

You note that E13, following E10, is clearly out of sequence. Hold this folio. It looks, anyway, like more eye-witness copy.

20 00

PAC   RUSHFULL.

43-PLANE.

THE BOAC SPOKESMAN ADDED THAT CAPT ERIC MILES,

BOAC'S 707 FLIGHT MANAGER, INTERVIEWED THE CAPTAIN

AND CREW AFTER THE INCIDENT AND SAID THEY HAD DONE A

MARVELLOUS JOB.

IN A STATEMENT, CAPT MILES AID: "IT WAS A PERFECT

LANDING DESPITE THE FACT THAT THE ENGINE WAS ON FIRE

AND, OF COURSE, CONTINUED TO BURN.

"THERE WAS NO QUESTION OF THE TAIL FALLING OFF

OR THE AIRCRAFT BREAKING ITS BACK".

THE BOAC SPOKESMAN SAID THE AIRLINER HAD BEEN IN

FLIGHT ONLY TWO MINUTES BEFORE CRASHING.

-M.F.

A considerable strengthening of the intro feature on pilot's skill. With half-an-hour to copy deadline should you begin work on the intro and the rejig—the marrying of all your new copy and the third edition type? If you have the proof of the WITNESS section now (closed fifteen minutes earlier), you have three parts of the puzzle physically available for shaping: you have the third-edition proof; the proof of the witness section; your notepad notes for the intro. You are still running SURVIVOR copy and will need to close it fairly soon if there is to be any hope of having a proof. So for the next five minutes concentrate on the rejig and intro. Keep one eye open for any further Flashes on the number of survivors and any other folio on SURVIVORS which will enable you to close the section. We therefore ignore Rushfull E11 PLANE (SCENE) and RUSHFULL E12 (SCENE) which are still more eye-witness copy around 8 p.m., but quickly edit another two folios on survivors at **8.6** p.m. (D3) and **8.7** p.m. (D4). Paste the two on one copy sheet and close this section.

PAC ~~RUSHFULL~~ ~~D9 (PLANE~~ (SURVIVORS 5)

[ONE OF THE SURVIVORS TAKEN TO HILLINGDON HOSPITAL,
75-YEAR-OLD MISS MARJORIE RASSELL, OF HOLLAND PARK,
WEST LONDON, ~~WHO WAS ON HER WAY TO TEHERAN FOR A~~
~~HOLIDAY IN PERSIA AND INDIA.~~

~~MISS RASSELL~~ SAID that AFTER THE PLANE HAD BEEN AIRBORNE
FOR JUST A FEW MINUTES, SHE LOOKED OUT FROM HER PORT-
SIDE SEAT AND SAW WHAT SHE THOUGHT WAS PART OF THE
WING FALL OFF. FLAMES BEGAN TO SHOOT OUT OF THE
ENGINE.

PAC ~~RUSHFULL~~ ~~D4 PLANE (SURVIVORS)~~

MISS RASSELL ~~SAID~~ (NP) [THERE WAS NO PANIC AS THE AIR-
CRAFT ~~TOUCHED DOWN. AS IT~~ CAME TO A STOP, THE CABIN
BEGAN TO FILL WITH DENSE BLACK, OILY SMOKE.

~~SHE SAID SHE GATHERED HER TWO BAGS TOGETHER~~
AND GOT TO THE EMERGENCY EXIT. WHEN SHE FELL FROM
THE BOTTOM OF THE ESCAPE CHUTE ON TO THE TARMAC
THAT SHE HURT HER LEGS.

"I WAS HURRYING AWAY WHEN I SUDDENLY FELT THE
~~HEAT AND THE AIRCRAFT SEEMED TO BE ON FIRE," SHE~~
~~SAID.~~

end - early proof, please

~~MF BH~~

As you contemplate the material for the intro, you have the third edition proof (left) and the PA Second Lead (right):

MORE THAN 100 passengers are known to have escaped from a BOAC Boeing jetliner bound for Sydney and Auckland which crashed on fire at Heathrow Airport, London, yesterday. A BOAC spokesman in London said there are 103 survivors.

There were 126 on board including 11 crew who all escaped. A BOAC spokesman in London said there were 103 survivors. London Fire Brigade said three bodies had been recovered.

According to an airport police spokesman three women, one man and a child died.

MORE THAN 100 people were alive tonight after their Australia-bound jetliner crashed and burst into flames only four minutes after take-off at London's Heathrow Airport. Five people are known to have died—three women, one man and one child.

A BOAC spokesman said: 'We know there are 103 survivors, but we cannot account for anyone else.' It was understood there were 126 people on board, including 11 crew.

All the crew escaped, said the spokesman.

Your intro notes are:

Pall of smoke visible 10 miles away.

Engine fell in gravel pit five miles away.

Pilot skill—plane 'rocked' but took it down 'beautifully'.

'No panic—marvellous landing'—survivor.

You also have the pilot's details—Captain Charles Taylor, 47, New Zealander, who once piloted the Queen and Prince Philip. What you seek in writing the three or four paragraphs of intro is to cover all the highlights succinctly, leaving the elaboration for the running story.

You could write the first paragraph as follows:

] MORE THAN 100 people were alive last night after a BOAC pilot flew his burning jetliner with 126 on board back to Heathrow London Airport. An engine fell in flames from the plane minutes after take-off, but in a pall of smoke visible 10 miles away, Captain Charles Taylor made what a survivor called a "marvellous landing"

Let that go as PLANE REJIG I. If there is a further official figure on the number saved it can now go as an Insert: 'more than 100' covers it. You have covered the fire, the escape and the pilot's skill. The second folio of the intro must give details of casualties and of the flight. On casualties you have the following copy in addition to the PA Lead and the third edition proof:

PAC   RUSHFULL 31 PLANE

A LONDON AMBULANCE SERVICE SPOKESMAN SAID TONIGHT:

"WE REMOVED 25 CASUALTIES TO HILLINGDON HOSPITAL,

(MIDDLESEX) AND FOUR DEAD TO HILLINGDON. SEVEN

CASUALTIES WERE TAKEN TO ASHFORD HOSPITAL (MIDDLESEX)

BY PRIVATE CAR."

ABOUT 25 AMBULANCES WERE SENT TO THE CRASH. HE

ADDED.

M.F. B.O.S.

PAC   RUSHFULL 35 PLANE.

AN ASHFORD HOSPITAL SPOKESMAN SAID TONIGHT

NINE CASUALTIES FROM THE 707 HAD BEEN BROUGHT TO

THE HOSPITAL.

TWO HAD BEEN ADMITTED, TWO WERE AWAITING THE

RESULTS OF X-RAYS, AND FIVE HAD BEEN TREATED FOR

MINOR CUTS AND DISCHARGED.

THE TWO ADMITTED WERE

"NOT SERIOUSLY HURT1, HE SAID.

M.F. B.O.S.

PAC   RUSHFULL 32 PLANE.

NORMAL SERVICES WERE RESUMED AT HEATHROW AIRPORT
AT 18.30 HRS.

Write the second folio of the intro, PLANE REJIG 2:

[All the crew escaped, but five people
are known to have died — three women,
one man and a child ○ Four dead
and 25 casualties were taken to
Hillingdon Hospital (Middlesex) ○ Seven
more casualties went to Ashford
Hospital (Middlesex) ○   mf

Spike the Rushfulls 31, 32, and 35. Get the details of the flight and a preliminary on what happened into the third folio. You have Rushfulls 39 and 43 to supplement the New Lead and the third edition proof.

PAC   RUSHFULL   39-PLANE.

ALMOST IMMEDIATELY AFTER TAKING OFF FROM RUNWAY 24
RIGHT, THE CAPTAIN HAD RADIOED THAT AN ENGINE WAS ON
FIRE AND THAT HE WAS RETURNING TO LAND, SAID THE
SPOKESMAN.

HE DID A HALF CIRCUIT AND CAME IN ON RUNWAY 05.

THE AIRLINER APPEARED TO TOUCH DOWN AND CRASH
AT THE SAME TIME.   IT BURST INTO FLAMES SIMULTANEOUSLY.
MF BH

PAC   RUSHFULL.

43-PLANE.

THE BOAC SPOKESMAN ADDED THAT CAPT ERIC MILES,
BOAC'S 707 FLIGHT MANAGER, INTERVIEWED THE CAPTAIN
AND CREW AFTER THE INCIDENT AND SAID THEY HAD DONE A
MARVELLOUS JOB.

IN A STATEMENT, CAPT MILES AID: "IT WAS A PERFECT
LANDING DESPITE THE FACT THAT THE ENGINE WAS ON FIRE
AND, OF COURSE, CONTINUED TO BURN.

"THERE WAS NO QUESTION OF THE TAIL FALLING OFF
OR THE AIRCRAFT BREAKING ITS BACK".

THE BOAC SPOKESMAN SAID THE AIRLINER HAD BEEN IN
FLIGHT ONLY TWO MINUTES BEFORE CRASHING.
-M.F.

Use PLANE 39 as the basis of your PLANE REJIG 3 but write in other details: e.g., from Rushfull 43 you take only the length of time the plane was in the air. Therefore still retain PLANE 43, but cross off the paragraph you have used.

[The Australia-bound plane, a Boeing, Flight No 712, took off at 4.27⊙ Almost immediately 47-year-old Captain Taylor radioed that an engine was on fire and that he was returning to land. He did half ⓐ circuit and two minutes later came in on a cross runway in front of Queen's Building ⊙ The airliner appeared to touch down and crash at the same time. It burst into flames simultaneously⊙ (my

Spike the PA Lead now that you have milked it.

The next step is to follow the new intro with the narrative, taking what you can from:

(i) Your third edition type.

(ii) Your section in type marked WITNESS.

(iii) Your section in type marked SURVIVOR.

Try to imagine the galleys of type as you work on the rejig. Make the marks clearly for the compositor who has to lift sections of it. When you have finished you must have accounted for every line of type: some you will kill, some you will lift. Everything must be clearly marked.

You decide to use some (but not all) of the type from the third edition. Therefore this proof, with your marks, becomes PLANE REJIG 4:   ..

THE RUNNING STORY 271

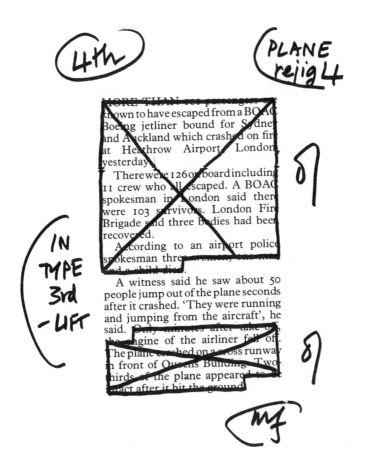

At this point it suits the narrative best to leave the third-edition type and to begin the stories of the survivors. These are in type, catchlined SURVIVORS. If you don't have a proof you do as follows for PLANE 5

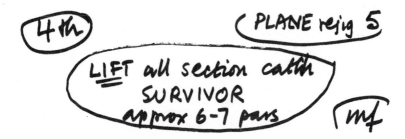

If you do have a proof, you do this:

(4th)

(PLANE reject 5

IN TYPE catch Survivor .LIFT

One survivor was Mark Wynter, the pop star, flying to Australia to be married. He was treated for minor injuries.

Two middle-aged sisters on the Boeing, Dorothy and Helena Taylor, of Mill Hill, London, said they heard a slight bang and someone said there was a fire. 'There was no panic at all.'

Another survivor, Canon Wilfred Henn, 64, formerly vicar at Branscombe, Seaton, Devon, said he and his wife, sitting on the starboard side just level with the wings, saw flames coming out of the port-side engine.

'The wing began to burn and a steward came up the aisle telling us to put our heads down on our laps.

'He said there was no need to worry. We felt the aircraft coming down, but it was a marvellous landing.'

The canon added: 'There was no panic, one or two children were crying, that was all. There were one or two small explosions after we got down. My wife and I slid down an escape chute and were told to get away from the plane before it exploded.'

One of the survivors taken to Hillingdon Hospital, 75-year-old Miss Marjorie Rassell, of Holland Park, West London, said that after the plane had been airborne for just a few minutes she looked out from her port-side seat and saw what she thought was part of the wing fall off. Flames began to shoot out of the engine.

There was no panic. As the aircraft came to a stop, the cabin began to fill with dense, black, oily smoke.

(mf

Part of the WITNESS section proof is PLANE REJIG 6:

The crash scene was marked by a pall of smoke which could be seen clearly over 10 miles away at Ealing (Middlesex) and Brentford.

Aircraft were still coming into land and taking off as rescuers worked among the debris on Runway 05 right. A member of the Airport Fire Brigade staff said: 'She was well alight when she came down and there was a series of explosions.' The port wing was destroyed and the fire had spread to fuselage and tail sections.

Broken debris covered the runway as firemen showered white foam on to the aircraft's still smouldering interior. The frame stood out like a skeleton.

Other firemen carried armfuls of debris from the wreckage. They brought out burnt cases, charred summer dresses belonging to the women passengers and recovered a baby's bath tub.

Break off here and use Rushfull E10 (SCENE) which you have put aside. It becomes PLANE REJIG 7.

~~PAG RUSHFULL E 10 PLANE (SCENE)~~ (Plane rejig 7

A MAN WHO SAW IT ALL FROM THE FIRST FLICKER OF FLAME TO THE GREAT FLASH AND PALL OF SMOKE SAID: "IT WAS THE MOST FANTASTIC THING I HAVE EVER SEEN."

MR. BERNARD KEITH WAS IN HIS GARDEN AT EGHAM, SURREY, WHEN HE HEARD THE ~~ILL-FATED~~ BOEING ROAR OFF FROM HEATHROW.

"I LOOKED UP AND THE FIRST THING I NOTICED WAS THE SUN SHINING ON THE BRIGHT SILVER OF THE AIRCRAFT. SUDDENLY THERE WAS A BRILLIANT RED STREAK ON THE INBOARD ENGINE—JUST AS IF AN ARTIST HAD SPLASHED IT WITH A PAINTBRUSH. THE AIRLINER SEEMED TO BE ABOUT 3,000 FEET UP AND WAS JUST COMING TO EGHAM HILL.

M.F. ~~B.O.S~~

Now pick up the WITNESS section proof:

4th

IN TYPE
—catch
Witness

PLANE rejig 8

LIFT

All afternoon dramatic messages of rescue operations were flashed to London Fire Brigade headquarters and hope increased for survivors.

'Boeing 707 broken back on landing. About two-thirds of aircraft involved in fire ... passenger casualties being recovered from tail ...

possible 70 escaped after crash landing . . . search of fuselage for further
casualties in progress using breathing apparatus . . .'

The crash scene was marked by
a pall of smoke which could be seen
clearly over 10 miles away at Ealing
(Middlesex) and Brentford.

The Rev. Stephen Blood, vicar
of St. Hilda's, Ashford, five miles
from Heathrow, stood among the
rescuers. 'I said a prayer that the
passengers would be all right. Some
were running to ambulances. They
seemed to be badly shocked.'

Mr. Henry Jones of Hayes,
Middlesex, and Mr. Ronald Revell,
of Hanworth, Middlesex, also described what happened.

'When the aircraft came in its
engine was in flames,' said Mr.
Jones. 'When it came down and
stopped the fire engines were about
200 yards behind. Then the aircraft
blew up. Black smoke and flame was
everywhere.'

Mr. Revell said: 'After it had
landed the engine went and I saw
people running away. They must
have used the emergency doors.
About 20 or 30 scattered across the
runway.'

The blazing engine fell away as
the 707 was passing over the village
of Thorpe (Surrey), five miles from
Heathrow. Mr. Ian McDonald said:
'As I looked up I saw flames pouring
out of the inboard port engine. The
plane circled round and the engine
fell off and went smack into the
centre of the water in the gravel pit
in Green Lane, Thorpe.

'Had the engine fallen seconds
later, it would probably have hit
the shopping centre of Staines
(Middlesex). Flames were still pouring from the aircraft as it passed
over the town.'

Another airport witness, Mr. Bert
Watts of Ashford, said: 'I saw it land
all right, then I heard the pilot put on
the reverse thrust to try and slow her
down. There was a bang and she
burst into flames.

'I saw people push open the emergency hatch and run across the wing.
Within minutes the whole centre of
the plane was alight and the tail
plane.

'There was no panic, although
people moved very quickly from the
plane. Many of them flopped down
on the grass. They seemed shocked
and shattered. I saw children's push
chairs lying among the charred
wreckage. There was a child's doll
in one of the push chairs.'

A witness at the gravel pit, Mr.
Anthony d'Marco, said: 'I watched
the plane the whole time it was in
difficulty and I have nothing but
admiration for the way the pilot
handled it. It was only about 200
yards in the air and I saw the wing
was on fire—a tremendous orange
glow, looking much more than it
really was because it was reflected
in the shining metal of the fuselage.
The plane was almost overhead when
the engine fell.'

Mr. d'Marco said the engine
splashed into the water in the gravel
pit. 'I was tensed up, thinking of the
emotions the pilot must have been
going through. When the engine
fell, the plane tilted from side to side
and rocked, but the pilot kept it on
course, kept it in a straight line for
London Airport.

'He made a very steady descent.
He took the blazing plane beautifully
into London Airport about four
miles away. It dropped out of view.
Then I saw a column of black smoke
rise about 100ft.

'Being so near to London Airport
we are familiar with the take-off and
landing of aircraft. He took this
crippled machine down beautifully.'

You still have PLANE 43 (the interview with the BOAC Flight Manager), which fits in neatly here as REJIG 9. PLANE 42, thoroughly milked, can be spiked.

~~PAC RUSHFULL.~~

~~43 PLANE~~. *(Plane rejig 9*

~~THE BOAC SPOKESMAN ADDED THAT~~ [CAP*tain* ERIC MILES, BOAC'S 707 FLIGHT MANAGER, *who* [INTERVIEWED THE CAPTAIN AND CREW ~~AFTER THE INCIDENT AND~~ SAID THEY HAD DONE A MARVELLOUS JOB.

~~IN A STATEMENT, CAPT MILES AID.~~ "IT WAS A PERFECT LANDING DESPITE THE FACT THAT THE ENGINE WAS ON FIRE AND/ OF COURSE/ CONTINUED TO BURN."

~~"THERE WAS NO QUESTION OF THE TAIL FALLING OFF OR THE AIRCRAFT BREAKING ITS BACK".~~

~~THE BOAC SPOKESMAN SAID THE AIRLINER HAD BEEN IN FLIGHT ONLY TWO MINUTES BEFORE CRASHING.~~

 M.F.

There still remains the rest of the third-edition type unaccounted for. Use what you want and mark the rest for kill.

4th **PLANE** Rejig 10

~~Almost immediately after take-off he pilot, Captain Charles Taylor, radioed that he had an engine on fire and was returning. The liner executed a left turn and immediately on touch-down crashed and burst into flames. The plane, call sign Whisky Echo, took off at 4.27 from the main runway.~~

∂

Mr. Jimmy Shand, head of Shand News and Press Services at Heathrow, was an eye-witness. 'We were almost on top of the crash scene', he said. 'We were about 300 yards from the runway and heard a terrific noise due to another plane overshooting the runway because, we were told, the Boeing was in trouble.

∂

IN TYPE 3rd - LIFT

~~We went back into the office. Then, just a fraction later, there was a terrific bang.~~

'We dashed out of the office again and saw the Boeing on the main runway. It appeared to be taxi-ing, almost in the centre of the airport, and almost 500 or 600 yards from the main buildings in the central area. There was a terrific pall of black smoke and flames coming from the aircraft. Two-thirds of it appeared to be intact, with the tail-end still sticking up. But where the galley is appeared to have burnt out'.

~~Mr. Shand continued: 'We heard at least four distinct bangs which would have been some of the petrol going up, and then we saw a lot of people getting out. They were jumping from the plane and running quickly away. It was only seconds after it had come down.~~

'We estimated that at least 50 got out and perhaps as many as 70 others might also have got out, but the smoke prevented us from keeping a continual watch. White smoke came from the tail end of the plane which was surrounded by fire engines.

'There seemed a good chance that the pilot and crew were safe because the nose appeared to be perfectly intact.

'At the same time as we saw the black smoke when it first crashed, we saw quite a lot of flames, but these did not appear to be anywhere near as great as the smoke. There were flames coming from the tail end.'

A Board of Trade spokesman said later: 'A BOAC Speedbird bound for Zurich developed some form of trouble immediately after take-off at 3.27 and a port engine then fell out. The aircraft executed a left-hand turn and was cleared for an emergency landing.

'When it landed at 3.30 it was already on fire. The fire gained in intensity and the wing fell off. The aircraft came to a stop and the emergency services which had already been called out began to deal with the fire.'

All available RAC patrols in the area were drafted to London Airport after police appealed for help to control traffic. Main roads in the area were jammed with rescue vehicles, homegoing motorists and sightseers.

An airport spokesman said the wreckage of the engine fell in Thorpe and other parts fell in Wraysbury, near Windsor.

The arrival and departure rate at the airport was greatly reduced owing to the total involvement of rescue services.

A BOAC spokesman said the flight number was BA 712. The chairman and vice-chairman of BOAC went to the scene.

Note that on PLANE REJIG 10 I have now marked 'end'. This means you are now in the happy position of having covered all points in the story; accounted for all the type; and closed a long story early enough; expect a proof before going to press. What do you do now? Sieve the rest of the copy on your desk—the section (v) material and the other copy which has been arriving as you worked on the intro. You can now be highly selective about this copy and what else comes. Much of the desk copy will have been overtaken by events; some is of minor importance in the light of the way the news has developed. Don't brood over it or worry about minor details. There may be time for that later. What you must do now is clear the decks and write the headlines. Spike what you can.

Good paragraphs which deserve a better place than the end of the long story should be sent as INSERTS. Only very good material is worth the trouble of an Insert (since it requires being marked on a proof). ADD matter is easier to place since it simply goes on the end of the story. Add matter should be self-contained—it should make sense on its own at the end of the narrative.

Of the section (v) copy on your desk—Flash 33, Rushfulls 26, 28, 29, 30, 32 and Flash 34, 35—spike everything except one paragraph worth sending:

4th

(1 Add PLANE

[Some planes were diverted to Gatwick but normal services were resumed at 6.30₀ Sir Giles GUTHRIE, chairman of BOAC, who was on the scene, promised to establish the cause of the accident ☉

end Add

The next paragraph can also be sent as an Add.

2007

~~PAC RUSHFULL 44 PLANE.~~ (Add Plane 2

[*The* SEARCH OF THE WRECKAGE WAS HELD UP FOR ABOUT TEN MINUTES ~~TONIGHT~~ AS FIREMEN SEARCHED FOR RADIO ACTIVE MATERIAL.

BUT THE WRECKAGE WAS CLEARED AND THE SEARCH CONTINUED. *end Add*)

~~M.F. B.O.S.~~

2011

PAC RUSHFULL D5 PLANE (SURVIVORS)

MISS RASSELL WAS ONE OF SIX PEOPLE ON A SPECIAL MIDDLE EAST TOUR, ORGANISED BY THE WINGS HOLIDAY COMPANY.

AN AMERICAN, MR. WILLIAM RAWSON, 35, OF ANNANDALE, VIRGINIA, WAS ON HIS WAY TO TEL AVIV ON AMERICAN GOVERNMENT BUSINESS.

"THERE WAS AN EXPLOSION AND THE PLANE LURCHED. I LOOKED OUT OF THE WINDOW AND IT LOOKED AS THOUGH ONE OF THE ENGINES BURNING," HE SAID.

"I WAS SCARED BUT YOU DON'T KNOW WHAT TO THINK WHEN

SOMETHING LIKE THIS IS HAPPENING TO YOU. THE MAN NEXT

TO ME SAID, "THIS IS IT - WE ARE GOING TO DIE." BUT

I THOUGHT WE HAD A GOOD CHANCE BECAUSE THE PILOT WAS

BRINGING THE PLANE IN VERY WELL INDEED."

MF BH

The last par has a good line. Send as A INSERT PLANE editing on copy to produce:

~~PAC   RUSHFULL   D5 PLANE (SURVIVORS)~~ (A Insert Plane

~~MISS RASSELL WAS ONE OF SIX PEOPLE ON A SPECIAL~~

~~MIDDLE EAST TOUR, ORGANISED BY THE WINGS HOLIDAY~~

~~COMPANY.~~ [One survivor said:

~~AN AMERICAN, MR. WILLIAM RAWSON, 75, OF ANNANDALE,~~

~~VIRGINIA, WAS ON HIS WAY TO TEL AVIV ON AMERICAN~~

~~GOVERNMENT BUSINESS.~~

~~"THERE WAS AN EXPLOSION AND THE PLANE LURCHED.~~

~~I LOOKED OUT OF THE WINDOW AND IT LOOKED AS THOUGH~~

~~ONE OF THE ENGINES BURNING," HE SAID.~~

~~"I WAS SCARED BUT YOU DON'T KNOW WHAT TO THINK WHEN~~

~~SOMETHING LIKE THIS IS HAPPENING TO YOU.~~" THE MAN

NEXT TO ME SAID, "THIS IS IT - WE ARE GOING TO DIE."

BUT I THOUGHT WE HAD A GOOD CHANCE BECAUSE THE PILOT

WAS BRINGING THE PLANE IN VERY WELL INDEED."

~~MF BH~~   (end A)

---

20 12

PAC   RUSHFULL D7 PLANE (SURVIVORS)

MR RAWSON SAID HEWAS JUST LEAVING THE BOEING
THROUGH THE EMERGENCY EXIT ON THE STARBOARD SIDE –
THE SIDE OPPOSITE THE BURNING WING – WHEN THE FLAMES
STARTED UP.

"JUST AS I WAS GETTING OUT, THERE WAS
EXPLOSION AND, WHEN I REACHED THE GROUND AND BEGAN
TO RUN AWAY, THERE WAS ANOTHER ON".

HE SAID IT WAS SO HOT THAT HE BURNED HIS HAND ON
THE STARBOARD WING AND THE BACK OF HIS HAIR WAS
SINGED.

THE CREW HELPED TO GET PEOPLE AS QUICKLY AS
POSSIBLE FROM THE AIRCRAFT.

HE SAID HE SAW A WOMAN WITH A CHILD IN HER ARMS
SLIDING DOWN THE ESCAPE CUTE.

M.F. RJW   RJW

D6 not yet arrived and this is not worth inserting. Put on one side.

2012

PAC   RUSHFULL

D 8 PLANE (SURVIVORS)

MR RAWSON WORKS FOR THE US GOVERNMENT–SPONSORED
NATIONAL SCIENCE FOUNDATION AND WAS ON HIS WAY TO
ISRAEL IN CONNECTION WITH THREE GOVERNMENT PROJECTS

IN TEL AVIV. HE WAS DRESSED IN HIS TROUSERS, SHIRT
AND PULLOVER.

"I LOST EVERYTHING ELSE, INCLUDING ALL MY
COMPARTMENT DOCUMENTS AND MY PASSPORT".

IN THE NEXT SEAT TO MR RAWSON WAS ANOTHER AMERICAN
WORKING FOR THE SAME FOUNDATION - MR SELIM SELCUK
OF ARLINGTON VIRGINIA.

MR SELCUK SAID HE SAW THE FLAMES SHOOTING
SEVERAL FEET FROM THE OUTER ENGINER ON THE PORT WING
AND ALSO PRAISED THE CREW FOR THE WAY THEY HANDLED
THE EMERGENCY.

Spike D7 and 8 but the next folio, the missing D6, should be edited
and sent as B INSERT.

20 13

~~PAO RUSHFULL D6 PLANE (SURVIVORS)~~   *(Plane Insert* **B**

IRENE MOLYNEAUX, 17, OF WALWORTH, SOUTHEAST
LONDON SAID SHE LOOKED OUT THE WINDOW AND SAW THE
BLAZING ENGINE.

~~SHE TOLD HER FATHER, WHO PICKED UP HIS SON
JOHN, NINE, AND PUT HIM BETWEEN HIS KNEES.~~

"THE WINDOWS WERE CRACKING WITH THE HEAT BUT
VERY FEW PEOPLE PANICKED. ~~SHE SAID.~~

"ONE MAN WHO HAD TO BE PICKED UP AND THROWN
DOWN THE CHUTE, WHEN WE LANDED".   *(end B)*

20 15

PAC RUSHFULL CORRECTION IN 'D5 PLANE'.

READ FOR LONG LINE IN THIRD PARA....

".....AS THOUGH ONE OF THE ENGINES WAS

BURNING," ETC.

END CORRECTION BH

Hard to know where this fits. Put on one side for checking later.

20 15

PAC   RUSHFULL 45 PLANE.

IT IS UNDERSTOOD THERE WERE TWO PACKAGES

CONTAINING RADIO ACTIVE MATERIAL IN ONE OF THE

AIRCRAFT'S REAR HOLDS.

ONE OF THEM BROKE ON IMPACT BUT NONE OF THE

RADIO ACTIVE CONTENTS WERE SPILLED.

IT IS ALSO UNDERSTOOD THE PACKAGES WERE REMOVED

BEFORE POLICE WHO CLEAREDTHE AREA AROUND THE WRECK

DURING THE 10 MINUTE SEARCH HAD BEEN INFORMED THEY

WERE ON BOARD.

M.F. B.O.S.

Point covered. Hold for next edition.

2017

PAC   RUSHFULL E14 PLANE   SCENE)

    RUNWAY 05 RIGHT IS KNOWN TO THE AIRPORT STAFF
AS RUNWAY TWO.   THISIS WHERE CAPTAIN CHARLES TAYLOR
FINALLY BROUGHT THE B.O.A.C. 707 CODE NAMED "WHISKY
ECHO" DOWN.

    A PRESS ASSOCIATION REPORTER WATCHED FIREMEN
PROBING AMONG THE WRECKAGE IN A SEA OF WHITE FOAM.
"THIS IS A HELL OF A THING TO HAPPEN," SAID ONE.

    ANOTHER SAID HIS CREW HAD BROUGHT FOUR DEAD
PASSENGERS.

M.F. B.O.S.

Spike.

2019

PAC RUSHFULL 46 (PLANE.3 Add)

[AS DUSK FELL, POLICE SEARCHED THE WRAYSBURY
AREA, WHERE THERE ARE MANY GRAVEL PITS, FOR PARTS
OF THE BOEING WHICH FELL OFF IN FLIGHT. (end add)

M.F. B.O.S.

    Worth sending as an Add paragraph. This ideal Add paragraph is
information like this which is self-contained.

20 25

PAC   RUSHFULL.

D9 PLANE (SURVIVORS)

MR BILL DEITSCH, 27, OF NEW YORK CITY, SAID HE
WAS ONE OF A THREE-MAN TEAM OF SCIENTOLOGY LECTURERS
TRAVELLING TO PERTH, WESTERN AUSTRALIA, AS PART OF
A ROUND-THE-WORLD TOUR TO PROMOTE SCIENTOLOGY.

"WE WERE SITTING IN THE AIRCRAFT AND DIRECTLY
ACROSS THE AISLE OPPOSITE WE SAW A WALL OF FLAME.
THIS WAS ABOUT TWO MINUTES AFTER TAKE-OFF AND THE
FLAME WAS COMING FROM THE ENGINE.

"ONE OF MY COLLEAGUES ASKED ME IF THE ENGINE
ALWAYS FLAMED LIKE THIS ON TAKE-OFF. I LAUGHED AND
SAID, 'NO, ONLY AT NIGHT'. THE QUESTION THEN WAS
WHETHER THE PILOT COULD BRING THE AIRCRAFT DOWN
BEFORE THE WING DROPPED OFF OR BEFORETHE FUEL TANKS
EXPLODED.

- M.F. -

Not worth using by itself. But the next folio strengthens the lead
emphasis on the pilot's skill. Transfer the attribution to D10, spike D9.
Take the first two paragraphs on D10 as shown below. Delete the rest.
Send as C INSERT.

20 27

PAC ~~RUSHFULL.~~

(*Plane* C
insert)

~~D10 PLANE (SURVIVORS)~~

[Mr Bill Deitsch said that on the plane he saw a ~~"THAT WAS THE WHOLE CRUX OF THE MATTER. THE~~ "wall of flame ... the) ~~FIRE WAS~~ GROWING ALL THE TIME AND THE PILOT BROUGHT THE AIRCRAFT ROUND AND WE LANDED THREE MINUTES LATER.]

"IT WAS A BEAUTIFUL LANDING. THE PILOT WAS BRILLIANT. YOU ALWAYS SAY THIS, BUT HE REALLY WAS BRILLIANT."

end C

~~MRS ALLISON PARKHOUSE, 33, SAID SHE WAS TRAVELL-~~
~~ING WITH MR DEITSCH TO PERTH AND SAID: "I MADE THE~~
~~REMARK ABOUT THE ENGINE. I KNEW ALL THE TIME IT~~
~~DIDN'T FLAME LIKE THAT BUT I WAS JUST HOPING I~~
~~MIGHT BE WRONG.~~

~~"WHEN THE PILOT BROUGHT THE AIRCRAFT DOWN, THE~~
~~STEWARDESS SAID: 'LADIES AND GENTLEMEN, PLEASE DO NOT~~
~~PANIC. WE ARE OPENING THE EMERGENCY EXITS NOW'.~~

~~"PEOPLE WERE VERY, VERY QUIET. THE EMERGENCY~~
~~EXITS WERE OPENED AND THEY PUT OUT LONG CUTES TO THE~~
~~GROUND AND WE SLID DOWN.~~

~~-M.F.~~

(Plane Insert +)
D

~~PAC   RUSHFULL.~~

~~D11 PLANE (SURVIVORS)~~

[LYNAIRE WILLIAMSON, a 23-YEAR-OLD SECRETARY ON
HER WAY HOME TO NEW ZEALAND, ~~AFTER SPENDING THREE
YEARS IN LONDON WAS SITTING IN THE MIDDLE OF THE
PLANE.~~

~~SHE~~ SAID: ~~"I SAW FLAMES ON THE WING AND AT THAT
MOMENT THE STEWARD TOLD EVERYONE TO KEEP CALM.
THE PLANE TURNED, BUT MADE A PERFECT LANDING. ALL
THE WHILE I HAD MY HEAD BETWEEN MY KNEES I JUST
COULD NOT BELIEVE IT WAS HAPPENING."~~

"AFTER WE LANDED, TWO ESCAPE CHUTES WERE OPENED
AND I GOT OUT QUICKLY. CHILDREN WERE SCREAMING AND
THE FLAMES SEEMED TO INCREASE AS WE SLID DOWN THE
CHUTE. WHEN I WAS ABOUT 100 YARDS AWAY FROM THE
PLANE I HEARD THREE BIG EXPLOSIONS".

—M.F.   (end D)

Let this be your last folio, as a D INSERT. You will now have a proof
of the lead, less the Inserts and Adds. Mark on the proof where the
Inserts should go (after the paragraph on Mark Wynter). The Add paragraphs can safely be left to go on the end, where Adds should go.
Simply mark the foot of the proof: TAKE IN ADD PARS 1, 2, 3.

The PA Third Lead has arrived too late for you. Scan it to check you have all the key points covered. You have. Now keep it for possible use next edition.

2030

PAC   RUSHFULL

PLANE (1-THIRD LEAD)

JETLINER CRASHES: "MIRACLE" ESCAPE FOR 103

PILOT LANDS AFTER ENGINE DROPS OFF.

CREW SAFE: FIVE PASSENGERS DEAD.

A 47-YEAR-OLD NEW ZEALANDER, WHO HAS PILOTED

THE QUEEN, BROUGHT HIS BURNING BOEING JETLINER

BACK TO HEATHROW AIRPORT TODAY AND SAVED OVER

100 PEOPLE ABOARD.

THE BOAC AUSTRALIA-BOUND PLANE, CARRYING 126

PEOPLE, INCLUDING 11 CREW, TOOK OFF ON ITS FIRST

LEG FOR ZURICH AT 1621 AND ALMOST IMMEDIATELY FLASHED

OUT A "MAY DAY" MESSAGE THAT IS INNER PORT ENGINE

WAS ON FIRE.

TWO MINUTES LATER IT CRASH-LANDED AND BURST

INTO FLAMES ON A CROSS RUNWAY IN FRONT OF QUEEN'S

BUILDING.   THE BURNING ENGINE HAD FALLEN INTO A

GRAVEL PIT FIVE MILES AWAY.

FIVE POEPLE ARE KNOWN TO HAVE DIED -- THREE

WOMEN, ONE MAN AND ONE CHILD.

"BEAUTIFUL" WAS THE WAY ONE EYEWITNESS DESCRIBED

CAPTAIN CHARLES TAYLOR'S DESCENT. "I WATCHED THE
PLANE THE WHOLE TIME IT WAS IN DIFFICULTY AND HAVE
NOTHING BUT ADMIRATION FOR THE WAY THE PILOT HANDLED
IT."
MF   BH

FOURTH EDITION PROOF

MORE THAN 100 people were alive last night after a BOAC pilot flew his burning jetliner with 126 on board back to Heathrow London Airport. An engine fell in flames from the plane minutes after take-off, but in a pall of smoke visible 10 miles away Captain Charles Taylor made what a survivor called a 'marvellous landing'.

All the crew escaped, but five people are known to have died— three women, one man and a child. Four dead and 25 casualties were taken to Hillingdon Hospital (Middlesex). Seven more casualties went to Ashford Hospital (Middlesex).

The Australia-bound plane, a Boeing, Flight No. 712, took off at 4.27. Almost immediately 47-year-old Captain Taylor radioed that an engine was on fire and that he was returning to land. He did a half-circuit and two minutes later came in on a cross runway in front of Queens Building. The airliner appeared to touch down and crash at the same time. It burst into flames simultaneously.

A witness said he saw about 50 people jump out of the plane seconds after it crashed. 'They were running and jumping from the aircraft', he said.

One survivor was Mark Wynter, the pop star, flying to Australia to be married. He was treated for minor injuries.

Irene Molyneaux, 17, of Walworth, South East London, said she looked out of the window and saw the blazing engine. 'The windows were cracking with the heat but very few people panicked. One man had to be picked up and thrown down the chute when we landed.'

Mr. Bill Deitsch said that on the plane he saw a 'wall of flame . . . the fire was growing all the time and the pilot brought the aircraft round and we landed three minutes later. It was a beautiful landing. The pilot was brilliant. You always say this, but he really was brilliant.'

Lynaire Williamson, a 23-year-old secretary, on her way home to New Zealand, said: 'After we landed two escape chutes were opened and I got out quickly. Children were screaming and the flames seemed to increase as we slid down the chute. When I was about 100 yards away from the plane I heard three big explosions.'

Two middle-aged sisters on the Boeing, Dorothy and Helena Taylor, of Mill Hill, London, said they heard a slight bang and someone said there was a fire. 'There was no panic at all.'

Another survivor, Canon Wilfred Henn, 64, formerly vicar at Branscombe, Seaton, Devon, said he and his wife, sitting on the starboard side just level with the wings, saw flames coming out of the port-side engine.

'The wing began to burn and a steward came up the aisle telling us to put our heads down on our laps.

'He said there was no need to worry. We felt the aircraft coming down, but it was a marvellous landing.'

The canon added: 'There was no panic, one or two children were crying, that was all. There were one or two small explosions after we got down. My wife and I slid down an escape chute and were told to get away from the plane before it exploded.'

One of the survivors taken to Hillingdon Hospital, 75-year-old Miss Marjorie Rassell, of Holland Park, West London, said that after the plane had been airborne for just a few minutes she looked out from her port-side seat and saw what she thought was part of the wing fall off. Flames began to shoot out of the engine.

There was no panic. As the aircraft came to a stop, the cabin began to fill with dense, black, oily smoke.

One survivor said: 'The man next to me said "This is it—we are going to die". But I thought we had a good chance because the pilot was bringing the plane in very well indeed.'

All afternoon dramatic messages of rescue operations were flashed to London Fire Brigade headquarters and hope increased for survivors.

'Boeing 707 broken back on landing. About two-thirds of aircraft involved in fire . . . passenger casualties being recovered from tail . . . possible 70 escaped after crash landing . . . search of fuselage for further casualties in progress using breathing apparatus . . .'

The crash scene was marked by a pall of smoke which could be seen clearly over 10 miles away at Ealing (Middlesex) and Brentford.

Aircraft were still coming into land and taking off as rescuers worked among the debris on Runway 05 right. A member of the Airport Fire Brigade staff said: 'She was well alight when she came down and there was a series of explosions.' The port wing was destroyed and the fire had spread to fuselage and tail sections.

Broken debris covered the runway as firemen showered white foam on to the aircraft's still smouldering interior. The frame stood out like a skeleton.

Other firemen carried armfuls of debris from the wreckage. They brought out burnt cases, charred summer dresses belonging to the women passengers and recovered a baby's bath tub.

A man who saw it all from the first flicker of flame to the great flash and pall of smoke said: 'It was the most fantastic thing I have ever seen.'

Mr. Bernard Keith was in his garden at Egham, Surrey, when he heard the Boeing roar off from Heathrow.

'I looked up and the first thing I noticed was the sun shining on the bright silver of the aircraft. Suddenly there was a brilliant red streak on the inboard engine—just as if an artist had splashed it with a paintbrush. The airliner seemed to be about 3,000 feet up and was just coming to Egham Hill.'

The Rev. Stephen Blood, vicar of St. Hilda's, Ashford, five miles from Heathrow, stood among the rescuers. 'I said a prayer that the passengers would be all right. Some were running to ambulances. They seemed to be badly shocked.'

Mr. Henry Jones of Hayes, Middlesex, and Mr. Ronald Revell, of Hanworth, Middlesex, also described what happened.

'When the aircraft came in its engine was in flames,' said Mr. Jones. 'When it came down and stopped the fire engines were about 200 yards behind. Then the aircraft blew up. Black smoke and flame was everywhere.'

Mr. Revell said: 'After it had landed the engine went and I saw people running away. They must have used the emergency doors. About 20 or 30 scattered across the runway.'

The blazing engine fell away as the 707 was passing over the village of Thorpe (Surrey), five miles from Heathrow. Mr. Ian McDonald said: 'As I looked up I saw flames pouring out of the inboard port engine. The plane circled round and the engine fell off and went smack into the centre of the water in the gravel pit in Green Lane, Thorpe.

'Had the engine fallen seconds later, it would probably have hit the shopping centre of Staines (Middlesex). Flames were still pouring from the aircraft as it passed over the town.'

Another airport witness, Mr. Bert Watts of Ashford, said: 'I saw it land all right, then I heard the pilot put on the reverse thrust to try and slow her down. There was a bang and she burst into flames.

'I saw people push open the emergency hatch and run across the wing. Within minutes the whole centre of the plane was alight and the tail plane.

'There was no panic, although people moved very quickly from the plane. Many of them flopped down on the grass. They seemed shocked and shattered. I saw children's push chairs lying among the charred wreckage. There was a child's doll in one of the push chairs.'

A witness at the gravel pit, Mr. Anthony d'Marco, said: 'I watched the plane the whole time it was in difficulty and I have nothing but admiration for the way the pilot handled it. It was only about 200 yards in the air and I saw the wing was on fire—a tremendous orange glow, looking much more than it really was because it was reflected in the shining metal of the fuselage. The plane was almost overhead when the engine fell.'

Mr. d'Marco said the engine splashed into the water in the gravel pit. 'I was tensed up, thinking of the emotions the pilot must have been going through. When the engine fell, the plane tilted from side to side and rocked, but the pilot kept it on course, kept it in a straight line for London Airport.

'He made a very steady descent. He took the blazing plane beautifully into London Airport about four miles away. It dropped out of view. Then I saw a column of black smoke rise about 100ft.

'Being so near to London Airport we are familiar with the take-off and landing of aircraft. He took this crippled machine down beautifully.'

Captain Eric Miles, BOAC's 707 Flight Manager, who interviewed the captain and crew, said they had done a marvellous job. 'It was a perfect landing despite the fact that the engine was on fire and of course continued to burn.'

Mr. Jimmy Shand, head of Shand News and Press services at Heathrow was an eyewitness. 'We were almost on top of the crash scene', he said. 'We were about 300 yards from the runway and heard a terrific noise due to another plane overshooting the runway because, we were told, the Boeing was in trouble.

'We dashed out of the office again and saw the Boeing on the main runway. It appeared to be taxi-ing, almost in the centre of the airport, and almost 500 or 600 yards from the main building in the central area.

There was a terrific pall of black smoke and flames coming from the aircraft. Two thirds of it appeared to be intact with the tail end still sticking up. But where the galley is appeared to have burnt out.'

An airport spokesman said the wreckage of the engine fell in Thorpe and other parts fell in Wraysbury near Windsor.

The arrival and departure rate at the airport was greatly reduced owing to the total involvement of rescue services.

Some planes were diverted to Gatwick, but normal services were resumed at 6.30. Sir Giles Guthrie, chairman of BOAC, who was on the scene, promised to establish the cause of the accident.

The search of the wreckage was held up for about 10 minutes as firemen searched for radioactive material. But the wreckage was cleared and the search continued.

As dusk fell, police searched the Wraysbury area, where there are many gravel pits, for parts of the Boeing which fell off in flight.

Fifth Edition

The news focus is now sharp: the escape of more than 100 people and the skill of the pilot. It is a bifocal lead. What we have in type in the fourth edition is a tolerably clear narrative but in the next two-and-a-half hours to the fifth edition at 11 p.m. we should be able to improve on the structure of the story, avoid some of the incidental repetition, and exploit any good new material. By this time in any running story, you will have become quite discriminating in what you consider worth setting.

In the early stages of a running story you are glad of any scraps of information. As copy builds up from many more witnesses, you spike a higher proportion. This is not a reflection on the judgment of the agency sending copy. The agency provides a service and it is up to the newspaper to decide how to use it. Rightly the agency will always err on the side of sending too much. Rightly, in a disaster story, you will receive a flood of witness copy, some of it overlapping, some of it in either verbose or rather banal terms. At this stage also the executive editor may have decided that the length of the disaster story in fourth edition is about right for text; other things are happening in other parts of the world which need space and by now, too, dramatic pictures have arrived which need space—and which will supply visually some of the information you have until now had to supply textually. Altogether it is up to you to see that the folios which are superseded or better related in other ways are spiked.

With two-and-a-half hours to fifth edition, we can lengthen the period of judgment before we again set copy. We start reading at 8.30 p.m. with the fourth edition proof (or later a clipping from the fourth edition as it is printed); and two folios of overmatter—Rushfull 45 on radio-active material and the beginning of the PA Third Lead. This material is now supplemented with the new copy for the next hour. I set out the new material below.

The action to take is indicated in the superimposed rough-editing marks; and in the comments. Rough-editing marks are made *as we read* the copy. Rough editing or rough cutting is the editing you do when you expect to want to incorporate copy in the final narrative but you are not yet sure where it will fit best. We therefore do not bother with type marks or catchline. We simply delete what we will clearly not want to use and especially duplication which might, in a hurry, slip into type. It is a moment's work to add later whatever type instructions and catchlines are appropriate.

You cannot afford to read the copy word for word and then rough cut it. You must try to do the reading and the rough cutting almost in the same instant: you can, with practice. In this way you absorb the information and you save time. (In the examples below I have rough-edited only the first two takes: you can imagine your treatment of the others.) You should again be envisaging the story in several sections, so when you have rough cut new copy put it in distinctly separate groups in front of you. One section, for instance, will still be on survivors' stories, another on statements by ground witnesses. If possible keep the folios in these sections in sequence.

2031

PAC   RUSHFULL.

47-PLANE.

B.O.A.C. OFFICIALS AT HEATHROW ~~WERE STILL~~ *said it seemed*

~~UNCERTAIN ABOUT THE CASUALTIES LATER TONIGHT.~~

~~ONE SENIOR OFFICIAL SAID: "WE ARE STILL~~

~~CHECKING WITH LOCAL HOSPITALS. IT WOULD SEEM~~

PROBABLE ~~THAT~~ THERE ARE NOT ~~(REPEAT NOT)~~ MORE

THAN 12 DEAD".

IT WAS FEARED THAT A STEWARDESS WAS AMONG

THOSE KILLED.

--M.F.

Rough edited and retained. The fear about the stewardess contradicts the earlier statement that the crew of eleven was safe.

2035

PAC   RUSHFULL D12 PLANE (SURVIVORS)

Allison Parkhouse said:

MRS ~~PARKHURST ADDED~~: "ONE MIDDLE-AGED LADY

SEEMED A BIT AFRAID TO GO DOWN. SHE WAS SITTING

THERE AT THE TOP BLOCKING US ALL. ONE OR TWO OF US

GAVE HER A PUSH AND SHE SLID AWAY.

"I GOT INTO THE CHUTE AND WENT DOWN. AS I WAS

GOING DOWN, THERE WAS A TERRIFIC EXPLOSION. ~~THE~~

~~PLANE WENT UP. I SHOT OUT OF THE CHUTE AND LOST MY~~

~~HANDBAG. I HURT MY BOTTOM AS WELL. I PICKED~~

~~MYSELF UP AND RAN OFF. SURE, I WAS FRIGHTENED, BUT~~

~~THERE WAS NOTHING I COULD DO ABOUT IT. I HAD TO BE~~

~~CALM.~~"

MF   BH

Rough edit and retain in SURVIVOR pile under paperweight. But who
is Mrs Parkhurst? The 8.38 correction enables you to write in the name.

2037

PAC   RUSHFULL   D13 PLANE (SURVIVORS)

ASKED IF SHE WOULD TRAVEL BY AIR AGAIN, MRS

PARKHURST SAID: "YES, WE HAVE JUST LOST A DAY.

THERE WASN'T ANY TIME ACTUALLY TO GET FRIGHTENED."

AS THE SURVIVORS TOLD THEIR STORIES, GROUPS OF

ANXIOUS RELATIVES BEGAN TO ARRIVE AT THE AIRPORT

SEEKING NEWS OF RELATIVES WHO HAD BEEN ON THE
AIRCRAFT.

AMONG THEM WAS A YOUNG GIRL, ANXIOUS TO KNOW
THE WHEREABOUTS OF HER AUNT: AN OLD LADY SEEKING
NEWS OF RELATIVES, AND A WOMAN NEAR TO TEARS, WITH
THREE YOUNG CHILDREN, CONSTANTLY QUESTIONED AIRLINE
OFFICIALS.

MFL   BH

Spike: Not worth its space.

2038

PAC   RUSHFULL.

CORRECTION.

IN D6 PLANE (SURVIVORS) (TIMED 2013) PLEASE
READ IN FOURTH PARA "MRS ALLISON PARKHOUSE" INSTEAD
OF "MISS ALISON PARKHOUSE" AS SENT.

PLEASE AMEND NAME IN SUBSEQUENT TAKES.

–END

Correct D 12 then spike this correction.

2043

PAC

RUSHFULL 48 PLANE

A BOAC SPOKESMAN SAID TONIGHT THAT 103 OF THE
115 PASSENGERS AND CREW OF 11 HAD SURVIVED THE CRASH

FIVE HAD DIED AND 18 WERE UNACCOUNTED FOR.

"THE 18 PEOPLE UNACCOUNTED FOR ARE NOT NECESSARILY DEAD. THEY COULD BE IN HOSPITAL OR CASUALTY DEPARTMENT OF HOSPITALS, WE JUST DON'T KNOW. BUT THAT IS THE FINAL TOTAL".

HE SAID THE AIRCRAFT WAS CARRYING A NUMBER OF RADIOACTIVE ISOTOPES BUT THEY WERE SAFELY HOUSED IN LEAD CASES. THEY HAD EARLIER BEEN SOUGHT BY STAFF WITH GEIGER COUNTERS. THEY HAD BEEN LOCATED.

M.F. RJ

Spike. Point covered.

2045

PAC RUSHFULL.

PLANE (2-THIRD LEAD)

THE EYEWITNESS , MR ANTHONY D'MARCO, WAS SUPERVISING THE BUILDING OF A BRIDGE WHEN HE SAW A TREMENDOUS ORANGE GLOW ON ONE OF THE PLANE'S WINGS.

HE SAID IT WAS ALMOST OVERHEAD WHEN THE ENGINE FELL, ABOUT 100 YARDS FROM WHERE HIS WORKMEN WERE.

"THE PLANE TILTED FROM SIDE TO SIDE AND ROCKED, BUT THE PILOT KEPT IT ON COURSE, KEPT IT IN A STRAIGHT LINE FOR LONDON AIRPORT. HE MADE A VERY

STEADY DESCENT. HE TOOK THE PLANE BEAUTIFULLY INTO
LONDON AIRPORT".

ALL THE CREW ESCAPED, SAID A BOAC SPOKESMAN.
"IT WOULD SEEM PROBABLY THAT THERE ARE NOT (REPEAT
NOT) MORE THAN 12 DEAD".

— M.F.

Hold with PLANE I—which you received as the last edition went—
for fifth-edition intro. Note this repeats that all crew saved.

2048

D 14 PLANE (SURVIVORS) (INSERT AFTER D2)

MR WYNTER, 25 - REAL NAME TERRY LEWIS - WAS
DISCOVERED SINGING FOR A "LARK" AT A DANCE IN
SOUTH LONDON.

"VENUS IN BLUE JEANS" SOLD MORE THAN 470,000
COPIES.

ONE OF THE QUIETEST OF POP SINGERS, MARK'S
OTHER HITS INCLUDE DURING EIGHT YEARS IN SHOW
BUSINESS "SHY GIRL" "GO AWAY LITTLE GIRL", "IT'S
ALMOST TOMORROW".

HE STARTED SINGING EARLY - THOUGH NOT POP. AT
SEVEN HE WAS A BOY SOPRANO IN THE ELEPHANT AND
CASTLE CHURCH CHOIR.

M.F. RJW

Spike. Since he survived his biography is superfluous.

20 50

PAC RUSHFULL.

D15-PLANE (SURVIVORS)

MRS MELDA WILDAY OF MANOR ROAD, SOLIHULL,
WARWICKSHIRE, WAS ON HER WAY WITH HER HUSBAND
JOHN TO PERTH.

SHE SAID AS THE AIRFRACT WAS TAKING OFF SHE
FELT A SLIGHT BUMP. AFTER THE PLANE HAD BEEN
AIRBORNE FOR JUST A FEW MINUTES SHE LOOKED OUT
AND SAW THE ENGINE BURST INTO FLAMES. "THE FLAMES
SUDDENLY BECAME A HUGE WALL OF FIRE AND SEEMED TO
SWEEP THE WHOLE WING.

"TO ME IT NOW SEEMS JUST LIKE A HORROR FILM
OR A BAD DREAM". HER HUSBAND ADDED: "AS THE WING
WAS ABLAZE, WE PRAYED. I DON'T KNOW WHAT WE SAID
TO EACH OTHER".

-M.F.

Rough edit and retain with the SURVIVOR copy.

20 53

PAC RUSHFULL   F1 PLANE (STATMENT)

PLANE MADE "NORMAL" LANDING SAYS BOAC.

A B.O.A.C. SPOKESMAN SAID TONIGHT THAT ACCORDING
TO CAPTAIN ERIC MILES, FLIGHT MANAGER OF B.O.A.C.'S

707S, IT SEEMED THAT SOON AFTER TAKE OFF, PRESUMABLY
WITHIN A FEW SECONDS, AN ENORMOUS FIRE DEVELOPED IN
THE LEFT WING OF THE AIRLINER.

IN A STATEMENT ISSUED THROUGH B.O.A.C'S LONDON
HEADQUARTERS, CAPTIN MILES SAID: "ALMOST IMMEDIATELY
AFTERWARDS, THE CONTROL TOWER RECEIVED A MAYDAY
CALL FROM THE AIRCRAFT.

"IT SEEMS THAT THIS WAS ALMOST CERTAINLY ALL THAT
CAPTAIN TAYLOR HAD TIME FOR.

MF BH

A new sub-section. Rough edit and retain.

2054

PAC   CORRECTION

IN PAGE "PLANE (1-THIRD LEAD)" TIMES 2030 HEADED
"JETLINER CRASHES: "MIRACLE" ESCAPE FOR 103" ETC

PLEASE READ IN SECOND PARA "ITS FIRST LEG FOR
ZURICH AT 1627" ETC THUS SUBSTITUTING "1627" FOR
"1621"

END CORRECTION   RJW

Correct PLANE I. Spike correcting folio.

20 54

PAC   RUSHFULL.

D16-PLANE (SURVIVORS)

MR WILDAY SAID, "WHEN THE PLANE CAME TO A STOP AND THE EMERGENCY DOORS WERE OPENED I WAS JUST IN FRONT OF MY WIFE GETTING OUT.

"I GOT ON TO THE WING AND HAD TO JUMP. I FELL SEVERAL FEET AND BROKE MY WRIST. THE DENSE BLACK SMOKE WAS COMING INTO THE PLANE MORE QUICKLY AND I WAITED FOR MY WIFE TO FOLLOW ME BUT THERE WAS NO SIGN OF HER. I WAS DESPERATELY WORRIED. I THOUGHT SHE WAS STILL INSIDE".

MRS WILDAY AGAIN TOOK UP THE STORY.

"WHEN IT WAS MY TURN TO GO THROUGH THE EMERGENCY EXIT I COULD NOT SEE BECAUSE OF THE SMOKE. SO I HAD TO TURN ROUND AND GO BACK INTO THE CABIN. I WAS REALLY FRIGHTENED AT THIS STAGE.

"SOME OF THE CREW GUIDED ME TO THE MAIN DOOR - THE DOOR THROUGH WHICH WE HAD ENTERED THE PLANE BEFORE IT TOOK OFF.

-M.F.

Rough edit and retain with D15 SURVIVOR copy.

20 55

PAC   RUSHFULL   F2 PLANE (STATEMENT)

"THE TOWER RESPONDED AT ONCE AND THE AIRCRAFT
WAS CLEARED TO LAND IMMEDIATELY. BY THIS TIME THE
AIRCRAFT HAD LOST AN ENGINE.

"THE CAPTAIN GOT HIMSELF PERFECTLY IN POSITION
FOR HIS FINAL APPROACH ON ZERO FIVE RUNWAY, AND
SINCE THE RUNWAY IS SHORTER THAN NORMALLY USED THE
AIRCRAFT SEEMS TO HAVE TOUCHED DOWN RIGHT ON THE
THRESHOLD".

CAPTAIN MILES SAID IT HAD BEEN A PERFECTLY NORMAL
LANDING. THE PASSENGERS WERE INSTRUCTED TO LEAVE
THE AEROPLANE BY THE ESCAPE SLIDES AND THIS THEY
DID.

NF BH

Put with F1, rough edited.

20 55

PAC   RUSHFULL

E15 PLANE (SCENE)

SURVIVORS WERE TAKEN FROM THE ALCOCK-BROWNE
SUITE AT THE AIRPORT TO THE SKYWAYS HOTEL.

SIR GILES GUTHRIE, CHAIRMAN OF BOAC ARRIVED AT
THE SCENE TO INSPECT THE CHARRED HULK OF THE AIR-
CRAFT AND SAID, "THIS IS A TERRIBLE TRAGEDY THERE

IS NO REASON THAT I CAN THINK OF WHERE THERE SHOULD
HAVE BEEN A FIRE. I SHALL BE CONDIOTING MY OWN
INVESTIGATION APART FROM THAT OF THE BOARD OF TRADE.

"I SHALL BE TRYING TO FIND OUT WHY THE FIRE
EXTINGUISHERS WERE NOT (REPEAT NOT) WORKING, WHY
THE FIRE WARNING SYSTEM WAS NOT (REPEAT NOT) WORK-
ING AND WHY THE ENGINE CAUGHT FIRE".

M.F. RJW

20 56

PAC   RUSHFULL   F3-PLANE (SCENE)

A CHECK CAPTAIN, CAPTAIN MOSS, HAD BEEN IN THE
"JUMP SEAT" OF THE AEROPLANE AND ASSISTED CAPTAIN
TAYLOR.

CAPTAIN MILES SAID IT WAS ONLY BACAUSE OF
CAPTAIN TAYLOR'S SKILL THAT A "VERY MUCH MORE SERIOUS"
ACCIDENT HAD BEEN AVOIDED.

MFL BH

The numbering gives a pause. Presumably SCENE and STATEMENT
numbering have been confused, since Captain Miles is also on F2 PLANE
(STATEMENT). It is a small matter, but query with the agency. In the
meantime, retain and rough edit.

---

21 00

PAC   SNAP OFFICIAL CORRECTION.

IN PAGE 42-PLANE PLEASE READ IN FINAL PARA
"IN 1954 CAPT TAYLOR WAS FIRST OFFICER AND CO-PILOT

ON THE AIRCRAFT CARRYING THE QUEEN" ETC THIS

SUBSTITUTES "WAS FIRST OFFICER AND CO-PILOT ON"

FOR "COMMANDED".

- END CORRECTION

Correct on proof and spike. Retain proof.

21 00

KV

PAC RUSHFULL   D17 PLANE (SURVIVORS)

"BY NOW THEY HAD GOT THE SHUTE DOWN AND I SLID

ONTO THE RUNWAY, BUT I WAS WORRIED BECAUSE ID DID

NOT KNOW WHERE MY HUSBAND WAS.

"I STARTED TO CALL FOR HIM AND THEN HEARD HIM

CALLING ME."

MR. AND MRS WILDAY WERE WAITING TONIGHT AT THE

HOSPITAL FOR THEIR MARRIED SON TO COME TO PICK THEM

UP AT HILLINGDON HOSPITAL. MRS WILDAY ESCAPED WITH

ONLY A GRAZED LEG.

SHE SAID THAT AS THE PLANE WAS RETURNING TO THE

AIRPORT HER MIND WAS A BLANK - "I DON'T THINK I

REALLY THOUGHT ABOUT ANYTHING."

MF BH

Spike: it does not add much.

2I 02

PAC RUSHFULL   E16 PLANE(SCENE)

SIR GILES SAID THE AIRCRAFT WAS INVOLVED IN AN
UNDERCARRIAGE ACCIDENT IN HONOLULU LAST NOVEMBER.

IT WAS TAKEN OUT OF SERVICE AND HAD UNDERGONE A
THOROUGH OVERHAUL.   YESTERDAY IT UNDERWENT A TEST
AND WAS SATISFACTORY.

DURING THE RESCUE OPERATION, THE BOEING WAS
SEARCHED WITH GEIGER COUNTERS FOR RADIO ACTIVE
MATERIAL BELIEVED TO BE ON BOARD.

THE PILOT CAPT. CHARLES TAYLOR AFTERWARDS DECLINED
TO SEE WAITING REPORTERS.   MEANWHILE AIRPORT WORKERS
RECOVERED THE MISSING ENGINE WHICH HAD FALLEN INTO
A RESERVOIR SITE AT WRAYSBURY, NEAR STAINES.

WORKMEN ON THE SITE RANG THE BRITISH AIRPORT'S
AUTHORITY AND ASKED "WE HAVE FOUND AN AIRCRAFT ENGINE.
WHAT SHALL WE DO WITH IT?"

MFL BH

Rough edit and retain with F copy (STATEMENT).

21 17

PAC RUSHFULL.

 PLANE (3-THIRD LEAD).

THE PLANE, CALL SIGN WHISKY ECHO, TOOK OFF AT
1627 HOURS EN ROUTE FOR SYDNEY AND AUCKLAND AND HAD
ONLY BEEN IN THE AIR A FEW MINUTES WHEN CAPT TAYLOR
RADIOED HE HAD AN ENGINE BLAZE AND WAS RETURNING.

THERE WAS A SERIES OF EXPLOSIONS AS THE PLANE
TOUCHED DOWN FROM ABOUT 2,000 FEET. A FLEET OF
FIRE ENGINES AND AMBULANCES SCRAMBLED TO THE SCENE
-- MARKED BY A PALL OF SMOKE CLEARLY VISIBLE MORE
THAN 10 MILES WAY.

WHISKY ECHO, NEARLY SIX YEARS OLD, WAS INVOLVED
IN AN UNDERCARRIAGE ACCIDENT IN HONOLULU LAST
NOVEMBER.

MR BERNARD KEITH, IN HIS GARDEN AT THE TIME THE
ILL-FATED BOEING ROARED OFF FROM HEATHROW, SAID:
"SUDDENTLY, THERE WAS A BRILLIANT RED STREAK ON THE
INBOARD ENGINE - JUST AS IF AN ARTIST HAS SPLASHED IT
WITH A PAINTBRUSH.... THE ENGINE DROPPED OFF....
TURNED OVER AND OVER.......IT MUST HAVE BEEN A MIRACLE
THAT SAVED ALL THOSE PEOPLE ON BOARD".
-M.F.

Retain with PLANE 1 and 2 LEAD.

21 17

RUSHFULL 48 PLANE

A BOAC SPOKESMAN SAID TONIGHT THAT 103 OF THE

115 PASSENGERS AND CREW OF 11 HAD SURVIVED THE

CRASH FIVE HAD DIED AND 18 WERE UNACCOUNTED FOR.

"THE 18 PEOPLE UNACCOUNTED FOR ARE NOT

NECESSARILY DEAD. THEY COULD BE IN HOSPITAL OR

CASUALTY DEPARTMENTS OF HOSPITALS, WE JUST DON'T

KNOW, BUT THAT IS THE FINAL TOTAL".

HE SAID THE AIRCRAFT WAS CARRYING A NUMBER OF

RADIOACTIVE ISOTOPES BUT THEY WERE SAFELY HOUSED

IN LEAD CASES. THEY HAD EARLIER BEEN SOUGHT BY

STAFF WITH GEIGER COUNTERS. THEY HAD BEEN LOCATED.

M.F. RJ.

Retain for intro—but this later information on the radioactive
material means you can now spike PLANE 45, held over from the fourth
edition. You can also delete the paragraph on the fourth-edition proof
and the E16 reference to geiger counting.

21 25

PAC RUSHFULL.

PLANE (4-THIRD LEAD)

ANOTHER EYEWITNESS SAID: "I SAW PEOPLE OPEN

THE EMERGENCY HATCH AND RUN ACROSS THE WING. WITH-

IN MINUTES THE WHOLE CENTRE OF THE PLANE WAS ALIGHT

AND THE TAIL PLANE.

"THERE WAS NO PANIC, ALTHOUGH PEOPLE MOVED VERY
QUICKLY FROM THE PLANE, MANY OF THEM FLOPPING DOWN
ON THE GRASS. THEY SEEMED SHOCKED AND SHATTERED".

AT 9 P.M. TONIGHT A BOAC SPOKESMAN SAID THAT 103
OF THE 115 PASSENGERS AND CREW OF 11 HAD SURVIVED
THE CRASH. FIVE HAD DIED AND 18 WERE UNACCOUNTED FOR.

"THE 18 PEOPLE UNACCOUNTED FOR ARE NOT
NECESSARILY DEAD. THEY COULD BE IN HOSPITAL OR
CASUALTY DEPARTMENTS OF HOSPITALS, WE JUST DON'T
KNOW", SAID THE SPOKESMAN.

-END LEAD

Put with PLANE LEAD 1, 2, 3. Pause a moment to skim through the new lead. You'll see that the new lead covers much of PLANE 48 on casualties. Delete those first two paragraphs on PLANE 48, retaining only the one paragraph on the radioactive material.

21 29

PAC   RUSHFULL.

49-PLANE.

SIR GILES GUTHRIE ALSO SAID "THIS WAS THE
PLANE'S FIRST FLIGHT OUT EXCEPT FOR A TEST FLIGHT,
FOLLOWING A MAJOR OVERHAUL. I CAN'T UNDERSTAND WHAT
HAPPENED.

- M.F.

Retain with previous Guthrie remarks which you see are running in two sections E15 and E16 and now in PLANE 49 and 50. Here is a case where you ignore the PA numbering—it seems astray in any event—and keep the subject together despite the different numbering.

21 30

PAC RUSHFULL.

50-PLANE.

"THE ONLY THING THAT I CAN SAY NOW IS THAT THE
SYSTEM TO STOP THE ENGINE FIRE DID NOT WORK.

"THE PLANE WAS 'ON TOP LINE'. LAST NOVEMBER
IT HAD TO ABANDON TAKEOFF IN HONOLULU AND WAS
SLIGHTLY DAMAGED. IT HAS BEEN OUT OF SERVICE SINCE
THEN.

"WE HAVE JUST INTRODUCED A NEW RE-WORK PROGRAMME
WHEREBY A PLANE FLIES 60,000 MILES RATHER THAN THE
NORMAL 30,000 BEFORE HAVING A COMPLETE OVERHAUL".

- M.F.

Retain with other Guthrie copy. Glancing back at E16, we see that
its first two paragraphs are covered here. Delete from E16, which now
has only the one paragraph about the lost engine.

2131

PAC   RUSHFULL

51-PLANE.

"I THINK THE CASUALTY FIGURES WERE KEPT DOWN
BY THE EXCELLENT DISCIPLINE ON THE PART OF BOTH THE
CREW AND THE PASSENGERS.   IT WAS EXTREMELY GOOD.

"WE WILL BE HOLDING OUR OWN INQUIRY AND THE BOARD
OF TRADE WILL ALSO HOLD ONE".

-M.F.

Useful support for the intro. Retain.

2132

RUSHFULL F5 PLANE (STATEMENT)

CAPTAIN MILES SAID OF CAPTAIN TAYLOR'S LANDING:
"HE HAS DONE A MARVELLOUS JOB, THIS WAS A BRILLIANT
LANDING DESPITE THE FACT THAT THE ENGINE WAS ON FIRE
AND OF COURSE CONTINUED TO BURN.

"THERE WAS NO QUESTION OF THE TAIL DROPPING OFF
OR ANYTHING OF THAT KIND".

M.F.L.   RJW

Already covered in the fourth-edition proof. Spike.

21 32

PAC RUSHFULL E17 - PLANE (SCENES)

AS DARKNESS FELL SPOTLIGHTS WERE TURNED ON TO
HELP THE 100 FIREMEN AND POLICE STILL SEARCHING AND
SORTING OUT THE SCARRED, TWISTED HULK. FLAMES HAD
EATEN AWAY THE PORT WING AND HALF THE PORT SIDE.

PILES OF CHARRED CLOTHES AND **PERSONAL EFFECTS**
WERE LIFTED FROM THE FOAM-COVERED RUNWAY IN CARD-
BOARD BOXES. A PILE OF TWISTED LONG-PLAYING RECORDS,
PLASTIC LIPSTICK CASES THAT HAD MELTED IN THE HEAT,
A DAMP CHILD'S DOLL, TIES AND POSTCARDS.

FIREMEN WERE TRYING TO SORT OUT PILES OF LETTERS
WHICH HAD SOMEHOW MANAGED TO ESCAPE BEING FULLY
DESTROYED.

MFL BH

Retain.

21 34

PAC

RUSHFULL 52 PLANE

AIRPORT SWITCHBOARD WERE JAMMED BY CALLERS WHO
HAD RELATIVES OR FRIENDS ENTERING OR LEAVING LONDON
TODAY.

A BRITISH AIRPORTS AUTHORITY SPOKESMAN SAID SOME
OF THE CALLS HAD COME FROM NEW YORK, PARIS, AND
AUSTRALIA – THE PLANE'S EVENTUAL DESTINATION.
M.F.L.

Spike.

2I 40

PAC

RUSHFULL D19 PLANE (SURVIVORS)

HE HAD A SORT OF PLEASING EXPRESSION ON HIS FACE
BUT HIS FACE WAS AS WHITE AS A SHEET".

MR WYNTER HAD JUST COME FROM HOSPITAL WHERE HE
WAS BEING TREATED FOR SPRAINS TO HIS FEET AND
ANKLES. HE JUMPED OFF THE WING OF THE AIRCRAFT.

HE SAID "FIRST OF ALL I LOOKED OUT TO THE LEFT
OF THE PLANE. I WAS SITTING ON THE RIGHTHAND SIDE
OF THE PLANE NEAR THE WING.

"WE HAD BEEN IN THE AIR ABOUT ONE AND A HALF
MINUTES.

M.F. RdW.

Your last D take was D17, which was spiked. Here it is not clear who is
speaking: hold in D pile of folios.

21 42

PAC

RUSHFULL D20 PLANE (SURVIVORS)

"I SAW THIS ORANGE FLAME WHICH I THOUGHT WAS THE
SUN REFLECTED ON THE WING.

"A STEWARD WAS SITTING IN FRONT OF ME. WE HAD
JUST LOST SIGHT OF THE GROUND. THE PLANE WAS GOING
UP INTO THE CLOUDS. WE STILL HAD OUR SAFETY BELTS
ON.

THE STEWARD JUMPED UP 'KEEP CALM, KEEP CALM
EVERYBODY' HE SAID.

"I WAS ADJACENT TO THE LEFTHAND WING. I NOTICED
A GIRL SITTING BY THAT WING WAS TURNING AWAY FROM IT
I SAW THE FLAMES LEAPING UP. THERE WAS A CLOUD OF
BLACK SMOKE.
M.F. RJ

---

21 43

PAC RUSHFULL D18 PLANE (SURVIVORS)

PILOTED DOWN LIKE A LIFT.

MARK WYNTER, THE POP STAR, SAID IN LONDON TONIGHT
"IT SEEMED THAT THE PILOT BROUGHT THE PLANE DOWN "AS
IF IT WERE A LIFT."

HE DESCRIBED THE CREW OF THE AIRCRAFT AS
"MARVELLOUS".

HE SAID THEY WERE SO BRISK AND EFFICIENT."

HE SPOKE ABOUT A STEWARD WHO AS THE PLANE WAS
COMING DOWN WALKED UP AND DOWN THE AIRCRAFT. "HE WAS
MARVELLOUS. HE KEPT SAYING 'KEEP CALM, KEEP CALM
EVERYBODY".

MF   BH

Now you can deal with D section. It is clearly Mark Wynter who is
speaking on D19 and D20. Take D18–20 and rough edit these folios in
correct order for the D section pile. Continue with this as other D copy
in sequence arrives in the next ten minutes.

22 00

PAC   RUSHFULL.

E 18-PLANE (SCENE)

A BOAC SPOKESMAN SAID THE INCIDENT REFERRRED
TO BY SIR GILES GUTHRIE IN HONOLULU LAST NOVEMBER
WAS A FIRE IN NUMBER FOUR ENGINE – OUTSIDE STAR-
BOARD.

THE AIRCRAFT WAS ABOUT TO TAKE OFF WHEN THE
FIRE WAS DETECTED AND PILOT CAPTAIN KENNETH EMMOTT
BROUGHT THE MACHINE TO A STANDSTILL. FOUR PASSENGERS
WERE SLIGHTLY INJURED.

ALL ENGINES HAD SINCE BEEN CHANGED.

THE FIRE TODAY WAS IN THE INNER-PORT ENGINE.

–M.F.

A previous fire? Retain for intro.

It is now 10 p.m., one hour to copy deadline. We have not retained a great volume of copy for setting, but this is about the right moment to break off from the reading and rough editing to try and construct a new story—a rejig of set and unset material. We can ignore the other copy as we survey the facts we must build into the intro. All we have to do is glance at the arriving copy, and let it pile up unless it is a Flash, the PA mark of priority. At **10.3** and **10.4** p.m. there are two Flashes.

PAC   FLASH

36. PLANE

    BOAC SPOKESMAN CONFIRMED 121 PEOPLE SURVIVED.

MF

PAC   FLASH

37. PLANE

    100 WERE PASSENGERS 10 WERE CREW MEMBERS. OUT

OF 5 DEAD 4 WERE PASSENGERS AND 1 HSXXX A HOSTESS.

MFL

So there are now four elements for the intro—these two flashes and the two intros already written. These are the fourth edition intro and the PA New Lead.

FOURTH EDITION INTRO

MORE THAN 100 people were alive last night after a BOAC pilot flew his burning jetliner with 126 on board back to Heathrow London Airport. An engine fell in flames from the plane minutes after take-off, but in a pall of smoke visible 10 miles away Captain Charles Taylor made what a survivor called a 'marvellous landing'.

PA NEW LEAD

A 47-year-old New Zealander who has piloted the Queen, brought his burning Boeing jetliner back to Heathrow Airport today—and saved over 100 people aboard.

The BOAC Australia-bound plane, carrying 126 people, including 11 crew, took off on its first leg for Zurich at 16.27 and almost immediately flashed out a 'Mayday' message that its inner port engine was on fire.

The PA New Lead is better for emphasising the pilot's skill so eloquently confirmed by now. But both intros suffer from being un-specific. Why not use the pilot's name right away? The point about the Queen is worth giving but it obtrudes too early into the story of a near-disaster. So we write something like this—and have it set:

PLANE REJIG 1

CAPTAIN CHARLES TAYLOR made a perfect landing last night with a blazing Boeing 707 airliner —and saved the lives of 121 people.

Five people died—four passengers and a stewardess—as the BOAC jetliner Whisky Echo exploded in flames two minutes after leaving Heathrow on the first leg of a flight to Australia.

PLANE REJIG 2

Almost immediately after take-off at 4.27 Captain Taylor, a 47-year-old New Zealander, flashed out a Mayday message that his inner port engine was on fire.

As he turned back to Heathrow the burning engine fell off. 'The plane tilted from side to side and rocked', said an eyewitness, 'but the pilot kept it on course. He took the plane beautifully into London Airport'.

Last night survivors joined in praising the pilot and crew. There was no panic. One survivor, emerging from the smoking wreck said: 'It was a marvellous landing.'

We have covered many of the points in the first three paragraphs of the fourth edition and in the PA New Lead 1 and 2: the pilot's skill; the numbers saved; how the accident happened. We have not much colour of what it was like when the plane landed, but let us now see what we can sub on copy and proof. We have spent long enough writing our own words. Spike PA New Lead 1 and 2, and Rushfull 47, whose information has been superseded and pick up the story on PA 3 Third Lead.

The second paragraph of this New Lead follows well—but the fourth paragraph on the previous accident is better covered by E18. Decide to deal with this aspect of the previous fire a little later after covering the drama at the airport. Therefore, edit the PA Lead as shown (the quote in the last paragraph is in type in the fourth-edition proof and we can lift that later).

PAC RUSHFULL.

PLANE (3 THIRD LEAD).

(Plane rejig 3)

THE PLANE, CALL SIGN WHISKY ECHO, TOOK OFF AT 1627 HOURS EN ROUTE FOR SYDNEY AND ACUKLAND AND HAD ONLY BEEN IN THE AIR A FEW MINUTES WHEN CAPT. TAYLOR RADIOED HE HAD AN ENGINE BLAZE AND WAS RETURNING.

THERE WAS A SERIES OF EXPLOSIONS AS THE PLANE TOUCHED DOWN FROM ABOUT 2,000 FEET. A FLEET OF FIRE ENGINES AND AMBULANCES SCRAMBLED TO THE SCENE, MARKED BY A PALL OF SMOKE CLEARLY VISIBLE MORE THAN 10 MILES AWAY.

WHISKY ECHO, NEARLY SIX YEARS OLD, WAS INVOLVED IN AN UNDERCARRIAGE ACCIDENT IN HONOLULU LAST NOVEMBER.

MR BERNARD KEITH, IN HIS GARDEN AT THE TIME THE ILL-FATED BOEING ROARED OFF FROM HEATHROW, SAID: "SUDDENTLY THERE WAS A BRILLIANT RED STREAK ON THE INBOARD ENGINE - JUST AS IF AN ARTIST HAS SPLASHED IT WITH A PAINTBRUSH.... THE ENGINE DROPPED OFF.... TURNED OVER AND OVER.......IT MUST HAVE BEEN A MIRACLE THAT SAVED ALL THOSE PEOPLE ON BOARD".

-M.F.

Complete intro section by going to PLANE 4 Third Lead.

~~PAC RUSHFULL.~~

~~PLANE (4-THIRD LEAD).~~ (Plane rejig 4)

~~ANOTHER EYE~~[A]WITNESS SAID: "I SAW PEOPLE OPEN THE
EMERGENCY HATCH AND RUN ACROSS THE WING. WITHIN
MINUTES THE WHOLE CENTRE OF THE PLANE WAS ALIGHT
AND THE TAIL PLANE.

["THERE WAS NO PANIC, ALTHOUGH PEOPLE MOVED VERY
QUICKLY FROM THE PLANE, MANY OF THEM FLOPPING DOWN
ON THE GRASS. THEY SEEMED SHOCKED AND SHATTERED".

~~AT 9 P.M. TONIGHT A BOAC SPOKESMAN SAID THAT~~
~~103 OF THE 115 PASSENGERS AND CREWE OF 14 HAD~~
~~SURVIVED THE CRASH. FIVE HAD DIED AND 18 WERE~~
~~UNACCOUNTED FOR.~~

~~"THE 18 PEOPLE UNACCOUNTED FOR ARE DNOT NECESSARILY~~
~~DEAD. THEY COULD BE IN HOSPITAL OR CASUALTY DEPART-~~
~~MENTS OF HOSPITALS, WE JUST DON'T KNOW", SAID THE~~
~~SPOKESMAN.~~ (mf)

~~- END LEAD -~~

We have deleted the last paragraph because it is already covered.

Since the scene at the airport has now been subbed, we can deal with Whisky Echo's previous fire. This is best tackled by taking E18 and marrying it with the Guthrie section which we have rough cut. You may remember from the PA Lead, discarded, that Whisky Echo was nearly six years old.

~~PAC~~ ~~RUSHFULL.~~

~~E18 - PLANE (SCENE).~~ *(Plane refig 6)*

[This is the second time Whisky Echo, nearly
~~A BOAC SPOKESMAN SAID THE INCIDENT REFERRED~~
six years old, has been on fire.]
~~TO BY SIR GILES GUTHRIE~~ IN HONOLULU LAST NOVEMBER there

WAS A FIRE IN NUMBER FOUR ENGINE — OUTSIDE STAR-

BOARD.

THE AIRCRAFT WAS ABOUT TO TAKE OFF WHEN THE

FIRE WAS DETECTED ~~AND PILOT CAPTAIN KENNETH EMMOTT~~

~~BROUGHT THE MACHINE TO A STANDSTILL.~~ FOUR

hurt. Since then,
PASSENGERS WERE ~~SLIGHTLY INJURED.~~

ve
ALL ENGINES HAD ~~SINCE~~ BEEN CHANGED. [Yesterday's

~~THE~~ FIRE ~~TODAY~~ WAS IN THE INNER-PORT ENGINE.]

- M.F.

~~PAC   RUSHFULL~~

~~15 PLANE (SCENE)~~ *(Plane rejig 6)*

~~SURVIVORS WERE TAKEN FROM THE ALCOCK-BROWNE~~

~~SUITE AT THE AIRPORT TO THE SKYWAYS HOTEL.~~

[SIR GILES GUTHRIE, CHAIRMAN OF BOAC ,who ARRIVED

~~AT THE SCENE~~ TO INSPECT THE CHARRED HULK OF ~~THE~~

Whisky Echo,
~~AIRCRAFT AND~~ SAID: "~~THIS IS A TERRIBLE TRAGEDY~~

~~THERE IS NO REASON THAT I CAN THINK OF WHERE~~

~~THERE SHOULD HAVE BEEN A FIRE.~~ I SHALL ~~BE~~

~~CONDUCTING MY OWN INVESTIGATION APART FROM THAT~~

~~OF THE BOARD OF TRADE.~~

"~~I SHALL BE~~ TRY~~ING~~ TO FIND OUT WHY THE FIRE

EXTINGUISHERS WERE NOT ~~(REPEAT NOT)~~ WORKING, WHY

THE FIRE WARNING SYSTEM WAS NOT ~~(REPEAT NOT)~~

WORKING, AND WHY THE ENGINE CAUGHT FIRE".

PAC   RUSHFULL.

49-PLANE.   *(Plane rejig 7)*

he said,
~~SIR GILES GUTHRIE ALSO SAID~~ [THIS WAS] THE PLANE'S

FIRST FLIGHT OUT EXCEPT FOR A TEST FLIGHT, FOLLOWING

A MAJOR OVERHAUL.   ~~I CAN'T UNDERSTAND WHAT HAPPENED.~~

- M.F.

PA's Rushfull 50-Plane can now be spiked.

We have still to process the following material which should be quickly visible in the little groups of copy in front of us:

(i) Sir Giles' compliment to the pilot on PLANE 51.

(ii) The rest of the fourth edition type.

(iii) The new set of folios retained on SURVIVORS.

(iv) The E17 folio on the airport scene at night.

(v) The F1 PLANE STATEMENT, basically on the pilot's manoeuvres.

(vi) A folio on the recovery of the missing engine (E16).

(vii) A paragraph on radioactive material on PLANE 48.

(viii) The new material still arriving, which seems as if it is all D section SURVIVOR copy.

We have covered all the main points in the story—the numbers alive, the pilot's skill, the engine falling off, the airport drama, and the fact that it was the second fire in Whisky Echo. The task now is to complete telling the main parts of the story with good detail. There is nothing to add on the numbers alive, but there are one or two details on the pilot's skill and a lot of copy from the survivors on what it was like on the plane. These two should now take priority.

First, do the pilot's skill. Everything that is worth reporting directly on this should now be covered (except, incidentally, you should not return to the subject lower down in the story). The same will apply when we deal with the survivors' stories. Each section should be self-contained. How, then, should we link the end of the intro section to detail on the pilot and then pass on to the survivors' stories? The Guthrie tribute on PLANE 51 can be a bridge to the section on pilot skill. This section is make up of three elements—the Guthrie folio; the F-numbered PLANE (STATEMENT), and a few paragraphs in type in the fourth-edition proof. This is how to do it.

PAC RUSHFULL.

51 - PLANE. [Sir Giles added:

(Plane rejig 8)

"I THINK THE CASUALTY FIGURES WERE KEPT DOWN BY
THE EXCELLENT DISCIPLINE ON THE PART OF BOTH THE
CREW AND THE PASSENGERS. IT WAS EXTREMELY GOOD."

"WE WILL BE HOLDING OUR OWN INQUIRY AND THE
BOARD OF TRADE WILL ALSO HOLD ONE".

M.F.

5th

(PLANE rejig 9)

[The man they wr all praising last night,
Captain Taylor, is a New Zealander who served
with the RAF in the war and joined BOAC in 1947.
In 1954 he commanded the aircraft carrying
the Queen and Prince Philip from Aden to
Entebbe and Entebbe to Tobruk. (mf 9½ folos)

(PLANE rejig 9½)

IN TYPE 4K -LIFT

Captain Eric Miles, BOAC's 707
Flight Manager, who interviewed
the captain and crew, said they had
done a marvellous job. 'It was a
perfect landing despite the fact that
the engine was on fire and ~~of course~~ δ7
continued to burn.'

(mf 10 folos)

F1 PLANE is spiked, but we continue with F2:

~~PAC RUSHFULL~~ ~~F2 PLANE~~ ~~(STATEMENT)~~ *rejig 10*

~~"THE TOWER RESPONDED AT ONCE AND THE AIRCRAFT~~
~~WAS CLEARED TO LAND IMMEDIATELY. BY THIS TIME~~
~~THE AIRCRAFT HAD LOST AN ENGINE.~~

["THE CAPTAIN GOT HIMSELF PERFECTLY IN POSITION
FOR HIS FINAL APPROACH ON ZERO FIVE RUNWAY, AND
SINCE THE RUNWAY IS SHORTER THAN NORMALLY USED
THE AIRCRAFT SEEMS TO HAVE TOUCHED DOWN RIGHT ON
THE THRESHOLD."

~~CAPTAIN MILES SAID IT HAD BEEN A PERFECTLY~~
~~NORMAL LANDING. THE PASSENGERS WERE INSTRUCTED~~
~~TO LEAVE THE AEROPLANE BY THE ESCAPE SLIDES AND~~
~~THIS THEY DID.~~

MF ~~BH~~

~~PAC RUSHFULL~~ ~~F3 PLANE~~ ~~(SCENE)~~ (*Plane rejig 11*)

[A CHECK CAPTAIN, CAPTAIN MOSS, HAD BEEN IN THE
Boeing's *a spare seat near the pilot,*
"JUMP" SEAT", ~~OF THE AEROPLANE~~ AND ASSISTED CAPTAIN
TAYLOR.

~~CAPTAIN MILES SAID IT WAS ONLY BECAUSE OF~~
~~CAPTAIN TAYLOR'S SKILL THAT A "VERY MUCH MORE~~
~~SERIOUS" ACCIDENT HAD BEEN AVOIDED.~~

MF. BH.

PLANE *rejig* 12

A witness at the gravel pit, Mr. Anthony d'Marco, said: 'I watched the plane the whole time it was in difficulty and I have nothing but admiration for the way the pilot handled it. It was only about 200 yards in the air and I saw the wing was on fire—a tremendous orange glow, looking much more than it really was because it was reflected in the shining metal of the fuselage. The plane was almost overhead when the engine fell.'

Mr. d'Marco said the engine splashed into the water in the gravel pit. 'I was tensed up, thinking of the emotions the pilot must have been going through. When the engine fell, the plane tilted from side to side and rocked, but the pilot kept it on course, kept it in a straight line for London Airport.

'He made a very steady descent. He took the blazing plane beautifully into London Airport about four miles away. It dropped out of view. Then I saw a column of black smoke rise about 100ft.

'Being so near to London Airport we are familiar with the take-off and landing of aircraft. He took this crippled machine down beautifully.'

The D-section copy of SURVIVORS provides a neat link between the pilot section and the survivor section. These are the folios you use:

~~PAC RUSHFULL D18 PLANE (SURVIVORS)~~

~~PILOTED DOWN LIKE A LIFT.~~ *(Plane rejig 13*

[Survivor,
MARK WYNTER, THE POP STAR, SAID ~~IN LONDON TONIGHT~~

~~"IT SEEMED THAT~~ THE PILOT BROUGHT THE PLANE DOWN "AS

IF IT WERE A LIFT". *Wynter,*

~~HE~~ DESCRIBED THE CREW OF THE AIRCRAFT AS

"MARVELLOUS".

~~HE SAID "THEY WERE SO BRISK AND EFFICIENT."~~

~~HE SPOKE ABOUT A STEWARD WHO~~ AS THE PLANE WAS COMING
one steward, he said,
DOWN WALKED UP AND DOWN THE AIRCRAFT. "HE WAS

MARVELLOUS. HE KEPT SAYING 'KEEP CALM, KEEP CALM

EVERYBODY'.

MF ~~BH~~

~~PAC RUSHFULL D21 PLANE (SURVIVORS)~~ *(Plane rejig 14*

["A VOICE CAME OVER THE INTECOM TELLING US TO

TIGHTEN OUR SEAT BELTS AS MUCH AS WE COULD AND TO

PUT OUR HEADS ON OUR KNEES.

EVERYONE WAS LOOKING TOWARDS WHERE THE FLAMES

WERE ROARING.

MF ~~BH~~

(Plane rejig 15)

D22 PLANE (SURVIVORS)

(NP) "HEARD SOMEONE SHOUT 'EMERGENCY'.

"I THOUGHT MY NUMBER WAS UP.

(M.F.) ~~NEW~~

(Plane rejig 16)

~~BAG RUSHFULL~~ D23-PLANE (SURVIVORS)

["AS WE HIT THE/STEWARD WAS AT THE EMERGENCY EXIT. *ground the*

HE PUSHED IT OPEN AND SAID 'EVERYBODY OUT'."

~~HE SNATCHED UP THE BAG UNDER HIS SEAT THAT HAD~~

~~HIS MUSIC IN IT AND OTHER THINGS. HE WAS ABOUT~~

~~THREE FEET FROM THE EMERGENCY EXIT. THERE WAS~~

~~NO SENSE OF HEAT.~~

"~~THE STEWARD KNOCKED THE BAG OUT OF MY HAND.~~"

~~SAID MR WINTER~~ "I GOT OUT ON THE WING *and* ~~& JUMPED~~

~~OFF THE WING. I BELIEVE MY WALLET WAS FOUND AND~~

~~MY PASSPORT. AFTER I JUMPED OFF I IMMEDIATELY~~

~~LOOKED UP AT THE WING ABOVE ME.~~ THERE WAS ~~THIS~~ *an*

EXPLOSION ON THE OTHER SIDE OF THE PLANE AND

SEVERAL PIECES OF THE PLANE WERE THROWN UP IN THE

AIR."

(MF) ~~BH~~

(PLANE rejig 17

[A survivor,

run on

~~A witness said he saw about 30 people jump out of the plane seconds after it crashed. 'They were running and jumping from the aircraft', he said.~~

~~One survivor was Mark Wynter, the pop star, flying to Australia to be married. He was treated for minor injuries.~~

IN TYPE -4th

Irene Molyneaux, 17, of Walworth, South East London, said she looked out of the window and saw the blazing engine. 'The windows were cracking with the heat but very few people panicked. One man had to be picked up and thrown down the chute when we landed.'

Mr. Bill Deitsch said that on the plane he saw a 'wall of flame . . . the fire was growing all the time and the pilot brought the aircraft round and we landed three minutes later. It was a beautiful landing. The pilot was brilliant. You always say this, but he really was brilliant.'

,27, who was on the plane,

Lynaire Williamson, a 23-year-old secretary, on her way home to New Zealand, said: 'After we landed two escape chutes were opened and I got out quickly. Children were screaming and the flames seemed to increase as we slid down the chute. When I was about 100 yards away from the plane I heard three big explosions.'

mf

The run of copy is such that we can be even more discriminating with some of the D-section SURVIVOR copy awaiting subbing. Spike D12, D19, D20; as REJIG 18 kill one of the interviews on the fourth edition proof; and continue with REJIG 19 on copy.

PLANE
rejig 18

Two middle-aged sisters on the Boeing, Dorothy and Helena Taylor, of Mill Hill, London, said they heard a slight bang and someone said there was a fire. 'There was no panic at all.'

Another survivor, Canon Wilfred Henn, 64, formerly vicar at Branscombe, Seaton, Devon, said he and his wife, sitting on the starboard side just level with the wings, saw flames coming out of the port-side engine.

'The wing began to burn and a steward came up the aisle telling us to put our heads down on our laps.

'He said there was no need to worry. We felt the aircraft coming down, but it was a marvellous landing.'

The canon added: 'There was no panic, one or two children were crying, that was all. There were one or two small explosions after we got down. My wife and I slid down an escape chute and were told to get away from the plane before it exploded.'

IN
TYPE
4th
-KILL

~~D15*PLANE (SURVIVORS)~~ (Plane rejig 19

[MRS MELDA WILDAY, OF ~~MANOR ROAD,~~ SOLIHULL,

WARWICKSHIRE, WAS ON HER WAY WITH HER HUSBAND JOHN

TO PERTH.)

[SHE SAID: ~~AS THE AIRCRAFT WAS TAKING OUT SHE FELT~~

~~A SLIGHT BUMP.~~ (STET) ~~AFTER THE PLANE HAD BEEN AIRBORNE~~

~~FOR JUST A FEW MINUTES SHE LOOKED OUT AND SAW THE~~ (STET)

~~ENGINE BURST INTO FLAMES.~~ "THE FLAMES SUDDENLY

BECAME A HUGE WALL OF FIRE AND SEEMED TO SWEEP THE

WHOLE WING.)

["TO ME IT NOW SEEMS JUST LIKE A HORROR FILM OR A

BAD DREAM".

[Mrs Wilday said:

~~HER HUSBAND ADDED:~~ ~~"AS THE WING WAS ABLAZE, WE~~

~~PRAYED.~~ ~~I DON'T KNOW WHAT WE SAID TO EACH OTHER".~~

—M.F. —

~~PAO RUSHFULL.~~

~~D16*PLANE (SURVIVORS).~~ [Mr Wilday said: "As the wing

~~MR WILDAY SAID,~~ was ablaze, we prayed₆]

WHEN THE PLANE CAME TO A STOP

AND THE EMERGENCY DOORS WERE OPENED I WAS JUST IN

FRONT OF MY WIFE IN GETTING OUT.

["I GOT ON TO THE WING AND HAD TO JUMP. I FELL

SEVERAL FEET AND BROKE MY WRIST. THE DENSE BLACK

(Plane rejig 20

SMOKE WAS COMING INTO THE PLANE MORE QUICKLY AND I

WAITED FOR MY WIFE TO FOLLOW ME BUT THERE WAS NO

SIGN OF HER. I WAS DESPERATELY WORRIED. I THOUGHT

SHE WAS STILL INSIDE".

MRS WILDAY ~~AGAIN TOOK UP THE STORY.~~ *explained* :

"WHEN IT WAS MY TURN TO GO THROUGH THE EMERGENCY

EXIT I COULD NOT SEE BECAUSE OF THE SMOKE. SO I HAD

TO TURN ROUND AND GO BACK INTO THE CABIN. I WAS

REALLY FRIGHTENED AT THIS STAGE.

SOME OF THE CREW GUIDED ME TO THE MAIN DOOR."

~~THE DOOR THROUGH WHICH WE HAD ENTERED THE PLANE~~

~~BEFORE IT TOOK OFF.~~

—M.F.—

(PLANE rejig 21

One of the survivors taken to Hillingdon Hospital, 75-year-old Miss Marjorie Rassell, of Holland Park, West London, said that after the plane had been airborne for just a few minutes she looked out from her port-side seat and saw what she thought was part of the wing fall off. Flames began to shoot out of the engine.

There was no panic. As the aircraft came to a stop, the cabin began to fill with dense, black, oily smoke.

One survivor said: 'The man next to me said "This is it—we are going to die". But I thought we had a good chance because the pilot was bringing the plane in very well indeed.'

IN TYPE 4th- LIFT

(m.f.

That accounts for all the SURVIVOR section copy we held before beginning to write the intro. Four further folios have arrived:

2201

PAC   RUSHFULL.

D27-PLANE (SURVIVORS)   LECTURERS.

   THREE SURVIVORS WERE SCIENTOLOGY LECTURERS
BILL DEITCH AGED 27 FROM NEW YORK: BRIAN RESO AGED
28 FROM JOHANNESBURG AND MRS ALLISON PARKHOUSE AGED
33 FROM CAPE TOWN.

   MRS PARKHOUSE, THE MOTHER OF THREE CHILDREN,
SAID: "WE HAD BEEN CLIMBING FOR ABOUT TWO MINUTES
WHEN I LOOKED OUT OF THE PORTHOLE AND SAW FLAMES
COMING FROM THE ENGINE.

   "I TURNED TO BILL AND HE ALSO LOOKED.   I THOUGHT
IT WAS USUAL, BUT HE SAID IT WAS NOT AND RAN UP THE
AISLE TO TELL THE CAPTAIN.

—M.F.

2203

PAC   RUSHFULL.

D28-PLANE (SURVIVORS).

   "BY THIS TIME THE FLAMES WERE GOING LIKE HELL
AND WE WERE STILL CLIMBING.

   "WE TURNED TWO OR THREE MINUTES LATER AND I HEARD
A STEWARDESS TELLING THE CHILDREN TO PUT THEIR HEADS

DOWN AND THEIR HANDS OVER THEIR HEADS. IT WAS A VERY
SMOOTH LANDING.

"IMMEDIATELY AFTERWARDS I HEARD THE CAPTAIN TELL-
ING US TO USE THE EMERGENCY EXIT. I PICKED UP MY
BAGS BEFORE MAKING FOR THE EXIT.

"I WAS HALFWAY DOWN THE EMERGENCY SHOOT WHEN
THE ENGINE EXPLODED.

2205

PAC   RUSHFULL.

D29-PLANE (SURVIVORS).

"I WAS BLOWN OFF THE SHOOT ONTO THE TARMAC AND
WAS NOT BADLY HURT ALTHOUGH I LOST ONE OF MY SHOES
AND MY HANDBAG".

MR BILL DEITCH WHO HAD BEEN STAYING IN TUNBRIDGE
WELLS, KENT, WITH THE TWO OTHER MEMBERS OF THE
LECTURE TEAM SAID: "I REMEMBER THINKING AFTER I HAD
SEEN THE ENGINE ON FIRE 'WE HAVE GOT A CHOICE, EITHER
HE LANDS, OR THE WING WILL FALL OFF AND WE WILL HAVE
HAD IT'.

"I REMEMBER TURNING TO ALLISON AND SHE WAS
ONVIOUSLY THINKING THE SAME THING BECAUSE WE BOTH
LAUGHED. IT WAS SO INAPPROPRIATE.

"THE ONLY SIGHT OF PANIC WERE THE MOTHERS SCREAMING
FOR THEIR CHILDREN, BUT ON THE WHOLE I'D SAY EVERYONE
WAS FANTASTICALLY CALM. - M.F.

22 06

PAC   RUSHFULL.

D30-PLANE (SURVIVORS)

"I DON'T KNOW HOW MANY PEOPLE WERE LEFT BEHIND ME
AFTER I LEFT THE PLANE.   I WAS NOT CARING TOO MUCH
ABOUT THEM".

THE THREE ARE ON A WORLD LECTURE TOUR FROM THE
CHURCH OF SCIENTOLOGY OF CALIFORNIA.

ADDED MR DEITCH   "AS SOON AS WE CAN GET INTO
SOME CLEAN CLOTHES WE WILL TRY AND BE ON OUR WAY
AGAIN.   WE HAVE A LECTURE IN PERTH, AUSTRALIA TO GET
TO".

— M.F.L.

We already have Mr Deitsch. There is nothing much new here. Spike
these folios. At 10.20 p.m. there is no further Survivor copy, so pro-
visionally decided to end the section on survivors in the running story.
Very good Survivor copy, if any, can always be sent as an Insert. The
most urgent task now is to complete the rejig and specially to account
for all the fourth-edition type, either by killing it or lifting it into fifth
edition. Begin to deal with that now. As you do, glance at further copy
arriving and copy as yet unplaced, in case it fits in with the section of the
story you are currently editing. When we mark the fourth-edition proof,
for instance, we will see that the existing E7 folio on the scene at the
airport can be interleaved.

PLANE rejig 22

All afternoon dramatic messages of rescue operations were flashed to London Fire Brigade headquarters and hope increased for survivors.

'Boeing 707 broken back on landing. About two-thirds of aircraft involved in fire . . . passenger casualties being recovered from tail . . . possible 70 escaped after crash landing . . . search of fuselage for further casualties in progress using breathing apparatus . . .'

The crash scene was marked by a pall of smoke which could be seen clearly over 10 miles away at Ealing (Middlesex) and Brentford.

IN TYPE 4th -LIFT

mf

PLANE rejig 23

Aircraft were still coming into land and taking off as rescuers worked among the debris on Runway 05 right. ~~A member of the Airport Fire Brigade staff said: 'She was well alight when she came down and there was a series of explosions. The port wing was destroyed and the fire had spread to fuselage and tail sections.~~

Broken debris covered the runway as firemen showered white foam on to the aircraft's still smouldering interior. The frame stood out like a skeleton.

IN TYPE 4th -LIFT

mf

~~PAC RUSHFULL E17 PLANE (SCENES)~~ (Plane rejig 24

[AS DARKNESS FELL, SPOTLIGHTS WERE TURNED ON TO HELP THE 100 FIREMEN AND POLICE STILL SEARCHING AND SORTING OUT THE SCARRED, TWISTED HULK. FLAMES HAD EATEN AWAY THE PORT WING AND HALF THE PORT SIDE.

[PILES OF CHARRED CLOTHES AND PERSONAL EFFECTS WERE LIFTED FROM THE FOAM-COVERED RUNWAY IN CARD- BOARD BOXES. A PILE OF TWISTED LONG-PLAYING RECORDS, PLASTIC LIPSTICK CASES THAT HAD MELTED IN THE HEAT, A ~~DAMP~~ CHILD'S DOLL ~~, TIES AND POSTCARDS.~~

~~FIREMEN WERE TRYING TO SORT OUT PILES OF LETTERS WHICH HAD SOMEHOW MANAGED TO ESCAPE BEING FULLY DESTROYED.~~

MF/ BH

PLANE
rejig 25

Other firemen carried armfuls of debris from the wreckage. They brought out burnt cases, charred summer dresses belonging to the women passengers and recovered a baby's bath tub.

IN TYPE
4th
-KILL

PLANE rejig 26

A man who saw it all from the first flicker of flame to the great flash and pall of smoke said: 'It was the most fantastic thing I have ever seen.'

Mr. Bernard Keith was in his garden at Egham, Surrey, when he heard the Boeing roar off from Heathrow.

'I looked up and the first thing I noticed was the sun shining on the bright silver of the aircraft. Suddenly there was a brilliant red streak on the inboard engine—just as if an artist had splashed it with a paintbrush. The airliner seemed to be about 3,000 feet up and was just coming to Egham Hill.'

IN TYPE 4th -LIFT

PLANE rejig 27

The Rev. Stephen Blood, vicar of St. Hilda's, Ashford, five miles from Heathrow, stood among the rescuers. 'I said a prayer that the passengers would be all right. Some were running to ambulances. They seemed to be badly shocked.'

Mr. Henry Jones of Hayes, Middlesex, and Mr. Ronald Revell, of Hanworth, Middlesex, also described what happened.

'When the aircraft came in its engine was in flames,' said Mr. Jones. 'When it came down and stopped the fire engines were about 200 yards behind. Then the aircraft blew up. Black smoke and flame was everywhere.'

Mr. Revell said: 'After it had landed the engine went and I saw people running away. They must have used the emergency doors. About 20 or 30 scattered across the runway.'

ON 4th -KILL

PLANE rejig 28

The blazing engine fell away as the 707 was passing over the village of Thorpe (Surrey), five miles from Heathrow. Mr. Ian McDonald said: 'As I looked up I saw flames pouring out of the inboard port engine. The plane circled round and the engine fell off and went smack into the centre of the water in the gravel pit in Green Lane, Thorpe.

'Had the engine fallen seconds later, it would probably have hit the shopping centre of Staines (Middlesex). Flames were still pouring from the aircraft as it passed over the town.'

IN TYPE 4rg – LIFT

mf

PLANE rejig 29

Another airport witness, Mr. Bert Watts of Ashford, said: 'I saw it land all right, then I heard the pilot put on the reverse thrust to try and slow her down. There was a bang and she burst into flames.

'I saw people push open the emergency hatch and run across the wing. Within minutes the whole centre of the plane was alight and the tail plane.

'There was no panic, although people moved very quickly from the plane. Many of them flopped down on the grass. They seemed shocked and shattered. I saw children's push chairs lying among the charred wreckage. There was a child's doll in one of the push chairs.'

Mr. Jimmy Shand, head of Shand News and Press services at Heathrow was an eyewitness. 'We were almost on top of the crash scene', he said. 'We were about 300 yards from the runway and heard a terrific noise due to another plane overshooting the runway because, we were told, the Boeing was in trouble.

'We dashed out of the office again and saw the Boeing on the main runway. It appeared to be taxi-ing, almost in the centre of the airport, and almost 500 or 600 yards from the main building in the central area. There was a terrific pall of black smoke and flames coming from the aircraft. Two thirds of it appeared to be intact with the tail end still sticking up. But where the galley is appeared to have burnt out.'

IN TYPE KILL

mf

(PLANE rejig 30)

(IN TYPE 4th)

An airport spokesman said the wreckage of the engine fell in Thorpe and other parts fell in Wraysbury near Windsor.

The arrival and departure rate at the airport was greatly reduced owing to the total involvement of rescue services.

Some planes were diverted to Gatwick, but normal services were resumed at 6.30. Sir Giles Guthrie, chairman of BOAC, who was on the scene, promised to establish the cause of the accident.

The search of the wreckage was held up for about 10 minutes as firemen searched for radioactive material. But the wreckage was cleared and the search continued.

As dusk fell, police searched the Wraysbury area, where there are many gravel pits, for parts of the Boeing which fell off in flight.

MORE THAN 100 people were alive last night after a BOAC pilot flew his burning jetliner with 126 on board back to Heathrow London Airport. An engine fell in flames from the plane minutes after take-off, but in a ball of smoke visible 10 miles away Captain Charles Taylor made what a survivor called a 'marvellous landing'.

All the crew escaped, but five people are known to have died—three women, one man and a child. Four dead and 2 casualties were taken to Hillingdon Hospital (Middlesex). Seven more casualties went to Ashford Hospital (Middlesex).

The Australia-bound plane, a Boeing, Flight No. 712, took off at 4.27. Almost immediately 47-year-old Captain Taylor radioed that an engine was on fire and that he was returning to land. He did a half-circuit and two minutes later came in on a cross runway in front of Queens Building. The airliner appeared to touch down and crash at the same time. It burst into flames simultaneously.

All the fourth-edition type has now been accounted for. But do not close the story just yet. Examine the copy that has arrived and also the copy you still have in the groups you started in front of you. Two facts remain to be noticed—the recovery of the engine on E16 and the radio-active material. The engine recovery follows naturally on the eye-witness who saw the burning engine fall, so make that REJIG 31. Part of the information is on E16 and part has arrived at 10.13 on PLANE 54. Paste PLANE 54 on the foot of E16 and send as one sheet.

~~PAC RUSHPULL E16 PLANE (SCENE)~~ (Plane resig 31

~~SIR GILESAID THE AIRCRAFT WAS INVOLVED IN AN~~
UNDERCARRIAGE ACCIDENT IN HONOLULU LAST NOVEMBER.

IT WAS TAKEN OUT OF SERVICE AND HAD UNDERGONE
A THOROUGH OVERHAUL. YESTERDAY IT UNDERWENT A TEST
AND WAS SATISFACTORY.

DURING THE RESCUE OPERATION, THE BOEING WAS
SEARCHED WITH GEIGER COUNTERS FOR RADIO ACTIVE
MATERIAL BELIEVED TO BE ON BOARD.

THE PILOT CAPT. CHARLES TAYLOR AFTERWARDS
~~DECLINED TO SEE WAITING REPORTERS. MEANWHILE AIR~~
Air PORT WORKERS later RECOVERED THE MISSING ENGINE ~~WHICH HAD~~
~~FALLEN INTO A RESERVOIR SITE AT WRAYSBURY, NEAR~~
~~STAINES.~~

~~WORKMEN ON THE SITE RANGE THE BRITISH AIRPORT'S~~
~~AUTHORITY AND ASKED "WE HAVE FOUND AN AIRCRAFT ENGINE.~~
~~WHAT SHALL WE DO WITH IT?"~~

~~MFL BH~~

~~PAC RUSHPULL~~

~~54 PLANE.~~

PIECES OF THE ENGINE COWLING WERE FOUND ~~TONIGHT~~
SCATTERED AT HYTHE END, WRAYSBURY ~~(BUCKS) ABOUT~~
~~FOUR MILES FROM THE AIRPORT.~~

(-M.F.)

The radioactive material is dealt with in folios 53 and 55 and an earlier paragraph on PLANE 48. Use the information from PLANE 55 to complete PLANE 53. We then spike PLANE 55 and also the superseded PLANE 48. When we have edited PLANE 53, we close the whole rejig there.

~~PAC RUSHFULL~~ *(Plane rejig 39)*

~~53 PLANE (SEE ALSO 44 PLANE)~~

~~A B.O.A.C. LONDON H.Q. SPOKESMAN SAID THERE HAD~~ *container* *low-strength* ~~BEEN~~ A ~~SMALL QUANTITY~~ OF RADIOACTIVE ISOTOPES ON BOARD THE CRASHED PLANE *was found with*

~~THEY WEIGHED ABOUT FIVE POUNDS, AND WERE VERY~~

~~HEAVILY PROTECTED WITH LEAD PACKING.~~

~~THE SHIPPERS SEARCHED THE WRECKAGE WITH~~ GEIGER *It was being exported for medical* COUNTERS ~~AND FOUND THE ISOTOPES UNDAMAGED.~~ *use and, though scorched, was* ~~HE SAID, "THERE WAS NO RISK AT ANY TIME".~~ ~~HE~~ *unbroached* ~~THOUGHT THEY WERE BEING EXPORTED FOR MEDICAL PURPOSES.~~

~~M.T. RJW~~

The rejig is completed. All the fourth-edition type has now been accounted for. So has all the copy we selected from 8.30 p.m. Now write the headlines, then read the new copy which arrives. There are five things we can do with this new copy:

Spike it.

Hold it for next edition.

Add it to the end of the story.

Insert it high up in the story or with its relevant sub-section.

Make it the basis of a Substitute intro or Line flash above the intro.

Keep a high standard of judgment, especially for Substitute intros and Inserts. A profusion of only marginally relevant Inserts and Adds creates production difficulties. A Substitute intro is only justified in this running story if the number of casualties is drastically changed. An Insert is justified only for worthwhile new information. If the type is in the forme, the compositor may have to lift it to cope with an Insert. This is a delay and risks paragraphs being transposed. (Inserts create similar problems in photoset when the film is already stripped in.) Add material is easier to cope with in production, but you should be discriminating about Add paragraphs. Avoid the untidiness of adding anything which belongs to an earlier section of the story. The best kind of Add paragraphs are self-contained new points.

Taking these standards, these are the useful pieces of copy to our 11 p.m. deadline.

22 21

PAC   RUSHFULL

56-PLANE.

IN A STATEMENT ISSUED THROUGH BOAC HQ. CAPTAIN
TAYLOR SAID: "WE CALLED MAYDAY AND THE TOWER
IMMEDIATELY CLEARED US TO LAND ON 05 RIGHT, WHICH
WAS PERFECT.   THE WHOLE OF THE CREW WERE QUITE
WONDERFUL IN THEIR BEHAVIOUR AND TECHNICAL
COMPETENCE".

- M.F.L

The first remark from Captain Taylor, and therefore worth an Insert. Edit it as follows:

PAC RUSHFULL.

56 PLANE.

(Insert A Plane

IN A STATEMENT ISSUED THROUGH BOAC HQ, CAPTAIN

later:

TAYLOR SAID "WE CALLED MAYDAY AND THE TOWER

IMMEDIATELY CLEARED US TO LAND ON 05 RIGHT, WHICH

WAS PERFECT. THE WHOLE OF THE CREW WERE QUITE

WONDERFUL IN THEIR BEHAVIOUR AND TECHNICAL

COMPETENCE".   end A

- M.F.L.

2225

PAC   RUSHFULL

D. 33 PLANE (SURVIVORS)

A SPOKESMAN AT BOAC LONDON HQ SAID TONIGHT THAT

ONE OF THE FATALITIES WAS JACQUELINE COOPER, NINE,

TRAVELLING WITH HER MOTHER AND FATHER, MR AND MRS

BRIAN COOPER AND BROTHERS KEVIN AND ANDREW.

THEY WERE BELIEVED TO BE EMIGRATING TO PERTH,

WESTERN AUSTRALIA. MR AND MRS COOPER, KEVIN AND

ANDREW SURVIVED, SAID THE SPOKESMAN.

THE SPOKESMAN CONFIRMED THAT STEWARDESS BARBARA

HARRISON WAS AMONG THOSE KILLED. MISS HARRISON

WAS BORN IN BRADFORD AND JOINED BOAC IN JUNE,1966.

MFL   SF

Edit as follows and send as an INSERT B.

PAC RUSHFULL.

D.33 PLANE (SURVIVORS)   (Insert B Plane

~~A SPOKESMAN AT BOAC LONDON HQ SAID TONIGHT THAT~~

                        dead included   *aged*
~~ONE OF~~ THE ~~FATALITIES WAS~~ JACQUELINE COOPER, NINE,

TRAVELLING WITH HER MOTHER AND FATHER, MR AND MRS

BRIAN COOPER, AND BROTHERS KEVIN AND ANDREW. *The*

~~THEY WERE BELIEVED TO BE EMIGRATING TO PERTH,~~

~~WESTERN AUSTRALIA, MR AND MRS COOPER, KEVIN AND~~

~~ANDREW SURVIVED, SAID THE SPOKESMAN.~~

                                         who died was
~~THE SPOKESMAN CONFIRMED THAT~~ STEWARDESS BARBARA

HARRISON ~~WAS AMONG THOSE KILLED. MISS HARRISON~~

~~WAS BORN IN BRADFORD AND JOINED BOAC IN JUNE 1966.~~   *end B*

MFL SF

2238

PAC RUSHFULL.

A7-PLANE (BOAC)

IN JUNE 1965 THERE WAS ANOTHER "MIRACLE"

LANDING WHEN A STARBOARD ENGINE OF A BOEING 707

CAUGHT FIRE AND DROPPED OFF WHEN TAKING OFF FROM

SAN FRANCISCO FOR HAWAII.

THE ENGINE TOOK ABOUT 20 FEET OF THE WINGTIP

WITH IT.

THE PILOT LANDED THE PLANE WITH 143 PASSENGERS
AND A CREW OF NINE SAFELY AND AT AN INQUIRY HE WAS
PRAISED FOR HIS CALMNESS.

THE PILOT, CAPT CHARLES KIMES SAID THE AIRCRAFT
REACHED 700 FEET WHEN "SHE BLEW".

-M.F.L.

This goes with the sub-section on the previous accident to Whisky
Echo. Edit and send as INSERT C.

~~PAC RUSHFULL.~~

~~A7 PLANE (BOAC)~~

(Insert C Plane

IN JUNE 1965 THERE WAS ANOTHER "MIRACLE"
LANDING WHEN A STARBOARD ENGINE OF *another* ~~#~~ BOEING 707
CAUGHT FIRE AND DROPPED OFF WHEN TAKING OFF FROM
SAN FRANCISCO ~~FOR HAWAII.~~

~~THE ENGINE TOOK ABOUT 20 FEET OF THE WINGTIP~~
~~WITH IT.~~

THE PILOT LANDED THE PLANE *safely* ~~WITH~~ 143 PASSENGERS
AND A CREW OF NINE ~~SAFELY AND AT AN INQUIRY HE WAS~~
~~PRAISED FOR HIS CALMNESS.~~ **(end C)**

~~THE PILOT, CAPT CHARLES KIMES SAID THE AIRCRAFT~~
~~REACHED 700 FEET WHEN "SHE BLEW".~~

~~M.F.L~~

Once again, remember to let the stone know (by marked galley proof
is best) where these inserts are to go. Then await your new proofs:

CAPTAIN CHARLES TAYLOR made a perfect landing last night with a blazing Boeing 707 airliner —and saved the lives of 121 people.

Five people died—four passengers and a stewardess—as the BOAC jetliner Whisky Echo exploded in flames two minutes after leaving Heathrow on the first leg of a flight to Australia.

Almost immediately after take-off at 4.27 Captain Taylor, a 47-year-old New Zealander, flashed out a Mayday message that his inner port engine was on fire.

As he turned back to Heathrow the burning engine fell off. 'The plane tilted from side to side and rocked', said an eyewitness, 'but the pilot kept it on course. He took the plane beautifully into London Airport'.

Last night survivors joined in praising the pilot and crew. There was no panic. One survivor, emerging from the smoking wreck said: 'It was a marvellous landing.'

There was a series of explosions as the plane touched down from about 2,000ft. A fleet of fire engines and ambulances scrambled to the scene—marked by a pall of smoke clearly visible more than 10 miles away.

A witness said: 'I saw people open the emergency hatch and run across the wing. Within minutes the whole centre of the plane was alight and the tail plane.

'There was no panic, although people moved very quickly from the plane, many of them flopping down on the grass. They seemed shocked and shattered.'

The dead included Jacqueline Cooper, aged nine, travelling with her mother and father, Mr. and Mrs. Brian Cooper, and brothers Kevin and Andrew, who survived. The stewardess who died was Barbara Harrison.

This is the second time Whisky Echo, nearly six years old, has been on fire. In Honolulu last November there was a fire in number 4 engine —outside starboard. The aircraft was about to take off when the fire was detected. Four passengers were hurst. Since then all engines have been changed. (Yesterday's fire was in the inner port engine.)

In June, 1965, there was another 'miracle' landing when a starboard engine of another Boeing 707 caught fire and dropped off when taking off from San Francisco. The pilot landed the plane safely with 143 passengers and a crew of nine.

Sir Giles Guthrie, chairman of BOAC, who arrived to inspect the charred hulk of Whisky Echo, said 'I shall try to find out why the fire extinguishers were not working, why the fire warning system was not working, and why the engine caught fire.'

This was, he said, the plane's first flight out except for a test flight, following a major overhaul.

Sir Giles added: 'I think the casualty figures were kept down by the excellent discipline on the part of both the crew and the passengers. It was extremely good.'

The man they were all praising last night, Captain Taylor, is a New Zealander who served with the RAF in the war and joined BOAC in 1947. In 1945 he was first officer and co-pilot on the aircraft carrying the Queen and Prince Philip from Aden to Entebbe and Entebbe to Tobruk.

Captain Taylor said later: 'We called Mayday and the Tower immediately cleared us to land on 05 right, which was perfect. The whole of the crew were quite wonderful in their behaviour and technical competence.'

Captain Eric Miles, BOAC's 707 Flight Manager, who interviewed the captain and crew, said they had done a marvellous job. It was a perfect landing despite the fact that the engine was on fire and continued to burn.

'The captain got himself perfectly in position for his final approach on zero five runway and since the runway is shorter than normally used the aircraft seems to have touched down right on the threshold.'

A check captain, Captain Moss, had been in the Boeing's 'jump seat', a spare seat near the pilot, and assisted Captain Taylor.

A witness at the gravel pit where the engine fell, Mr. Anthony d'Marco, said: 'I watched the plane the whole time it was in difficulty and I have nothing but admiration for the way the pilot handled it.

'It was only about 200 yards in the air and I saw the wing was on fire—a tremendous orange glow looking much more than it really was because it was reflected in the shining metal of the fuselage.

'When the engine fell the plane tilted from side to side and rocked but the pilot kept it on course, kept it on a straight line for London airport. He took this crippled machine down beautifully.'

Survivor Mark Wynter, the pop star, said the pilot brought the plane down 'as if it were a lift'. Wynter described the crew as 'marvellous'. As the plane was coming down one steward, he said, walked up and down the aircraft. 'He was marvellous. He kept saying "Keep calm everybody, keep calm everybody".

'A voice came over the intercom telling us to tighten our seat belts as much as we could and to put our heads on our knees. Everyone was looking towards where the flames were roaring.

'I heard someone shout "Emergency". I thought my number was up.

'As we hit the ground the steward was at the ground emergency exit. He pushed it open and said "Everybody out". I got out on the wing and jumped off. There was an explosion at the other side of the plane and several pieces of the plane were thrown up in the air.'

A survivor, Irene Molyneaux, 17, of Walworth, South East London, said she looked out of the window and saw the blazing engine. 'The windows were cracking with the heat but very few people panicked. One man had to be picked up and thrown down the chute when we landed.'

Mr. Bill Deitsch, 27, who was on the plane, said he saw a 'wall of flame . . . the fire was growing all the time. The pilot brought the aircraft round and we landed three minutes later. It was a beautiful landing. The pilot was brilliant. You always say this, but he really was brilliant.'

Lynaire Williamson, a 23-year-old secretary, on her way home to New Zealand, said 'After we landed two escape chutes were opened and I got out quickly. Children were screaming and the flames seemed to increase as we slid down the chute. When I was about 100 yards away from the plane I heard three explosions.'

Mrs Melda Wilday, of Solihull, Warwickshire, was on her way with her husband John to Perth. She said after the plane had been airborne for just a few minutes she looked out and saw the engine burst into flames. 'The flames suddenly became a huge wall of fire and seemed to sweep the whole wing. To me it now seems just like a horror film or a bad dream.'

Mr. Wilday said: 'As the wing was ablaze, we prayed. When the plane came to a stop and the emergency doors were opened, I was just in front of my wife in getting out.

'I got on to the wing and had to jump. I fell several feet and broke my wrist. The dense black smoke was coming into the plane more quickly and I waited for my wife to follow me but there was no sign of her. I was desperately worried. I thought she was still inside.'

Mrs. Wilday explained: 'When it was my turn to go through the emergency exit I could not see because of the smoke. So I had to turn round and go back into the cabin. I was really frightened at this stage. Some of the crew guided me to the main door.'

One of the survivors taken to Hillingdon hospital, 75-year-old Miss Marjorie Rassell of Holland Park, West London, said that after the plane had been airborne for just a few minutes she looked out from her port-side seat and saw what she thought was part of the wing fall off. Flames began to shoot out of the engine.

There was no panic. As the aircraft came to a stop, the cabin began to fill with dense, black, oily smoke.

One survivor said: 'The man next to me said: "This is it—we are going to die". But I thought we had a good chance because the pilot was bringing the plane in very well indeed.' .

All afternoon dramatic messages of rescue operations were flashed to London Fire Brigade headquarters and hope increased for survivors.

'Boeing 707 broken back on landing . . . about two-thirds of aircraft involved in fire . . . passenger casualties being recovered from tail . . . possible 70 escaped after crash landing . . . search of fuselage for further casualties in progress using breathing apparatus . . .'

The crash scene was marked by a pall of smoke which could be seen clearly over 10 miles away at Ealing (Middlesex) and Brentford.

Aircraft were still coming into land and taking off as rescuers worked among the debris on Runway 05 right.

Broken debris covered the runway as firemen showed white foam on the aircraft's still smouldering interior. The frame stood out like a skeleton.

As darkness fell, spotlights were turned on to help the 100 firemen and police still searching and sorting out the scarred, twisted hulk. Flames had eaten away the port wing and half the port side.

Piles of charred clothes and personal effects were lifted from the foam covered runway in cardboard boxes. A pile of twisted long-playing records, plastic lipstick cases that had melted in the heat—and a child's doll.

A man who saw it all from the first flicker of flame to the great flash and pall of smoke said: 'It was the most fantastic thing I have ever seen.'

Mr. Bernard Keith was in his garden at Egham, Surrey, when he heard the Boeing roar off from Heathrow.

'I looked up and the first thing I noticed was the sun shining on the bright silver of the aircraft. Suddenly there was a brilliant red streak on the inboard engine—just as if an artist had splashed it with a paintbrush. The airliner seemed to be about 3,000 ft. up and was just coming to Egham Hill.'

The blazing engine fell away as the 707 was passing over the village of Thorpe (Surrey) five miles from Heathrow. Mr. Ian McDonald said: 'As I looked up I saw flames pouring out of the inboard port engine. The plane circled round and the engine fell off and went smack into the centre of the water in the gravel pit in Green Lane, Thorpe.

'Had the engine fallen seconds later, it would probably have hit the shopping centre of Staines (Middlesex). Flames were still pouring from the aircraft as it passed over the town.'

Airport workers later recovered the missing engine. Pieces of the engine cowling were found scattered at Hythe End, Wraysbury.

A container of low-strength radioactive isotopes on board the crashed plane was found with geiger counters. It was being exported for medical use and, though scorched, was unbroached.

For any further edition—and it would be quite usual for a morning paper to have a Sixth, say about 2 a.m.—this story can obviously be polished, even if there are no further major developments. There are two main blemishes. Over-reliance on direct quotes, for all their immediacy, wastes space that is perhaps better given to narrative; and we could with advantage give a crisper description, earlier in the story, of the scene as passengers scrambled from the burning, exploding aircraft. Such changes can be done neatly on proof, by means of Inserts, Subst pars, and so on—exactly the same techniques used during the evening when the copy seemed to tumble on you incessantly while the clock raced on. You kept your head then, so keep it now. They will be grateful on the stone, where they have shared with you (if you have done your job well) the exhilaration and sense of accomplishment that good, controlled desk work under pressure can bring.

Appendix

The Linotype tabulation overleaf is to assist casting off. It lists characters by pica ems from 10 to 36 ems measure (across the table) for alphabet lengths from 73 to 250 points (shown at the sides).

Two further tables give character counts (p. 356) and alphabet lengths (p. 357).

These are followed by comparative tables for the three systems of type measurement (pp. 358–9).

	36	35	34	33	32	31	30	29	28	27	26	25	24	23	22	21	20	19	18	17	16	15	14	13	12	11	10	
73	157	152	148	143	139	135	131	126	122	117	113	108	104	100	96	91	87	82	78	74	70	65	61	56	52	48	44	73
75	153	149	145	140	136	132	128	123	119	115	111	106	102	98	94	89	85	81	77	72	68	64	60	55	51	47	43	75
76	151	147	143	138	134	130	126	122	118	113	109	105	101	96	92	88	84	80	76	71	67	63	59	54	50	46	42	76
77	149	145	141	137	133	129	125	120	116	112	108	104	100	95	91	87	83	79	75	70	66	62	58	54	50	46	42	77
79	146	142	138	134	130	126	122	117	113	109	105	101	97	93	89	85	81	77	73	69	65	61	57	53	49	45	41	79
80	144	140	136	132	128	124	120	116	112	108	104	100	96	92	88	84	80	76	72	68	64	60	56	52	48	44	40	80
81	142	138	134	130	126	122	119	115	111	107	103	99	95	91	87	83	79	75	71	67	63	59	55	51	47	43	40	81
82	140	136	133	129	125	121	117	113	109	105	101	97	94	90	86	82	78	74	70	66	62	58	55	51	47	43	39	82
83	138	135	131	127	123	119	116	112	108	104	100	96	92	88	85	81	77	73	69	65	62	58	54	50	46	42	39	83
84	137	133	129	125	122	118	114	110	106	102	99	95	91	87	84	80	76	72	68	64	61	57	53	49	46	42	38	84
86	135	131	128	124	120	116	113	109	105	101	98	94	90	86	83	79	75	71	68	64	60	56	53	49	45	41	38	86
87	133	129	126	122	118	115	112	108	104	100	96	92	89	85	81	77	74	70	67	63	59	55	52	48	44	40	37	87
88	131	128	124	120	117	113	110	106	102	98	95	91	88	84	80	76	73	69	66	62	58	54	51	47	44	40	37	88
90	130	126	122	118	115	111	108	104	101	97	94	90	86	82	79	75	72	68	65	61	58	54	50	46	43	39	36	90
91	128	124	121	117	114	110	107	103	99	95	92	88	85	81	78	74	71	67	64	60	57	53	50	46	43	39	36	91
93	126	122	119	115	112	108	105	101	98	94	91	87	84	80	77	73	70	66	63	59	56	52	49	45	42	38	35	93
94	124	120	117	113	110	107	104	100	97	93	90	86	83	79	76	72	69	65	62	58	55	51	48	44	41	38	35	94
96	122	119	115	112	109	105	102	98	95	91	88	85	82	78	75	71	68	64	61	57	54	50	48	44	41	38	34	96
98	121	117	114	110	107	104	101	97	94	90	87	83	80	77	74	70	67	63	60	57	54	50	47	43	40	37	34	98
100	119	115	112	109	106	102	99	95	92	89	86	82	79	76	73	69	66	62	59	56	53	49	46	43	40	36	33	100
102	117	114	111	107	104	101	98	94	91	88	85	81	78	75	72	68	65	62	59	55	52	49	46	42	39	36	33	102
104	115	112	109	105	102	99	96	93	90	86	83	80	77	73	70	67	64	61	58	54	51	48	45	41	38	35	32	104
106	113	110	107	104	101	98	95	91	88	85	82	79	76	72	69	66	63	60	57	53	50	47	44	41	38	35	32	106
108	112	108	105	102	99	96	93	90	87	84	81	77	74	71	68	65	62	59	56	53	50	46	43	40	37	34	31	108
110	110	107	104	101	98	95	92	88	85	82	79	76	73	70	67	64	61	58	55	52	49	46	43	40	37	34	31	110
112	108	105	102	99	96	93	90	87	84	81	78	75	72	69	66	63	60	57	54	51	48	45	42	39	36	33	30	112
	36	35	34	33	32	31	30	29	28	27	26	25	24	23	22	21	20	19	18	17	16	15	14	13	12	11	10	

	36	35	34	33	32	31	30	29	28	27	26	25	24	23	22	21	20	19	18	17	16	15	14	13	12	11	10
114	106	103	100	97	94	91	89	86	83	80	77	74	71	68	65	62	59	56	53	50	47	44	41	38	35	32	30
116	104	101	99	96	93	90	87	84	81	78	75	72	70	67	64	61	58	55	52	49	46	43	41	38	35	32	29
118	103	100	97	94	91	88	86	83	80	77	74	71	68	65	63	60	57	54	51	48	46	43	40	37	34	31	29
120	101	98	95	92	90	87	84	81	78	75	73	70	67	64	62	59	56	53	50	47	45	42	39	36	34	31	28
122	99	96	94	91	88	85	83	80	77	74	72	69	66	63	61	58	55	52	50	47	44	41	39	36	33	30	28
124	97	94	92	89	86	83	81	78	76	73	70	67	65	62	59	57	54	51	49	46	43	40	38	35	33	29	27
127	95	92	90	87	85	82	80	77	74	71	69	66	64	61	58	55	53	50	48	45	42	39	37	34	32	29	27
129	94	91	88	85	83	80	78	75	73	70	68	65	62	60	57	54	51	49	47	44	42	39	36	33	31	28	26
132	92	89	87	84	82	79	77	74	71	68	66	63	61	58	56	53	51	48	46	43	41	38	36	33	31	28	26
135	90	87	85	82	80	77	75	72	70	67	65	62	60	57	55	52	50	47	45	42	40	37	35	32	30	27	25
138	88	85	83	80	78	76	74	71	69	66	64	61	59	56	54	51	49	46	44	41	39	36	34	31	30	27	25
142	86	84	82	79	77	74	72	69	67	64	62	60	58	55	53	50	48	45	43	40	38	36	34	31	29	26	24
146	85	82	80	77	75	73	71	68	66	63	61	58	56	54	52	49	47	44	42	40	38	35	33	30	28	26	24
150	83	81	78	76	74	71	69	66	64	62	60	57	55	53	51	48	46	43	41	39	37	34	32	30	28	25	23
154	81	79	77	74	72	70	68	65	63	61	59	56	54	52	50	47	45	43	41	38	36	34	32	29	27	25	23
158	79	77	75	72	70	68	66	64	62	59	57	55	53	50	48	46	44	42	40	37	35	33	31	28	26	24	22
162	77	75	73	71	69	67	65	62	60	58	56	54	52	49	47	45	43	41	39	36	34	32	30	28	26	24	22
166	76	73	71	69	67	65	63	61	59	57	55	52	50	48	46	44	42	40	38	36	34	31	29	27	25	23	21
170	74	72	70	68	66	64	62	59	57	55	53	51	49	47	45	43	41	39	37	35	33	31	29	27	25	23	21
175	72	70	68	66	64	62	60	58	56	54	52	50	48	46	44	42	40	38	36	34	32	30	28	26	24	22	20
180	70	68	66	64	62	60	59	57	55	53	51	49	47	45	43	41	39	37	35	33	31	29	27	25	24	21	20
185	68	66	65	63	61	59	57	55	53	51	49	47	46	44	42	40	38	36	34	32	30	28	27	25	23	21	19
190	67	65	63	61	59	57	56	54	52	50	48	46	44	42	41	39	37	35	33	31	30	28	26	24	22	20	19
195	65	63	61	59	58	55	54	52	50	48	47	44	43	41	40	38	36	34	32	30	29	27	25	23	22	20	18
200	63	61	60	58	56	54	53	51	49	47	46	44	42	40	39	37	35	33	32	30	28	26	25	23	21	19	18
206	61	59	58	56	54	52	51	49	48	46	44	42	41	39	37	35	34	32	31	29	27	25	24	22	20	18	17
212	59	57	56	54	53	51	50	48	46	44	43	41	40	38	36	34	33	31	30	28	26	24	23	22	20	18	17
218	58	56	54	52	51	49	48	46	45	43	42	40	38	36	35	33	32	30	29	27	26	24	22	21	19	17	16
225	56	54	53	51	50	48	47	45	43	41	40	38	37	35	34	32	31	29	28	26	25	23	22	20	19	17	16
233	54	52	51	49	48	46	45	43	42	40	39	37	36	34	33	31	30	28	27	25	24	22	21	19	18	16	15
241	52	50	49	47	46	45	44	42	41	39	38	36	35	33	32	30	29	27	26	24	23	21	20	18	17	16	15
250	50	49	48	46	45	43	42	40	39	37	36	35	34	32	31	29	28	26	25	23	22	21	20	18	17	15	14
	36	35	34	33	32	31	30	29	28	27	26	25	24	23	22	21	20	19	18	17	16	15	14	13	12	11	10

	Across 9 ems					Across 11 ems					Across 13 ems					
	7pt	8pt	9pt	10pt	12pt	7pt	8pt	9pt	10pt	12pt	7pt	8pt	9pt	10pt	12pt	14pt
Intertype faces																
Galaxy	32	26	—	21	18	—	32	—	27	22	—	38	—	32	26	—
Ideal	25	24	22	20	17	31	30	28	26	21	37	36	34	31	35	—
Imperial	27	24	22	20	18	34	30	28	26	22	40	36	34	31	26	—
Plantin with Italics	—	27	26	24	19	—	34	32	30	24	—	41	38	36	29	98
Royal	26	24	22	20	18	32	30	28	26	23	38	36	34	31	27	—
Times Roman	29	27	25	23	18	37	34	31	29	23	44	41	37	35	27	—
Vogue Bold Cond.	—	35	—	29	25	—	43	—	37	31	—	52	—	44	37	—
Linotype faces																
Corona	26	24	21	20	—	32	30	27	26	—	38	36	33	31	—	—
Excelsior	25	23	21	19	18	31	29	27	25	22	37	35	32	30	26	—
Helvetica	—	26	—	20	18	—	32	—	26	22	—	38	—	31	26	—
Ionic	25	22	20	18	—	31	28	26	23	—	37	34	31	28	—	—
Jubilee	27	25	23	21	18	34	31	29	27	23	41	37	35	33	28	—
Modern																
Metroblack 2	—	26	—	20	18	—	33	—	26	22	—	39	—	31	26	100

All with bold unless otherwise stated.

Typeface	5	5¼	6	6½	7	7½	8	9	10	11	12
Ionic with Italic & Sm. Caps	84	94	110	110	114	—	127	139	152	—	—
Ionic with Boldface No. 2	84	94	110	110	114	—	127	139	152	—	—
Ionic with Doric	84	94	110	110	114	—	128	139	—	—	—
Excelsior with Italic & Sm. Caps	—	—	107	—	115	—	123	132	143	—	170
Excelsior with Boldface No. 2	—	—	108	—	114	—	123	132	143	—	170
Excelsior with Doric	—	—	107	—	115	—	123	132	142	—	—
Paragon with Italic & Sm. Caps	—	101	107	—	120	—	129	136	145	—	—
Paragon with Paragon Bold	—	101	107	—	120	—	129	136	145	—	—
Corona with Italic	—	—	103	—	112	118	118	129	138	—	—
Corona with Boldface No. 2	—	94	103	—	112	118	118	129	137	146	—
Jubilee with Italic & Sm. Caps	—	—	95	—	103	—	113	122	129	141	152
Jubilee with Bold	—	—	95	—	103	—	113	122	129	141	151
Times Roman with Italic & Sm. Caps	—	83	87	—	99	105	109	118	125	135	152
Times Roman with Heavy	—	84	87	—	100	—	109	118	125	135	152
Plantin with Italic & Sm. Caps	—	—	88	—	96	—	107	116	120	130	149
Plantin with Plantin Bold	—	—	88	—	97	—	107	116	121	131	150
Granjon with Italic & Sm. Caps	—	—	—	—	—	—	97	108	117	126	137
Century with Italic & Sm. Caps	—	—	95	—	107	—	119	128	142	149	162
Imperial with Italics & Sm. Caps	—	90	98	—	108	—	117	129	141	143	159
Imperial with Bold	—	90	98	—	108	—	118	129	141	143	159
Royal with Italic	4¾	88	100	—	111	114	119	130	139	147	155
Royal with Bold	84	88	101	—	111	114	119	129	138	147	155
Royal with Doric	84	88	101	—	111	114	119	129	138	—	—
Ideal News with Doric	—	93	100	—	117	—	119	—	—	—	—
Ideal News with Italic and Sm. Caps	—	93	105	—	117	—	119	129	142	—	172
Ideal News with Bold	—	93	105	111	117	—	119	129	141	—	174
Typeface No. 108	—	—	—	—	—	—	118	—	—	—	—

The Anglo-American system

The standard of measurement is the 0·166 in. pica and the 0·01383 in. point, or one-twelfth of the pica. (Thus 1,000 lines of pica or 12pt matter measure 166 in., and 1,000 lines of 6pt matter measure 83 in., and so on.)

Points	in.	mm		Points	in.	mm
1	0·01383	0·35		10	0·1383	3·51
2	0·0277	0·70		11	0·1522	3·87
3	0·0415	1·05		12	0·1660	4·22
4	0·0553	1·40		14	0·1936	4·92
$4\frac{3}{4}$	0·0657	1·67		16	0·2213	5·62
5	0·0692	1·76		18	0·2490	6·32
$5\frac{1}{2}$	0·0761	1·93		20	0·2767	7·03
6	0·0830	2·11		24	0·3320	8·43
$6\frac{1}{2}$	0·0899	2·28		30	0·4150	10·54
7	0·0968	2·46		36	0·4980	12·65
$7\frac{1}{2}$	0·1037	2·63		42	0·5810	14·76
8	0·1107	2·81		48	0·6640	16·87
9	0·1245	3·16				

The Mediaan system

Used principally in Belgium, the unit is 0·01374 in. The Mediaan em or *cicero* measures 0·165 in., i.e. less than the Anglo-American pica.

Points	in.	mm		Points	in.	mm
1	0·01374	0·35		10	0·1374	3·49
2	0·0275	0·70		11	0·1511	3·84
3	0·0412	1·05		12	0·1649	4·18
4	0·0550	1·40		14	0·1924	4·89
$4\frac{3}{4}$	0·0653	1·65		16	0·2198	5·58
5	0·0687	1·74		18	0·2473	6·28
$5\frac{1}{2}$	0·0755	1·92		20	0·2748	7·00
6	0·0824	2·09		24	0·3298	8·38
$6\frac{1}{2}$	0·0893	2·27		30	0·4122	10·47
7	0·0962	2·44		36	0·4946	12·56
$7\frac{1}{2}$	0·1031	2·62		42	0·5771	14·66
8	0·1099	2·79		48	0·6598	16·75
9	0·1237	3·14				

The Didot system

Used in France and most of Continental Europe except Belgium. The *cicero* is the basic unit. The *cicero* equals 12 *corps* or 0·178 in. and the Didot *corps* or point measures exactly 0·01483 in., i.e. it is bigger than the Anglo-American point.

Points	in.	mm			
1	0·01483	0·38	10	0·1483	3·77
2	0·0296	0·75	11	0·1631	4·14
3	0·0445	1·13	12	0·1780	4·52
4	0·0593	1·51	14	0·2076	5·27
4¾	0·0704	1·79	16	0·2373	6·03
5	0·0742	1·88	18	0·2669	6·78
5½	0·0816	2·07	20	0·2966	7·53
6	0·0890	2·26	24	0·3559	9·04
6½	0·0964	2·45	30	0·4449	11·30
7	0·1038	2·64	36	0·5339	13·56
7½	0·1112	2·82	42	0·6229	15·82
8	0·1186	3·01	48	0·7118	18·08
9	0·1335	3·39			

References

Chapter 1

1 Elementary: Excelsior is a typeface which has been cut only in small sizes for linecasting in metal; but filmsetters can produce 24pt or any other size by photographically enlarging the small sizes.

2 Harris-Intertype at Slough, Bucks, produce a handy pocket-size gauge. Monotype at Redhill, Surrey, produce a larger desk gauge. Both have type scales subdivided from the smaller sizes to 12pt, and an inch scale. In the US, try Mergenthaler Linotype Co, 29 Ryerson Street, Brooklyn 5, New York.

3 The Anglo-American point system is different from Europe's. The basic unit in most Continental countries is the Didot point, which is fractionally larger at 0·0148 in. or 0·38mm. There is also the Mediaan system, mainly used in Belgium, where the unit is fractionally smaller than the US point. Throughout this book the references to point sizes are to the Anglo-American standard. *See* Appendix.

4 Some European papers give type sizes in millimetres—3mm being equal to 8pt. *See* Appendix.

5 There is a good general account of the reading process in *Alphabets and Reading*, by Sir James Pitman and John St John (London: Pitman, 1969), Chapter 2. *See also: The Psychology of Perception*, by M D Vernon (Harmondsworth: Penguin, 1970); and *A Psychological Study of Typography*, by Sir Cyril Burt (London: Cambridge University Press, 1959).

6 A lucid analysis of international reading research is in *The Visible Word, Problems of Legibility*, by Herbert Spencer (London: Lund Humphries, in association with the Royal College of Art, 1969). Current research is reviewed in *The Journal of Typographic Research* (c/o The Cleveland Museum of Modern Art, Cleveland, Ohio, USA; quarterly).

7 Pitman and St John, op. cit., p. 17.

8 Lower-case signifies small letters, of course, in contrast to upper-case or capital letters. The expression lower-case, used throughout this book, derives from the days when all type was handset and the small letters were kept close to the typesetter in the part of the printer's case. Caps were kept in the upper part of the case.

9 Spencer, op. cit., p. 14.

10 Spencer, op. cit., pp. 25–6.

11 Spencer, op. cit., p. 31.

12 Spencer, op. cit., p. 27.

13 Stanley Morison's Introduction to Burt's *Psychological Study*, op. cit. *See also: Memorandum on a Proposal to Revise the Typography of the Times* (London, 1930), p. 29.

14 Vincent Steer, in *Printing Design and Layout* (Coulsdon: Virtue and Co, second edition 1957), p. 186, on the need of a sans such as Gill for wider letter-spacing to prevent words running into one another. *See also* Edwin W Shaar, designer of Imperial, in *Penrose Annual 1958* (London: Lund Humphries, 1958), p. 20, on the serif as a 'key to readability'.

15 Peggy Lang, *Alphabet and Image, No. 2* (Shenval Press, 58 Frith Street, London W1), September 1946, p. 8.

16 Burt, op. cit. Beatrice Warde, supporting the relevance of aesthetics, suggested that the aesthetic preference

lay in the pleasantness of familiarity: *Penrose Annual 1956* (London: Lund Humphries, 1956), pp. 51–5.

17 Alison Shaw, *Print for Partial Sight* (London: The Library Association, 1969).

18 D Cheetham and B Grimbly, article, Design Analysis: Typeface in 1964, in *Design 186*, June 1964 (London: The Design Centre, 1964).

19 Morison, *Times Memorandum*, op. cit., p. 29.

20 Alison Shaw, op. cit., p. 48, reports that an increase in weight achieved an improvement in reading performance of 9 per cent (compared with a 16 per cent improvement after an increase in type size).

21 Address to a conference 'Newspaper Design' at the Royal College of Art, London, July 1971, sponsored by the Association Typographique Internationale, headquarters London.

22 Article in *Penrose Annual 1958* (London: Lund Humphries, 1958), p. 19 *et seq.*

23 Stanley Morison is the author of the unsigned article, The Editorial Test, in *The Monotype Recorder*, Vol. XXXV, Spring 1936, pp. 3–6 (London: The Monotype Corporation Ltd, 1936) which insists, magisterially, on standardisation of the types of the text. 'The English reader', he declared, 'dislikes altering the focus of his vision'. Standardisation of headline types was desirable for economy, for the readers' familiarity, and because 'sub-editors never will be typographers'.

24 Morison, op. cit., p. 5. The authorities of *The Times*, he says, made three decisions: 1, to retain the proportions of Monotype Modern; 2, to increase the weight of the face by relating it to Ionic; and 3, to dilute the heaviness of Ionic.

25 Allen Hutt, article, *Journal of Typo-graphic Research*, Vol. IV, No. 3, Summer 1970.

26 There is an excellent discussion of type behaviour in different printing conditions, with genuinely comparable examples, in *The Bowater Papers*, No. 3, 1954 (London: Bowater Corporation, 1954). The article, pp. 42–7, is by Beatrice Warde.

27 The design committee, appointed by Times Newspapers Executive Board, and chaired by the author, comprised Edwin Taylor, Director of Design, *The Sunday Times*; Robert Harling, typographical consultant; Jeanette Collins, designer, *The Times*; John Webb, then production director for Times Newspapers Ltd; and Walter Tracy, typographical consultant to *The Times*. Herbert Spencer and Allen Hutt gave advice.

Chapter 2

1 Burt, op. cit.

2 For a fuller discussion see Walter Tracy, article, Typographic Agora-phobia, *Studio International* (Chatham, Kent: Cory, Adams and Mackay Ltd, 1968), Vol. 176, No. 903, September 1968, pp. 115–17.

3 R Fabrizio, I Kaplan and G Teal, article on readability as a function of the straightness of right-hand margins, in *The Journal of Typographic Research*, January 1967, pp. 90–5.

4 Spencer, op. cit.

5 C H Evers, *The Journal of Typo-graphic Research*, Vol. II, No. 1, January 1963, pp. 59–74.

6 Spencer, op. cit., p. 37.

7 Letter to the author, 1970. Unjustified setting was only one of a number of design changes and it was the combination of all, suddenly, which apparently upset conservative readers.

8 *Journal of Experimental Psychology*, XXX (Lancaster, Pennsylvania: American Psychological Association;

and Evanston, Illinois: North-Western University), pp. 1574–6.

9 Burt, op. cit.

10 Spencer, op. cit., p. 37.

11 Patterson and Tinker, *see* ref. 8 to this chapter, *above*.

12 *What's Happening in News Display*, by the Associated Press Managing Editors' Display Committee (New York: Associated Press, undated but around 1970), p. 10.

13 Raymond Roberts, *Typographic Design* (London: Ernest Benn, 1966), p. 77 in student's edition.

14 *Research Institute Bulletin* of the American Newspaper Publishers' Association (Production Department, PO Box 598, Easton, PA 18042) December 1968. Published annually, this is a valuable index of American newspaper production practices.

15 Roberts, op. cit., p. 77.

16 *Research Institute Bulletin*, ANPA, 1972.

17 *What's Happening in News Display*, op. cit., p. 3.

18 *Editor and Publisher* magazine (850 Third Avenue, NY 10022), 20 July 1968, p. 15.

19 *Editor and Publisher*, 6 May 1967, p. 17, article by Howard Copley.

20 The Measurement of Legibility, a paper given in February 1968, by Christopher Poulton, Medical Research Council, Applied Psychology Unit, Cambridge, and in *Printing Technology* (London: Institute of Printing), pp. 72–6, 88–9.

21 Spencer, op. cit., pp. 7–8.

22 They must, of course, be modern numerals lining up with capitals.

23 Drug labels printed in 6pt caps are more easily discriminated than lower-case, though this was not demonstrated with 10pt type. Research by M Hailstone and J J Foster reported in *Journal of Typographic Research*, Vol. I, No. 3, July 1967, pp. 275–84.

Chapter 3

1 Roberts, op. cit., p. 79.

2 In a paper to the 11th Congress of the Association Typographique Internationale, Prague, June 1960, published by the Association in 1970 as *Typographic Opportunities in the Computer Age* pp. 52–5.

Chapter 7

1 *See* Appendix. Copy-fitting tables by Linotype & Machinery Ltd, Kingsbury Works, Kingsbury Road, London NW9.

2 In the excellent short pamphlet, *How to make Layouts Accurate*, by Caspar Mitchell, for Harris-Intertype Ltd, Slough, Bucks.

3 Monotype Ltd, 43 Fetter Lane, London EC4, sell, through the Publicity Department, a book called *Copyfitting Tables* which uses a system of factor numbers.

4 Caspar Mitchell, op. cit.

5 Charles Fyffe, *Basic Copy Fitting* (London: Studio Vista; New York: Watson-Guptill, 1969).

Bibliography

ARNOLD, Edmund C. *Modern Newspaper Design.* New York: Harper and Row, 1969.

BARNHART, Thomas F. *Weekly Newspaper Make-up and Typography.* Minneapolis: University of Minnesota Press; London: Oxford University Press, 1949.

BARTRAM, Alan and SUTTON, James. *An Atlas of Typeforms.* London: Lund Humphries, 1968.
Handsomely illustrated large book analysing the development of type design. Especially useful pull-out of more than fifty specimen text settings.

BERRY, W Turner, JOHNSON, A F, and JASPERT, W P. *The Encyclopaedia of Typefaces.* London: Blandford Press, Third edition, 1962.
Nearly 2,000 showings of typefaces, each with a brief note.

FYFFE, Charles. *Basic Copy Fitting.* London: Studio Vista; New York: Watson-Guptill, 1969.
How to fit the words into the space allowed; how to find out what space the words need. Very useful for fitting type to odd-shaped areas.

HUTT, Allen. *Newspaper Design.* London: Oxford University Press, Second edition, 1967.
Authoritative study, especially in descriptive passages on mechanics of newspaper production and text setting, and discussion of title-pieces.

Journal of Typographic Research Quarterly. Cleveland: The Press of Case Western Reserve University, 11000 Cedar Avenue, Cleveland, Ohio 44106.
Nearly always something of value for newspaper typographers.

LEWIS, John. *Typography. Basic Principles.* London: Studio Books; New York; Reinhold, 1966.
Perhaps the best single short introduction to typography and design and what they can do to help us communicate.

Index